The Case to Reclaim our Nationwide Privileges and Immunities

Helping to Solve the Mystery of Their Disappearance

Brian S. Messenger

First Hardcover Edition, March 2026

ISBN 979-8-218-93849-9

Published and Printed in the United States of America

For Cathy
my loving wife of thirty-six years and counting

Table of Contents

Table of Exhibits

Table of Figures

Table of Tables

Introduction

A year before the *Declaration of Independence*, Patrick Henry of Virginia spoke the immortal words[1] "*Give me Liberty or Give me Death*". 250 years ago, our forefathers risked their lives and fortunes to obtain the freedoms, liberties and rights that we have today. Regrettably, some of our present leaders are chipping away at these rights as we speak. Their reasons are heartfelt and often arise from fear and uncertainty. Unfortunately, their solutions invariably lead to a reduction in individual rights to achieve their goal for the "greater good". Patrick Henry described the alternative to liberty when he said "*What would they have? Is life so dear, or peace so sweet, as to be purchased at the price of chains and slavery?*".

This book is written for all Americans since it pertains to our collective individual rights. It is not written to propose "pie-in-the-sky" ideas. Instead, it is written to identify standing Supreme Court precedents, and detailed legal history that define these rights. The intention is that it can be used now to defend and reclaim many of our rights today.

I have been a lifelong citizen of California. My forefathers settled in Connecticut Colony in the 1630s, and I am a 10th generation American. My relatives fought in the Revolutionary War, the War of 1812, and my great-great Grandfather died fighting for the Union Army in the Civil War. Over the last three decades, I have seen an enormous reduction of the rights and liberties that my relatives fought to obtain and protect. Living in California through the COVID-19 pandemic was especially illustrative of these losses.

As Americans, we are used to hearing about our 1st and 2nd Amendment rights. These protect our freedom of speech, freedom of the press, freedom of religion, right to assemble, and the right to bear arms. Unfortunately, before and after the Civil War, many state govern-

---

1 Henry, Patrick. March 23, 1775, Speech Transcript.
Yale Law School, Lillian Goldman Law Library, The Avalon Project. (2026, Feb. 22). https://avalon.law.yale.edu/18th_century/patrick.asp

ments infringed upon these rights, primarily for African Americans. The 14th Amendment was approved in 1868 to provide African Americans with the full rights of citizenship, but the demise of Reconstruction and a series of Supreme Court decisions delayed this by many decades. The Supreme Court has tried to enforce our 1st and 2nd Amendment rights upon the states through what is called "incorporation". For some other amendments in the *Bill of Rights*, this slow and cumbersome process has taken over a century.

This detailed analysis will show that the Privileges and Immunities clause of the Constitution should be the primary means for protecting these rights. Ideally, the Privileges and Immunities Clause should be acting as a partner to the *Bill of Rights;* as opposed to being a long-lost sibling. The problem is that it takes significant historical research to understand and apply it. As you read this analysis it will become clear that the Clause intentionally does not list the individual rights that it protects. In addition, many of those rights were defined prior to the *Declaration of Independence*. This requires an analysis of English Law and Colonial American history and goes back over 900 years.

Early in our nation's history, the first of three "Butterfly" effects sowed the seeds for future confusion regarding the Privileges and Immunities Clause. These effects will be explained in detail since they help to solve the mystery as to what has happened. After the Civil War and the 14th Amendment, there was a lot of focus on using the Bill of Rights and other Constitutional provisions to protect the newly freed slaves. Unfortunately, one approach that was not tried was a strong argument based on Privileges and Immunities that had been recognized decades earlier. People lost focus of the real power and meaning of the Privileges and Immunities Clause to the detriment of our nation.

To add even more confusion, in the late 1800's and early 1900's, many Supreme Court cases attempted to stretch the idea of Nationwide Privileges and Immunities. A multitude of cases reached the Supreme Court that pertained to very particular grievances. These included things such as proposing: "the right to obtain a liquor license", "the right to publish a horse racing chart at an establishment where the association had sold the right to another company", "the right for sheep owners to use the public lands equally with cattle ranchers", "the right to be in a fraternity when a student at the University of Mississippi", and "the right to refuse to take a required military science class at the University of California". In most of these Supreme Court decisions, it was found that the protections of these non-historical rights were left to the states These distractions caused people to lose interest in trying to utilize the Privileges and Immunities Clause for issues of national importance.

This book will study pertinent historical Supreme Court decisions, and help the reader to understand the perspectives and context that shaped them. Supreme Court Chief Justice John Roberts said in his confirmation hearing: "*I will remember that it's my job to call balls and strikes, and not to pitch or bat.*" When the Supreme Court has deeply divided decisions, both sides must see the pitch very differently. It will be shown that when Justices are focused on outcomes, as opposed to fidelity to the Constitution and precedents, they can create upheaval for our nation. Unfortunately, Supreme Court Justices are not exposed to formal cross examination for their opinions. Such a process might highlight that instead of calling balls and strikes, some justices are trying to throw us "*wild pitches*" in the form of illogical arguments, or are "*batting away*" obvious precedents and meanings.

In developing this case to reclaim our Nationwide Privileges and Immunities, historical context is provided throughout. Importantly, extensive Exhibits, Figures, Tables and Appendices are provided for the more legally inclined. Footnotes are intentionally shown on each page as a means to reduce the clutter of formal legal references in the text. They are also used to show additional writings and documentation. This book provides extensive legal precedents to fight to reclaim our rights now. It is also intended to proactively provide a template to protect our rights in the future should something such as COVID-19 ever happen again.

Studying the history of the Privileges and Immunities Clause is a very complex puzzle. It is a form of a forensic analysis of history, legal precedents and human behavior. I will explain the many missing pieces of the puzzle that I have uncovered. Using that knowledge, I will also show and explain what I believe went wrong. Between narration of the original sources, I try to add perspective for the less legally inclined reader. This is done using movie, book, and other modern analogies that they may be familiar with.

The fact that I am not a lawyer provides me with an additional power that typical writers in this field do not have. I am not worried about offending my law firm through my writings. I am not worried about offending justices that I may be practicing in front of. I am not worried about destroying my legal career. That makes me willing to review and comment on mistakes that the Supreme Court has made without fear of retribution. I sincerely hope that this unique perspective helps to provide our present Supreme Court with the ammunition to use this knowledge for our common good.

In the final chapter of the book, existing Supreme Court precedent regarding Privileges and Immunities are used to identify immediate opportunities for change. Beyond our 1st and 2nd Amendment rights, issues such as voting rights, Sanctuary cities, and birthright citizenship are also analyzed. This book is written to empower the reader. Whether you are defending our American rights at the Thanksgiving dinner table, at your book club, or in front of the United States Supreme Court, the detailed analysis presented in this book should empower you to make your case.

CHAPTER 1

Our English History

(Up Through the Declaration of Independence)

The *Declaration of Independence*[1] declares that all men are "*endowed by their Creator with certain unalienable Rights*" and that "*Governments are instituted among Men, deriving their just powers from the consent of the governed*" to secure those rights. If the power of government comes from the consent of the governed, it rationally follows that the governed should be able to understand the government that they have formed. The United States Supreme Court has emphasized[2] this principle for over 200 years by saying: "*The Constitution was written to be understood by the voters; its words and phrases were used in their normal and ordinary as distinguished from technical meaning;*" This is an extremely powerful statement. It means that if you are reading this book, you should be able to understand the Constitution's meaning exactly. There aren't some secret codes or handshakes required to do that. Similarly, any United States Supreme Court decision should be understandable in its description and analysis. Unfortunately, for all American citizens, the meaning of the Privileges and Immunities Clause of the Constitution has been distorted, lost, and ignored over the last 250 years. As stated in the introduction, the primary purpose of this book is to pro-

1 United States National Archives and Records Administration. (2026, Feb. 22). https://www.archives.gov/founding-docs/declaration-transcript

2 Cases that have emphasized this principle include *Martin v. Hunter's Lessee* (1816), *Gibbons v. Ogden* (1824), *United States v. Sprague*(1931), *District of Columbia v. Heller* (2008), and *McDonald v. Chicago* (2010)

vide any reader with a complete case that will make them a subject matter expert in Privileges and Immunities. The topic may seem specific and nuanced, but it impacts every facet of our daily lives. To start to develop the background material for this case, we need to start well before the founding of our country.

This Chapter focuses on England's use and understanding of "*privileges and immunities*" prior to the Revolutionary War. To try to keep the reader engaged, easily understood arguments will be accompanied by detailed exhibits, precedents and appendices for those who are legally inclined. The author would never want to be accused of performing a "*mind-numbing technical query*" or had it said that his "*legalize is a smokescreen*". Instead of providing detailed history lessons, quick overviews will be described. It is hoped that the reader will be encouraged to independently research, verify and study selected events and cases that are of interest to them.

Most Supreme Court opinions are written considering the *United States Constitution*[3], prior precedents and historical perspectives. In the history of the United States, the first document where we find mention of "*privileges and immunities*" is in the *Articles of Confederation*[4] which was approved in 1777. This precedent will be analyzed in detail in the next chapter. Before we can understand the meaning of "*privileges and immunities*", we must look much further back in time. The first permanent English Colony in what is now the United States of America was founded in 1607 at Jamestown (*Virginia Colony*). This was 169 years before the signing of the *Declaration of Independence.* If the average child was born when a parent was 25, then this would be over six generations of experience prior to the American Revolution. For a modern perspective, if we went back in time from the year 2026 by 169 years, we would arrive in America in 1857. That was four years before the American Civil War and only 81 years after the founding of our country. Since the *Articles of Confederation* weren't written out of thin air, the tremendous history of colonial America must be understood to determine their meaning.

As a thought experiment, what would you say to an 18-year-

3 United States National Archives and Records Administration. (2026, Feb. 22). https://www.archives.gov/founding-docs/constitution-transcript

4 United States National Archives and Records Administration. (2026, Feb. 22). https://www.archives.gov/milestone-documents/articles-of-confederation#transcript

old George Washington if you could travel back in time to the English colony of Virginia in 1749 to meet him? If you traveled back on March 25th and suddenly became tongue-tied you could say "Happy New Year!". How can that be? Hasn't New Years always been January 1? The short answer is no, and the Bible unlocks the reason. We can't look at the history of both England and the United States without understanding the importance of Christianity to their development.

Every year, March 25 is celebrated as the *Feast of the Annunciation* in the Christian calendar (it is called *Lady Day* in England). In the *Gospel of Luke*[5] , the *Angel Gabriel* explains to the *Virgin Mary* that the *Holy Spirit* will come over her, and that she will give birth to Jesus who is the son of God. Backing up 9 months from Jesus' birth on December 25 (Christmas Day), the *Holy Spirit* came over Mary on March 25. The tremendous joy and importance of this singular event, and how it brought about an entirely new era for mankind, is the reason that it was celebrated as the New Year. For those who love art, the Smithsonian National Gallery of Art in Washington, DC has many beautiful Medieval paintings[6] that commemorate the Annunciation. Before the invention of the printing press in approximately the year 1440, artwork was a key means to teach history and religion.

When George Washington was 20, the English Parliament aligned

---

5 Bible, King James Version. Luke Chapter 1, verses 26:35
"And in the sixth month the angel Gabriel was sent from God unto a city of Galilee, named Nazareth, To a virgin espoused to a man whose name was Joseph, of the house of David; and the virgin's name was Mary. And the angel came in unto her, and said, Hail, thou that art highly favoured, the Lord is with thee: blessed art thou among women. And when she saw him, she was troubled at his saying, and cast in her mind what manner of salutation this should be. And the angel said unto her, Fear not, Mary: for thou hast found favour with God. And, behold, thou shalt conceive in thy womb, and bring forth a son, and shalt call his name JESUS. He shall be great, and shall be called the Son of the Highest: and the Lord God shall give unto him the throne of his father David: And he shall reign over the house of Jacob for ever; and of his kingdom there shall be no end. Then said Mary unto the angel, How shall this be, seeing I know not a man? And the angel answered and said unto her, The Holy Ghost shall come upon thee, and the power of the Highest shall overshadow thee: therefore also that holy thing which shall be born of thee shall be called the Son of God."

6 Medieval Paintings at the Smithsonian National Gallery of Art include: "The Coronation of the Virgin with Six Angels" (circa 1390 by Agnolo Gaddi), "The Presentation of the Virgin in the Temple" (circa 1398 by Paolo di Giovanni Fei), "The Annunciation" (circa 1423 by Masollino de Panicale) and "The Annunciation" (circa 1445 by Fra Carnevale)

England's Julian Calendar with the Gregorian Calendar. The Julian calendar had been instituted by Julius Caesar 45 years before the birth of Christ. Pope Gregory XIII had established the Gregorian Calendar in 1582 to better account for the actual observed solar year. In addition to the New Years change, there was also an 11-day shift having to do with the recognition of leap years. For someone such as George Washington who lived across this transition, and was born between January 1 and March 25,, this meant that his birthday suddenly changed one year and 11 days! How efficiently do you think present-day departments in charge of issuing state driver's licenses could have handled that change?

In a search for English legal precedents for uses of the terms privileges and immunities we can find an early example from over 600 years before George Washington was born. King Henry I ruled England. Henry was the youngest son of William the Conqueror, whose Normand conquest in 1066 created the present English Monarchy. In the time of King Henry I, laws were handwritten on scrolls since the printing press wouldn't be invented for over 300 years. At that time, the Pope in Rome ran the Church of England. This was over 400 years before King Henry VIII took control of the Church of England away from the Pope. He did this when he was frustrated with the Pope for not allowing him to have his first marriage to Catherine of Aragon annulled.

Most people have heard of the medieval Knights Templar from movies or books such as *Raiders of the Lost Ark(1981)*, *Indiana Jones and the Last Crusade(1989)*, or *The Da Vinci Code(2003)*. The Knights Templar were appointed by the Pope in Rome, but could travel far and wide throughout the world. Even though they could have swords, armor and other weaponry, King Henry I provided them with additional rights and protection by granting them extensive privileges and immunities. In the 1600's, Sir Edward Coke wrote about this in his authoritative description of English Law referred to as the *Institutes*. This law operated for approximately 200 years during the Middle Ages. Through the law[7], the Knights Templar "*obtained so great and large privileges, liberties and immunities for themselves, their Tenants and Farmers, etc. as no other order had the like.*"

Continuing a search forward through English History from King Henry I's time, we find a recurring theme: the threat of Civil War forced English monarchs to provide their subjects more rights in order to maintain power. We will see how in one instance, a refusal to compromise resulted in a full-blown Civil War in which the King not only lost his power but lost his head. The first of these threats to the Monarchy occurred under King John, and resulted in the *Magna Carta* in 1215. It helped to establish England as a Constitutional Monarchy (as opposed to the present-day United States of America, which is a Constitutional Republic).

The *Magna Carta (1215)*

The *Magna Carta* is so important to our collective history with England that a copy is maintained by the National Archives . Interestingly, the 37th paragraph of the *Magna Carta* ties back to the law of King

7 Coke, Edward. *The Second Part of the Institutes of the Laws of England, 6th Edition*, page 431, "For the better understanding of this Statute; it is to be known that the order of the Templers, otherwise Knights of the Temple being men professed mere by Gelasius the Pope founded Anno Domini 1117, which was Anno 18 H. 1.These were called Templarii, because they were first founded in some of the edifices adjoining and belonging to the Temple, and had the charge and keeping of the Lords Sepulchre, and not only entertained Pilgrims that came to the Sepulchre, etc. but in their armour conducted Christians that had a desire to see the City of Jerusalem, and other places in the Land of Palestine, and to guard them from the Saracens and Infidels. Soon after, viz. Anno Domini 1120, which was in Anno 21 H. 1. The Hospitallers, commonly called Milites Sancti Johannis Jerosolymitani, being professed Friers of S. John of Jerusalem, under the rule of S. Augustine, were founded, Honorius then being Pope, and they were called Hospitularii, Hospitallers, because they had the care of hosting and providing Hospitals for Pilgrims, etc. travelling to Jerusalem, etc. and for their safe-conduct against Saracens and Infidels. These two orders, (but especially the Templars) did so overspread throughout Christendom, and so exceedingly increased in possessions, revenues and wealth, and specially in England, as you will wonder to read in approved Histories, and withall obtained so great and large privileges, liberties, and immunities for themselves, their Tenants and Farmers, etc. as no other order had the like."

Henry I regarding the Knights Templar. It says[8]: "*... all liberties and free customs shall be preserved to archbishops, bishops, abbots, priors, Templars, Hospitallers, earls, barons and all others, both ecclesiastical and secular persons, just as they formerly had.*"

The *Magna Carta* recognizes religious freedom for the Church of England[9], it recognizes inheritance rights, it provides for judicial due process, and it acknowledges private property rights. When describing individual rights for Englishmen, it makes a powerful statement regarding trade which is shown in Exhibit 1[10].

In the coming sections, it will be shown how trade was closely tied to privileges and immunities and how it impacted the *Declaration of Independence*, the *Articles of Confederation*, and the *United States Constitution*. The famous English legal authority William Blackstone wrote[11] about the section of the *Magna Carta* shown in Exhibit 1. His quote is a form of a "*two for the price of one*" quote since he uses

8 United States National Archives and Records Administration. (2026, Feb. 22). https://www.archives.gov/exhibits/featured-documents/magna-carta/translation.html

9 Magna Carta, §1, "...the English Church is to be free and to have all its rights fully and its liberties entirely."

10 United States National Archives and Records Administration. (2026, Feb. 22). https://www.archives.gov/exhibits/featured-documents/magna-carta/translation.html

11 Blackstone, William. *Commentaries on the Laws of England Book I: The Rights of Persons: Chapter 7 – Of the King's Prerogative.*

Exhibit 1 - Protections for Foreign Merchants, Magna Carta §30

> "All merchants, unless they have been previously and publicly forbidden, are to have safe and secure conduct in leaving and coming to England and in staying and going through England both by land and by water to buy and to sell, without any evil exactions, according to the ancient and right customs, save in time of war, and if they should be from a land at war against us and be found in our land at the beginning of the war, they are to be attached without damage to their bodies or goods until it is established by us or our chief justiciar in what way the merchants of our land are treated who at such a time are found in the land that is at war with us, and if our merchants are safe there, the other merchants are to be safe in our land."

statements by the French philosopher Montesquieu to help make his argument. Blackstone said: *"But it is somewhat extraordinary, that it should have found a place in the magna carta, a mere interior treaty between the king and his natural-born subjects; which occasions the learned Montesquieu to remark with a degree of admiration, 'that the English have made protection of foreign merchants one of the articles of their national liberty.' But indeed it well justifies another observation which he has made 'that the English know better than any other people on earth, how to value at the same time these three great advantages, religion, liberty and commerce.'"*

The three great advantages of religion, liberty and commerce that Montesquieu described were also tightly coupled with the rationale for founding the English colonies in America. In 1578, Queen Elizabeth I of England granted Charters to Sir Humphrey Gilbert for parts of what is now Canada, and to Sir Walter Raleigh for parts of what is now the United States of America. Supreme Court Justice Joseph Story wrote[12] extensively about the Colonial development of the United States in his *Commentaries on the Constitution of the United States(1833)*. He described how Sir Walter Raleigh's writings about the newly discovered lands impacted Queen Elizabeth I with the following: "*such was the splendor of the description of the soil and climate and productions of that region given by the first adventurers, that Elizabeth was proud to bestow upon it the name of Virginia, and thus to connect it with the reign of a virgin Queen.*" It will be left to the reader to consider some of the parallels between the role of the Virgin Mary in the birth of Christianity and the role of the Virgin Queen in the birth of the United States.

Before moving onto the history of Colonial America, the *Magna Carta* describes various rights of all Englishmen that our forefathers inherited. The *Magna Carta* went through different versions and stabilized with the 1297 version that is used in this book. Appendix 1 analyzes all 37 sections of the document. The 1297 *Magna Carta* used in Appendix 1 was translated by Professor Nicholas Vincent for Sotheby's. Many of the sections only apply to England, and are so noted. Other sections have direct applicability to our country, and are identified as MC1-MC37. Specific privileges and immunities from the *Magna Carta* will be discussed later in this chapter.

---

12 Story, Joseph. *Commentaries on the Constitution of the United States.* Volume 1, Chapter II

Colonial American Timeline

Next, we will move on to analyze the 169-year history of Colonial America to help to identify and understand the reasons for "privileges and immunities". The goal here is not to teach a full history lesson for Colonial America, but to highlight key events that later impacted the privileges and immunities clause of the United States Constitution. One way to do this concisely is with the visual timeline shown as "Figure 1 – Colonial America Timeline 1600-1775".

Reviewing the first row of Figure 1, each of the English Monarchs that reigned during this timeframe is shown. The 1600's were an extremely tumultuous century for England. The gap from 1649-1660 corresponds to overthrow of King Charles I, his eventual beheading, the English Commonwealth and the eventual restoration of the monarchy with King Charles II. A second overthrow of the monarchy occurred in 1688 when King James II was forced to abdicate in what is known as the "Glorious Revolution". It is amazing that the English Colonies in America survived these decades of turmoil. By the time of the American Revolution, frustration with the King had reached the boiling point. An important description regarding feelings about the entire monarchy comes from Thomas Paine in his book *Common Sense*[13] *(1776)*. In flowery language, Paine described that *"England, since the conquest, hath known some few good monarchs, but groaned beneath a much larger number of bad ones; yet no man in his senses can say that their claim under William the Conqueror is a very honorable one. A French bastard landing with armed banditti, and establishing himself king of England..."*

After the English monarchs, the next row of Figure 1 shows Key English Parliament Acts that impacted the rights of Englishmen. William Blackstone's *Commentaries on the Laws of England* were published in 1769. This was less than a decade before the American Revolution. Blackstone discussed the rights of Englishmen extensively, and he indicates that their liberties come from the *Magna Carta(1215)*, the *Petition of Right(1628)*[14]

13 Paine, Thomas. *Common Sense.* Pages 13-14

14 United Kingdom National Archives. (2026, Feb. 22). Petition of Right. https://www.legislation.gov.uk/aep/Cha1/3/1/enacted

Figure 1 - Colonial America Timeline 1600-1775

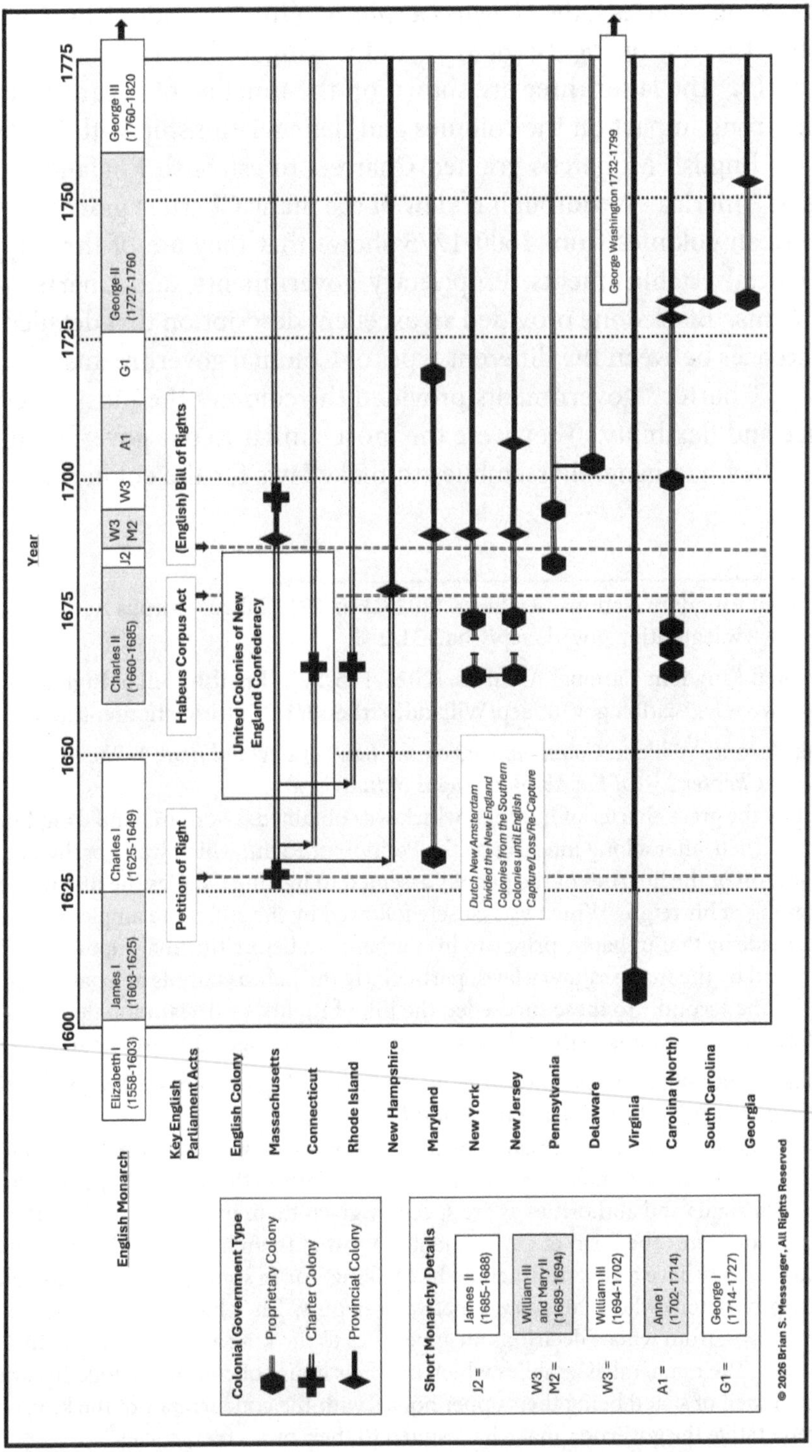

under King Charles I, the *Habeus Corpus Act(1680)*[15] under King Charles II, and the *Bill of Rights(1688)*[16] under King William III and Queen Mary II[17]. The latter three are shown on the timeline of Figure 1 due to their strong impact on the colonies and their relationship with England.

English Monarchs granted Charters to establish England's colonies in America. A thorough review of the many Charters granted to the American colonies from 1600-1775 shows that they are of three types: Provincial establishments, Proprietary governments, and Charter governments. Blackstone provided an excellent description that detailed the differences between the different types of Colonial governments.

Charter[18] governments provided the colonies the most independence and flexibility. They were the most similar to our government today. They had general assemblies to make laws for the colony. Provin-

---

15 United Kingdom National Archives. (2026, Feb. 22). Habeus Corpus Act. https://www.legislation.gov.uk/aep/Cha2/31/2

16 United Kingdom National Archives. (2026, Feb. 22). [English] Bill of Rights. https://www.legislation.gov.uk/aep/WillandMarSess2/1/2/introduction/enacted

17 Blackstone, William. *Commentaries on the Laws of England Book 1: The Rights of Persons: Chapter 1 – Of the Absolute Rights of Individuals:*
"First by the great charter of liberties, which was obtained, sword in hand from king John; ...Then, after a long interval, by the Petition of Right; which was a parliamentary declaration of the liberties of the people, assented to by king Charles the first in the beginning of his reign. Which was closely followed by the still more ample concessions made by that unhappy prince to his parliament, before the final rupture between them; and by the many salutary laws, particularly the habeas corpus act, passed under Charles the second. To these succeeded the Bill of Rights, or declaration delivered by the lords and commons to the prince and princess of Orange 13 February 1688;"

18 Blackstone, William. *Commentaries on the Laws of England Book I, Section 4 – Of the Countries Subject to the Laws of England.*
"Charter governments, in the nature of civil corporations, with the power of making bye-laws for their own interior regulation, not contrary to the laws of England; and with such rights and authorities as are specially given them in their several charters of incorporation. The form of government in most of them is borrowed from that of England. They have a governor named by the king, (or in some proprietary colonies by the proprietor,) who is his representative or deputy. They have courts of justice of their own, from whose decisions an appeal lies to the king and council here in England. Their general assemblies which are their house of commons, together with their council of stated being their upper house, with the concurrence of the king or his representative the governor, make laws suited to their own emergencies."

cial[19] establishments basically had a Governor who was appointed by the King and were the default case. They provided the King with the most control over the colony. Proprietary[20] governments were given to individuals and/or corporations and were operated more like a business.

Reviewing Figure 1, it can be seen that many colonies had their type of Charter government change over time. For instance, Virginia started as a Proprietary Colony in 1607, but switched to a Provincial Colony when its Charter was revoked in 1624. Supreme Court Justice Joseph Story provided[21] the commentary on the origins and charters for the colonies used to generate Figure 1.

Each of the Colonial Charters referred to how the Colonists were subject to English Law. This fact is critical for understanding the legal history of the United States. Exhibit 2[22] is from the Virginia Charter of 1606. Similar sections are included in all of the colonial Charters, but the style and verbiage also changes over time and across monarchs. What is critical for our analysis is that colonists had the same fundamental rights as people born in England.

Approximately 30 years after the Glorious Revolution in England (1688), and 10 years before the birth of George Washington, Cato's Letters[23] were anonymously published in the London Journal. This amazing

---

19 Blackstone, William. *Commentaries on the Laws of England Book I, Section 4 – Of the Countries Subject to the Laws of England.*
"Provincial establishments, the constitutions of which depend on the respective commissions issued by the crown to the governors, and the instructions which usually accompany those commissions; under the authority of which, provincial assemblies are constituted, with the power of making local ordinances, not repugnant to the laws"

20 Blackstone, William. *Commentaries on the Laws of England Book I, Section 4 – Of the Countries Subject to the Laws of England.*
"Proprietary governments, granted out by the crown to individuals in the nature of feudatory principalities, with all the inferior regalities, and subordinate powers of Legislation, which formerly belonged to the owners of counties palatine: yet still with these express conditions, that the ends for which the grant was made be substantially pursued, and that nothing be attempted which may derogate from the sovereignty of the mother-country."

21 Story, Joseph. *Commentaries on the Constitution of the United States.* Volume 1, Book 1, History of the Colonies. Pages 3-183

22 Lucas, Samuel. *Charters of the Old English Colonies in America.* Page 6

23 Trenchard, John and Gordon, Thomas. *CATO's Letters: Or, Essays on Liberty, Civil and Religious, and other important Subjects.*

Exhibit 2 - Virginia Charter I by King James I (1606), Paragraph XV

"Also we do, for us, our heirs, and successors, declare, by these presents, that all and every the persons, being our subjects, which shall dwell and inhabit within every or any of the said several colonies and plantations, and every of their children, which shall happen to be born within any the limits and precincts of the said several colonies and plantations, shall have and enjoy all liberties, franchises, and immunities, within any of our other dominions, to all intents and purposes, as if they had been abiding and born within this our realm of England, or any other of our said dominions."

group of 144 essays were originally printed in the newspaper weekly between 1720 and 1723. The concept of "*Freedom of the Press*" didn't exist in England in the 1720's, and this is why the letters were published anonymously under the ancient name Cato. Their authors were later identified as former member of Parliament John Trenchard and his publishing friend Thomas Gordon.

Cato's Letters cover a tremendous range of topics involving liberty, government, corruption, religion and life. Many of the subjects that are discussed are timeless in nature, and it is surprising how applicable some of the letters are to issues of modern-day America. Decades after their newspaper publication, Cato's Letters were compiled into four volumes. They became popular references in the American Colonies leading up to the American Revolution. These essays have been quoted in many Supreme Court decisions because they provide an excellent perspective as to the rights of Englishmen at that time.

Possessing the legal rights of Englishmen was extremely critical to the colonists. It was so important that the fear of losing the rights of English Law was a grievance[24] that was written in the *Declaration of Independence*. Cato's Letter #48 explains[25] why English Law was so im-

24 *Declaration of Independence* – "For abolishing the free System of English Laws in a neighbouring Province, establishing therein an Arbitrary government, and enlarging its Boundaries so as to render it at once an example and fit instrument for introducing the same absolute rule into these Colonies:"

25 Trenchard, John and Gordon, Thomas. *CATO's Letters: Or, Essays on Liberty, Civil and Religious, and other important Subjects: Cato's Letter #48, The general unhappy State of the World, from the Baseness and Iniquity of its Governors in most Countries.* Published Saturday, October 14, 1721. (Thomas Gordon)

portant saying: "*Let us therefore remember the mighty difference between ourselves and other nations, and the glorious cause of it, and always cherish it. We are not the prey of monks, or janizaries, or dragoons, nor the blind slaves of unaccountable will and pleasure. Our lives and properties are secured by the best bulwark in the world, that of laws made by ourselves, and executed by our magistrates, who are likewise made by us;*".

What are Privileges and Immunities?

While the Virginia Charter of 1606 refers to "*liberties, franchises and immunities*", the third Virginia Charter in 1612 refers[26] to "*freedoms, liberties, franchises, privileges, immunities,...*". We will see how different terminology is often used to describe the same concepts in the writings of the time. When describing the sources of the rights of Englishmen, Blackstone uses language from philosophical theories such as John Locke's[27] to describe both privileges and immunities. In Exhibit 3[28],

26 Lucas, Samuel. *Charters of the Old English Colonies in America.* Page 24, Par. X

27 John Locke lived from 1632-1704. His philosophical writings impacted the Declaration of Independence, he was a leading political theorist, and he also helped to write the Carolina Charter of 1669. His most famous publication was *The Second Treatise of Government.*

28 Blackstone, William. *Commentaries on the Laws of England Book 1: The Rights of Persons: Chapter 1 – Of the Absolute Rights of Individuals*

Exhibit 3 – Description of Privileges and Immunities, Blackstone

"The rights themselves thus defined by these several statutes consist in a number of private immunities; which will appear, from what has been premised, to be indeed, no other than either residuum [remainder] of natural liberty, which is not required by laws of society to be sacrificed to public convenience; or else those civil privileges, which society has engaged to provide, in lieu of the natural liberties so given up by individuals. ... And these may be reduced to three principal or primary articles; the right of personal security, the right of personal liberty; and the right of private property: Because as there is no other known method of compulsion, or of abridging man's natural free will, but by an infringement or diminution of one or other of these important rights, the preservation of these, inviolate, may justly be said to include the preservation of our civil immunities in their largest and most extensive sense."

he indicates that when man enters society, he must sacrifice some liberty, and what is left are his private immunities. In addition, society may provide privileges to compensate for the natural rights given up. These privileges and immunities revolve around personal security, personal liberty, and private property. His reference to "these several statutes" refers to the *Magna Carta* and the acts of parliament shown in Figure 1.

As described by Blackstone, a right that is granted by the government can be called a privilege. Rights may include protection against prosecution for using the right, which can be called immunity. For instance, the "right to free speech" provides the privilege to speak freely and the immunity against prosecution for doing so. Some rights that provide specific legal protection, such as the "right to habeas corpus", may be thought of strictly as an immunity only. This is due to the fact that their purpose is to protect the person from government abuse. We shall see that it is also possible that a right describes an action that does not require legal protection. In this case, the right may be thought of strictly as a privilege only. In the days of Colonial America, there was no "right to free speech"; with one major exception. The English Parliament had a "right to free speech" as described[29] in the English Bill of Rights.

The English Parliament had many Privileges and Immunities. A valid question would be whether all of the Privileges and Immunities should be written down in a simple list? Exhibit 4[30] describes William Blackstone's reasons why this should never be done. He describes the fear that the crown (king or queen) could devise means to work around precisely defined privileges to harass parliament. Another problem is that the list could not be easily changed if something was forgotten. A further problem could be the implied prioritization of the rights based upon their position in a list. Is a right that is listed higher in the list more important than a right that is listed lower on the list? For centuries, the United States Supreme Court has grappled with the fact that Privileges and Immunities in the *United States Constitution* are not individually listed.

Provided with this framework for evaluating rights, we can turn

29 [English] Bill of Rights - "That the Freedom of Speech and Debates or Proceedings in Parliament ought not to be impeached or questioned in any Court or Place out of Parliament"

30 Blackstone, William. *Commentaries on the Laws of England Book 1: The Rights of Persons: Chapter 2 – Of the Parliament.*

Exhibit 4 – Reason to Not List Privileges & Immunities, Blackstone

"The privileges of parliament are likewise very large and indefinite; which has occasioned an observation that the principal privilege of parliament consisted in this, that its privileges were not certainly known to any but the parliament itself. … Privilege of parliament was principally established, in order to protect its members not only from being molested by their fellow-subjects, but also more especially from being oppressed by the power of the crown. It therefore all the privileges of parliament were once to be set down and ascertained, and no privilege to be allowed but what was so defined and determined, it were easy for the executive power to devise some new case, not within the line of privilege, and under pretense thereof to harass any refractory member and violate the freedom of parliament."

to the *Magna Carta*, the *Petition of Right*, the *Habeus Corpus Act*, and the *English Bill of Rights* to identify all of the rights that they enshrined. The Magna Carta's structure is different than the other three Acts of Parliament and it will be looked at first. The original text to generate the simplified rights listed below can be found in Appendix 1.

Simplified Rights Enshrined in the *Magna Carta(1215)*

- "Right for the Church of England to be free with full rights and liberties." {MC1}
- "Right for widows to inherit their husband's estates and to a formal due process to do so." {MC6, MC7}
- "Right to due process by the government in collection of fees and debts" {MC8, MC10, MC14, MC18, MC19}
- "Right to regular judicial proceedings in fixed locations" {MC11, MC12}
- "Right to due process in terms of who can run trials" {MC17}
- "Right to government compensation for property taken" {MC19, MC21}
- "Right to due process in the handling of land seized from felons" {MC22}
- "Right to due process regarding requirement to appear in court" {MC24}
- "Right to uniform weights and measures" {MC25}
- "Right to a free inquest for someone who has died" {MC26}
- "Right to bail with reliable witnesses" {MC27}
- "Right to a trial by jury" {MC29}
- "Right to a speedy trial" {MC29}
- "Right to due process in collection of taxes" {MC35}

{The rights described above are from the translation of the 1297 Magna Carta performed by Professor Nicholas Vincent for Sotheby's Inc.}

The other three Acts of Parliament listed grievances that were perpetrated by the King and his representatives. Following the grievances, Parliament petitioned the King to acknowledge a specific right. For purpose of analysis, each of the three grievance based Acts of Parliament is broken down in an attached Appendices to show the petitioned right, the corresponding grievance, and a simplified description of the right. Each of the rights is provided with an identifier based on the Act of Parliament and its order in the Act. To generalize the simplified rights, the term Parliament is replaced by "legislature" or "legislative" depending upon context.

Early in his monarchy, King Charles I was forced to accept the *Petition of Right* (1627). His commissioners had been charged with taxing subjects without Parliament's approval, imprisoning subjects without charging them, quartering soldiers and sailors in subjects' homes, and executing some subjects and refusing to prosecute other subjects through commissions operating under martial law. The complete breakdown of the Petition of Right is found in Appendix 2. The simplified rights that were extracted by Parliament in the Petition of Right are:

Simplified Rights Enshrined in the *Petition of Right(1627)*

- "Right not to be taxed without legislative approval" {PR1}
- "Right to being formally charged with a crime, and to due process, before being imprisoned" {PR2}
- "Right not to have soldiers or sailors quartered in your home" {PR3}
- "Right not to be tried and executed under martial law that is not approved by the legislature" {PR4}

During the monarchy of King James II, he was forced to accept the *Habeus Corpus Act*(1679). The grievances that Parliament had with the King were that some subjects were kept in prison when they should have been bailable to be released. There were also subjects who were transferred far away or overseas to be imprisoned. The complete breakdown of the *Habeus Corpus Act* is found in Appendix 3 but the simplified rights are shown here:

Simplified Rights Enshrined in the *Habeus Corpus Act (1679)*

- "Right to Habeus Corpus" {HC1}

- "Right not to be imprisoned overseas or far from home" {HC2}

In 1688, during the monarchy of Catholic King James II the surprise birth of a son, who would be raised Catholic, made it likely that a Catholic dynasty would rule England. England had been roiled by religious disagreements between Catholics and Protestants for decades. Protestants dominated the population and encouraged an invasion from the Dutch Prince William of Orange. William of Orange's Protestant wife Mary had been next in line of succession to the English crown prior to the surprise birth of King James II's son. King James II fled England and abdicated the crown; not wanting to repeat the fate of his father King Charles I. It could be said that this is one case in history where a country's ruler was thrown out of office for sleeping with his wife.

One of the features of the *Bill of Rights* (1688) was to guarantee that only Protestants could become English monarchs. The *Popish Recusants Act* (1672) had already blocked[31] Catholics from holding any government offices. The *Taxation Act*(1678) had blocked[32] Catholics from being members of Parliament by requiring an oath that denied the transubstantiation of the bread and wine into the body and blood of Christ. The *Toleration Act* (1688) was passed[33] within months of the *Bill of Rights.* Part of its purpose was to unify all Protestants in England in opposition to the Catholics who had been defeated with the abdication of King James II.

Parliament took the opportunity of allowing William III and Mary II to jointly take the crown to set up a more permanent set of rights for Englishmen. All of the declared rights were stated as "...*Vindicating and Asserting their ancient Rights and Liberties...*" This acknowledgment

31 United Kingdom National Archives. (2026, Feb. 22). Popish Recusants Act (1672). https://www.legislation.gov.uk/aep/Cha2/25/2/enacted/data.html

32 United Kingdom National Archives. (2026, Feb. 22). Taxation Act (1678). https://www.legislation.gov.uk/aep/Cha2/30/2/enacted/data.html
-required an Oath for Parliament that included "...That I doe believe that in the Sacrament of the Lords Supper there is not any Transubtantiation of the Elements of Bread and Wine into the Body and Blood of Christ..."

33 United Kingdom National Archives. (2026, Feb. 22). Toleration Act (1688). https://www.legislation.gov.uk/aep/WillandMar/1/18/paragraph/1n1/enacted
- listed its purpose as "Forasmuch as some ease to scrupulous Consciences in the Exercise of Religion may be an effectuall meanes to unite their Majesties Protestant Subjects in Interest and Affection..."

means that all of the rights listed in the English Bill of Rights had been around since ancient time. To enshrine the *Bill of Rights*, Parliament created a new requirement for Kings and Queens. Prior to coronation, the King and/or Queen had to take an oath which included "*...established by this present Parliament and shall stand and be the Law of this Realm forever...*". This workaround made it clear that these rights were not to be changed by either a new monarch or a new Parliament.

As in the case of prior Acts of Parliament, the *Bill of Rights* comes in the form of grievances and the corresponding declared rights. The complete breakdown of the rights is described in Appendix 4, but the simplified rights are shown below:

Simplified Rights Enshrined in the *(English) Bill of Rights(1688)*

- "Right not to have laws suspended without legislative approval" {EBR1}
- "Right not to be prosecuted for petitioning to be excused from laws" {EBR2}
- "Right not to be prosecuted by an Ecclesiastical Court" {EBR3}
- "Right not to have the government spend money not approved by the legislature"{EBR4}
- "Right to petition the government for a redress of grievances" {EBR5}
- "Right not to have a standing army without approval of the legislature" {EBR6}
- "Right for citizens to have arms for their personal defense" {EBR7}
- "Right to have free elections" {EBR8}
- "Right for members of the legislature to speak and debate freely" {EBR9}
- "Right to have only qualified jurors seated for trials" {EBR10}
- "Right not to have excessive bail required"{EBR11}
- "Right not to have excessive fines imposed" {EBR12}
- "Right not to have cruel or unusual punishments inflicted" {EBR13}
- "Right not to have pre-conviction fines and forfeitures" {EBR14}
- "Right to have frequent meetings of the legislature" {EBR15}

Of all the rights listed in the (English) *Bill of Right*, the "Right for citizens to have arms for their personal defense" {EBR7} requires additional discussion. In Appendix 4, it can be seen that the grievance for King James II's reign involved the disarming of Protestants. The resulting Declared Right was that "The Subjects which are Protestants may have Arms for their Defense suitable to their Conditions and as allowed by Law." The use of "Subjects" is key since that is the most general term for citizens of the England that could be used; as opposed to some privileged class. The use of "Protestants" makes total sense in the context of the Glorious Revolution and the fact that Catholics were a minority disfavored class. The purpose for subjects having Arms for their Defense makes it perfectly clear that this is an individual right. There are two excellent contemporaneous sources that describe important reasons for "Subjects" to be armed.

The ancient principle of Self Defense was described[34] by John Locke in his "*The Second Treatise of Government*". Locke said "*it being reasonable and just I should have a right to destroy that which threatens me with destruction.*" He also said: "*when all cannot be preserved, the safety of the innocent is to be preferred; and one may destroy a man who makes war upon him*". Locke goes on to describe[35] the right to kill a robber with "*This makes it lawful for a man to kill a thief who has not in the least hurt him, nor declared any design upon his life, any farther than by the use of force so to get him in his power as to take away his money...*".

Beyond the personal right to self-defense, there is another extremely important national defense perspective to having armed citizens. This was explained[36] in Cato's Letter #65 with "*In free countries, as people work for themselves, so they will fight for themselves: But in arbitrary countries, ... when a tyrant's army is beaten, his country is conquered: He has no resource; his subjects having neither arms, nor courage, nor reason to fight for him; He has no support but his standing forces; who, for enabling him to oppress, are sharers in his oppression;*" This letter goes on to explain how "*In attacks upon a free state, every man will fight to defend it, because every many has something to defend in it. He is in love with his condition, his ease, and property, and will venture his life rather than lose them; ...For these reasons, small free states have conquered the greatest princes; and the greatest princes have never been able to conquer free states, but either by surprising them basely, or by corrupting them, or by forces almost infinitely superior...*". A little over 50 years later, this was proven in the case of the American Revolution. Even with nearly "infinitely superior" forces, King

34 Locke, John. *The Second Treatise of Government.* §16

35 Locke, John, *The Second Treatise of Government.* §18

36 Trenchard, John and Gordon, Thomas. *CATO's Letters: Or, Essays on Liberty, Civil and Religious, and other important Subjects: Cato's Letter #65 Military Virtue produced and supported by Civil Liberty only.* published Saturday, February 10, 1721. (Thomas Gordon)

George III was unable to defeat the Continental Army of "free men" in the "small free states" led by General George Washington.

At the time of the (English) *Bill of Rights*(1688), it is interesting to see which of our present 1st and 2nd Amendment rights were possessed by an English citizen. The "Right to petition the government for a redress of grievances" that is found in our 1st Amendment was a clear right {EBR5}. The "Right for citizens to have arms for their personal defense", which is protected by our 2nd Amendment, was a clear right {EBR7}. "Freedom of Speech" and "Freedom of the Press" were rights that were possessed only by members of Parliament {EBR9}. There was no formal Freedom of Assembly, though the right to have a Parliament {EBR15}, and the right to have religious services would definitely qualify as rights to assemble. Finally, the *Magna Carta* had provided the Church of England with rights, but otherwise, "Freedom of Religion" was very circumscribed. Christianity was permitted, but Catholics were heavily disfavored. The colony of Maryland provided an extreme example of religious fidelity which can only be described as the opposite of "Freedom of Religion". In 1649, they passed a law[37] declaring that denying the holy Trinity, or making other comments constituting blasphemy, was punishable with death and confiscation of your lands and goods.

Privileges and Immunities for Trade

Trade and commerce were critical to the survival and prosperity of the colonies. In his 1689 publication of *The Second Treatise of Government*, John Locke described[38] an interesting thought experiment. He

---

37 Maryland State Archives. (2026, Feb. 22). Maryland Assembly Proceedings, April 2—21, 1649 P. 269.

https://msa.maryland.gov/megafile/msa/speccol/sc2900/sc2908/000001/000001/html/am1--244.html

"That whatsoever pson or psons within this Province and the Islands thereunto belonging shall from henceforth blaspheme God, that is Curse him, or deny our Saviour Jesus Christ to bee the sonne of God, or shall deny the holy Trinity the ffather sonne and holy Ghost, or the God-head of any of the said Three psons of the Trinity or the Vnity of the Godhead, or shall use or utter any reproachfull Speeches, words or language concerning the said Holy Trinity, or any of the said three psons thereof, shalbe punished with death and confiscaton or forfeiture of all his or her lands and goods to the Lord Proprietary and his heires,"

38 Locke, John. *The Second Treatise of Government*. §48

said: "*for I ask, what would a man value ten thousand or an hundred thousand acres of excellent land, ready cultivated, and well stocked too with cattle, in the middle of the inland parts of America, where he had no hopes of commerce with other parts of the world, to draw money by the sale of the product? It would not be worth the enclosing, and we should see him give up again to the wild of common nature whatever was more than would supply the conveniences of life to be had there for him and his family.*" At present day pricing[39] , an average acre of farmland in the eastern United States is worth approximately $5,000. Using John Locke's description, 100,000 acres would be valued at $500 Million today. Without any hope of commerce, he was indicating that the land would be worthless.

Referring back to the timeline for the English Colonies in Figure 1, the English colonies started off in Virginia and New England. For many decades, the Dutch colony of New Netherlands (centered around New Amsterdam which became New York City) separated the New England colonies from the Virginia and southern colonies. New Netherlands actually ranged from Delaware to Connecticut. Between 1664 and 1674, the colony of New Netherlands changed hands back and forth between the Dutch and the English during wars between them. It finally remained in English control starting in 1674, and would stay that way for over 100 years leading up to the Revolutionary War. To counter foreign and other threats, the United Colonies of New England was formed. Supreme Court Justice Joseph Story wrote about this confederation in Exhibit 5[40].

The United Colonies of New England was formed by individual colonies in what are now Massachusetts and Connecticut. As Justice Story described, Rhode Island was denied admission to the Confederation over a territorial disagreement with Plymouth Colony. The refusal to allow Rhode Island to join the Confederation was a little bit of a "mean girls" action. Rhode Island was a very small colony, and it was now surrounded by The United Colonies of New-England Confederation for all land routes leading into and out of the colony. When Rhode Island petitioned King Charles II for an updated Charter in 1662, they were able to

---

39 United States Department of Agriculture, National Agriculture Statistics Service. (2026, Feb. 22)
https://www.nass.usda.gov/Charts_and_Maps/graphics/farm_value_map.pdf

40 Story, Joseph. *Commentaries on the Constitution of the United States: Volume I.* §102

Exhibit 5 – United Colonies of New England Description, Joseph Story

"One of the most memorable circumstances in the history of New-England is the early formation and establishment of a confederation of the colonies ... the articles of the union were not finally adopted until 1643. In the month of May of that year the colonies of Massachusetts, Connecticut, New-Haven, and Plymouth formed a confederacy by the name of the United Colonies of New-England, and entered into a perpetual league of friendship and amity for offence and defence and mutual advice and succor. ... This union, so important and necessary for mutual defense and assistance during the troubles, which then agitated the parent country, was not objected to by King Charles the Second on his restoration; and with some few alterations it subsisted down to 1686, when all the charters were prostrated by the authority of King James [II]. Rhode Island made application to be admitted into this Union ; but was refused upon the ground, that the territory was within the limits of Plymouth colony."

include a trade and commerce rights section that differs from any other colonies' Charter. This section gives inhabitants of the Providence plantations the right to pass and repass through other English colonies for commerce and trade as shown in Exhibit 6[41].

Approximately 50 years after the Rhode Island Charter of 1662, John Trenchard discussed[42] the virtues and risks of trade in Cato's Letter

41 Lucas, Samuel. *Charters of the Old English Colonies in America*. Page 66

42 Trenchard, John and Gordon, Thomas. *CATO's Letters: Or, Essays on Liberty, Civil and Religious, and other important Subjects: Cato's Letter #64 Trade and Naval Power the Offspring of Civil Liberty only, and cannot subsist without it.* Saturday, February 3, 1721 (Trenchard, John)

Exhibit 6 – Rhode Island Charter (1662), Commerce & Trade Rights

"and that it shall be lawful to and for the inhabitants of the said colony of Providence plantation, without lett or molestation, to pass and repass with freedom into and through the rest of the English colonies, upon their lawful and civil occasions, and to converse, and hold commerce, and trade with such of the inhabitants of our other English colonies as shall be willing to admit them thereunto, they behaving themselves peaceably among them;"

#64. Trenchard described how trade can "*turn deserts into fruitful fields, villages into great cities, cottages into palaces, beggars into princes*". He wrote in flowery detail about the types of trading risks that Rhode Island was concerned with. For instance, he described raging corruption, bribery and extreme expense as risks with trading with arbitrary governments. With arbitrary governments, he described how a trader needs "*privileges and immunities*" to succeed and survive. The problem is that the only way to obtain them would be through bribery. In addition, the trader is at risk of a change of government officials, or the arbitrary and capricious nature of a specific official's requests. The entire Cato's Letter #64 is very interesting. In Exhibit 7[43], Trenchard describes the arbitrary government officials as bandits (banditti).

Trenchard then goes on to describe how even the best ruler, which he calls a "virtuous prince", cannot prevent problems such as a classic "bait and switch". He describes how "*Merchants shall be encouraged to import their goods, upon promises of easy and gentle usage; these goods when imported shall be subjected to exorbitant impositions and customs, perhaps confiscated upon frivolous pretences.*" These concerns clearly impacted Rhode Island in requesting their Charter of 1662. In the next

43 Trenchard, John and Gordon, Thomas. *Cato's Letters: Or, Essays on Liberty, Civil and Religious, and other important Subjects: Cato's Letter #64 Trade and Naval Power the Offspring of Civil Liberty only, and cannot subsist without it.*
"...grapple with and stem the raging corruptions in it, where virtue has nothing to do, and vice rides triumphant; where bribery, servile flattery, blind submissions, riotous expence, and very often lust and unnatural prostitutions, are the ladders to greatness;"

Exhibit 7 – Privileges and Immunities for Trade, Cato's Letter #64

"Now what encouragement or security can trade and industry receive from such a crew of banditti? No privileges and immunities, or even protection, can be obtained but for money, and are always granted to such who give most: and these again shall be curtailed, altered, abrogated, and cancelled, upon the change of a minister, or of his inclinations, interest, and caprices: ...Some merchants shall be openly encouraged and protected, and get exemptions from searches and duties, or shall be connived at in escaping them; others shall be burdened, oppressed, manacled, stopped, and delayed to extort presents, to wreak revenge, or to give preference of markets to favourites."

chapter, we will see how they impacted the development of the Privileges and Immunities Clause of the Articles of Confederation.

The Declaration of Independence

On April 19, 1775, the "Shot Heard Round the World" was fired at Lexington, Massachusetts Colony. The colonists were at war with England, but they didn't have a national government. Since the prior fall, each colony except for Georgia had representatives meeting in Philadelphia at what was called the First Continental Congress. When hostilities broke out[44], it was the colonists in Massachusetts that led the fighting. The Continental Congress worked to select George Washington to build and lead the Continental Army. He took over the army outside Boston on July 3, 1775. This was well after the Battle of Bunker Hill[45] had already been fought. That battle decimated the British Officer Corp even though the battle was a technical win for the British. As a last-ditch attempt towards peace, the Colonists sent King George III the "*Olive Branch Petition*". The King refused to read it, but the act of producing and sending it helped to generate support for a full dissolution of the ties to Great Britain. Remember that the round-trip time to send a message from the colonies to England would take many months since it included sailing each direction and generating a response.

During the Spring and early Summer of 1776, The Second Continental Congress developed, debated and rewrote their justification for separating from Great Britain. Finally, they announced and published the Declaration of Independence on July 4, 1776. In a form similar to the *Petition of Right*, *Habeus Corpus Act*, and the (English) *Bill of Rights* evaluated previously, the *Declaration of Independence* lists a long number of grievances that the colonists had against King George III. Since the *Declaration of Independence* involved breaking away from England, there was no reason to produce a list of corresponding rights that King George III needed to obey in the future. The signers of the *Declaration of Independence* stated that "*... we mutually pledge to each other our Lives,*

44 American Battlefield Trust. (2026, Feb. 22). https://www.battlefields.org/learn/articles/american-revolution-timeline

45 United States Department of Interior, National Park Service. (2026, Feb. 22). https://www.nps.gov/articles/000/the-battle-of-bunker-hill.htm

our Fortunes and our sacred Honor." It is abundantly clear that protecting these rights was worth sacrificing their lives for.

Appendix 5 takes the opening paragraphs, grievance list, and concluding paragraphs of the *Declaration of Independence* to clearly identify the "implied rights" that it identifies. For specific grievances, identifying the "implied right" is fairly simple. For the opening paragraphs of the *Declaration of Independence*, this takes a little more explanation. The entire structure and operation of this new government was different than from a monarchy. The most critical phrases regarding the structure of government are "*We hold these truths to be self-evident, that all men are created equal...*" and the phrase "*...Governments are instituted among Men, deriving their just power from the consent of the governed ...*". These definitions imply very powerful individual rights revolving around speech, press and assembly.

Under the English monarchy, speech was highly restricted. Parliament had the right to speak freely, but citizens did not. From Cato's Letter #15, it was said[46] that "*Whoever would overthrow the liberty of the nation, must begin by subduing the freedom of speech*". He then goes on to explain how King Charles I "*procured a proclamation to forbid the people to talk of Parliaments*". He explained how for King Charles II to live securely as a Catholic (papist), "*there was an act of Parliament made, declaring it treason to say that he was one.*" Can you imagine being convicted of treason for saying that the King was Catholic when it was true?

Since government is made by men, and all of its power comes from the consent of the governed, no citizen should have more right to speak or write than any other. All citizens must be able to speak and write about issues associated with governing the country. This includes, but is not limited to, anything regarding existing laws, proposed laws, policies, and the behavior and actions of anyone in government or working for the government. The right to speak and write freely are doubly evident since all citizens have a right to petition the government for a redress of grievances. In England, this was to protect them from retaliation by the King/Queen or their ministers. Since the government works for the people, the people have a right to complain about any wrongs or

---

46 Trenchard, John and Gordon, Thomas. *CATO's Letters: Or, Essays on Liberty, Civil and Religious, and other important Subjects: Cato's Letter #15 Of Freedom of Speech: That the same is inseparable from public Liberty.* Saturday, February 4, 1720, (Gordon, Thomas)

abuses that they see the government performing.

The right to assemble is another implied right from the Declaration of Independence. This comes from the ability to gather together in meetings to discuss anything related to the government. The right to redress grievances implies a right to assemble to support or to protest the actions of the government. Further, it implies a right to travel in groups to the location of the legislature to request a redress of grievances. The following are implied rights from the Declaration of Independence analyzed in Appendix 5.

Implied Rights in the *Declaration of Independence(1776)*

- "Right to speak and write about issues associated with the government (including regarding laws, policies, and members of the government)" {D1}
- "Right to assemble to support or protest the actions of the government" {D2}
- "Right to alter or abolish destructive governments" {D3}
- "Right to have a representative government that is responsive to the citizen's needs" {D4}
- "Right to have public records conveniently available for legislative use" {D5}
- "Right to an independent judiciary" {D6}
- "Right not to have targeted financial harassment from government officers or authorities"{D7}
- "Right not to have standing armies without legislative approval" {D8}
- "Right to have civilian control of the military" {D9}
- "Right not to have troops quartered in your home"{D10}
- "Right not to have complete trade embargoes with all other countries" {D11}
- "Right to a trial by jury" {D12}
- "Right to be tried near where a crime allegedly occurred"{D13}
- "Right to the existing System of English Laws" {D14}
- "Right not to have the government waging war against its citizens" {D15}
- "Right to petition government for a redress of grievances" {D16}

The Declaration of Independence significantly increased the rights of the former English colonists living in the "*13 united States of America*". In addition to the rights of Englishmen created by Parliament, and the implied rights created by the Declaration of Independence, there were other more ancient rights identified in the *Magna Carta*. These included the free practice of religion by the Church of England. In addition, the *Magna Carta* recognized the ancient rights of private property.

The foundational knowledge explained in this chapter will help the reader to understand the creation of the Privileges and Immunities Clauses in the coming chapters. Specific rights that Americans had as of the Declaration of Independence included those from the *Magna Carta* (Appx. 1, MC1-MC37) *Petition of Right* (Appx. 2, PR1-PR4), the *Habeus Corpus Act* (Appx. 3, HC1-HC2), the (English) *Bill of Rights* (Appx. 4, EBR1-EBR15), and the *Declaration of Independence* (Appx. 5, D1-D16). This chapter has explained the important reasons why Privileges and Immunities are critical for successful trade, and why they should not be formally listed. With the signing of the *Declaration of Independence*, the easy part was over. Our nation now had to successfully accomplish winning a war and founding a government.

CHAPTER 2

Our Nation in its Infancy

(1776 to the Signing of the Constitution)

After the Continental Congress adopted the Declaration of Independence, things went from bad to worse for George Washington's Continental Army. The British trounced Washington's army in battles across New York and New Jersey that fall. Things were so desperate for Washington in December 1776, that the British felt they had won the war. Many of the small remaining number of troops that Washington commanded had enlistments that would expire at the end of the year. His troops were encamped in Pennsylvania over the Delaware river from New Jersey. The British figured that fighting was probably over for the winter.

Desperate times call for desperate measures. Washington's crossing of the Delaware on Christmas night in 1776, and his amazing victory at the Battle of Trenton, turned a sure defeat for the infant nation of thirteen states into a tiny glimmer of hope[1]. This virtually divine event is memorialized in a 21-foot wide by 12-foot tall painting of *Washington Crossing the Delaware* by Emanuel Leutze. The painting was completed in 1851 and is displayed at the Metropolitan Museum of Art in New York City.

During 1777, Washington's Army started to have greater success. This led to the pivotal battles at Saratoga, New York. The second battle of Saratoga helped to encourage the French to enter the war in support of the United States. Washington's Army would experience the brutal winter at Valley Forge, Pennsylvania that winter,

1 O'Donnell, Patrick K. *The Indispensables: The Diverse Soldier-Mariners Who Shaped the Country, Formed the Navy, and Rowed Washington Across the Delaware.*

and a similarly awful winter at Morristown, New Jersey two years later. Serious fighting would continue for over four years until Washington's Victory at Yorktown, Virginia in late 1781. Peace with the British wouldn't be agreed to until the Treaty of Paris was signed in 1783.

The *Articles of Confederation(1777)*

While Washington was fresh off the victories in the battles at Saratoga, New York, the Continental Congress finalized the "Articles of Confederation" on November 15, 1777. All Colonial Charters written by Kings or Queens started with the calendar year and then the year of the reign of the Monarch. Taking this style, the opening paragraph of the Articles of Confederation indicates that it was agreed to on "*...the fifteenth day of November in the year of our Lord One Thousand Seven Hundred and Seventy seven, and in the Second Year of the Independence of America...*" The approval by Congress in 1777 still required all of the States to agree to the Articles. This didn't happen quickly, especially with the war going on. It was four years later on March 1, 1781, when the Articles of Confederation became the first Constitution for the United States of America. For most of the Revolutionary War, our country operated without a Constitution.

When the 13 original states agreed to the Articles of Confederation, they were creating a very weak central government with very powerful states. Article II said that "*Each state retains its sovereignty, freedom and independence, and every Power, Jurisdiction and right, which is not by this confederation expressly delegated to the United States, in Congress assembled.*" It has been said that "*the Federation*" in the original television show Star Trek was partially modeled upon the Articles of Confederation. The founding members of "*the Federation*" included humans, Vulcans(logically thinking pointy eared humanoids), Tellarites (who are pig like humanoids), and Andorians (who have blue skin and white hair). Which state do you think the Star Trek creators modeled the Vulcans after? On a more serious note, in Star Trek, "*the Federation*" was an abbreviation for the "*United Federation of Planets*". Throughout human history, people have used shorthand to simplify saying long things. This knowledge helps to unlock the meaning behind a part of the Articles of Confederation that has confused some people for centuries. What does it mean to be "in the several states"?

The Meaning of "in the several states"

In the present day southwest United States, on a Navajo Nation Reservation, lies the Four Corners Monument. It is the only place in our country where four states come together in a single point (Arizona, Utah, Colorado and New Mexico). It is so unique that people pay admission fees so that they can stand in several states (four) at the same time. Besides the fact that Arizona didn't become a state until 1912, and the land at the four corners wasn't part of the United States until the Treaty of Guadalupe Hidalgo in 1848, this concept ofbeing in several states at the same time is clearly not what the founders intended when they wrote "*in the several states*"!

When words in legal writing are confusing, there are standard rules to interpret them. At the time of the writing of the *Articles of Confederation*, William Blackstone provided[2] one of the best means of interpretation . His second rule of interpretation is that "*if words happen to be still dubious, we may establish their meaning from the context; with which it may be of singular use to compare a word, or a sentence, whenever they are ambiguous, equivocal, or intricate*". The reason that the phrase "*in the several states*" is so confusing is that "*the several states*" is a form of shorthand. Figure 2 shows how the opening sentence in Article III can be seen to explain the reasoning behind the use of the phrase "*the several states*". It is clearly derived from "*The said states hereby severally enter into a firm league of friendship...*". To provide further proof, it seems to be a universal rule of government that laws are written the most clearly and concisely to enable collecting taxes. Fortunately, Article VIII of the *Articles of Confederation* provides two examples using "*the several states*" when describing taxes. The meaning is abundantly clear, or else an entire state could get out of paying their taxes! Finally, the other place in the *Articles of Confederation* where the phrase "*the several states*" is used is in Article IV which will be discussed below. Looking at the definition in Article III and the three examples from the *Articles of Confederation*, it is perfectly clear that "*the several states*" is shorthand for "*all of the states that have severally entered into the Confederation*".

---

2 Blackstone, William. *Commentaries on the Laws of England Book 1: The Rights of Persons: Section 2 – Of the Nature of Laws in General.*

Figure 2 - Usage of "the several states", Articles of Confederation

Commentary

Article III. **The** said **states** hereby **severally** enter into a firm league of friendship with each other, for their common defence, the security of their Liberties, and their mutual and general welfare, binding themselves to assist each other, against all force offered to, or attacks made upon them, or any of them, on account of religion, sovereignty, trade, or any other pretence whatever.

The Confederation of states is defined as being created by "the said states hereby severally" joining together.

The phrase "the several states" is shorthand for "all of the states that have severally entered into the Confederation"

Article VIII. All charges of war, and all other expenses that shall be incurred for the common defence or general welfare, and allowed by the united states in congress assembled, shall be defrayed out of a common treasury, which shall be supplied by **the several states**, in proportion to the value of all land within each state, ... The taxes for paying that proportion shall be laid and levied by the authority and direction of the legislatures of **the several states** within the time agreed upon by the united states in congress assembled.

Article IV. ...shall be entitled to all privileges and immunities of free citizens in **the several states**;

There are 3 examples of "the several states" in the Articles of Confederation.

The associated actions are as follows:

"supplied by the several states"
"legislatures of the several states"
"free citizens in the several states"

These three cases can only make logical sense if "the several states" is equivalent to and shorthand for, "all of the states that have severally entered into the Confederation"

Replacing the King and his Kingdom

A year after the Declaration of Independence was signed, the writers of the *Articles of Confederation* were faced with an interesting problem. They were developing a new government, but wanted to protect the rights of Englishmen that had been acquired after over 500 years of struggles against their monarchs. In Chapter 1, the *Magna Carta(1215)*, the *Petition of Right(1627)*, the *Habeus Corpus Act(1679)* and the English

Bill of Rights(1688) were all described as producing the key rights of all Englishmen. In 1707, the combination of England, Scotland and Wales officially created Great Britain. At the time of the American Revolution, our country was fighting the British. From the perspective of our legal system though, we still refer to the English Common Law. Putting yourself in the shoes of a writer of the *Articles of Confederation*, how would view these rights of Englishmen? Just prior to the *Declaration of Independence*, King George III was supposed to protect your rights. Just like the Knights Templar in the Middle Ages, you had the privileges and immunities of Englishmen wherever you were in his Kingdom. Under King George III, you could have described this protection of rights as follows:

> **Exemplary Protection of Rights under King George III**
> *All subjects of the King shall be entitled to*
> *the privileges and immunities of Englishmen*
> *wherever they are in his Kingdom.*

Now, the King was gone, and you had a loose confederation of highly sovereign states to try to manage. Working from this exemplary goal, how could you adjust this for the newly formed confederation of states? The King was now replaced with sovereign states. Each state could decide whether to join, or not to join, this new confederation. The primary point of leverage over the states to force them to grant these common rights, was as part of their requirement for admission to this new government. Instead of subjects, people living in the individual states could now be called free inhabitants; since those who were not slaves or indentured servants were now free. This could change the exemplary phrase "*All Subjects of the King shall be entitled to*" to the phrase "*The free inhabitants of each of these states shall be entitled to*".

The next question would be what are the rights that are protected? The exemplary phrase "*the privileges and immunities of Englishmen*" needed to be replaced with something to reflect the people of this new confederation. The nationwide rights that were to be protected were now those of free citizens living in their respective states. This meant that the exemplary phrase "*the privileges and immunities of Englishmen*" could be replaced with "*the privileges and immunities of free citizens*". Slavery was inherited from England and King George III. Under the *Articles of Confederation*, the use of "free citizens" makes sense since it is the most powerful way to describe the rights.

How would you describe the coverage area for these common rights? The common rights nationwide would be those that every person held across the confederation. The exemplary phrase "*wherever they are in his Kingdom*" needed to be replaced with something that described anywhere within the states that made up the confederation. A long way to write this would have been "*in all of the states that severally make up this confederation*". We saw in the previous section that "*the several states*" came from "the said states hereby severally enter into a firm league of friendship" and is shorthand for "*all of the states that severally make up this confederation*". Therefore, the exemplary phrase "*wherever they are in his Kingdom*" could be replaced with "*in the several states*" for the case of the *Articles of Confederation.*

> **Exemplary Mapping to the Confederation of States**
> *The free inhabitants of each of these states shall be entitled to*
> *the privileges and immunities of free citizens*
> *in the several states.*

This mapping of the English rights to this new American confederation of states would have been short and concise. It cleanly matches how general rights would have been viewed across the British Empire. It generated a novel way to guarantee nationwide privileges and immunities for citizens of largely sovereign states. As we saw in Chapter 1, privileges and immunities are closely coupled with trade, and that still needed to be addressed. Therefore the work of describing privileges and immunities was not done yet.

With respect to trade, Chapter 1 showed that having privileges and immunities are critical. As a thought experiment, imagine that you are a trader and can take your goods to two possible countries to sell them. The first country has the same "*privileges and immunities*" as your country, but it has a 25% tariff to sell your goods into the country. The second country does not have the "*privileges and immunities*" of your country, but it has a no tariff to sell your goods there. Cato's Letter #64 (Exhibit 7) described the risks of being "*burdened, oppressed, manacled, stopped, and delayed...*" as means to extract bribes and to give preferences to favorite traders. The Rhode Island Charter of 1662 (Exhibit 6) similarly envisioned this problem. It required that Rhode Island's merchants be allowed "*without lett*[3] *or molestation, to pass and repass with freedom into and through the rest of the English colonies.*" Would you choose to risk being imprisoned for months based on committing a crime that you might not even know existed? Would you choose to risk not being able to be bailed out of jail if you didn't have sufficient funds? Is the greater profit selling in the second country worth the risk to you?

In the movie *Dirty Harry* (1971), Inspector Callahan (Clint Eastwood) posed a similar but more extreme sort of question. Inspector Callahan was asking a criminal whether the criminal had counted how many shots that Callahan had fired, and whether Callahan had any bullets left. After a flowery description of what could happen to the criminal if he was wrong, Inspector Callahan told the criminal that he had to ask himself, "do I feel lucky?". Needing to rely on luck is no way to inspire and encourage travel and trade.

Figure 3 shows a high level hierarchical breakdown of the extremely long first sentence in Article IV of the *Articles of Confederation*. This sentence has 148 words, 9 commas and 2 semicolons. As a modern day example, patent claims are required by law to be limited to a single sentence. The author has provided expert witness testimony for interpreting patent claims up to 256 words long with 10 semicolons and 9 commas. In this Articles of Confederation instance, this entire sentence describes privileges and immunities.

The first section describes Nationwide Privileges and Immunities Protection, and the second section describes Travel Rights and non-Discriminatory Trade Rights. Both of these features are critical for traveling between states. Traveling is made much more complex if you are going through multiple states that each have different "*privileges and immunities*". As a present-day analogy, imagine driving a car from Boston to Philadelphia. You would likely pass through Massachusetts, Connecticut, New York, New Jersey and Pennsylvania. If each state had different rules of the road, you would need to learn all of them. If each state had different vehicle requirements, you would need to evaluate the laws of all five states and make sure that your car met the requirements in each state. Otherwise, your car might be impounded and you could become stranded.

---

3 lett - an impediment or obstacle

Figure 3 - Privileges and Immunities Sentence, Articles of Confederation

Articles of Confederation: Article IV first sentence deconstruction into standalone phrases and their hierarchy	**Commentary**
The better to secure and perpetuate mutual friendship and intercourse among the people of the different states in this union, the free inhabitants of each of these states, paupers, vagabonds and fugitives from Justice excepted, shall be entitled to all privileges and immunities of free citizens in the several states;	**Nationwide Privileges and Immunities Protection** (Figure 4 will breakdown this complex phrase)
and the people of each state shall have free ingress and regress to and from any other state, and shall enjoy therein all the privileges of trade and commerce, subject to the same duties, impositions and restrictions as the inhabitants thereof respectively, provided that such restrictions shall not extend so far as to prevent the removal of property imported into any state, to any other State of which the Owner is an inhabitant; provided also that no imposition, duties or restriction shall be laid by any state, on the property of the united states, or either of them.	**Travel Rights and non-Discriminatory Trade Rights .** (Figure 5 will breakdown this complex phrase)

If you think about why people travel between states today, the reasons are similar to those reasons at the founding of our country. These include travel to visit family and friends, travel for business and trade, vacation travel, and travel for religious, political or other reasons. The purpose of the "*Privileges and Immunities*" section of the *Articles of Confederation* was to "*better secure and perpetuate mutual friendship and intercourse among the people of the different states in this union*".

Nationwide Privileges and Immunities Protection

The Articles of Confederation did not contain a "*Bill of Rights*" or any equivalent declaration of rights. States were their own sovereign entities[4] , and the only place to enforce commonality of rights between the states was as a condition of joining the confederation. This is much like any organization that you join that has requirements to maintain your membership. By declaring Nationwide Privileges and Immunities, Congress had the right to decide disagreements[5] between states. Congress also had a means to enforce their decision[6].

Figure 4 breaks down the Nationwide Privileges and Immunity section. The key section can be shortened to "*the free inhabitants of each of these states...shall be entitled to all privileges and immunities of free citizens in the several states*" by separating out the exceptions which will be described momentarily. Most importantly, this nationwide privileges and immunities phrase matches exactly the translation for the protection of Englishmen in the British Empire that was analyzed above.

The exception clause of "*paupers, vagabonds and fugitives from justice excepted*" requires some explanation. All three of these categories are what could be considered disfavored, and hence not felt to be deserving of complete rights. Paupers were extremely destitute individuals who relied on public support. Vagabonds were nomadic, or leading a carefree life and would not have been felt to be contributing to society. Fugitives

---

4 *Articles of Confederation*, Article II, "Each state retains its sovereignty, freedom and independence, and every Power, Jurisdiction and right, which is not by this confederation expressly delegated to the United States, in Congress assembled."

5 *Articles of Confederation*, Article IX, "...The united states, in congress assembled, shall also be the last resort on appeal, in all disputes and differences now subsisting, or that hereafter may arise between two or more states concerning boundary, jurisdiction, or any other cause whatever; which authority shall always be exercised in the manner following. Whenever the legislative or executive authority, or lawful agent of any state in controversy with another, shall present a petition to congress, stating the matter in question, and praying for a hearing, notice thereof shall be given, by order of congress, to the legislative or executive authority of the other state in controversy, ..."

6 *Articles of Confederation*, Article XIII, "...Every State shall abide by the determinations of the united states, in congress assembled, on all questions which by this confederation are submitted to them. And the Articles of this confederation shall be inviolably observed by every state, and the union shall be perpetual;"

Figure 4 - Nationwide Privileges and Immunities, Articles of Confederation

Articles of Confederation: Article IV first sentence deconstruction first complex section
(text size, **bold** and *italics* are used for descriptive purposes and are not in original)

Commentary

The better to secure and perpetuate mutual friendship and intercourse among the people of the different states in this union,

Purpose for Nationwide Privileges and Immunities

the free inhabitants of each of these states,

paupers, vagabonds and fugitives from Justice excepted,

Disfavored individuals not felt to be completely deserving of Nationwide Privileges and Immunities

shall be entitled to all privileges and immunities of free citizens in the several states;

Shown in Figure 2 to be shorthand for *"all of the states that severally entered into the Confederation"*. Making this substitution, the key bolded sections read as: *"the free inhabitants of each of these states, shall be entitled to all privileges and immunities of free citizens in all of the states that have severally entered into the Confederation."*.

Each state is agreeing to provide its inhabitants Nationwide Privileges and Immunities to join the Confederation.

from justice would lose[7] their rights if convicted, and a further part of Article IV explains the procedure for extraditing them between states.

Another factor that causes confusion is the use of free inhabitants

---

7 *Articles of Confederation,* Article IV "If any Person guilty of, or charged with, treason, felony, or other high misdemeanor in any state, shall flee from Justice, and be found in any of the united states, he shall upon demand of the Governor or executive power of the state from which he fled, be delivered up, and removed to the state having jurisdiction of his offence."

and free citizens. The sentence is written in the most powerful way possible for anyone living within the states of the confederation. Citizens were the highest general category for people in a state. In some states, citizens could mean only people eligible to vote. The way that the sentence is written, the more powerful rights of citizens are provided to all free inhabitants. The Articles of Confederation were written in the middle of the Revolutionary War. Many "*British Loyalists*" wanted to reunite with England, and would not want to be called citizens of this less than two-year-old nation. Others would be worried that if they were thought of as a citizen of this breakaway nation, they might be punished or hung if the British won the war. From a marketing perspective, this generosity regarding Privileges and Immunities might have helped to recruit people to the American side.

Travel Rights and Non-Discriminatory Trade Rights

Figure 5 breaks down the second part of the Privileges and Immunities found in Article IV of the Articles of Confederation. These Travel Rights and Non-Discriminatory Trade Rights create new fundamental rights for Americans that were recognized by all 13 of the original states. These include the right to freely travel into and out of any other state. This right was first seen and described in the Rhode Island Charter of 1662 (Exhibit 6). The right to Non-Discriminatory Trade when in other states was a new right. Finally, the right to take anything back to your home state that you brought into another state was enshrined. One of the purposes for this phrase would have been to protect the movement of slaves, but even after the abolition of slavery, it will be shown that this right still has meaning today. Finally, to avoid state versus state hostility, or state versus United States hostility, a further limitation said that you couldn't impound the property of other states or the United States.

Appendix 6 shows how Article IV of the Articles of Confederation produced three new fundamental rights for all Americans excluding paupers, vagabonds and fugitives from justice:

- Right to freely travel between states; paupers, vagabonds, and fugitives from justice excluded. {AC1}
- Right to non-discriminatory trade and commerce when in other

Figure 5 - Travel and Non-Discriminatory Trade, Articles of Confederation

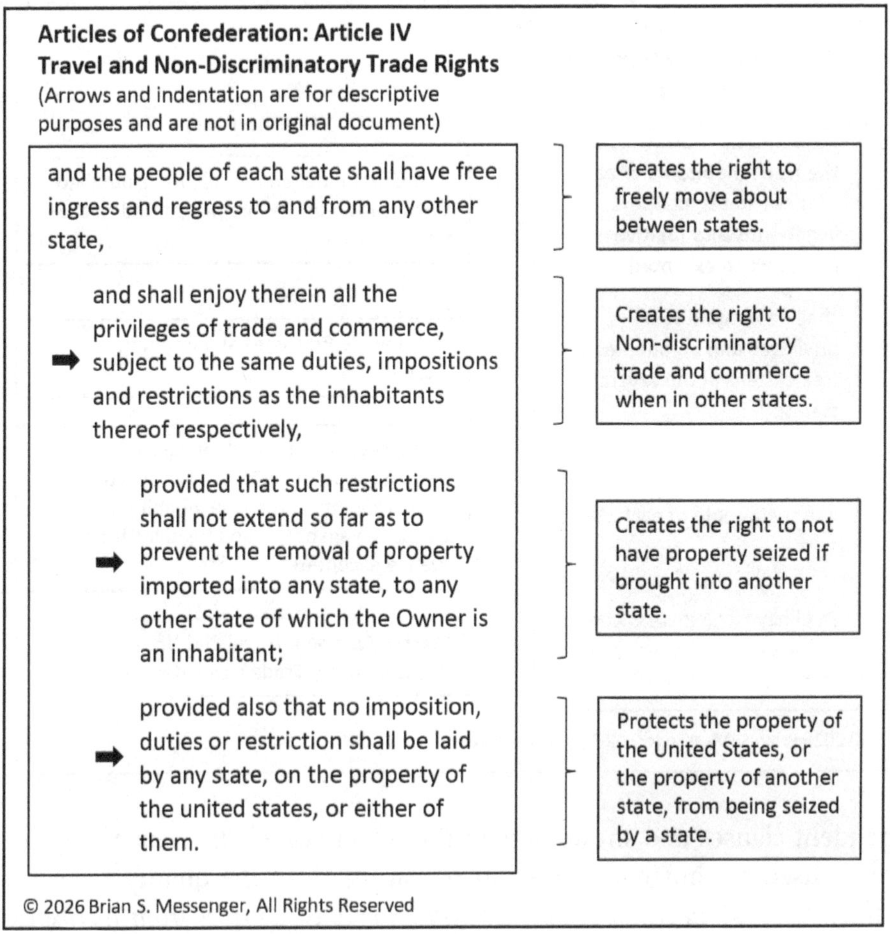

states; paupers, vagabonds, and fugitives from justice excluded.{AC2}

- Right to take property out of a state that you brought into the state; paupers, vagabonds, and fugitives from justice excluded. {AC3}

At this point, a reader might ask: "Why are you using the 'paupers, vagabonds, and fugitives from justice excluded' addition to these rights?" This is a good question, and it comes down to another case of shorthand. In Figure 5, the text starts with "and the people of each state". Remember that this is all one massive sentence that has a preamble and two independent clauses. Figure 6 breaks down the start of these inde-

Figure 6 - Use of "the people" as Apparent Shorthand

Articles of Confederation: Article IV first sentence deconstruction into qualifications and start of independent clauses.

	Commentary
the free inhabitants of each of these states, **paupers, vagabonds and fugitives from Justice excepted,**	In the first independent clause, a detailed qualification of the people entitled to the rights is used.
shall be entitled to all privileges and immunities of free citizens in the several states;	Nationwide Privileges and Immunity Description
and the **people** of each state	In the second independent clause, "the people" appears to be used as shorthand to avoid repeating "the free inhabitants ... paupers, vagabonds and fugitives from Justice excepted."
shall have free ingress and regress to and from any other state, ...	Start of Complex Travel and Non-Discriminatory Trade rights description

pendent clauses and shows how in the second one, "*the people*" appears to be used as shorthand to avoid repeating all of the qualifying words "*the free inhabitants, ... paupers, vagabonds and fugitives from Justice excepted*". It would seem illogical to explicitly deny Nationwide Privileges and Immunities to certain classes of people and then provide them with full travel and trade rights. From the perspective of Supreme Court decisions, this remains an open question.

Sixty years after the *Articles of Confederation*, the Supreme Court said in *City of New York v. Miln(1837)* that:[8] "*We think it as competent and as necessary for a state to provide precautionary measures against the moral pestilence of paupers, vagabonds, and possibly convicts; as it is to guard against the physical pestilence, which may arise from unsound and infectious articles imported, or from a ship...*" This sentence was repeated in lat-

8 City of New York v. Miln, 36 U.S. 102, 142-143 (1837) - Opinion of the Court

er Supreme Court cases, and as recently as *Edwards v. California(1941)*, the Supreme Court said[9] "*In none of these cases, however, was the power of a State to exclude 'paupers' actually involved.*" In later years, in welfare cases such as in *Shapiro v. Thompson(1969)*[10], the Supreme Court switched to referring to poor people on public assistance as "indigents." This avoided any use of the term "pauper".

As in the case of all of the rights from Appendices 1-5, the Nationwide rights from the *Articles of Confederation* can only be modified or eliminated by Constitutional changes. Later in this chapter, we will see how all of the rights specified in the Privileges and Immunities Clause of the *Articles of Confederation* were transferred to the *United States Constitution*. In the meantime, there is a very important concept regarding State Level Privileges and Immunities that must be discussed.

State Level Privileges and Immunities

In addition to Nationwide Privileges and Immunities it is also possible for individual states to create State Level Privileges and Immunities. Any Privilege or Immunity created at the state level only applies within the boundaries of that state. At the state level, there are also issues as to whether the privilege and immunities apply to citizens of the state or to anyone within the boundaries of the state. A further issue with State Level Privileges and Immunities relates to how they interact with Nationwide Privileges and Immunities. In general, the hope would be that these State Level Privileges and Immunities would add to the rights of the Nationwide Privileges and Immunities. Unfortunately, as will be described later, there can be instances where State Level Privileges and Immunities negatively affect specific Nationwide Privileges and Immunities.

The point of this book is not to attempt to define all of the types of State Level Privileges and Immunities that exist, but to help the reader understand the concept. Some specific examples of State Level Privileges and Immunities are shown below:

- The privilege to legally practice medicine, law, etc., in the state
- The privilege to hunt or fish in the state

---

9 Edwards v. California, 314 U.S. 160, 177 (1941) - Opinion of the Court

10 Shapiro v. Thompson, 394 U.S. 618 (1969) - Opinion of the Court

- The privilege to pay lower in-state college tuition
- The privilege to receive natural resource royalties such as with the Alaska Pipeline royalty
- The privileges and immunities associated with creating corporations
- The immunity from being required to prove legal status in the country
- The immunity from being required to prove United States Citizenship when registering to vote.
- The immunity from being required to show proper identification when voting in elections.
- The immunity from being charged with federal immigration law or Controlled Substance Act violations by state officials.

Articles of Confederation - State Level View Confusion

There have been some people who have tried to tie the fact that since states had to treat people from other states in a non-discriminatory fashion for trade (Figure 5), that this somehow meant that the privileges and immunities that citizens were entitled to (Figure 4) were all of the state level privileges and immunities of citizens for the specific state that you are in. In simpler words, they have tried to say that the intention was that "*when you are in a specific state, you are entitled to all of the state level privileges and immunities of citizens in that state*". Confusion regarding the meaning of "*in the several states*" helped to lead to this incorrect "state level view".

When a legal misunderstanding keeps coming back, it is important to put a "*stake through the heart of it*" as if it was a vampire[11] . Therefore, it is important to show from many directions why this "state level view" is incorrect. To refresh the reader's memory, the confusing phrase is "the free inhabitants of each of these states, … , shall be entitled to all privileges and immunities of free citizens in the several states;".

The first direction of additional refutation for the "state level view" comes from the text. Blackstone's first rule[12] of judicial interpretation is *"Words are generally to be understood in their usual and*

11 Stoker, Bram. *Dracula*. In the 1897 novel, Count Dracula was killed by simultaneous beheading and driving a Bowie knife into his heart. Traditionally, "staking" was considered a means of killing vampires.

12 Blackstone, William. *Commentaries on the Laws of England Book 1: The Rights of Persons: Section 2 – Of the Nature of Laws in General.*

most known signification; not so much regarding the propriety of grammar, as their general and popular use." In the analysis shown above, the nationwide privileges and immunities protection in the Articles of Confederation identically match what would have been expected.

If the intention was as claimed in the "state level view", the phrase could have been clearly written as: "the free inhabitants of each of these states, … , shall be entitled to all the privileges and immunities of free citizens in the state that they are presently in". The words "the state that they are presently in" would have replaced "the several states". This is not a simple grammatical error. It is not a simple alternative interpretation for the meaning of a single word. The authors of the *Articles of Confederation* were very detailed in their descriptions. There are myriad examples where the authors described in fine specificity people and their positions in states. These include:

- *"on demand of the Governor or executive power of the state from which he fled"* - Article IV
- *"and be found in any of the united states"* - Article IV
- *"and removed to the state having jurisdiction"* - Article IV
- *"the courts and magistrates of every other state" - Article IV*
- *"executive authority of the other state in controversy" - Article IX*
- *"congress shall name three persons out of each of the united states" - Article IX*
- *"with the Indians, not members of any of the states;" - Article IX*

Observing how the authors of the Articles of Confederation described positions of people relative to states, it is clear that they could have specied the state-level view if that had been their intent.

The second direction of additional refutation for the "state level view" is that it would strictly limit the ability of states to actually implement State Level Privileges and Immunities. If anyone who comes into a state is entitled to "all the privileges and immunities of the people of that state", then how could states give any preferences to being citizens of their state? This approach would throw into question all sorts of the previously described State Level Privileges and Immunities. These include professional licensing, in-state tuition, natural resource royalties for citizens, and many more. Since the states retained tremendous sovereignty under the *Articles of Confederation*, this would have been an extremely contradictory and misguided concept for them to have signed up to.

The third direction of additional refutation is that if the "state-level view" was correct, then there would have been no need for the phrase "*and shall enjoy therein all the privileges of trade and commerce, subject to the same duties, impositions and restrictions as the inhabitants thereof respectively,*". That phrase appears in a subsequent part of the very same sentence. It appears unfathomable to believe that such a complex description would have been added to the *Articles of Confederation* if it was already covered by the "state-level view" interpretation. The fundamental reason for nationwide privileges and immunities, and all of these additional directions to refute the state-level view make it absolutely clear what the Articles of Confederation intended to implement. To provide the reader with greater context as to the need for Nationwide Privileges and Immunities, we must think about life in 1700's America versus today.

The Need for Nationwide Privileges and Immunities

Privileges and immunities were meant to protect travelers and merchants from potential abuses by authoritarians and protectionists as shown in Chapter 1. American travelers and merchants in the 1700's had many of the same concerns as Americans today. They also had limitations that provided additional challenges. With respect to transportation, land transportation was done by horse, walking, or using wagons. The first railroads in our country wouldn't come for many decades. Water transportation was done using sailing ships on the ocean, and ferries or row boats on rivers or lakes within the country. Powered steamships would not be invented for many years. Money was carried in the form of gold and silver coins. Credit Cards and Automatic Teller Machines wouldn't become prevalent until the last half of the 20th century. Paper checks could be delivered to banks where a merchant had established accounts, but most travelers would not have access to using them.

How could authoritarians and protectionists abuse travelers and merchants? As a modern example, most people have seen a vehicle speed trap sometime in their lives. A typical situation occurs on a rural highway that passes through a small town or village. The Speed Limit can drop by 40 mile/hour in a short distance, and a hidden police officer can wait to ticket unsuspecting drivers who are unaware of, or slow to react to, the change. This can provide the city, county or state government with needed revenue; especially since it is pocketed from visitors to the area.

Unfortunately, there could have been many ways to achieve protectionist goals by harassing out of state merchants in non-financial ways. These methods did not need to involve different duties, impositions, or restrictions. The reader is asked to put themselves in the shoes of an authoritarian and/or protectionist striving to discriminate against outsiders. Harassment could involve stopping travelers and searching their wagons to delay or frustrate them. Imagine being told to unload an entire wagon load of goods on the side of the road due to some fictitious claim of searching for stolen pocket watches. Harassment could involve arresting people for saying something in a pub that offends the local officials. Harassment could involve arresting a merchant for a minor offense, and leaving his entire wagon load of goods on the side of the road at risk of being stolen. The ways that authoritarians and protectionists could harass and intimidate outsiders were endless.

The exception clause for both paupers and vagabonds in the *Articles of Confederation* would be discussed for centuries. Paupers were destitute and relied on either charity or the government for their support. States had an inherent interest in avoiding having paupers immigrating into them and becoming their responsibility. In future Chapters, we will see multiple Supreme Court cases that revolved around this specific issue. In a similar vein, vagabonds were nomadic and lived a carefree and unpredictable life. They were undesirable visitors to a state. People granted privileges and immunities were expected to be law-abiding with a reason for their travels.

Presuming that the travelers and merchants traveling between states are law-abiding does not eliminate their need for criminal justice protections. We saw earlier how searches and seizures can be used to harass outsiders. If people are taken into custody, then many other factors become important. This includes unreasonable bail or fines; especially when the only money you have access to is what you are carrying. Imagine being charged with a trumped-up serious crime far from home. An authoritarian Sheriff could hold you on charges for months, and then have a single judge convict you if you were not guaranteed a speedy trial and a trial by jury. In the next Chapter, we will be reviewing the *Bill of Rights*, and how there is significant synergy with the privileges and immunities of citizens that the Constitution already protected. In parallel with the development of the Articles of Confederation, most states were developing State Constitutions. Looking at individual State Constitutions provides us with additional context for the time.

Early State Level Constitutions

To understand rights during our nation's early years, a valuable resource is early State Constitutions. States were highly sovereign, and they also had conflicts between each other. For instance, disagreements between New Hampshire and New York over what is now Vermont kept Vermont from being included in the original 13 states. The citizens of Vermont were forced to declare themselves an independent Republic, but they fought alongside the other states in the Revolutionary War. Therefore, the Constitution of the Vermont Republic can also be reviewed to understand context. As another interesting fact, the *Articles of Confederation* permitted Canada to automatically[13] join the United States. Canada would have been the 14th state at the time, but they didn't take advantage of the opportunity.

The writers of some of the state constitutions were famous founding fathers including John Adams who wrote the Massachusetts Constitution, Benjamin Franklin who wrote the Pennsylvania Constitution, and George Mason who wrote the *Virginia Declaration of Rights*. Some of these were written before the Declaration of Independence, some were written shortly after the Declaration, and in two cases[14], the first State Constitutions weren't written for decades! Searching for rights in State Constitutions can show interesting concepts, commonalities and trends, but the absence of the declaration of a right is fairly meaningless. This is since it can just mean that the right was obvious. On the other hand, just as in patent cases, we shall see that certain State Constitutional provisions can indirectly provide invaluable insight regarding rights. Table 1 shows

13 *Articles of Confederation,* "Article XI. Canada acceding to this confederation, and joining in the measures of the united states, shall be admitted into, and entitled to all the advantages of this union: ..."

14 Connecticut's first State Constitution was adopted in 1818 and prior to that they used the government structure setup by the Charter of King Charles II from 1662. Rhode Island's first State Constitution was adopted in 1842 and prior to that they used the government structure setup by the Charter of King Charles II from 1663.

a breakdown of four 1st Amendment rights granted in State Constitutions prior to the development of the United States Constitution. The complete, and detailed, State Constitutional text is shown in Appendix 7. Very short summaries are broken down in Table 1, but the reader is encouraged to review the Appendix as the original source for areas of interest. In some instances, multiple State Constitutions or Bill of Rights were generated by a given State, and each of these is included at the proper point in sequential time.

The right to free speech in England had been very limited. It was shown in Chapter 1 how Parliament had the privilege and immunity to speak freely but not the general population. Cato's Letter #15 described how[15] "*Whoever would overthrow the liberty of the nation, must begin by subduing the freedom of speech; a thing terrible to publick traitors.*" When the *Declaration of Independence* was signed, the implied right to speak about anything associated with governing the country was created (see Identifier D1 in Appendix 5). The fact that the right to Freedom of Speech was so integral to the American founding is likely the reason that it was mentioned in only three of the State Constitutions and State Bill of Rights prior to the US Constitution; it was perceived as a nationwide right.

Freedom of the Press had been restricted heavily in England. Cato's Letters were published anonymously due to this risk. In Jacob Mchangama's book *"Free Speech: A History from Socrates to Social Media* " he describes[16] how "*Even though England had abolished prepublication censorship, English press freedom did not protect against post-publication punishment for speech crimes like blasphemy and sedition, which remained part and parcel of British common law.*" Mchangama then goes on to tell the story of Member of Parliament John Wilkes who lampooned the King and his ministers in an infamous publication called the "*North Briton No. 45*". Wilkes served over two years in prison and his newspaper was burned. According to Mchangama, this inspired "*American Patriots who adopted 'Wilkes and Liberty' and the number 45 as rallying cries*". Appendix 7 shows the interesting fact that most of the nine

15 Trenchard, John and Gordon, Thomas. *CATO's Letters: Or, Essays on Liberty, Civil and Religious, and other important Subjects: Cato's Letter #15 Of Freedom of Speech: that the same is inseparable from publick Liberty.* published Saturday, February 4,1720 (Gordon, Thomas)

16 Mchangama, Jacob. *Free Speech: A History from Socrates to Social Media.* Page 126

Table 1 - Summary of Early State Constitutional Speech, Press, Redress and Assembly Rights (prior to the United States Constitution)

State	Month/ Year[1]	Freedom of Speech	Freedom of the Press	Redress of Grievances	Freedom of Assembly
New Hampshire	Jan. 1776			Notes English failure to Redress grievances	
South Carolina	Mar. 1776			Notes English failure to Redress grievances	
Virginia Const. and Bill of Rights	June 1776		General Freedom of the Press	Notes English failure to Redress grievances	
New Jersey	July 1776				
Maryland	Aug. 1776		General Freedom of the Press	Right to petition government for Redress	
Pennsylvania	Sep. 1776	General Freedom of Speech	General Freedom of the Press	Right to petition government for Redress	General Right to Assemble
Delaware	Sep. 1776				
North Carolina	Dec. 1776		General Freedom of the Press	Right to petition government for Redress	General Right to Assemble
Georgia	Feb. 1777		General Freedom of the Press		
New York	Apr. 1777			Notes English failure to Redress grievances	
Vermont Republic	July 1777	General Freedom of Speech	General Freedom of the Press		General Right to Assemble
South Carolina	Mar. 1778		General Freedom of the Press		

1 If the Constitution has a date embedded in the document, that date is used. In some cases, a vote of the people was necessary, and this could have taken many months to complete the process. Using the date that the document was written provides the context as to what was happening at that specific time.

State	Month/ Year[1]	Freedom of Speech	Freedom of the Press	Redress of Grievances	Freedom of Assembly
Massachusetts	June 1780	General Freedom of Speech	General Freedom of the Press	Right to petition government for Redress	General Right to Assemble
New Hampshire *(Bill of Rights)*	Oct. 1783		General Freedom of the Press	Right to petition government for Redress	General Right to Assemble
New York *(Bill of Rights)*	Jan. 1787			Right to petition government for Redress	

references to Freedom of the Press in the early State Constitutions just declared how essential it is to liberty. This coincides with it being already perceived as a nationwide right (see Identifier D1 in Appendix 5).

In Chapter 1, it was shown that the Declaration of Independence listed many grievances against the King of England. In each case, the colonists declared that their grievances had not been resolved. The right to petition for a redress of grievances had been formalized almost a century before in the *English Bill of Rights* (see Appendix 4, EBR5 and Appendix 5, D16). Some early State Constitutions formalized this right at the state level, and some also affirmed the necessity to have frequent legislative sessions to deal with grievances. Other State Constitutions just noted the King's refusal to redress the colonists' grievances. This coincides with the "right to a redress of grievances" already being perceived as a nationwide right.

Freedom of Assembly was implied in the Declaration of Independence (Appendix 5, D2) by the phrase "*Governments are instituted among Men, deriving their just powers from the consent of the governed*" as shown in Chapter 1. The early State Constitutions had five instances where it was declared in one of two ways: "*the people have a right to assemble together, to consult for their common good*", and "T*he people have a right in an orderly and peaceable manner, to assemble and consult upon the common good...*". Since this right was implied by the Declaration of Independence, many states did not find it necessary to restate it. This coincides with "the right to assemble" being perceived as a nationwide right.

The right to bear arms, and the military & militia are two different but related things. Prior to the United States Constitution, various State Constitutional provisions addressed these two different topics. The complete, and detailed, constitutional text is shown in Appendix 8. Very short summaries are broken down in Table 2, but the reader is encouraged to review the Appendix as the original source for areas of interest.

The most powerful statement regarding the right to bear arms in these early Constitutions comes in an unlikely place. The Delaware Constitution of 1776 had an election provision[17] that "*To prevent any violence or force being used at the said elections, no person shall come armed to any of them, ...* ". At first glance, this might just seem common sense. What is amazing is that it was included in the State Constitution. You might ask yourself, "Why couldn't they just pass a law to outlaw this?". The answer is that bearing arms was such a fundamental right passed down from the *English Bill of Rights* (See Appendix 4, Identifier EBR7), that it could only be restricted by a state Constitution for very specific reasons. In this case, most people in Delaware would understand that avoiding intimidation at their voting locations was a good thing. Since only citizens of Delaware would be voting, this restriction would not impact people traveling through Delaware from other states.

The earlier someone is trained in arms, the more likely they will be proficient when they reach military age. The Vermont Republic Constitution of 1777 recognized this when it said, "*The freemen of this Commonwealth, and their sons, shall be trained and armed for its defence...*". The Virginia Constitution of 1776 recognized this when it said, "*That a well-regulated militia, composed of the body of the people, trained to arms, is the proper, natural, and safe defence of a free State;*". A *World War I* example provides excellent insight as to the value of being trained in arms prior to joining the military. Sergeant Alvin York was a Medal of Honor winner for leading a team of 6 men to capture 132 German soldiers. He was an expert marksman from years of hunting in Tennessee. The movie *Sergeant York(1941)* was released 6 months before the Japanese attack on Pearl Harbor that brought America into *World War II* against Japan and Germany. It shows Sergeant York's valor in detail, and it can be argued that his hunting training, actually saved 132 German lives.

The Minute Man National Historical Park in Massachusetts has

---

17 There was a similar provision in the New York Bill of Rights of January 1787. It said "That all elections shall be free and that no person by force of arms nor by malice or menacing or otherwise presume to disturb or hinder any citizen of this State to make free election upon pain of fine and imprisonment and treble damages to the party grieved."

Table 2 - Summary of State Constitutional Right to Bear Arms and Militia Structure (prior to the United States Constitution)

State	Month/ Year	Right to Bear Arms	Military and Militia Structure
New Hampshire	Jan. 1776		Legislature appoints militia officers
South Carolina	Mar. 1776	People armed to defend themselves and their properties.	Legislature appoints militia officers Civilian control of the military.
Virginia Const. and Bill of Rights	June 1776	People trained to arms are proper defense of a free state.	Civilian control of the military. Executive appointment of militia officers.
New Jersey	July 1776		Civilian control of the military. Legislature appoints militia officers.
Maryland	Aug. 1776		Civilian control of the military.
Pennsylvania	Sep. 1776	Right to bear arms to defend themselves and the state. General hunting rights.	Civilian control of the military. Executive appointment of military officers. Equal contributions required for military defense.
Delaware	Sep. 1776	People cannot come armed to elections to prevent violence.	Civilian control of the military. Legislature appoints militia officers. No muster of militia on election days.
North Carolina	Dec. 1776	Right to bear arms to defend the State.	Civilian control of the military
Georgia	Feb. 1777	Military officers cannot come to elections in military gear to prevent intimidation.	Executive appointment of military officers. Counties of 250 men "liable to bear arms" required to form battalions.
New York	Apr. 1777	Duty of every man to be prepared and willing to defend the State.	Civilian control of the military. Executive appointment of military officers. Equal contributions required for military defense.
Vermont Republic	July 1777	Right to bear arms to defend themselves and the state.	Equal contributions required for military defense. Legislature appoints militia officers.
South Carolina	Mar. 1778		Civilian control of the military. Legislature appoints militia officers
Massachusetts	June 1780	Right to keep and bear arms for the common defense.	Equal contributions required for military defense. Civilian control of the military. Legislature and Executive appoint militia officers.

State	Month/ Year	Right to Bear Arms	Military and Militia Structure
New Hampshire *(Bill of Rights)*	Oct. 1783	Duty of every man to be prepared and willing to defend the State.	Equal contributions required for military defense. Civilian control of the military.
New York *(Bill of Rights)*	Jan. 1787	People cannot come armed to elections to prevent violence.	

excellent contemporaneous descriptions for the start of the Revolutionary War. With regards to having arms and participating in the militia, their website[18] explains the following:

- The militia was a part time army in colonial Massachusetts responsible for the colony's defense. Every town was expected to maintain at least one company (approx. 60 men) commanded by a captain.

- According to the law, nearly all men between the ages of 16 and 60 were required to serve, keep arms and train.

- Most men exempted from training, including "Indians and Negroes" were still required to keep arms (or be provided by the master of the household) and were expected to have them inspected twice per year and to turn out in an emergency.

- Company-level training was required by law 6 days each year

- Serving in your town's militia company was required by law. Minute man companies were raised by volunteer. Whereas militia companies trained 6 days each year, minute man companies trained two days each week.

- Militiamen were required to be armed "as according to law." This meant that they were to have "a well fixt Firelock Musket, of Musket (69-75 caliber) or Bastard Musket (50-60 caliber) Bore, the Barrel not less than Three Foot and a half long; or other good Fire Arms, to the Satisfaction of the commission officer of the company..." They were also expected to have twenty bul-

18 United States Department of the Interior, National Park Service. (2026, Feb. 22). https://www.nps.gov/mima/learn/historyculture/the-militia-and-minute-men-of-1775.htm

> lets fit to their gun, one pound of powder, twelve flints, and a cutting sword. Later, bayonets were required for at least half the men in each company. As with the training, fines were levied against those who failed to provide themselves with these arms.

With the perspective provided by the *Minute Man National Historical Park*, it was not only a "right to bear arms", but for most people a responsibility to do so. People in the militia had to provide their own guns, powder and ammunition to defend the state. They were expected to keep their arms at home to be available as an immediate defense against attack. Anyone who aged out of militia requirements would still have their arms to continue to protect themselves, their homes, and their nation in an emergency. We will see later in our nation's history, how having arms distributed in homes not only provides immediate defense, but avoided having large stockpiles of guns that were vulnerable to capture.

All of the early State Constitutions emphasized civilian control of the militia. Officers were appointed and approved by the governor and/or legislature. One issue that arose was for people of religious faiths (such as the Quakers) that had a religious moral conviction against bearing arms. In the example of Pennsylvania's 1776 Constitution this was written as "*Nor can any man who is conscientiously scrupulous of bearing arms, be justly compelled thereto, if he will pay such equivalent...*". Other states had similarly written provisions where it was made clear that the alternative to militia requirements was making payments to the government that were established to be equivalent to performing that duty.

The rights of "freedom of speech", "freedom of the press", "right to assemble", "right to petition for a redress of grievances" and the "right to bear arms" were all clearly supported as nationwide privileges and immunities. Reviewing Appendix 7 and Appendix 8, there was not a single instance in any early State Constitution that would limit these fundamental rights. Freedom of religion was an entirely different story. Appendix 9 contains the original text of the religious provisions in the early State Constitutions, and Table 3 attempts to summarize them. Given the complexity of any discussion of religion, Table 3 is meant only to provide an overview to help the reader explore further.

Table 3 - Summary of State Constitutional Religious Provisions (prior to the United States Constitution)

State	Month/ Year	Religious Worship and Individual Rights	Government Restrictions
New Hamp-shire	Jan. 1776		
South Carolina	Mar. 1776	Significant grievance with England that the Catholic Province of Quebec was abutting the Protestant American colonies.	
Virginia Const. and Bill of Rights	June 1776	Privilege to worship God according to conscience. All expected to practice Christian forbearance, love and charity.	
New Jersey	July 1776	Privilege to worship God according to conscience.	No establishment of any one Protestant Religious Sect as State Religion. Only Protestants could be in government.
Maryland	Aug. 1776	Privilege to worship God according to conscience. All Christians equally free to worship God. Legislature had to approve land and gifts used to create religious buildings and schools.	Taxes to generally support Christian religions allowed. All government officials required to take an oath regarding belief in God and the Christian religion.
Pennsyl-vania	Sep. 1776	Privilege to worship God according to conscience. Acknowledgment of God provided people with civil rights of citizenship.	All government officials required to take an oath regarding belief in God and the Christian religion.
Delaware	Sep. 1776		No establishment of any one Protestant Religious Sect as State Religion. All government officials required to take an oath regarding belief in God and the Christian religion.

State	Month/ Year	Religious Worship and Individual Rights	Government Restrictions
North Carolina	Dec. 1776	Privilege to worship God according to conscience.	Religious leaders cannot serve in government. All government officials required to take an oath regarding belief in God and the Protestant Christian religion. No establishment of any one Protestant Religious Sect as State Religion.
Georgia	Feb. 1777	Free exercise of religion that is not repugnant to the peace and safety of the State	All government officials had to be of the Protestant religion. Religious leaders cannot serve in government.
New York	Apr. 1777	Free exercise of religion that is not repugnant to the peace and safety of the State	No establishment of any one Protestant Religious Sect as State Religion.
Vermont Republic	July 1777	Privilege to worship God according to conscience. All Protestants equally free to worship God and have full civil rights.	All government officials required to take an oath regarding belief in God and the Protestant Christian religion. Religious Societies encouraged and their privileges and immunities protected.
South Carolina	Mar. 1778	People who believe in God tolerated, but the Christian Protestant religion is the State Religion. Established Churches have to agree to five specific articles of faith.	Only Protestants could be in government. Religious leaders cannot serve in government.
Massachusetts	June 1780	Privilege to worship God according to conscience. All Protestants equally free to worship God and have full civil rights.	All government officials required to take an oath regarding belief in God and the Christian religion. Legislature could require towns to spend money on Protestant teachers of piety, religion and morality, and require attendance at stated times.

State	Month/ Year	Religious Worship and Individual Rights	Government Restrictions
New Hamp-shire *(Bill of Rights)*	Oct. 1783	All government officials required to take an oath regarding belief in God and the Christian religion. Legislature could require towns to spend money on Protestant teachers of piety, religion and morality, and require attendance at stated times.	Legislature could require towns to spend money on Protestant teachers of piety, religion and morality, and require attendance at stated times. Only Protestants could be in government.
New York *(Bill of Rights)*	Jan. 1787		

With respect to religion in 1787 America, the world was much different than it is today. If Table 3 were reviewed in a vacuum, there would be three clear common rights across most of the states. These would have been: "a right to worship God according to conscience", "a right to practice different Protestant religions and have full civil rights", and a "right to have only Protestants in government". The concept of "*Freedom of Religion*" meant you were free to practice any Protestant Christian religion. At that time, the concept of "*Separation of Church and State*" meant that religious leaders could not be in government. These policies applied to higher education too. The Massachusetts Constitution of 1780 discussed[19] the purpose of Harvard University as being "*the encouragement of arts and sciences, and all good literature, tends to the honor of God, the advantage of the Christian religion, and the great benefit of this and the other United States of America*". This was the status of the religious rights at the point where the United States Constitution was written in 1787.

The Constitutional Convention

In May of 1787, the Constitutional Convention started work on what would become our present Constitution. The Articles of Confederation had many well-known shortcomings, but they were the precedent or "prior art" that all of this work was done under. This is

19 Massachusetts Constitution of 1780, Chapter V, Article I, See Appendix 9 for full Constitutional text.

especially important with respect to the Privileges and Immunities Clause. During the convention debates, there were very few issues raised regarding privileges and immunities. One of these occurred on June 19, 1787. James Madison spoke[20] about problems with a United States Constitution proposal from New Jersey when he referred to: "*Acts of Virginia and Maryland which gave preferences to their own Citizens in cases where the Citizens of other States are entitled to equality of privileges by the Articles of Confederation.*" This complaint was in reference to the Maryland-Virginia Compact of 1785, and it had to do with the Travel Rights and Non-Discriminatory Trade Rights section.

The first draft of the *Constitution* on August 6, 1787 had the same text[21] for the main Nationwide Privileges and Immunities Clause as was agreed to in the final *Constitution* version. Figure 7 shows how the Nationwide Privileges from the *Articles of Confederation* were migrated to the *Constitution*. The phrase from the *Articles of Confederation* was simplified by removing the exception clause : *"paupers, vagabonds and fugitives from justice excepted"*. In the prior discussion of the *Articles of Confederation*, the terms "inhabitants", "citizens" and "people" were all used in the Privileges and Immunities sentence. It was explained that during the Revolutionary War, many people might not want to have been called citizens; especially if their sympathies were more towards the British. When the United States Constitution was written in 1787, the Revolutionary War had been over for four years. Any people that did not want to be "*citizens*" of this new country had had plenty of time to leave.

Privileges and Immunities are very powerful. The new United States Congress was tasked with creating[22] a "uniform Rule of Naturalization" for the whole country. People who wanted to become citizens would have had residency and other requirements to do so. They would not expect to have full rights of citizenship until they completed these requirements. The switch to citizens from inhabitants did not mean that

---

20 Ketcham, Ralph. *The Anti-Federalist Papers and Constitutional Convention Debates.* Signet Classics, 1986, page 62, Opposition to the New Jersey Plan (June 19)

21 Ketcham, Ralph. The Anti-Federalist Papers and Constitutional Convention Debates. Signet Classics, 1986, page 132, First Draft of the Constitution (August 6). In this draft, Article XIV said "The Citizens of each State shall be entitled to all privileges and immunities of citizens in the several States."

22 United States Constitution, Article I, Section 8. "The Congress shall have Power … To establish an uniform Rule of Naturalization,…"

Figure 7 - Nationwide Priviliges and Immunities in the Constitution

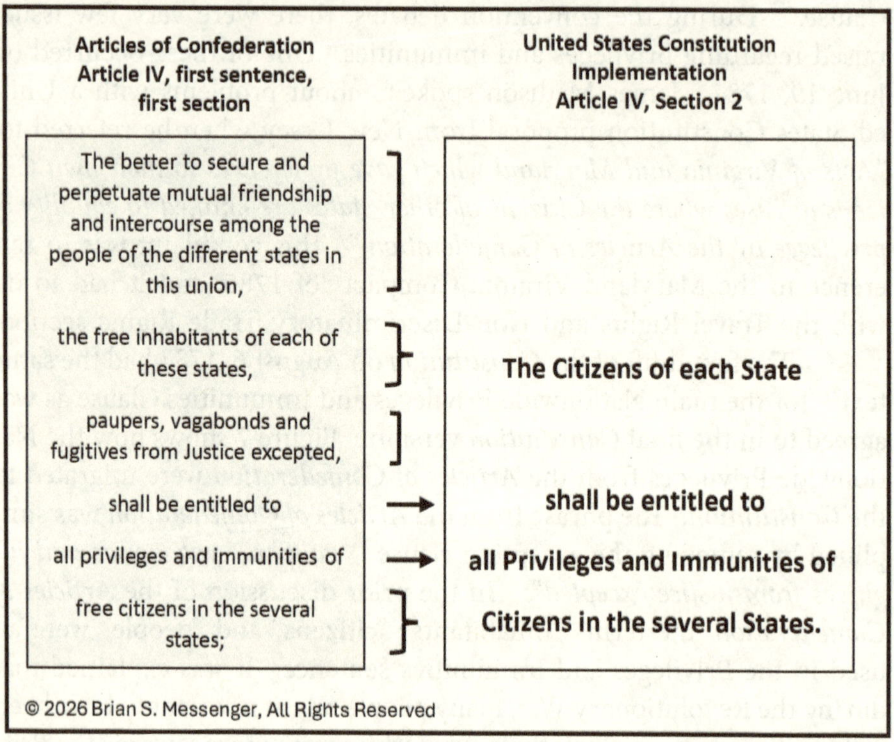

non-citizens would have no rights, but that Congress would have to decide what they were. For example, "Green Card Holders" (Permanent Residents) in 2025 must[23] "obey all laws", are "required to file tax returns", "must support a democratic form of government" and males between 18-25 "must register with the Selective Service". These are some of the requirements that could result in their status being revoked if they are not followed.

Under the *Articles of Confederation*, States were extremely powerful relative to the existing federal government. As the Constitution was written, this was still the case, and the states were protective of giving up too much power to the federal government being designed. It is necessary to have the perspective of a State centered world to understand

23 United States Department of Homeland Security, U.S. Citizenship and Immigration Services. (2026, Feb. 22). https://www.uscis.gov/green-card/after-we-grant-your-green-card/rights-and-responsibilities-of-a-green-card-holder-permanent-resident

why the Privileges and Immunities Clause is written the way it is. Each individual state would debate joining the country. In exchange for receiving the benefits of joining the nation, they were giving up some of their powers. The Privileges and Immunities Clause says that if a State joins the nation, it will guarantee to all citizens of the country Nationwide Privileges and Immunities in their state. This is why the phrase "*Citizens in the several States*" is written the way it is. As explained earlier, this can be read as "*Citizens in all of the States that have severally joined the United States*".

The components of the *Articles of Confederation*'s Travel Rights and Non-Discriminatory Trade Rights phrase were incorporated into various parts of the Constitution as shown in Figure 8. What is interesting about the incorporation, is that the Articles of Confederation phrase "and the people of each state shall have free ingress and regress to and from any other state" was not copied into the United States Constitution. Instead, it now fell under the Constitution's Privileges and Immunities clause. After the Articles of Confederation, these Nationwide Privileges and Immunities now included "the right to freely travel between states; paupers, vagabonds, and fugitives from justice excluded", and the other rights shown in Appendix 6.

Some might try to argue that since the "right to freely travel between the states ..." wasn't copied into the Constitution, it isn't a privilege and immunity. In Chapter 1, it was shown why privileges and immunities are not all individually listed. Unless a right is explicitly eliminated, it is implied that it still exists. There are two instances where prior "rights" were taken away by Constitutional Amendment. The horrible history of slavery will be discussed in detail in Chapter 4, but from the perspective of slave owners, their "right to own slaves" was prohibited[24] by the 13th Amendment to the Constitution. The 18th Amendment took away[25] the

24 United States Constitution, 13th Amendment: "Neither slavery nor involuntary servitude, except as a punishment for crime whereof the party shall have been duly convicted, shall exist within the United States, or any place subject to their jurisdiction."

25 United States Constitution, 18th Amendment: "After one year from the ratification of this article the manufacture, sale, or transportation of intoxicating liquors within, the importation thereof into, or the exportation thereof from the United States and all territory subject to the jurisdiction thereof for beverage purposes is hereby prohibited."

Figure 8 - Migration of Travel and Trade Rights to the Constitution

Articles of Confederation: Article IV first sentence, Travel and Non-Discriminatory Trade Section	United States Constitution Implementation
and the people of each state shall have free ingress and regress to and from any other state,	**Implied Nationwide Privilege and Immunity** "The right to freely travel between states"
and shall enjoy therein all the privileges of trade and commerce, subject to the same duties, impositions and restrictions as the inhabitants thereof respectively, provided that such restrictions shall not extend so far as to prevent the removal of property imported into any state, to any other State of which the Owner is an inhabitant;	**Article I, Section 9** No Tax or Duty shall be laid on Articles exported from any State. No Preference shall be given by any Regulation of Commerce or Revenue to the Ports of one State over those of another: nor shall Vessels bound to, or from, one State, be obliged to enter, clear, or pay Duties in another.
provided also that no imposition, duties or restriction shall be laid by any state, on the property of the united states, or either of them. → **Article 4, Section 3** The Congress shall have Power to dispose of and make all needful Rules and Regulations respecting the Territory or other Property belonging to the United States; and nothing in this Constitution shall be so construed as to Prejudice any Claims of the United States, or of any particular State.	**Article I, Section 8** "The Congress shall have Power To lay and collect Taxes, Duties, Imposts and Excises...; but all Duties, Imposts and Excises shall be uniform throughout the United States; The Congress shall have Power ... To regulate Commerce with foreign Nations, and among the several States, and with the Indian Tribes; **Article 4, Section 2** No person held to Service or Labour in one State, under the Laws thereof, escaping into another, shall, in Consequence of any Law or Regulation therein, be discharged from such Service or Labour, but shall be delivered up on Claim of the Party to whom such Service or Labour may be due.

"right to manufacture or purchase alcohol". This right was restored years later by the 21st Amendment.

The new United States Constitution explicitly created four new Nationwide rights, two rights that limited the federal government only, and one right that limited state governments only. These are shown in Appendix 10 and are summarized here:

Nationwide Rights created in the Constitution

- Right against bills of attainder (C1)
- Right against ex post facto laws (C2)
- Right to have a republican form of government for your state (C3)
- Right to have your state protected against invasion (C4)

Rights restricting Federal Government only in the Constitution

- Right to habeas corpus unless during rebellion, invasion, or if required for public safety. (CFG1)
- Right against being required to pass a religious office test (CFG2)

Rights restricting State Governments only in the Constitution

- Right not to have your obligation of contracts impaired by state law. (CSG1)

The "right against bills of attainder" and the "right against ex post facto laws" were new nationwide rights since the Constitution explicitly restricted both the national and state governments from enacting these types of laws. The new United States Constitution created a new "right to have a republican form of government for your state", and a "right to have your state protected against invasion". These rights applied to the citizens of each state which is the definition of a nationwide right.

The "right to habeas corpus" had existed since the Habeas Corpus Act of 1679 (HC1 in Appendix 3). This had been a privilege and immunity of all citizens since then, but the Constitution now set limits on when it could be suspended by Congress. At the time of the United States Constitution, most of the states (see Table 3 and Appendix 9) required religious oaths or affiliation to be officeholders. These were now explicitly eliminated at the national level by the United States Constitution with the "right against being required to pass a religious test to be in government".

To confirm the textual interpretation of "*the several states*" from

Table 4 - Use of "the several states" in the United States Constitution

Location	Phrase
Article I, Section 2	The House of Representatives shall be composed of Members chosen every second Year by the People of **the several States**
Article I, Section 2	Representatives and direct Taxes shall be apportioned among **the several States** which may be included within this Union, according to their respective Numbers…
Article I, Section 8	To regulate Commerce with foreign Nations, and among **the several States**, and with the Indian Tribes;
Article II, Section 2	The President shall be Commander in Chief of the Army and Navy of the United States, and of the Militia of **the several States**, when called into the actual Service of the United States;
Article IV, Section 2	The Citizens of each State shall be entitled to all Privileges and Immunities of Citizens in **the several States.**
Article V	The Congress, whenever two thirds of both Houses shall deem it necessary, shall propose Amendments to this Constitution, or, on the Application of the Legislatures of two thirds of **the several States.**
Article V	…when ratified by the Legislatures of three fourths of **the several States**, or by Conventions in three fourths thereof, as the one or the other Mode of Ratification may be proposed by the Congress;
Article VI	The Senators and Representatives before mentioned, and the Members of the several State Legislatures, and all executive and judicial Officers, both of the United States and of **the several States**, shall be bound by Oath or Affirmation, to support this Constitution

the *Articles of Confederation*, it is informative to review the usage of the phrase "*the several states*" in the United States Constitution. Table 4 lists and shows places where this phrase is used.

During the Constitutional Convention, there were strong concerns that the states of South Carolina and Georgia would not join the union[26] unless they were allowed to continue to import slaves. The Republic of Vermont had already been excluded from the confederation due to a territorial dispute, and had managed to independently act as its own nation. The desire to have "safety in numbers", and not to lose South Carolina and Georgia, contributed to Constitutional trade offs regarding

26 Ketcham, Ralph. *The Anti-Federalist Papers and Constitutional Convention Debates.* Signet Classics, 1986, pages 153-158, Slavery and the Constitution (August 21,22). The topic of slavery will be discussed in detail in Chapter 4 where it was profoundly intertwined with privileges and immunities.

slavery that would haunt the nation for decades to come. These will be discussed in detail in Chapter 4.

On September 17, 1787, the United States Constitution was finalized and signed. This was a "times up, pencils down" moment for our Constitution. The founders believed that their work was complete. There was no *Bill of Rights*. With the exception of the limited explicit rights in the Constitution, the protection of nationwide rights was done by the Privileges and Immunities Clause. The citizens of each state were entitled to all of the Privileges and Immunities of citizens of the country. These included, but were not limited to, the prior nationwide rights that were analyzed in Appendices 1-6. In the next Chapter, we will analyze the ratification of the Constitution and specifically the synergy between the *Bill of Rights* and the Privileges and Immunities Clause.

CHAPTER 3

The Early Years of Our Republic

(Constitutional Ratification through the Gold Rush)

As soon as the *United States Constitution* was signed by George Washington and 38 other delegates, the real work began. Before it could take effect, the Constitution had to be ratified by the states. Two competing camps (the *Federalists* and the *Anti-Federalists*) pushed for and against ratification. Initially, the *Federalist* camp was led by Alexander Hamilton and John Jay. Later, James Madison was added to the team when John Jay's health kept him from continuing his contributions. Hamilton, Madison and Jay anonymously published[1] 85 essays in two New York newspapers: the "*New York Packet*" and the "*Independent Journal*" to promote ratification. Years later, these were grouped together and republished as the *Federalist Papers*. We all know the outcome; the Federalists were successful. The ratification effort would take almost three years[2] , but the *Federalist Papers* were rapidly written over approximately 6 months from October 1787 to April 1788. They were a marketing and sales campaign to convince the public, and individual state legislatures, to support this dramatic change to the government's structure.

As described in the prior chapter, there was very little discussion of Privileges and Immunities in the Constitutional Convention debates. When James Madison arrived late to the team writing the *Federalist Papers,* he rapidly published 12 different essays *(Federalist 37-Federalist 48)*

---

1 United States Library of Congress. (2026, Feb. 23). https://guides.loc.gov/federalist-papers/full-text

2 Rhode Island became the last state to ratify the Constitution in May 1790.

between January 11, 1788 and February 1, 1788. That would be a tremendous feat for anyone. In the dark of winter, probably working late nights writing by candlelight, it was truly amazing. One of these essays, *Federalist 42*, described[3] a number of reasons for a stronger central government. One of the reasons Madison discussed in *Federalist 42* was to have nationwide rules for naturalization. He described how: "*The dissimilarity in the rules of naturalization has long been remarked as a fault in our system*". To add additional justification for his position, Madison discussed hypothetical issues with the Privileges and Immunities section of the Articles of Confederation (Article IV, Sentence 1 shown in Figure 3).

The Confusion Created by Federalist 42

When proclaiming the benefits of nationwide rules for naturalization in the new Constitution in *Federalist No. 42*, James Madison was trying to highlight the risks of each state having their own rules for naturalization under the *Articles of Confederation*. He tried to create a hypothetical where one state could have loose naturalization rules that allowed a person to obtain citizenship. Madison was worried that that person could then travel or move to a new state. He thought their citizenship from the one state would grant them all of the privileges and immunities of citizens of the new state. The problem is that Madison overlooked that the Nationwide Privileges and Immunities clause (Figure 4) was independent of the Travel Rights and Non-Discriminatory Trade Rights clause (Figure 5). It is hard enough to read this sentence with 148 words, 9 commas and 2 semicolons on a computer, but it would have been extremely difficult to do by candlelight.

Madison was intermingling the functions of these two independent clauses. In *Federalist 42* he acknowledged uncertainty with his interpretation when he said: "*or what was meant by superadding to 'all privileges and immunities of free citizens,' 'all the privileges of trade and commerce,' cannot easily be determined*". At this point, Madison realized that the way he was reading the *Articles of Confederation* had an issue. Chapter 2 of this book showed that under the *Articles of Confederation*,

---

3 "The Federalist Papers", Dover Publications, New York, "No. 42: The powers conferred by the Constitution further considered, James Madison", pages 203-209

all people could trade on equal footing throughout the states, but they were only entitled to Nationwide Privileges and Immunities when in other states. This understanding would have eliminated most of the citizenship concerns that Madison expressed in a detailed[4] hypothetical in *Federalist 42*.

What Madison was missing was that States could still have State Level Privileges and Immunities that had State citizenship requirements, as shown in Chapter 2. The different uses of "free inhabitants", "free citizens" and "people" did not create the problem that concerned Madison. From a marketing perspective, Madison's misunderstanding actually created more impetus to adopt the Constitution. What came next can only be described as a perfect example of what is called the "Butterfly Effect".

The First Privileges and Immunities Butterfly Effect

The term "Butterfly Effect" is used to describe how a small change in the initial conditions of a system can have much larger consequences later. One of the many descriptions that have been used is how the formation, location, and the future path of a tornado are significantly altered by the flapping of a butterfly's wings. We are all human, and we all make mistakes. It will be shown that a minor mistake made by James Madison (where he acknowledged multiple problems with his understanding) produced confusion that lasts to this day. How could a marketing cam-

---

4 "The Federalist Papers", Dover Publications, New York, "No. 42: The powers conferred by the Constitution further considered, James Madison", page 208, "It seems to be a construction scarcely avoidable, however, that those who come under the denomination of *free inhabitants* of a State, although not citizens of such State, are entitled, in every other State, to all the privileges of *free citizens* of the latter; that is, to greater privileges than they may be entitled to in their own State; so that it may be in the power of a particular State, or rather every State is laid under a necessity not only to confer the rights of citizenship in other States upon any whom it may admit to such rights within itself, but upon any whom it may allow to become inhabitants within its jurisdiction. But were an exposition of the term 'inhabitants' to be admitted which would confine the stipulated privileges to citizens alone, the difficulty is diminished only, not removed. The very improper power would still be retained by each State of naturalizing aliens in every other State. In one State, residence for a short term confirms all the rights of citizenship: in another, qualifications of greater importance are required. An alien, therefore, legally incapacitated for certain rights in the latter, may, by previous residence only in the former, elude his incapacity; and thus the law of one State be preposterously rendered paramount to the law of another."

paign document do such a thing? The answer comes from the fact that it was repeated in Joseph Story's *Commentaries on the Constitution* which was published[5] in 1833.

Joseph Story was nominated to the United States Supreme Court by none other than President James Madison in 1811. Story's three volume Commentaries became a primary reference for understanding the original Colonial Charters, the *Articles of Confederation* and the development of the Constitution. When Joseph Story wrote the Commentaries, former President Madison was still alive; and many thought of him as the "father of the Constitution". In reviewing the historical record for the Privileges and Immunities Clause in the Constitution, the only significant reference that Joseph Story could find[6] was *Federalist No. 42*. By 1833, when Story wrote the Commentaries, there had been no Supreme Court cases that had reviewed, or discussed in depth, the Constitution's Privileges and Immunities Clause. Story's inclusion comes near the end of a massive three volume set. Writing the Commentaries must have taken tremendous effort for Story to compile, while his "day job" was being a sitting United States Supreme Court Associate Justice. Unfortunately, Story's inclusion continued the confusion. By repeating Madison's small mistake from 46 years earlier, Story gave the mistake new life. The result has been confusion with the Privileges and Immunities Clause that, for some, has lasted to this day.

The Ratification Struggle for the *Constitution(1787)*

Stepping back to the winter of 1788, ratification of the Constitution started to run into serious trouble. The first five state ratifications for the federal Constitution went relatively smoothly. Massachusetts created the first major problem. It only ratified the federal Constitution by attaching a set of recommended constitutional amendments (Appendix 11) that it expected the Congress to consider. This set the precedent for five more states to recommend constitutional amendments. Table 5 shows the timing of the votes from each state and the appendices where

---

5 Story, Joseph. *Commentaries on the Constitution of the United States, Volume III*, §1799 and §1800.

6 Joseph Story also made a minor reference to the Appeals Court Case of *Corfield v. Coryell* which will be analyzed in detail later in this Chapter.

Table 5 - Ratification of the Constitution by State and Date

State	Constitutional Ratification Vote Date[1]	Vote	State Proposed Recommendatory Amendments
Delaware	December 7, 1787	unanimous	
Pennsylvania	December 12, 1787	46-23	
New Jersey	December 18, 1787	unanimous	
Georgia	January 2, 1788	unanimous	
Connecticut	January 9, 1788	128-40	
Massachusetts	February 6, 1788	187-168	See Appendix 11
Maryland	April 28, 1788	63-11	
South Carolina	May 23, 1788	149-73	See Appendix 12
New Hampshire	June 21, 1788	57-47	See Appendix 13
Virginia	June 25, 1788	89-79	See Appendix 14
New York	July 26, 1788	30-27	See Appendix 15
North Carolina	August 4, 1788	Rejected	See Appendix 16
North Carolina	November 1789	195-77	See Appendix 16
Rhode Island	May 1790	34-32	See Appendix 17

1 National Constitution Center. (2026, Feb. 23). Ratification Timeline. https://constitutioncenter.org/education/classroom-resource-library/classroom/4.5-info-brief-ratification-timeline.

Kickler, Dr. Troy, North Carolina History Project, *North Carolina's Ratification Debates Guaranteed Bill of Rights.* (2026, Feb. 23). https://northcarolinahistory.org/commentary/north-carolinas-ratification-debates-guaranteed-bill-of-rights/

Rhode Island Secretary of State, *Declaration of Rights 1790.* (2026, Feb. 23). https://docs.sos.ri.gov/documents/civicsandeducation/teacherresources/DeclarationOfRights.pdf recommended constitutional amendments are shown.

When these state conventions recommended federal Constitutional Amendments, they were stating what they thought would make this a "more perfect union". This was what the state thought was necessary to "join the team". These votes, and each state's recommended amendments provide powerful perspectives on how different states viewed issues of importance. They are a very important precedent, and they helped to drive the development of the *Bill of Rights.* Like a high school teacher trying to see if students copied each other's homework, the appendices show when different states copied or modified other states' amendments. This helps to complete the amendment picture.

The Federalists and Anti-Federalists had opposing views on whether a *Bill of Rights* should be included in the federal Constitution. James Wilson of Pennsylvania supported the Federalist position in a speech on October 6, 1787. He explained[7] in Exhibit 8 how in the proposed federal Constitution, the rights of new federal government were enumerated. Therefore, he felt that any rights that were not given to the federal government were reserved. He declared that it was absurd to list those rights.

7 "The Anti-Federalist Papers and the Constitutional Convention Debates", Signet Classics, 1986, Speech of James Wilson (October 6, 1787), page 182

Exhibit 8 - James Wilson Supporting Not Having a Bill of Rights

"But in delegating federal powers, another criterion was necessarily introduced, and the congressional power is to be collected, not from tacit implication, but from the positive grant expressed in the instrument of the union. Hence it is evident that, that the former case everything which is not reserved is given; but in the latter the reverse of the proposition prevails, and everything which is not given is reserved.

This distinction being recognized, will furnish an answer to those who think the omission of the bill of rights a defect in the proposed constitution; for it would have been superfluous and absurd to have stipulated with a federal body of our own creation, that we should enjoy those privileges of which we are not divested, either by intention or the act that has brought the body into existence."

Exhibit 9 - Patrick Henry Supporting a Bill of Rights

Here is a revolution as radical as that which separated us from Great Britain. It is as radical, if in this transition our rights and privileges are endangered, and the sovereignty of the States be relinquished: And cannot we plainly see, that this is actually the case? The rights of conscience, trial by jury, liberty of the press, all your immunities and franchises, all pretensions to human rights and privileges, are rendered insecure, if not lost, by this change so loudly talked of by some, and inconsiderately by others. Is this same relinquishment of rights worthy of freemen?

On the Anti-Federalist side, Patrick Henry of Virginia described[8] his view that this transition to a strong federal government risked all of the people's rights and privileges. He strongly supported a *Bill of Rights* in his speech of June 5, 1788 that is shown in Exhibit 9.

Speeches can provide context. The context here, and from the votes in Table 5 above, show that there were strong views on both sides. The Federalists were entirely comfortable with no *Bill of Rights.* This was the way that the federal Constitution was originally signed. The Anti-Federalists thought that all their rights were at risk. They produced a litany of recommended amendments that are found in their entirety in Appendices 11-17. Table 6 provides summaries of the recommended amendments for each of the 1st and 2nd Amendment rights by state. For cases where an amendment was proposed, the Appendix and Identifier are shown.

For any controversial issue, listening to two different individuals can provide two entirely different views and perspectives. This was shown from the speeches of James Wilson and Patrick Henry. Similarly, any author who writes a book, law article, or other publication will have their own inclinations, tendencies and predispositions. This makes quoting anything that is non-original source material of very limited value from a legal precedent. It is the reason that the appendices in this book are included. They provide any reader with the ability to review the actual evidence themselves.

In analyzing the recommended Constitutional amendments from different states, we are not seeing a single person's opinion. Instead, we

8 "The Anti-Federalist Papers and the Constitutional Convention Debates", Signet Classics, 1986, Speeches of Patrick Henry (June 5 and 7, 1788), page 200

Table 6 - First and Second Amendment related State Proposals

State	Freedom of Speech	Freedom of the Press	Redress of Griev-ances	Freedom of Assembly	Right of Con-science	Freedom of Religion	Right to Bear Arms
Massa-chusetts							
South Carolina							
New Hamp-shire					NHRA11 Appx. 13	NHRA11 Appx. 13	NHRA12 Appx. 13
Virginia	VRA16 Appx. 14	VRA16 Appx. 14	VRA15 Appx. 14	VRA15 Appx. 14	VRA20 Appx. 14	VRA20 Appx. 14	VRA17 Appx. 14
New York		NYRA17 Appx. 15	NYRA16 Appx. 15	NYRA16 Appx. 15	NYRA4 Appx. 15	NYRA4 Appx. 15	NYRA5 Appx. 15
North Carolina	VRA16 Appx. 14	VRA16 Appx. 14	VRA15 Appx. 14	VRA15 Appx. 14	VRA20 Appx. 14	VRA20 Appx. 14	VRA17 Appx. 14
Rhode Island	RIRA16 Appx. 17	RIRA16 Appx. 17	RIRA15 Appx. 17	RIRA15 Appx. 17	RIRA4 Appx. 17	RIRA4 Appx. 17	RIRA17 Appx. 17

are seeing the results from the debate and analysis of an entire state convention of people. In recommending amendments, they thought that these issues were so important that they did not want their state to join the United States unless they were addressed. In the summer of 1788, North Carolina became the first state to reject the new Constitution. Rhode Island was also a holdout. With all due respect to Rhode Island, the loss of North Carolina would have physically divided the nation at that time in two. It had to be addressed.

After his work on the Federalist Papers, James Madison was integral to the development of the *Bill of Rights*. On March 4, 1789 Congress proposed 12 Amendments to the Constitution. Congress' resolution[9] started with Exhibit 10, and clearly states that the purpose was to address the requests from the states that had proposed amendments that were either as a part of their agreeing to the Constitution, or were stopping them from joining the Constitution (North Carolina and Rhode Island).

As stated in the Joint Resolution of Congress, the *Bill of Rights* were developed to address the Recommended Amendments found in

9 United States National Archives and Records Administration. (2026, Feb. 23). https://www.archives.gov/founding-docs/bill-of-rights-transcript

Exhibit 10 - Congressional Joint Resolution for the Bill of Rights

THE Conventions of a number of the States, having at the time of their adopting the Constitution, expressed a desire, in order to prevent misconstruction or abuse of its powers, that further declaratory and restrictive clauses should be added: And as extending the ground of public confidence in the Government, will best ensure the beneficent ends of its institution.
RESOLVED by the Senate and House of Representatives of the United States of America, in Congress assembled, two thirds of both Houses concurring, that the following Articles be proposed to the Legislatures of the several States, as amendments to the Constitution of the United States, all, or any of which Articles, when ratified by three fourths of the said Legislatures, to be valid to all intents and purposes, as part of the said Constitution; viz.

Appendices 11-16 (Rhode Island's proposed Amendments were not proposed until a year later). The text of what are now the 1st and 2nd Amendments to the Constitution did not change after the March 4, 1789 Joint Resolution. The interesting thing to ask is how were the texts of these amendments developed?

The state recommendations that led to the religious phrase in the 1st Amendment are shown in Figure 9. This allows the reader to imagine being in James Madison's shoes and trying to create a final amendment for the federal Constitution. The first thing that can be seen is that Virginia's recommended amendment was extremely loquacious. The overall federal Constitution was very tightly written using extensive semicolons and brevity. Figure 9 shows the phrases that Madison combined to produce the 1st Amendment. He addressed both the "right of conscience" and restricted any establishment of a national religious sect by Congress.

Another issue that has caused surprising confusion was James Madison's construction of the 2nd Amendment. The first recommended amendment by New Hampshire (NHRA12, Appendix 13) forcefully exclaimed that "Congress shall never disarm any citizen". In Chapter 1, the 1688 Glorious Revolution was discussed where King James II had disarmed Protestants. This infringement of Englishmen's "rights to bear arms" had resulted in the formal declaration of this right in the English Bill of Rights (EBR7, Appendix 4). New Hampshire appears to have been worried about a similar risk from this new federal government and Congress.

By the time of the drafting of what became the 2nd amendment,

Figure 9 - 1st Amendment Religious Section Development

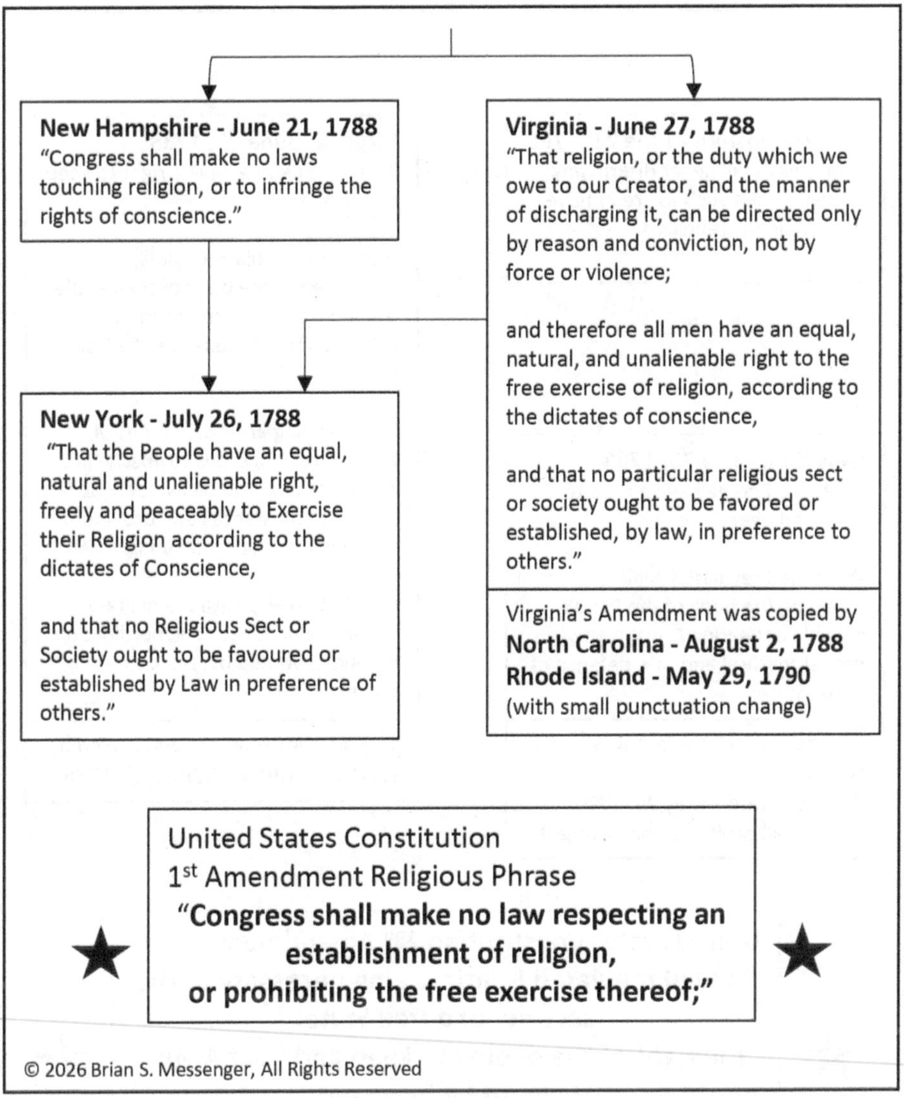

three other states (Virginia, New York and North Carolina) had all emphatically stated: "That the people have a right to keep and bear arms". They wanted this general right to be clearly stated for all Americans. Virginia's proposal was very detailed with four independent clauses. They also described the importance of a "well regulated militia", their disdain for "standing armies", and their requirement for "civilian control of the

Figure 10 - 2nd Amendment Right to Bear Arms Development

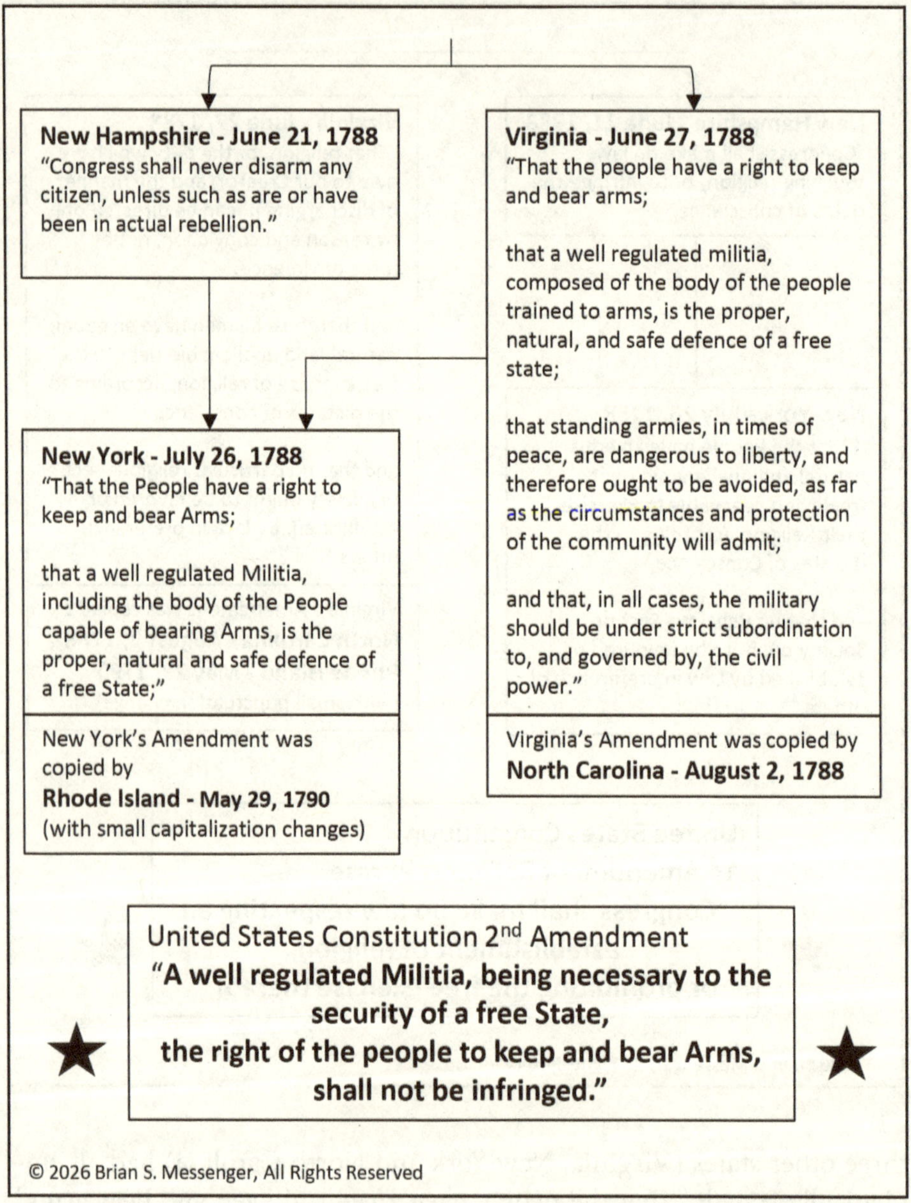

military". Taking the last three independent phrases from Virginia's proposal, Madison combined their intents to generate the first part of the 2nd Amendment to the Constitution. Figure 10 shows the recommended amendments from various states so that the reader can see the task that Madison was faced with. The 2nd Amendment was declaring a general right of all Americans. Merging the four states' proposals, Madison did not use the limitation of "Congress shall never" as New Hampshire had proposed, or as he had done in the 1st Amendment.

In addition to the 1st and 2nd Amendments described above, the recommended amendments in Appendices 11-17 show the sources for the other amendments in the *Bill of Rights*. The appendices also show how some proposals that were initially rejected for inclusion became Constitutional Amendments centuries later. Madison's Constitutional work completed on December 15, 1791. This was when the ten amendments referred to as the *Bill of Rights* were formally approved by the states. Some might have viewed this as an early Christmas present for our country. It was also a key success that helped to build up the reputation of James Madison who would later become our fourth President.

We all celebrate the *Bill of Rights*, but what about the recommended amendments that were not accepted? Table 7 shows the percentage of each state's amendments that were accepted by Congress that were proposed to the States. No state had more than 55% of their Recommended Amendments approved, nor did any state have less than 25%. The key is that all of the states were approving these "rights" to be integral to the Constitution. It will be seen that most of these "rights" integral to the Constitution are Nationwide Privileges and Immunities. Thinking back to the goals of privileges and immunities stated in the *Articles of Confederation*, any traveler or visitor to a state needs to have a baseline set of Nationwide privileges and immunities that they are entitled to. Otherwise, they will not know what they can safely do without risk of imprisonment.

The *Bill of Rights* has a very interesting difference between the 1st Amendment and all of the remaining Amendments. In the case of the 1st Amendment, it places a restriction on Congress specifically. This implies that the states have more flexibility on these issues. For instance, a state could establish a preferred state religion as had been done by some of the states already. Additionally, discussions of state restrictions on the speaking or publishing of anti-slavery abolitionist information will be discussed in the next chapter.

Later in this chapter, the Supreme Court decision in *Barron v.*

Table 7 - Success Rate for State Recommended Amendments

State	Recommended Amendments	Recommended Amendments in inital 12 Proposed Amendments	Success Rate Percentage for proposed Bill of Rights (12 Amendments)	Recommended Amendments in Bill of Rights (10 Amendments)	Success Rate Percentage for final Bill of Rights (10 Amendments)
Massachusetts	9	4	44	3	33
South Carolina	4	1	25	1	25
New Hampshire	12	7	58	6	50
Virginia	20	11	55	11	55
New York	57	15	26	14	25
North Carolina	46	15	33	14	30
Rhode Island	39	13	33	13	33

Baltimore[10]*(1833)* will be discussed in detail. This decision found that the *Bill of Rights* did not apply to the States. It does not change the Privileges and Immunities precedents or history explained in this book, but it provides context for Constitutional and court decisions that came later. In preparation for the discussion of *Barron v. Baltimore*, the rights identified in the *Bill of Rights* are analyzed with respect to crossover with the Nationwide Privileges and Immunities from the *Magna Carta*, the *Petition of Right*, the *Habeus Corpus Act*, the *[English] Bill of Rights*, the *Declaration of Independence*, and the *Articles of Confederation.* This analysis is shown in Appendix 18. In addition, the importance of the various sections of the *Bill of Rights* to travelers and merchants are considered. This is included since a key importance for privileges and immunities stated in the Articles of Confederation was to "*secure and perpetuate mutual friendship and intercourse among the people of the different states in the*

10 Barron v. Mayor and City Council of Baltimore, 32 U.S. 243 (1833)

union."

In Appendix 18, the Bill of Rights is broken down into a total of 19 separate and specific rights (some Amendments have multiple rights such as the 1st Amendment with five). At the time of our nation's founding, 13 of these 19 rights were directly addressed by foundational documents from England that were established to last for perpetuity, and/or by the *Declaration of Independence*. These rights were all discussed in Chapter 1. Four of the remaining six specific rights in the *Bill of Rights* are found in the 4th and 5th Amendment. These rights pertain to searches, warrants, double-jeopardy, and self incrimination. A complete analysis of English Common Law at the time of our founding would be necessary to determine which of these rights were of a foundational nature to our national character. If this was the case, then they would also have been considered privileges and immunities at our nation's founding.

In the famous Christmas movie *It's a Wonderful Life*(1946) George Baily (Jimmy Stewart) is shown by his guardian angel Clarence how the world would have looked like if he had never been born. An interesting question is how our legal world would have looked if the *Bill of Rights* had never been enacted. That premise may seem sacrilegious, or un-American, but a plausible argument can be made that it might have been better in some cases. How can that be you might ask? The answer is that when *Barron v. Baltimore* removed the protections of the *Bill of Rights* over actions by the states, a virtual landmine was set up that was triggered 50 years later. With the fall of Reconstruction in the Southern States in the late 1870's, states used this fact to justify their re-established discriminatory laws and practices. We will see how cases such as *United States v. Cruikshank(1876), The Civil Rights Cases(1883)*, and *Plessy v. Ferguson(1896)* might have been decided differently by the Supreme Court if the questions had revolved around Privileges and Immunities. In the meantime, the government created by the newly ratified Constitution had to be set up. The Presidency and the Supreme Court were totally new, and the Congress now consisted of both the House of Representatives and the Senate.

An Early Test of Press Freedoms

Within 10 years of the ratification of the Constitution, the question of Freedom of the Press came to the forefront of the public's discussion. John Adams was our second President. He had been a founding father who helped to write the strong freedom of the press protections[11] in the Massachusetts State Constitution. In 1798, Congress passed, and President Adams signed, the *Sedition Act.* The federal government was worried[12] about a possible war with France. They used that fear to restrict criticism of the government itself.

Prior to the internet, television, radio, or even the telephone, newspapers and books provided the greatest means to promote ideas and positions on issues. Without loudspeakers or megaphones, individual speakers might be heard by a few hundred people at a time. Newspapers and books could reach thousands and thousands. The 1st Amendment says that "*Congress shall make no law ... abridging the freedom of ... the press.*" The United States Congress in 1798 decided that it was alright to pass a law against publishing false or malicious information about the government. Not only that, but this "crime" could result[13] in a fine of $2,000 and up to two years in prison! If politicians belonging to the party out of power in our present century were held to such a standard, would there be any left?

---

11 Massachusetts State Constitution of 1780. "Article XVI. The liberty of the press is essential to the security of freedom in a state: it ought not, therefore, to be restrained in this commonwealth."

12 United States National Archives and Records Administration. (2026, Feb. 23). https://www.archives.gov/milestone-documents/alien-and-sedition-acts

13 Sedition Act of 1798, "SEC. 2. And be it farther enacted, That if any person shall write, print, utter or publish, or shall cause or procure to be written, printed, uttered or published, or shall knowingly and willingly assist or aid in writing, printing, uttering or publishing any false, scandalous and malicious writing or writings against the government of the United States, or either house of the Congress of the United States, or the President of the United States, with intent to defame the said government, or either house of the said Congress, or the said President, or to bring them, or either of them, into contempt or disrepute; or to excite against them, or either or any of them, the hatred of the good people of the United States, or to stir up sedition within the United States, or to excite any unlawful combinations therein, for opposing or resisting any law of the United States, or any act of the President of the United States, done in pursuance of any such law, or of the powers in him vested by the constitution of the United States, or to resist, oppose, or defeat any such law or act, or to aid, encourage or abet any hostile designs of any foreign nation against United States, their people or government, then such person, being thereof convicted before any court of the United States having jurisdiction thereof, shall be punished by a fine not exceeding two thousand dollars, and by imprisonment not exceeding two years."

Your initial reaction might be, "How wasn't the Sedition Act ruled unconstitutional by the Supreme Court?". The answer is that early in our republic, the Supreme Court had not yet established its ability to rule laws unconstitutional. It wasn't until five years later that the Supreme Court first did this in the case of *Marbury v. Madison(1803)* . The writers of the Sedition Act also wrote their law for a temporary emergency situation. They did this by having it expire in March 1801. Since this was two years before *Marbury v. Madison*, the Supreme Court never had the opportunity to determine the Sedition Act's constitutionality. In the world of political discourse, disagreements shouldn't result in imprisonment. Corresponding to the "right of freedom of speech" and the "right of freedom of the press" is a related responsibility that all citizens have to temper their feelings and to remain peaceful when they don't agree with each other . Unfortunately, America lost "a founding father" due to high political emotions.

Alexander Hamilton and the Horrible History of Dueling

As children, many of us learned the rhyme: "sticks and stones will break my bones, but words will never hurt me". Unfortunately, that is not always true. Words can damage people's reputations. For those who are unfamiliar with the history of dueling , it started in the Middle Ages and was used to defend men's honor. In a typical duel, men with loaded pistols start back-to-back and then march away from each other. At a certain distance they turn and wait for a signal to "fire". At this point, while looking at their opponent, they are both permitted to shoot at the same time. Some people come to their senses and back out by realizing that their argument isn't worth dying for. Each participant has a "second" to act as their assistant and witness, and hopefully to convince them to resolve their differences without resorting to dueling.

Most people are familiar with Alexander Hamilton from the Broadway show *Hamilton*(2015), or from the fact that he is in their wallets if they have a $10 bill. Hamilton was a critical founding father and was our nation's first Secretary of the Treasury under President George Washington. He might have become President, but his life was shockingly cut short in the summer of 1804. Hamilton died at the age of 49 in a duel. The amazing thing is that his opponent was the sitting Vice

President of the United States, Aaron Burr.

Hamilton and Burr both traveled to New Jersey from New York to participate in their duel. According to the National Park Service[14], "*dueling was outlawed in both states, but the penalties for dueling were less harsh in New Jersey*". The tragedy is that the concern about penalties might only apply to the "winner", since the "loser" would probably die of their wounds. During their duel, Hamilton's shot missed Burr and hit a tree. He had said days before that his plan was to throw away his first shot. In contrast, Burr's shot was accurate and hit Hamilton in the abdomen. The nation was shocked when Hamilton died from his wounds the next day. We lost one potential president with a duel, but two years later, a future president would not only kill a man in a duel, but suffer a dangerous wound himself.

In his excellent biography of Andrew Jackson, called *American Lion*, John Meacham describes[15] Jackson's duel as follows: "*At seven o'clock on the morning of Friday, May 30, 1806, on the Red River in Logan County, Kentucky, Jackson and Dickinson faced each other at twenty-four feet. Jackson let Dickinson shoot first, and he hit Jackson in the chest with a bullet. Though wounded, Jackson coolly leveled his own pistol at his opponent, and fired. The trigger caught halfway; Jackson cocked the gun again and fired, killing Dickinson. Only later, as his boot filled with blood after he had left the dueling ground, did the extent of Jackson's wound become clear. He carried Dickinson's bullet in his body until he died. Even in pain -- the wound complicated his health for decades -- Jackson never let his mask drop. 'If he had shot me through the brain, sir,' Jackson told a friend, 'I should still have killed him'*".

How does dueling fit into the discussion of privileges and immunities? For individual states in our country, there was a strong desire to stop this behavior. Appendix 19 shows the detailed provisions that states included in their constitutions regarding dueling, but these are summarized in Table 8.

There are multiple contextual things that can be learned by reading these state Constitutional Amendments. One observation is that

---

14 United States Department of the Interior, National Park Service, *Hamilton-Burr Duel: Dueling in the 18th and 19th Centuries*. (2026, Feb. 23). https://www.nps.gov/articles/000/hamilton-burr-duel.htm

15 Meacham, John. *American Lion: Andrew Jackson in the White House*. Page 26

Table 8 - Dueling Restrictions in State Constitutions 1812-1850

State	Date of Constitution	Dueling Provisions in State Constitution or [Law]
Louisiana	Apr. 30, 1812	Dueling Later Restricted by Constitution in 1845
Indiana	Dec. 11, 1816	Dueling Later Restricted by Constitution in 1851
Mississippi	Dec. 10, 1817	Assembly can disqualify from public office for dueling
Illinois	Dec. 3, 1818	Assembly can pass laws to prevent dueling
Alabama	Dec. 14, 1819	Assembly can pass laws to prevent dueling
Maine	Mar. 15, 1820	[State Laws were passed to prevent dueling]
Missouri	Aug. 10, 1821	[State Law declared killing someone in a duel was murder]
Arkansas	Jun. 15, 1836	Dueling Later Restricted by Constitution in 1874
Michigan	Jan. 26, 1837	Dueling Later Restricted by Constitution in 1850
Florida	Mar. 3, 1845	Cannot hold public office if engaging in duel
Texas	Dec. 29, 1845	Cannot hold public office if engaging in duel
Iowa	Dec. 28, 1846	Cannot hold public office if engaging in duel
Wisconsin	May 29, 1848	Cannot hold public office if engaging in duel
California	Sep. 9, 1850	Cannot hold public office if engaging in duel

since "the right to bear arms" was so universal, states were limited in what they could do to stop dueling. The states' most common response was to disqualify people from public office if they participated in a duel. Another observation is that multiple states recognized that their citizens might travel to other states to participate in a duel as Hamilton and Burr had done. Appendix 19 shows that Florida, Texas and California all wanted to extend their office holding restrictions to account for this case. While participating in a duel was barbaric, it forced people to evaluate their behavior and to potentially back down. Surprisingly, it wasn't until 61 years after the Hamilton-Burr duel that America had its first high level assassination. The cowardice of assassinations, that started with Abraham Lincoln's in 1865, have resulted in major turning points in our nation's history.

The 10-90 Rule of Second-Hand Historical Knowledge

In the days prior to computers and the internet, knowledge was passed down primarily through books, written publications and verbally. Obvious Privileges and Immunities of citizenship would have been verbally communicated from elders to children. To highlight how far this can go, consider the following thought experiment: A child at the age of 10 should be able to learn the basics of American History and to ask their elders questions about their elders' memories and understandings. Some percentage of people will live to the age of 90. Using this "10-90 Rule", there should be some living Americans today who learned directly from people who vividly remembered the horrors of the Civil War and Lincoln's assassination. As surprising as this may seem, a person born in 1851 would have been 10 when the Civil War started and should have had a good memory of those terrible times. If that person lived to 90, they would have passed away in 1941. Just prior to their death, they could have taught a young 10-year-old relative about their experiences. Since life expectancy has increased, that relative could still be alive at the age of 95 today.

In a court of law, there are a few exceptions where second-hand information is admissible. Using the "10-90" rule, second-hand information can be passed down verbally for over 160 years. In the short 72 years between the ratification of the Constitution and the start of the Civil War, this may help to explain why the Supreme Court had very few cases that discussed privileges and immunities. We shall see that many of the Supreme Court justices at that time remembered pre-Constitutional America. They would have understood privileges and immunities of citizenship from an early age. Prior to the 1850's, there was only a single Appeals Court case that broadly discussed the topic. That case was *Corfield v. Coryell(1823)*, and it involved harvesting oysters of all things.

The Case of *Corfield v. Coryell(1823)*

The appeal[16] in *Corfield v. Coryell* was argued in front of a single Circuit Court Justice: Bushrod Washington. During the early republic,

16 Corfield v. Coryell, 6 F. Cas. 546 (C.C.E.D. Pa. 1823) (No. 3230)

Supreme Court Justices "rode circuit" during part of the year and handled initial appeals for their assigned region. Bushrod Washington was a United States Supreme Court Associate Justice when he wrote the appellate decision in *Corfield v. Coryell.* He was also 27 years old when the United States Constitution was ratified, so he had a lifetime of knowledge regarding the privileges and immunities of United States citizens.

Ironically, Bushrod Washington was handling a case about harvesting oysters approximately 100 miles down the Delaware river from where General George Washington had crossed on Christmas Day in 1776. From the opinion, it involved a vessel that was "*...found engaged in taking oysters in Maurice river cove by means of dredges, was seized, condemned, and sold, ...*". It was found that the State of New Jersey had the right to regulate who and when people could harvest oysters, since that was not directly tied to commerce "*on the navigable waters belonging to the several states*". Bushrod Washington also found that "*The law does not inhibit the buying and selling of oysters after they are lawfully gathered, and become articles of trade;*".

The second question proposed by the defense lawyers had to do with whether New Jersey's oyster harvesting laws violated the Privileges and Immunities clause. In this case, the defendant was from Delaware. He was claiming that the Privileges and Immunities Clause of the United States Constitution allowed him equal rights to New Jersey's oyster fields. This is where Bushrod Washington made a number of key points related to the subject of this book. Exhibit 11 shows[17] how he described the fundamental and nationwide nature of privileges and immunities. In the text in Exhibit 11, the reference to "*the citizens of all free governments*" is a "*motherhood and apple pie*" sort of statement. It can only be true if every

17 Corfield v. Coryell, 6 F. Cas. 546, 551 (C.C.E.D. Pa. 1823) (No. 3230)

Exhibit 11 - Corfield v. Coryell Nationwide Privileges and Immunities

The inquiry is, what are the privileges and immunities of citizens in the several states? We feel no hesitation in confining these expressions to those privileges and immunities which are, in their nature, fundamental; which belong, of right, to the citizens of all free governments; and which have, at all times, been enjoyed by the citizens of the several states which compose this Union, from the time of their becoming free, independent, and sovereign.

free government is alike in the rights that they believe are important to their citizens. Therefore, while it may have sounded powerful to write, it really has no meaning. On the other hand, it is clear that Bushrod Washington views the Constitution's Privileges and Immunities as applying to nationwide rights.

As discussed in many places earlier, there was intentionally no formal list of privileges and immunities. In Exhibit 12, Washington explained this fact. He then goes on to propose a very general statement on various areas where these rights apply. He felt that rights apply to protection by the government, enjoyment of life and liberty, property rights, pursuit of happiness, and safety. These are incredibly general topics. What makes one person happy or safe may do the opposite for another. There is no obvious precedent for this definition, but later in the section, Washington refers to the opening sentence of the Articles of Confederation's Privileges and Immunities Clause. That sentence was dissected in Chapter 2. It referred to the purpose of privileges and immunities as being: "*the better to secure and perpetuate mutual friendship and intercourse among the people of the different states of the Union.*"

It must be repeated, that this case never reached the United States Supreme Court. What can be analyzed is how the specific rights that Washington identified in his opinion match up to the fundamental privileges and immunities that have been identified in prior chapters. He specifically listed six rights that are shown in Table 9. Corfield v. Coryell was the first court case to clearly show that some rights listed in the *Constitution*, the *Bill of Rights* and the *Articles of Confederation* were nationwide privileges and immunities of all citizens.

In Chapter 2, the "state level view" was shown to be an improper interpretation. That view felt that any citizen who entered another state immediately had all of the privileges and immunities of the citizens of

Exhibit 12 - Corfield v. Coryell Determining Fundamental Rights

What these fundamental principles are, it would perhaps be more tedious than difficult to enumerate. They may, however, be all comprehended under the following general heads: Protection by the government; the enjoyment of life and liberty, with the right to acquire and possess property of every kind, and to pursue and obtain happiness and safety; subject nevertheless to such restraints as the government may justly prescribe for the general good of the whole.

Table 9 - Corfield v. Coryell Declared Rights

Text from *Corfield v. Coryell*[1] Opinion	Prior References as Nationwide Privileges and Immunities	Notes regarding prior precedents
The right of a citizen of one state to pass through, or to reside in any other state, for purposes of trade, agriculture, professional pursuits, or otherwise	Articles of Confederation, Appendix 6, AC1- AC3	Excellent alignment with the Articles of Confederation defined rights
To claim the writ of habeas corpus	Habeus Corpus Act(1679), Appendix 3, HC1 United States Constitution Appendix 10, C1	Excellent alignment with the English Habeus Corpus Act and the United States Constitution
To institute and maintain actions of any kind in the courts of the state	United States Constitution 7th Amendment - "In Suits at common law, where the value in controversy shall exceed twenty dollars, the right of trial by jury shall be preserved, and no fact tried by a jury, shall be otherwise re-examined in any Court of the United States, than according to the rules of the common law."	The United States Constitution 7th Amendment ties back to English Common Law
To take, hold and dispose of property, either real or personal	Magna Carta	Excellent alignment
an exemption from higher taxes or impositions than are paid by the other citizens of the state	In 1823, the United States Constitution Article I, Section 8[2] Article I, Section 9[3]	Excellent alignment with Constitution in 1823. The Sections were changed in 1913 by ratification of the 16th Amendment that permitted the income tax.

1 Corfield v. Coryell, 6 F. Cas. 546, 551 (C.C.E.D. Pa. 1823) (No. 3230)

2 The original Article I, Section 8 of the Constitution said: "The Congress shall have Power To lay and collect Taxes, Duties, Imposts and Excises, to pay the Debts and provide for the common Defence and general Welfare of the United States; but all Duties, Imposts and Excises shall be uniform throughout the United States;"

3The original Article I, Section 9 of the Constitution said: "No Capitation, or other direct, Tax shall be laid, unless in Proportion to the Census or enumeration herein before directed to be taken."

Text from *Corfield v. Coryell*[1] Opinion	Prior References as Nationwide Privileges and Immunities	Notes regarding prior precedents
the elective franchise, as regulated and established by the laws or constitution of the state in which it is to be exercised.	United States Constitution Article 1, Section 4[4] Article II, Section 1[5]	Excellent alignment with Constitution

4 United States Constitution, Article I, Section 4: "The Times, Places and Manner of holding Elections for Senators and Representatives, shall be prescribed in each State by the Legislature thereof; but the Congress may at any time by Law make or alter such Regulations, except as to the Places of chusing Senators."

5 United States Constitution, Article II, Section 1: "Each State shall appoint, in such Manner as the Legislature thereof may direct, a Number of Electors, equal to the whole Number of Senators and Representatives to which the State may be entitled in the Congress: but no Senator or Representative, or Person holding an Office of Trust or Profit under the United States, shall be appointed an Elector."

that state. Exhibit 13 clearly shows that Justice Bushrod Washington believed that the citizens of states can have privileges and immunities that exceed those of visiting citizens from other states. This matches the extensive analysis previously shown in Chapter 2.

Only ten years after the *Corfield v. Coryell* case, Supreme Court Associate Justice Joseph Story published his *Commentaries on the Constitution of the United States.* It was previously discussed[18] that Story included Madison's confusing interpretation of the privileges and immu-

18 Story, Joseph, *Commentaries on the Constitution of the United States Volume III.* Chapter XL, §1800

Exhibit 13 - Corfield v. Coryell Rejection of "State Level View"

But we cannot accede to the proposition which was insisted on by the counsel, that, under this provision of the constitution, the citizens of the several states are permitted to participate in all the rights which belong exclusively to the citizens of any particular state, merely upon the ground that they are enjoyed by those citizens; much less, that in regulating the common property of the citizens of such state, the legislature is bound to extend to the citizens of all the other states the same advantages as are secured to their own citizens. ... that of fishing belongs to all the citizens or subjects of the state. It is the property of all; to be enjoyed by them in subordination to the laws which regulate its use.

Exhibit 14 - Joseph Story's Comments on Corfield v. Coryell

> Connected with the exclusive power of naturalization in the national government, it puts at rest many of the difficulties, which affected the construction of the article of confederation. It is obvious, that, if the citizens of each state were to be deemed aliens to each other, they could not take, or hold real estate, or other privileges, except as other aliens. The intention of this clause was to confer on them, if one may so say, a general citizenship ; and to communicate all the privileges and immunities , which the citizens of the same state would be entitled to under the like circumstances.

nities clause. Story also referenced *Corfield v. Coryell.* Unfortunately, Justice Bushrod Washington had passed away four years earlier. Justice Story noted correctly that since Congress now controlled naturalization, many of the problems with the *Articles of Confederation* were removed. Exhibit 14 shows Story's comments regarding *Corfield v. Coryell.* The phrase "*the intention of this clause was to confer on them, if one may say so, a general citizenship*" is another way of describing Nationwide Privileges and Immunities as discussed in this book so far. A potential problem arises in the ambiguity of the second phrase of the last sentence of Exhibit 14. Unfortunately, he used the phrase "*and to communicate all the privileges and immunities, which citizens of the same state would be entitled to under the like circumstances*". If this meant the ability to "*take, or hold real estate*", that would be correct. It could also be interpreted as the "state level view" that was shown to be incorrect and was definitely not supported by *Corfield v. Coryell* (see Exhibit 13).

The Expansively Restrictive Decision in *Barron v. Baltimore(1833)*

Early in this chapter, we discussed how many of the founding fathers and state conventions did not believe that a *Bill of Rights* was necessary for the United States Constitution. The court decision in *Barron v. Baltimore* moved the country back towards this position by removing any protections in the *Bill of Rights* from affecting State governments. The suit revolved around the 5th Amendment clause[19] that "*nor shall private property be taken for public use, without just compensation.*" Supreme

19 United States National Archives and Records Administration. (2026, Feb. 23). https://www.archives.gov/founding-docs/bill-of-rights-transcript

Court Chief Justice John Marshall was our longest serving Chief Justice, and this was the final opinion that he wrote.

In simple terms to describe the case, a wharf owner in Baltimore sued the city for paving roads and rerouting streams that caused silt to build up in the water in front of his wharf. Over many years, this made his wharf useless[20]. If Chief Justice Marshall had wanted to be a "wise guy", he could have thrown the case out on the grounds that it wasn't a "taking" since Barron's property was being added to. Suffice it to say, that approach would not have been befitting of a Supreme Court opinion.

Chief Justice Marshall wrote an opinion with a very strong[21] State's Rights argument. He said "*The constitution was ordained and established by the people of the United States for themselves, for their own government, and not for the government of the individual states. Each state established a constitution for itself, and, in that constitution, provided such limitations and restrictions on the powers of its particular government as its judgement dictated.*" Another problem with allowing a case such as Barron's to be tried in Federal Court under the 5th Amendment, is that the possible workload would be tremendous. In a present-day analogy to this case, anytime a highway was going to be routed so that it reduced travelers going by a store, the owner could sue that he was suffering a taking.

Chief Justice Marshall declared that this part of the 5th Amendment only applied to actions by the United States government by saying[22]: "*We are of opinion, that the provision in the fifth amendment to the constitution, declaring that private property shall not be taken for public*

---

20 Barron v. Baltimore, 32 U.S. 243, 243-244 (1833), "The city, in the asserted exercise of its corporate authority over the harbour, the paving of streets, and regulating grades for paving, and over the health of Baltimore, directed from their accustomed and natural course, certain streams of water which flow from the range of hills bordering the city, and diverted them, partly by adopting new grades of streets, and partly by the necessary results of paving, and partly by mounds, embankments and other artificial means, purposely adapted to bend the course of the water to the wharf in question. These streams becoming very full and violent in rains, carried down with them from the hills and the soil over which they ran, large masses of sand and earth, which they deposited along, and widely in front of the wharf of the plaintiff. The alleged consequence was, that the water was rendered so shallow that it ceased to be useful for vessels of any important burthen, lost its income, and became of little or no value as a wharf.

21 Barron v. Baltimore, 32 U.S. 243, 247 (1833)

22 Barron v. Baltimore, 32 U.S. 243, 250-251 (1833)

use without just compensation, is intended solely as a limitation on the exercise of power by the government of the United States, and is not applicable to the legislation of the states." If he had left this issue there, it is expected that most people would have been happy. Instead, he fired a proverbial shotgun blast at the entire *Bill of Rights.*

He left the protection of these fundamental rights entirely up to the states[23] when he said: "*Had the people of the several states, or any of them, required changes in their constitutions; had they required additional safeguards to liberty from the apprehended encroachments of their particular governments the remedy was in their own hands, and would have been applied by themselves.*" This simple, and non-controversial, court decision at the time buried a landmine that would explode after the Civil War. Future Constitutional Amendments would be written to explicitly apply to both the federal government and to the states. In the meantime, this had the practical effect of leaving the individual states free to govern how they wished; while leaving their citizens with no declared rights from the *Bill of Rights.* Chief Justice Marshall was replaced by Chief Justice Taney who would find a more draconian means to deny individuals their rights. In the meantime, the country was growing and the right to travel between states was reaching the Supreme Court.

Arriving Immigrant Concerns in *The Passenger Cases(1849)*

In 2026, if you heard someone complaining about other countries emptying out their mental institutions and sending their people to the United States, you might not be surprised[24]. If you heard that Massachusetts had a law regarding passengers arriving by ship that said: "*If, on such examination, there shall be found among said passengers any lunatic, idiot, maimed, aged or infirm person, incompetent, in the opinion of the officer so examining, to maintain themselves, or who have been paupers in any other country, no such alien passenger shall be permitted to land until the master, owner, consignee, or agent of such vessel shall have given to such city or town a bond in the sum of one thousand dollars, with good and*

---

23 Barron v. Baltimore, 32 U.S. 243, 249 (1833), Chief Justice Marshall

24 President Trump Inaugural Address – January 20, 2025: "*Our government ... fails to protect our magnificent, law-abiding American citizens but provides sanctuary and protection for dangerous criminals, many from prisons and mental institutions, that have illegally entered our country from all over the world.*"

sufficient security, that no such lunatic or indigent passenger shall become a city, town, or State charge within ten years from the date of said bond.", you might believe you were in an alternate universe. This Massachusetts law, and a similar law from New York, were the basis of the United States Supreme Court's *Passenger Cases*(1849) decision.

The *Passenger Cases* had multiple issues that were related to the Privileges and Immunities Clause of the Constitution. The Court decision was fractured with multiple opinions. It ruled[25] that States could not place a tax on people arriving since that "*was a regulation of commerce, and not being within the power of the State, the act imposing the tax is void.*" Chief Justice Taney, in his dissent, made the argument[26] that compelling states "*to receive and to retain among them persons whom the State may deem dangerous to its peace, or who may be tainted with crimes or infectious diseases, or who may be a burden upon its industrious citizens, would subject its domestic concerns and social relations to the powers of the Federal government.*"

Chief Justice Taney was a former Democrat slave holder from Maryland. He was appointed Chief Justice by President Andrew Jackson in 1836, and he served until his death during the Civil War in 1864. Taney's view entailed a more traditional States Rights approach. He felt that the Federal Government should not control what happened within the states themselves. Part of Chief Justice Taney's dissent was used as a positive description for the Privileges and Immunities Clause many years later. The explanation that he used is shown[27] in Exhibit 15. Chief Justice Taney's description would later be used as a "*gold standard*" description of the importance for American citizens to be able to freely move about

25 Passenger Cases, Justice Wayne's Opinion 48 U.S. 283, 410 (1849)

26 Passenger Cases, Chief Justice Taney Dissent 48 U.S. 283, 476-477 (1849)

27 Passenger Cases, Chief Justice Taney Dissent 48 U.S. 283, 492 (1849)

Exhibit 15 – Chief Justice Taney's explanation for Travel Freedoms

"For all the great purposes for which the Federal government was formed, we are all one people, with one common country. We are all citizens of the United States; and, as members of the same community, must have the right to pass and repass through every part of it without interruption, as freely as in our own States."

our country. Unfortunately, his idea of who were "citizens" would rock the nation eight years later. In the next Chapter, will discuss his infamous *Dred Scott* decision. During the interim, the right to pass and repass through every part of the country without interruption helped to facilitate the California Gold Rush.

The Gold Rush and California's Constitution of 1849

California was a sleepy and remote Mexican territory until the *Mexican American War* broke out in the summer or 1846. It was an independent republic for a short time, and was then occupied by the American military. After the United States defeated Mexico in the war, the *Treaty of Guadalupe Hidalgo*[28] was negotiated and approved by both countries in May of 1848. Based on the treaty, the United States bought the territory that included California from Mexico for a total of $15 Million[29] . What is utterly amazing is that California became a state slightly over two years after formally being purchased from Mexico by the United States. That was all thanks to gold.

Gold was discovered on January 24, 1848, but it took many months for the news to reach the east coast. People from around the country who wanted to "strike it rich" started heading for California. Many took a harrowing journey by covered wagon that could last six months or more. Most started their journey on the previously established Oregon Trail[30] . Many cutoff to cross the desert of Nevada, and the steep, snowy and high Sierra Nevada mountains. One of the most harrowing stories regarding this route was that of the Donner Party. Many of their group perished. Of those who survived, most resorted to cannibalism when trapped in the treacherous Sierra Nevada mountains through a very snowy winter.

Americans heading to California would be traveling with all of their belongings through many states. For instance, someone from New

---

28 United States National Archives and Records Administration. (2026, Feb. 23). https://www.archives.gov/milestone-documents/treaty-of-guadalupe-hidalgo

29 Treaty of Guadalupe Hidalgo: "Article XII – In consideration of the extension acquired by the boundaries of the United States, as defined in the fifth article of the present treaty, the Government of the United States engages to pay to that of the Mexican Republic the sum of fifteen million of dollars."

30 United States Department of the Interior, National Park Service. (2026. Feb. 23). https://www.nps.gov/oreg/index.htm

Hampshire would likely travel overland through Massachusetts, New York, Pennsylvania, Ohio, Indiana, Illinois and Missouri before reaching the western territories. For many northerners, their travels through Missouri to the city of Independence where the Oregon Trail started may have been their first exposure to slavery. Fortunately, since they were citizens of one country, they could be confident that their privileges and immunities as Americans would protect them on their travels through existing states. They knew what their rights were. Their privileges and immunities helped to protect them from harassment or abuse by local, state, or government officials. Given what lay ahead, they needed all the help that they could get. Those who survived the trip to California had to find work and build a new life. It is very interesting to think about the types of jobs that they could do when they arrived.

We are very fortunate to have a census[31] from California for 1850 when it became a state (and an additional Congressionally mandated census from 1852). The census is very valuable since it tells us a lot about the population who wrote California's first Constitution. In 1850, there were roughly 100,000 people in California[32]. The population was approximately[33] 92% male! California was a territory and a state that did not have slavery; and the 'Free Colored' population made up approximately 1% of the state's population. The top five professions for people in California were *Miners(57,797)*, *Merchants (3,284)*, *Traders (2,410)*, *Laborers (2,159)*, and *Farmers (1,486)*. Approximately 75% of all men working in the state were *Miners*!

California became the 31st State on September 9, 1850 as a "*Free State*". In the next chapter, we will discuss the overall issue of slavery and how it interacted with the Privileges and Immunities of American citizens. Most of the people living in California in 1850 had moved

---

31 United States Department of Commerce, U.S. Census Bureau. (2026, Feb. 23). https://www2.census.gov/library/publications/decennial/1850/1850a/1850-census-report-california.pdf

32 Unfortunately, the 1850 census numbers for San Francisco, Santa Clara, and Contra Costa counties were lost. In 1852, these counties had 36,154, 6,764 and 2,786 people respectively. The 1850 census without those three counties had a total population of 92,597.

33 Excluding lost San Francisco, Santa Clara and Contra Costa county records, the state had 84,708 White Males, 6, 927 White Females, 872 Free Colored Males, and 90 Free Colored Females. Slavery was outlawed in California.

there in the last year or two from every other state, as well as from many other countries. The first California Constitution[34] came 63 years after the *United States Constitution* and approximately 60 years after the *Bill of Rights*. Therefore, it is an interesting milestone in understanding how States viewed rights; especially those protected by the 1st and 2nd Amendments.

Appendix 20 shows California's *Declaration of Rights*. The rights are listed in the order that they are found in the State Constitution, which can sometimes indicate importance. Starting with the 1st Amendment Rights, Section 4 in California's list provides an extensive statement on Freedom of Religion. It declares that "*The free exercise and enjoyment of religious profession and worship, without discrimination or preference, shall forever be allowed in this state;*". Next, Section 9 in California's list provides an extensive description of Freedom of Speech and of the Press. It declares "*Every citizen may freely speak, write, and publish his sentiments on all subjects, being responsible for the abuse of that right;*". Section 9 goes on by extensively explaining how the truth can be used as a defense in libel prosecutions. Finally, Section 10 declares that "*The people shall have the right freely to assemble together to consult for the common good, to instruct their representatives, and to petition the legislature for redress of grievances.*" California's Constitution clearly repeated and further defined the 1st Amendment rights from the United States Constitution. This was needed, since the 1st Amendment restricted Congress but not the States.

In a similar vein, California's Constitution added additional context to other rights found in the *Bill of Rights*. For instance, the 7th Amendment to the Constitution produced a particular problem. It declares that "*where the value of controversy shall exceed twenty dollars, the right to trial by jury shall be preserved,*". This could create a huge backlog of civil court cases, so Section 3 of California's Constitution provides that "*a jury trial may be waived by the parties,*". In the case of Excessive Bail described in the 8th Amendment to the United States Constitution, Section 7 of California's Constitution added "*All persons shall be bailable, by sufficient sureties, unless for capital offences, when the proof is evident or*

34 California Secretary of State, California State Archives. (2026, Feb. 23). https://archives.cdn.sos.ca.gov/pdf/1849-california-constitution-for-website-9-16-20.pdf

the presumption great."

What about gun rights? Approximately 75% of all men were miners. Their horse, pistol and rifle were the equivalent of an armored truck today. Many of California's citizens had come across the country in vulnerable covered wagons. They needed guns for protection, hunting and their very survival. Section 1 of California's Constitution declared that among people's inalienable rights were "*defending life and liberty*" and "*protecting property*". California's Constitution also said that you would lose your right to vote or hold government office if you were involved in dueling (Article XI, Section 2). What did California's Constitution directly say about the 2nd Amendment "*right to bear arms*"? It said absolutely nothing.

After the Supreme Court decision in *Barron v. Baltimore*, the *Bill of Rights*, including the 2nd Amendment, did not apply to the states. Clearly, the writer's of the California Constitution knew that gun ownership was a Nationwide Privilege and Immunity. Otherwise, an omission of an equivalent to the 2nd Amendment in the California State Constitution would have been the pinnacle of legal malpractice. If the reader doesn't believe that guns were integral to 1850 California society, the author has the Golden Gate Bridge that he would like to sell you.

In 1849, California's Constitution made a strong declaration outlawing slavery[35]. This was expanded upon to produce the 13th Amendment to the United States Constitution which outlawed slavery in 1865. Unfortunately, those 16 intervening years saw the horrible Civil War and the abhorrent arguments leading up to it. The next Chapter will show how the battle over slavery had a strong relationship to the Privileges and Immunities Clause of the Constitution.

---

35 California Constitution of 1849, Declaration of Rights, Section 18 - "Neither slavery, nor involuntary servitude, unless for the punishment of crimes, shall ever be tolerated in this state."

CHAPTER 4

Slavery, Civil War, and Freedom

(1850 through the 14th Amendment)

There is no way to understand what has happened to the Privileges and Immunities Clause without understanding the history of slavery in the United States. Multiple critical Supreme Court cases in the 1800's were decided, and directly impacted, by this evil institution. The fact that it was a disgusting part of our country's history must not preclude studying the causes, effects and results. Those factors directly resulted in an awful Civil War for all Americans. This was followed by many decades of heartache and additional suffering for African Americans after the collapse of Reconstruction. Objectively, understanding the demographics, attitudes and fears in the country during this period can help us to learn not to repeat actions that may be similar or that produce similar results.

The Founding Fathers of the 1700's had a biblical history that would have shaped each person's views on slavery differently. The *Book of Exodus* is the second book of the Bible. It is understood by all Christians and Jews around world since it is a key part of the Old Testament. Exodus describes how the Israelites were enslaved in Africa by the Egyptian Pharaohs for over 400 years. The famous movie *The Ten Commandments(1956)* stars Charlton Heston as Moses. It helps modern Americans to understand the amazing story of God working through Moses to help the Israelites escape their slavery in Egypt.

By studying the history of ancient Greece and Rome, the founders were also aware that both societies had extensive slavery. We have James Madison's notes from the Constitutional Convention debates to provide us with a unique window on how different delegates thought about slavery. In the Constitutional debates on slavery from August 21-22, 1787, we have the records of 13 delegates who spoke on the topic. Two of the delegates specifically referenced the negatives of slavery in Greece and Rome. George Mason of Virginia[1] "*mentioned the dangerous insurrections of the slaves in Greece and Sicily*", while John Dickinson of Delaware described[2] how "*Greece and Rome were unhappy by their slaves* ". These notes give a unique perspective on the opinions regarding slavery from different parts of the country.

The debate notes help to explain the founders' views regarding how slavery was brought to the colonies by the English. George Mason of Virginia described[3] how "*This infernal traffic originated in the avarice of British Merchants. The British Government constantly checked the attempts of Virginia to put a stop to it.*" To show that the British had not had a problem with slavery, Charles Pinckney of South Carolina made the excuse[4] that "*the Royal assent before the Revolution had never been refused to South Carolina*".

From a humanitarian standpoint, Luther Martin of Maryland said[5] that slavery "*was inconsistent with the principles of the revolution and dishonorable to the American character to have such a feature in the Constitution* ". Oliver Ellsworth of Connecticut said[6] of slavery "*that if it was to be considered in a moral light we ought to go farther and free those already in the Country* ". George Mason of Virginia worried about a potential enemy arming slaves when he said[7]: "*The evil of having slaves was experienced during the late war. Had slaves been treated as they might have been by the Enemy, they would have proved dangerous instruments in their hands.*" In the same discussion, George Mason described how during the English Civil War, Oliver Cromwell did this to Virginia to ob-

1 The Anti-Federalist Papers and the [Constitutional Convention Debates], Signet Classics, 1986, page 155, Slavery and the Constitution (August 21, 22), Madison's notes for COLONEL MASON (George Mason)

2 Ibid., page 157, Madison's notes for MR. DICKINSON (John Dickinson)

3 Ibid., page 155, Madison's notes for COLONEL MASON (George Mason)

4 Ibid., page 156, Madison's notes for GENERAL PINCKNEY (Charles Pinckney)

5 Ibid., pages 153-154, Madison's notes for MR. L. MARTIN (Luther Martin)

6 Ibid., page 155, Madison's notes for MR. ELLSWORTH (Oliver Ellsworth)

7 Ibid., page 155, Madison's notes for COLONEL MASON (George Mason)

tain control over the colony when he said: "*and the instructions given by Cromwell to the Commissioners sent to Virginia, to arm the servants and slaves, in case other means of obtaining its submission should fail.*"

Before proceeding with the Constitutional Convention Debates, it is important to understand the government of the United States at that time. Remembering back to the analysis in Chapter 2, each of the States under the Articles of Confederation were sovereign, free and independent. They each controlled their own immigration and any importation of slaves. The National government had no control over these functions. It is in this context of individual sovereign states, that the delegates were asked to form a Constitution for the entire nation.

To provide additional context, we can look at the population of each state at the time. Fortunately, we have the official United States Census data from 1790. This is a good approximation since it was only three years after the Constitutional Convention. The census data from 1790 includes three main categories: "Free Whites", "Other Free People", and "Slaves". Appendix 21 shows a summary of the data with two additional columns. The additional columns show the percent of the population made up by "Other Free People" and "Slaves" for each state. The Northern States (Vermont, New Hampshire, Maine[8] , Massachusetts, Rhode Island and Connecticut) all had less than 2% Slaves. In the case of Massachusetts, they had already abolished slavery. On the other end of the spectrum, the deepest Southern States all had a significant part of their populations in slavery: South Carolina (43%), Virginia (39%), Georgia (36%), Maryland (32%) and North Carolina(25%).

Provided with that context, we can now look at the rest of the Constitutional Convention discussions to observe the arguments from all sides. During the debates, there was a "First Draft of the Constitution from August 6, 1787". The proposed sections that addressed slavery are shown in Exhibit 16 (the section numbers changed in the final Constitution): The draft Constitution from August 6 had tax, representation and slavery importation provisions. In the original Constitution, there was no income tax. Taxes were distributed amongst the states directly based upon a calculated population for the state. How slaves and indentured servants were calculated for representation purposes in the House of Representatives would indirectly impact how each state was

8 In 1790, Maine was still part of Massachusetts, but its numbers were broken out.

Exhibit 16 - First Draft Constitutional Slavery Provisions (August 6, 1787)

Article VII, Sect. 3. The proportions of direct taxation shall be regulated by the whole number of white and other free citizens and inhabitants, of every age, sex and condition, including those bound to servitude for a term of years, and three fifths of all persons not comprehended in the foregoing description (except Indians not paying taxes) which number shall, within six years after the first meeting of the Legislature, and within the term of every ten years afterwards, be taken in such manner as the Legislature shall direct.

Article VII, Sect. 4. No tax or duty shall be laid by the Legislature on articles exported from any State; nor on the migration or importation of such persons as the several States shall think proper to admit; nor shall such migration or importation be prohibited.

taxed too. Northern states, who desired an abolition of slavery, would have preferred that slaves would have zero impact for representation purposes, that the importation of slaves would be prohibited, and that slaves would be taxed as anyone else. Southern states, who desired to continue slavery, would have preferred that slaves would be fully counted for representation purposes, and that the National Government would have no ability to restrict importation or resale of slaves.

The August 6th Draft Constitution incorporated what is known as the 3/5 Compromise. It tried to balance the views between the Northern and Southern States. Northern States were not happy with the fact that Southern States received congressional representation that counted slaves (even if only at a 3/5 rate). Since slaves were literally property with no opportunity to vote, Northern States felt that the 3/5 Compromise encouraged Southerners to import more. As an example, Luther Martin of Maryland said[9] that it "*would leave encouragement to this traffic* ". In the 21st century, we hear a similar debate. How can states receive Congressional representation for people who are living in the country illegally? Doesn't this incentivize states to encourage more illegal immigration and settlement? Reviewing the Constitutional Convention Debate records, we can break out the arguments regarding importation of slaves and the new National governments ability to regulate slavery. Exhibit 17 shows both the pro and con positions taken by the delegates at the Constitutional Convention.

9 Ibid., page 153, Madison's notes for MR. L. MARTIN (Luther Martin)

Exhibit 17 - Summary of Slavery Arguments at the Convention

[Pro Slavery Arguments]

- *Importing slaves increases economic activity for all the states.*[1]
- *If South Carolina and Georgia were not permitted to import slaves, they would not join the union.*[2]
- *States should individually decide on slavery.*[3]

[Anti-Slavery Arguments]

- Slavery weakened the Slave holding states and the other states would have to protect them.[4]
- Maryland and Virginia had already prohibited importation of slaves, and North Carolina had almost done so.[5]
- *If South Carolina and Georgia could continue to import slaves, they would be transported through them to states further west.*[6]
- The National Government should control the increase of slavery.[7]

---

1 Ibid., Constitution Convention Debates, page 156 - Madison's notes for GENERAL PINCKNEY (Charles Pinckney of South Carolina), page 154 - for MR. RUTLEDGE (John Rutledge of South Carolina)

2 Ibid., Constitution Convention Debates, Madison's Notes, page 158 - for MR. RUTLEDGE , page 158 - for MR. KING (Rufus King of Massachusetts), pages 155-156 - for MR. ELLSWORTH (Oliver Ellsworth of Connecticut), page 156 - for GENERAL PINCKNEY, page 157 - for MR. WILLIAMSON (Hugh Williamson of North Carolina), pages 156-157 - for MR. BALDWIN (Abraham Baldwin of Georgia)

3 Ibid., Constitution Convention Debates, Madison's Notes, page 157 –for MR. GERRY (Elbridge Gerry of Massachusetts), page 154 - for MR. SHERMAN (Roger Sherman of Connecticut), page 154 -for MR. ELLSWORTH, page 154 – for MR. PINCKNEY (Charles Pinckney of South Carolina), page 158 – for MR. RUTLEDGE, Page 156 – for MR. BALDWIN

4 Ibid., Constitution Convention Debates, pages 153-154, Madison's notes for MR. L. MARTIN. (Luther Martin of Maryland)

5 Ibid., Constitution Convention Debates, page 155, Madison's notes for COLONEL MASON. (George Mason of Virginia)

6 Ibid., Constitution Convention Debates, page 155, Madison's notes for COLONEL MASON. (George Mason of Virginia)

7 Ibid., Constitution Convention Debates, Madison's Notes, page 155 – for COLONEL MASON (George Mason of Virginia), page 158 –for MR. LANGDON (John Langdon of New Hampshire), page 157 - for MR. DICKINSON (John Dickinson of Delaware)

- States should individually decide on slavery.[8]
- The National Government should tax the importation of slaves.[9]

8 Ibid., Constitution Convention Debates, Madison's Notes, page 157 –for MR. GERRY (Elbridge Gerry of Massachusetts), page 154 - for MR. SHERMAN (Roger Sherman of Connecticut), page 154 -for MR. ELLSWORTH (Oliver Ellsworth of Connecticut), page 154 – for MR. PINCKNEY (Charles Pinckney of South Carolina), page 158 – for MR. RUTLEDGE (John Rutledge of South Carolina), Page 156 – for MR. BALDWIN (Abraham Baldwin of Georgia)

9 Ibid., Constitution Convention Debates, James Madison's Notes, page 157 – for MR. WILSON (James Wilson of Pennsylvania), page 156 – for GENERAL PINCKNEY (Charles Pinckney of South Carolina), Page 158 – for MR. King (Rufus King of Massachusetts)

It is easy to "Monday morning quarterback", over 235 years after the Constitution was written, about what the framers should have done. If they had disallowed the importation of slaves, it is clear that South Carolina and Georgia wouldn't have stayed in the country. If they had tried to outlaw slavery immediately, North Carolina, Virginia, Maryland and Delaware likely would not have joined either. If all 13 states hadn't stayed in the Union, the remaining states might not have survived upcoming wars such as the War of 1812; especially if the excluded states had allied with a European foreign power. If that had been the case, we Americans might not be here to debate this today.

After the debates of August 6-7, the framers of the Constitution did what everyone who argues for bipartisanship always demands. They compromised to reach the final Constitution that we have today. The Constitution was modified to show that both taxes and representation were based on the same formula. That formula used a 3/5 ratio for slaves. As another compromise, instead of the open-ended importation of slaves for the future, Congress was allowed to ban importing new slaves as early as 1808. At the time, that was 21 years in the future. Finally, instead of duty-free importation of slaves, a $10 per slave duty was instituted to economically discourage the practice. The sections that were shown in Exhibit 16 were finalized and are shown in Exhibit 18 below.

The Constitutional debates also included many predictions on what would happen under various alternative approaches. Those predictions help to show why the practice of slavery was eliminated in the Northern States, but metastasized in the South in the decades that

Exhibit 18 - Final United States Constitution Slavery Provisions

Article I, Section 2. Representatives and direct Taxes shall be apportioned among the several States which may be included within this Union, according to their respective Numbers, which shall be determined by adding to the whole Number of free Persons, including those bound to Service for a Term of Years, and excluding Indians not taxed, three fifths of all other Persons. The actual Enumeration shall be made within three Years after the first Meeting of the Congress of the United States, and within every subsequent Term of ten Years, in such Manner as they shall by Law direct.

Article I, Section 9. The Migration or Importation of such Persons as any of the States now existing shall think proper to admit, shall not be prohibited by the Congress prior to the Year one thousand eight hundred and eight, but a Tax or duty may be imposed on such importation, not exceeding ten dollars for each Person.

followed the signing of the Constitution. The 1860 Census results are shown in Appendix 22. They show the abolition of slavery in the northern states, and the expansion of slavery in the southern and western states 73 years after the Constitution was written. Comparing the 1790 census results with the 1860 census results, we can see how dramatically the country changed leading up to the Civil War. We can also evaluate how accurate the predictions of the framers of the Constitution were.

Predictions during the Convention Debates

- George Mason of Virginia predicted that slavery would move to the new western states.[10]

  [Came True] - By 1860, slavery had expanded to all of the new Southern States. The percentage of slaves in these states were as follows: Florida (44%), Alabama(45%), Mississippi(55%), Kentucky(20%), Tennessee(25%), Louisiana(47%), Arkansas(26%), Missouri(10%), and Texas(30%).

- Luther Martin of Maryland predicted that the 3/5 apportionment for

10 Ibid., Constitution Convention Debates, pages 155, Madison's notes for COLONEL MASON. (George Mason of Virginia) *"The Western people are already calling out for slaves for their new lands, and will fill that country with slaves if they can be got through South Carolina and Georgia".*

representatives would encourage the slave trade.[11]

[**Came True**] - The percentage of the population that were slaves increased dramatically in the Southern states that opposed limits on importing new slaves. The percentage of slaves in Georgia increased from 36% to 44% between 1790 and 1860. In South Carolina it increased from 43% to 57%. In North Carolina, it increased from 26% to 33%.

- Oliver Ellsworth of Connecticut predicted that increases in poor non-slave laborers would eliminate the need for slavery.[12]

  [**Came Partially True**] - It is true that slavery was abolished in the Northern states by 1860, but it increased in the Southern States.

- John Rutledge of South Carolina predicted that slave insurrections would not be a problem.[13]

  [**False**] This prediction came across as audaciously ignorant. As evidence of possible danger, in 1803, the entire nation of Haiti was taken over in a slave insurrection. This resulted in the French being driven from the island, and 20,000 soldiers and 60,000 white civilians being killed[14]. Nat Turner's slave insurrection (Turner's Rebellion) happened in Southampton County, Virginia in 1831. David Reynolds described[15] the rebellion in his book John Brown Abolitionist as follows: "*On the night of Sunday, August 31, the revolt began. Turner and six cohorts, armed with swords and axes, went from plantation to plantation, killing men, women, and children as they slept. Not until they had killed fifty-five were the whites in the area able to organize*

---

11 Ibid., Constitution Convention Debates, pages 153, Madison's notes for MR. L. MARTIN. (Luther Martin of Maryland) "*as five slaves are to be counted as 3 free men in the apportionment of Representatives; such a clause would leave an encouragement to this traffic.*"

12 Ibid., Constitution Convention Debates, pages 156, Madison's notes for MR. ELLSWORTH. (Oliver Ellsworth of Connecticut) "*As population increases poor laborers will be so plenty as to render slaves useless. Slavery in time will not be a speck in our Country. Provision is already made in Connecticut for abolishing it. And the abolition has already taken place in Massachusetts.*"

13 Ibid., Constitution Convention Debates, pages 154, Madison's notes for MR. RUTLEDGE (John Rutledge of South Carolina) "*He was not apprehensive of insurrections and would readily exempt the other States from the obligation to protect the Southern against them.*"

14 Reynolds, David. *John Brown Abolitionist.* page 109

15 Reynolds, David, *John Brown Abolitionist.* page 53

a pursuit. An untold number of blacks – reportedly hundreds – were slaughtered in the chase." In 1859, John Brown attempted to organize a massive slave insurrection by taking over the arsenal at Harpers Ferry, Virginia. Though the attempt failed, and John Brown was hanged, this event massively increased the animosity between the North and South.

- George Mason of Virginia predicted[16] that slavery would bring the judgment of heaven down upon the country.

  [**Came True**] The Civil War would result in massive death and destruction for the entire United States. It finally resulted in the elimination of slavery.

Unfortunately, many of the predictions from the Constitutional Convention turned out to be true. Slavery increased dramatically in the South to the point where two states (South Carolina and Mississippi) had populations where slaves outnumbered whites. The Missouri Compromise[17] of 1820 brought additional Slave states into the union. The Compromise of 1850 allowed California to enter the union, but tightened the Fugitive Slave Laws dramatically. In 1854, the Kansas-Nebraska Act led to the infamous "Bleeding Kansas" battles between Northern Abolitionists and Southern Pro-Slavery forces. The animosity between the Slave States and the Free States continued to increase throughout the 1850's. As the division grew, the 1857 United States Supreme Court decision in the Dred Scott case added a ton of fuel to the fire.

The *Dred Scott(1857)* Supreme Court Decision

Though it may be painful to read the Dred Scott Supreme Court opinions, there are remarkable insights that can be gleaned from them. For purposes of this book, the fundamental question that was addressed was whether African Americans could be citizens of the United States.

---

16 The Anti-Federalist Papers and the [Constitutional Convention Debates], Signet Classics, 1986, page 155, Madison's notes for COLONEL MASON. (George Mason of Virginia) *"Every master of slaves is born a petty tyrant. They bring the judgment of heaven on a Country. As nations can not be rewarded or punished in the next world they must be in this. By an inevitable chain of causes and effects providence punishes national sins by national calamities."*

17 United States National Archives and Records Administration. (2026, Feb. 23). https://www.archives.gov/milestone-documents/missouri-compromise

Due to the case's infamy, most readers likely know that the Supreme Court decided that African Americans could not be citizens of the United States (in a 7-2 vote). This flew in direct opposition to the history of African Americans being citizens of many Northern states even though they generally did not have the right to vote[18]. From a voting perspective, they were treated no differently than white women at that time, who were also citizens but could not vote.

How did the Supreme Court reach this decision? The Opinion of the Court was written by Chief Justice Roger Taney. He wrote the *Passenger Cases* dissent that was analyzed in Chapter 3. Chief Justice Taney had already been Chief Justice for over 20 years. Clearly, we cannot excuse inexperience or ignorance for the result. Chief Justice Taney was born in 1777 in the early days of the Revolutionary War. This was before the Articles of Confederation. He was a teenager when the *Constitution* was ratified, and when the *Bill of Rights* was approved. If anyone on the Supreme Court of the 1850's understood the rights of American citizens, it was Chief Justice Taney.

Table 10 shows the makeup of the Supreme Court for the Dred Scott decision. Chief Justice Taney was seven years older than the next oldest judge, but seven of the nine Supreme Court Justices were born in the 1700's. Five of the Justices were from Slave States and four of the Justices were from Free States.

There was incredible chicanery that went along with the Dred Scott decision. In 1856, Democrat James Buchanan was elected president. Until 2021, he was the only person born in Pennsylvania to become President. Historically, James Buchanan has also been considered to be one of the worst Presidents in our nation's history. Even before he started his term in office, he was working behind the scenes to influence the Supreme Court on the timing and the result for the *Dred Scott* decision. For those who are interested in some of the captivating intrigue surrounding the case, Paul Finkelman published[19] "Scott v. Sandford: The Court's Most Dreadful Case and How It Changed History" (2007) in the Chicago-Kent Law Review. For those interested in learning more

18 New York's Constitution of 1821 permitted wealthy African American men to vote.

19 Finkelman, Paul. *Scott v. Sandford: The Court's Most Dreadful Case and How It Changed History.* Chicago-Kent Law Review, 2007, Pages 27-47. (2026, Feb. 23). https://scholarship.kentlaw.iit.edu/cklawreview/vol82/iss1/2/

Table 10 – Supreme Court Makeup for the Dred Scott Decision

Justice	Home State	Court Tenure	Birth Year	Opinion
Roger Taney (Chief)	Maryland	1836-1864	1777	Opinion of the Court[1]
John McLean	Ohio	1829-1861	1785	Dissent [2]
James Wayne	Georgia	1835-1867	1790	Concurring Opinion[3]
John Catron	Tennessee	1837-1865	1786	Concurring Opinion[4]
Peter Daniel	Virginia	1842-1860	1784	Concurring Opinion[5]
Samuel Nelson	New York	1845-1872	1792	Concurring Opinion[6]
Robert Grier	Pennsylvania	1846-1870	1794	Concurring Opinion[7]
Benjamin Curtis	Massachusetts	1851-1857	1809	Dissent[8]
John Campbell	Alabama	1853-1861	1811	Concurring Opinion[9]

1 Chief Justice Taney's Opinion of the Court, 60 U.S. 393, 399

2 Justice McLean's Dissent, 60 U.S. 393, 529 – Provides Extensive historical analysis regarding slavery

3 Justice Wayne's Concurring Opinion, 60 U.S. 393, 454 - justifies voiding the Missouri Compromise

4 Justice Catron's Concurring Opinion, 60 U.S. 393, 518 - justifies voiding the Missouri Compromise

5 Justice Daniel's Concurring Opinion, 60 U.S. 393, 469 - makes further justifications based on history

6 Justice Nelson's Concurring Opinion, 60 U.S. 393, 457 makes argument based on Missouri Law.

7 Justice Grier's Concurring Opinion, 60 U.S. 393, 469 agrees with Justice Nelson's opinion too.

8 Justice Curtis' Dissent, 60 U.S. 393, 564 – Dissent covering all angles

9 Justice Campbell's Concurring Opinion, 60 U.S. 393, 493

about James Buchanan's life and how it shaped his views on slavery, the Smithsonian Magazine published[20] an article about his long friendship with William Rufus King of Alabama, who's career culminated as Vice President for Franklin Pierce.

20 Balcerski, Thomas. *The 175-Year History of Speculating About President James Buchanan's Bachelorhood.* Smithsonian Magazine, August 27, 2019. (2026, Feb. 23). https://www.smithsonianmag.com/history/175-year-history-examining-bachelor-president-james-buchanans-close-friendship-william-rufus-king-180972992/

The *Dred Scott* case was so impactful that a summary would have been published in every major newspaper in the country. A reader might ask: "*Why are you worried about the Dred Scott decision?*". The answer is that a huge part of the reason for deciding that African Americans could not be citizens was to deprive them of Nationwide Privileges and Immunities. Understanding the reasons why the Slave states were at extreme risk of survival helps to unlock the mystery of this dreadful case. It helps to explain why Chief Justice Taney, in a single court decision, wrecked his reputation (at least in the Northern States). If the South had won the Civil War, the Dred Scott decision might have been heralded as one of the greatest decisions in the history of Supreme Court. Thankfully, that did not happen, but the decision still provides amazing insights.

One possible way to view the Dred Scott decision is that Chief Justice Taney was "*looking into a crystal ball*" with "*a gun to his head*" and he was making a "*death-bed confession*". Imagining the future, it was obvious that the risks of Northerners helping slaves to revolt was growing. Two years after the Dred Scott decision, John Brown would attempt to incite a massive slave revolt. He and his men temporarily took over the arsenal at Harpers Ferry, Virginia. They were attempting to arm slaves with guns and pikes to inspire a slave insurrection as Nat Turner had done over 25 years before. Chief Justice Taney was under duress and fear of free African Americans from Northern states coming into Slave States to help free the slaves. He knew that if they were United States citizens, the Constitution gave them powerful Privileges and Immunities wherever they were in the country. This overruled the ability of Slave States to selectively discriminate against them from a police and safety perspective. Finally, the Dred Scott decision implicitly acknowledged that the country was on an irreconcilable path towards a death of the union between Free and Slave States.

What did Chief Justice Taney say about Privileges and Immunities? Like a "broken record", he stated over and over that if "negros" were citizens of the United States, they would possess Nationwide Privileges and Immunities wherever they were in the country. He said this not once, not twice, but a total of 12 different times in various sections! Appendix 23 breaks down key quotations from the decision into those regarding Privileges and Immunities, and those regarding the Articles of Confederation. They are also broken down between Chief Justice Taney's Opinion of the Court and Associate Justice Curtis' strong dissent. Chief

Justice Taney's decision that "negros" could not be United States citizens drew all of the ire and attention in the Northern States. This resulted from him needing to deny "negros" the Privileges and Immunities guaranteed by the Constitution.

Insights from the Dred Scott Opinions

Both Chief Justice Taney's Opinion and Justice Curtis' Dissent made tremendously strong acknowledgments regarding the Privileges and Immunities in the Constitution being nationwide. For instance, Chief Justice Taney said[21]: "*And if persons of the African race are citizens of a State, and of the United States, they would be entitled to all of these privileges and immunities in every State and the State could not restrict them; for they would hold these privileges and immunities under the paramount authority of the Federal Government, and its courts would be bound to maintain and enforce them, the Constitution and laws of the State to the contrary notwithstanding.*" In a very similar vein, the dissent by Justice Curtis declared[22]: "*In selecting those who are to enjoy these national rights of citizenship, how are they described? As citizens of each State. It is to them these national rights are secured. The qualification for them is not to be looked for in any provision of the Constitution or laws of the United States. They are to be citizens of the several States, and, as such, the privileges and immunities of general citizenship, derived from and guarantied by the Constitution, are to be enjoyed by them.*"

To complement their understanding of Nationwide Privileges and Immunities, Chief Justice Taney's Opinion of the Court, and Justice Curtis' Dissent both explain specific State Level Privileges and Immunities. Justice Taney referred to states having voting and other special rights when he said[23]: "*But so far as mere rights of person are concerned, the provision in question is confined to the citizens of a State who are temporarily in another State without taking up residence there. It gives them no political rights in the State, as to voting or holding office, or in any other respect. For a citizen of one State has no right to participate in the government of another.*" From Justice Curtis' dissent, we see a similar proclama-

---

21 Dred Scott, 60 U.S. 393, 422-423 (1857), Chief Justice Taney Opinion of the Court

22 Dred Scott, 60 U.S. 393, 580 (1857), Justice Curtis Dissent

23 Dred Scott, 60 U.S. 393, 422 (1857), Chief Justice Taney Opinion of the Court

tion[24] with: "*Thus, if the laws of a State require, in addition to citizenship of the State, some qualification for office, or the exercise of the elective franchise, citizens of all other States, coming thither to reside, and not possessing those qualifications, cannot enjoy those privileges, not because they are not to be deemed entitled to the privileges of citizens of the State in which they reside, but because they, in common with the native-born citizens of that State, must have the qualifications prescribed by laws for the enjoyment of such privileges, under its Constitution and laws.*"

As another interesting insight, Chief Justice Taney's Opinion of the Court and Justice Curtis' Dissent both discussed citizenship under the Articles of Confederation. Chief Justice Taney argued that the change of the Privileges and Immunities clause to "citizens" in the United States Constitution from "free inhabitants" in the Articles of Confederation was meant to exclude African Americans. He said[25] : "*The word citizen excluded, and no doubt intended to exclude, foreigners who had not become citizens of some one of the States when the Constitution was adopted; and also every description of persons who were not fully recognized as citizens in the several States. This upon any fair construction of the instruments to which we have referred, was evidently the object and purpose of this change of words.*" Justice Curtis argued in his dissent that this was a simple change of terminology when saying[26]: "*An examination of the forms of expression commonly used in the State papers of that day, and an attention to the substance of this article of the Confederation, will show that the words 'free inhabitants,' as then used, were synonymous with citizens.*" As a "coup de grace" in his excellent dissent, Justice Curtis explained[27] that under the *Articles of Confederation* in 1778, South Carolina had introduced an Amendment to change "free inhabitants" to "free white inhabitants" in the Privileges and Immunities clause. They were resoundingly defeated in an 8-2 vote by the other states (see Appx. 22, section on *Articles of Confederation*).

To understand some of the commentary by both Chief Justice Taney and Justice Curtis, the very limited rights of free African Americans in Slave States must be understood. These limited rights existed be-

---

24 Dred Scott, 60 U.S. 393, 583-584 (1857), Justice Curtis Dissent

25 Dred Scott, 60 U.S. 393, 419 (1857), Chief Justice Taney Opinion of the Court

26 Dred Scott, 60 U.S. 393, 584 (1857), Justice Curtis Dissent

27 Dred Scott, 60 U.S. 393, 575 (1857), Justice Curtis Dissent

fore the Dred Scott decision; and were exactly the ones that Chief Justice Taney wanted to remain limited. By declaring African Americans not to be citizens, they had no Nationwide Privileges and Immunities. Slave states had Special Laws and Police Regulations that dramatically restricted the rights of African Americans in their states. Figure 11 shows the perspective of the relative rights for whites versus free African Americans in Slave States.

Another area that requires additional context is Freedom of Speech. At the time of the Dred Scott Decision in 1857, states could restrict speech and the press. Slave States notoriously restricted Abolitionist literature and books such as Harriet Beecher Stowe's *Uncle Tom's Cabin(1852)*. This was done to avoid inciting slave revolts. As a legal ex-

Figure 11 - Relative Rights in Slave States

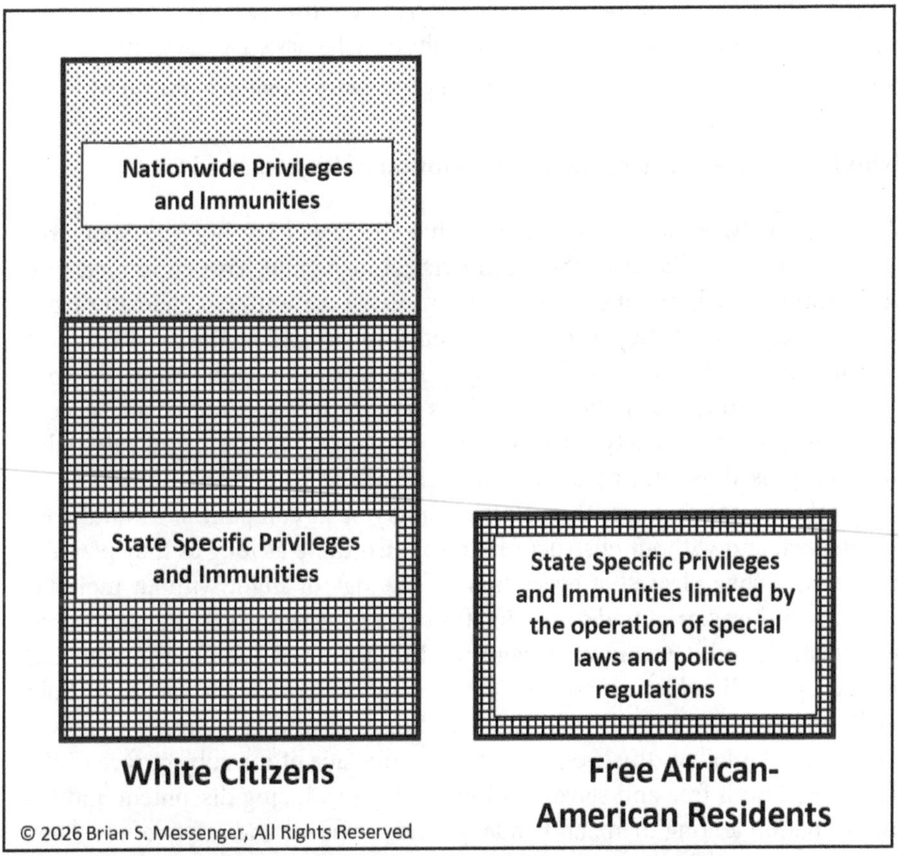

ample, according to Missouri's archives, Missouri passed[28] a law in 1837 to: "*prohibit the publication, circulation, and promulgation of the abolition doctrines.*" A conviction subjected the offending person to a maximum fine of $1000 and two years in the state penitentiary. A second offense brought twenty years in prison; and a third offense translated to a life sentence.

Nationwide Privileges and Immunities - Dred Scott Opinions

Discussing Privileges and Immunities, there is one passage where Chief Justice Taney describes exactly the many fears that he had regarding African Americans being citizens. Taken in the context of Figure 11 above, the passage[29] in Exhibit 19 provides great insight into both National and State Level Privileges and Immunities for citizens of the United States. The first part of Exhibit 19 provides a retrospective view that Slave States

28 Missouri Secretary of State, Missouri State Archives. (2026, Feb. 23). https://www.sos.mo.gov/archives/education/aahi/earlyslavelaws/slavelaws.asp

29 Dred Scott, 60 U.S. 393, 417 (1857), Chief Justice Taney Opinion of the Court

Exhibit 19 - Chief Justice Taney's Description of Rights, Dred Scott

More especially, it cannot be believed that the large slaveholding States regarded them as included in the word citizens, or would have consented to a Constitution which might compel them to receive them in that character from another State. For if they were so received, and entitled to the privileges and immunities of citizens, it would exempt them from the operation of the special laws and from the police regulations which they considered to be necessary for their own safety. It would give to persons of the negro race, who were recognised as citizens in any one State of the Union, the right to enter every other State whenever they pleased, singly or in companies, without pass or passport, and without obstruction, to sojourn there as long as they pleased, to go where they pleased at every hour of the day or night without molestation, unless they committed some violation of law for which a white man would be punished; and it would give them the full liberty of speech in public and private upon all subjects upon which its own citizens might speak; to hold public meetings upon political affairs, and to keep and carry arms wherever they went. And all of this would be done in the face of the subject race of the same color, both free and slaves, and inevitably producing discontent and insubordination among them, and endangering the peace and safety of the State.

would never have signed a Constitution where "negros" could have been citizens of the United States. This would have meant that they could travel to Slave States and would have to be treated as citizens with the same rights as the white citizens in those states. They could not be discriminated against by the State using "special laws and from the police regulations".

The various rights that Chief Justice Taney describes are very important. They touch on almost all of the rights that are protected by the 1st and 2nd Amendments, but they go further. They recognize the rights of assembly and bearing arms as extending Nationwide and across state lines. Figure 12 breaks down the second part of Exhibit 19 into various nationwide rights of citizens that the Dred Scott decision recognized. It should be noted that there were no disagreements regarding the specific nationwide rights in any of the Dred Scott opinions. The disagreement was whether African Americans were entitled to them.

When reading the opinion text in Appendix 23, there are a few instances where Chief Justice Taney's remarks may sound like the incorrect state-level approach that "when you are in a specific state, you are entitled to all of the privileges and immunities of citizens in that state". One instance is when Chief Justice Taney said[30]: "*But if he ranks as a citizen in the State to which he belongs, within the meaning of the Constitution of the United States, then, whenever he goes into another-State, the Constitution clothes him, as to the rights of person, with all the privileges and immunities which belong to citizens of the State.*" Reviewing the massive inequality of rights shown in Figure 11 above, he is referring to the fact that African American citizens would be entitled to all of the rights shown for white citizens in the Slave States. First, they would now obtain the Nationwide Privileges and Immunities of citizens. Second, they could not be discriminated against from a State law perspective and would have equal state-level privileges and immunities with the white citizens. Justice Taney's next sentence provides convincing proof of this interpretation when he said[31] "*And if persons of the African race are citizens of a State, and of the United States, they would be entitled to all of these privileges and immunities in every State, and the State could not restrict them;*"

30 Dred Scott, 60 U.S. 393, 422-423 (1857) Chief Justice Taney's Opinion of the Court

31 Dred Scott, 60 U.S. 393, 423 (1857) Chief Justice Taney's Opinion of the Court

Figure 12 - Nationwide Privilege and Immunities Description, Dred Scott

Sentence fragment deconstruction using standard rules of punctuation

Sentence fragment	Description
"… the right to enter every other state whenever they pleased,	Nationwide Right to travel between states and to do all of the following:
singly or in companies, without pass or passport, and without obstruction; to sojourn there as long as they pleased, to go where they pleased at every hour of the day or night without molestation, unless they committed some violation of law for which a white man would be punished;	Nationwide Right to Assemble in groups and travel. Rejects discriminatory travel regulations for classes of citizens.
and it would give them the full liberty of speech in public and in private upon all subjects upon which its own citizens might speak;	Rejects discriminatory speech regulations for classes of citizens.
to hold public meetings upon political affairs,	Nationwide Right to Assemble and speak about political affairs.
and to keep and carry arms wherever they went."	Nationwide Right to keep and carry arms wherever a person goes.

In Chief Justice Taney's Opinion of the Court in the Dred Scott decision, he forecast the need for a Constitutional change to determine nationwide citizenship. He attempted to excuse[32] his opinion by saying: "*It is not the province of the court to decide upon the justice or injustice, the policy or impolicy, of these laws. The decision of that question belonged to the political or law-making power; to those who formed the sovereignty and framed the Constitution.*" His opinion would not only become a factor in leading to the Civil War, but it would require the 14th Amendment to the Constitution to reverse the court's findings.

The Second Privileges and Immunities Butterfly Effect

There has been a major misconception regarding the Dred Scott decision. Many people think that it was overruled by the Supreme Court. That is patently not true. As shown in the discussion above, all of the concurring and dissenting opinions agreed upon many issues. The question of citizenship was the primary disagreement, and it required the death of approximately[33] 600,000 Americans to resolve. For over 10 years, the complete Dred Scott decision was the law of the land. In 1868, the part of the decision saying that African Americans could not be United States citizens was changed by the 14th Amendment.

Unfortunately, when people are reading such an overtly racist decision as in the case of Dred Scott, it is immensely challenging to parse out the legal precedents. The problem is that decisions must be reviewed in the context of the time that they were written. One person who reviewed the Dred Scott decision was a former Congressman from Illinois. He would be assassinated eight years later after leading the Union to victory in the Civil War. That man was Abraham Lincoln. In his famous "House Divided" speech in 1858, Lincoln spoke about a key purpose of the Dred Scott decision (Figure 13). Lincoln held the strong view that the purpose of the Chief Justice Taney's decision was to deny "negros" the privileges and immunities of citizens. The only way to guarantee this was for Chief Justice Taney to argue that no African American could ever be a citizen. This confirms that Lincoln agreed that the Nationwide Privileges

32 Dred Scott, 60 U.S. 393, 405 (1857), Chief Justice Taney Opinion of the Court

33 American Battlefield Trust. (2026, Feb. 23). https://www.battlefields.org/learn/articles/civil-war-casualties

Figure 13 - Abraham Lincoln's Dred Scott Discussion

From Abraham Lincoln's House Divided Speech, June 16, 1858	Explanation & Commentary
The several points of the Dred Scott decision ...	
First, that no negro slave, imported as such from Africa, and no descendant of such slave can ever be a citizen of any State, in the sense of that term as used in the Constitution of the United States.	Lincoln describing how the goal of the Dred Scott decision was to make sure that 'negros' could never become a citizen of any State.
This point is made in order to deprive the negro, in every possible event, of the benefits of this provision of the United States Constitution, which declares that – "The citizens of each State shall be entitled to all privileges and immunities of citizens in the several States."	Lincoln describing that the reason for this was to make sure that they were not entitled to the privileges and immunities of citizens from the United States Constitution.

and Immunities of citizens were very strong.

Each of the powerful Nationwide Privileges shown in Figure 12 was previously discussed in this book in other contexts. What some people have overlooked is the extraordinarily forceful descriptions and acknowledgment that they are given by the Dred Scott decision. Our nation fought a dreadful war to provide these rights to all Americans, and it is our responsibility to never forget them. The following list of Nationwide Privileges and Immunities were the first precedents to be recognized by the Supreme Court. This book will use the abbreviation SCP (Supreme Court Precedent) for active precedents moving forward.

- SCP_DS_1 - *The right to enter any other state whenever you please, and in groups of any size.* (This was previously recognized in the Articles of Confederation, Appendix 6, AC1)

- SCP_DS_2 – *The right to enter every other state, and to travel freely around a state wherever you please unless committing a legal violation.* (This was previously recognized in the Articles of Confederation, Appendix 6, AC1)
- SCP_DS_3 – *The right to speak freely in any other state with the same rights as any of its own citizens.* (This was previously implied in the Declaration of Independence, Appendix 5, D1)
- SCP_DS_4 – *The right to hold public meetings in any other state upon political affairs.* (This was previously implied in the Declaration of Independence, Appendix 5, D2)
- SCP_DS_5 – *The right to enter every other state, and to keep and carry arms wherever you go.* (This was originally recognized in the [English] Bill of Rights, Appendix 4, EBR7)

As stated above, all of these rights were discussed in depth in previous chapters. These Supreme Court precedents help to add additional context. Within four years of the Dred Scott decision, the nation would be embroiled in the Civil War. During the war, the very survival of the nation was at stake, and there were no key Supreme Court cases that reflected on Privileges and Immunities.

In 1864, in the middle of the Civil War, Chief Justice Taney passed away at the age of 87. Though they had opposite views on slavery, President Abraham Lincoln attended his funeral. It would be four more years until the citizenship question that Chief Justice Taney had decided in the Dred Scott decision was reversed. In the meantime, President Lincoln had a war to win and a Supreme Court Chief Justice to appoint. He appointed Salmon Chase who had been his Secretary of the Treasury during most of the Civil War, and who had run against Abraham Lincoln for the Republican nomination in 1860.

During the slightly over four years Lincoln was in office, he appointed five[34] Supreme Court Justices (Noah Swayne, Samuel Miller, David Davis, Stephen Field, and Chief Justice Salmon Chase). Of these men, Justice Samuel Miller would have the greatest impact on the subject of Privileges and Immunities. After the war, and before the 14th Amend-

34 Supreme Court of the United States. (2026, Feb. 23). https://www.supremecourt.gov/about/members_text.aspx

ment was approved, there is one additional Supreme Court case that was decided regarding the right to travel. That case[35] was *Crandall v. State of Nevada (1868).*

The Case of *Crandall v. State of Nevada(1868)*

The case of *Crandall v. State of Nevada* was an interesting case about travel through a state. As Justice Miller said[36] in his Opinion of the Court: "*The proposition to be considered is the right of a State to levy a tax upon persons residing in the State who may wish to get out of it, and upon persons not residing in it who may have occasion to pass through it.*" This resulted from[37] a law passed by the Nevada Legislature that said "*there shall be levied and collected a capitation tax of one dollar upon every person leaving the State by any railroad, stage coach, or other vehicle engaged or employed in the business of transporting passengers for hire*". If a person did not have the money for the tax, Nevada was treating them like the Eagles song *Hotel California(1977)* which claimed that "*You can check-out any time you like, But you can never leave!*"

In all seriousness, there were two unique points regarding Justice Miller's Opinion of the Court. The first involves the questions that were decided by the court. The Supreme Court of Nevada had thought there were two parts of the United States Constitution that were[38] implicated: "*…namely: that which forbids any State, without the consent of Congress, to lay any imposts or duties on imports or exports, and that which confers on Congress the power to regulate commerce with foreign nations and among the several States.*" Neither of the questions being considered involved the Privileges and Immunities Clause of the United States Constitution. How did this happen?

The Supreme Court chooses the questions to be argued. In 1867, when Crandall v. State of Nevada was argued, there were five relatively new members of the Court including the Chief Justice. The Supreme Court had not directly answered a question regarding the Privileges and Immunities Clause as a formal question to decide a prior case. Chief Jus-

35 Crandall v. State of Nevada, 73 U.S. 35 (1868) Opinion of the Court

36 Crandall v. State of Nevada, 73 U.S. 35, 39 (1868) Opinion of the Court

37 Crandall v. State of Nevada, 73 U.S. 35, 36 (1868) Opinion of the Court

38 Crandall v. State of Nevada, 73 U.S. 35, 41 (1868) Opinion of the Court

tice Taney had died, and was not around to discuss the applicability of the Privileges and Immunities Clause as shown in *Dred Scott.* Justice Curtis had resigned from the Supreme Court after the *Dred Scott* decision, and was not around to discuss the powerful Privileges and Immunities Clause commentary he had written in his *Dred Scott* Dissenting Opinion. This was a classic situation where the Supreme Court should have had a different question argued by the plaintiffs and defendants. Justice Miller wrote the Opinion of the Court based on the questions asked.

After finding that the two questions that were argued did not resolve this issue, Justice Miller went on to write his own novel argument. He wrote[39] that "*government has a right to call to this point any or all of its citizens to aid in its service, as members of Congress, of the courts, of the executive departments, and to fill all its other offices; and this right cannot be made to depend upon the pleasure of a State over whose territory they must pass to reach the point where these services must be rendered.*" Ironically, five years later, he corrected the oversight of the Privileges and Immunities Clause in his *The Slaughterhouse Cases(1873)* decision that will be discussed in the next chapter.

The other interesting thing about *Crandall v. State of Nevada* was that Justice Miller referenced[40] former Chief Justice Taney's dissenting opinion in the *Passenger Cases* in two locations (discussed in the previous chapter). In the second instance, Justice Miller actually copied the text from the *Passenger Cases* that included the entire quotation shown in Exhibit 15 in Chapter 3. These observations are made in anticipation of a "case of amnesia" that Justice Miller exhibited in *The Slaughterhouse*

---

39 Crandall v. State of Nevada, 73 U.S. 35, 43 (1868) Opinion of the Court

40 Crandall v. State of Nevada, 73, U.S. 35, 40 (1868) Opinion of the Court,
"Chief Justice Taney, while he differed from the majority of the court, and held the law to be valid, said of the tax levied by the analogous statute of Massachusetts, that 'its payment is the condition upon which the State permits the alien passenger to come on shore and mingle with its citizens, and to reside among them. ...'"
Crandall v. State of Nevada, 73, U.S. 35, 48 (1868) Opinion of the Court,
"But the principles here laid down may be found more clearly stated in the dissenting opinion of the Chief Justice in those cases, and with more direct pertinency to the case now before us than anywhere else. ... He then adds: 'Living as we do under a common government, charged with the great concerns of the whole Union, every citizen of the United States from the most remote States or territories, is entitled to free access, not only to the principal departments established at Washington, but also to its judicial tribunals and public offices in every State in the Union ...'"

Cases that will be discussed in the next chapter. First, the nation ratified the 14th Amendment in 1868.

The 14th Amendment to the Constitution - 1868

At the conclusion of the horrible Civil War, the 13th Amendment freed all of the remaining slaves in the United States in December of 1865. This was not until over six months after the end of the major fighting. Surprisingly, the last three states that had legal slavery were Delaware, Kentucky, and New Jersey. The slaves in the Southern Slave States were legally freed in 1863 by Lincoln's Emancipation Proclamation. This was a legal action, but at the time it was made, those states were part of a breakaway country: the Confederate States of America. After the Civil War, Federal troops worked to keep the peace, and occupied the States that had been in rebellion. The societal upheaval and battle to incorporate the former slaves into the populace was just getting started.

During the Civil War, the Union Army occupied the strategic islands around Beaufort County, South Carolina. In that area, President Lincoln encouraged the prototyping of a means to incorporate former slaves into the society and economy. Today, the Reconstruction Era National Historic Park helps to explain the history of this effort. In states such as South Carolina and Mississippi, the newly freed slaves outnumbered the white population. The 14th Amendment was developed to provide the former slaves with full citizenship, and to attempt to restrict the States from violating their new-found rights. President Lincoln's assassination clearly slowed this effort.

It took three years after the Civil War ended for the 14th Amendment to be ratified. The 14th Amendment has five sections, but for purposes of analyzing general Privileges and Immunities, only the first section is pertinent. The second section will come into play with the perspective of voting rights that are analyzed in the next chapter. The first section of the 14th Amendment is broken out in Figure 14.

The first part of Section 1 of the 14th Amendment addressed the denial of citizenship to African Americans from the *Dred Scott* Supreme Court decision. It granted them both United States citizenship and State citizenship based upon where the person lived. By granting African Americans United States citizenship, they were automatically granted the

Figure 14 - Breakdown of 14th Amendment, Section 1

14th Amendment, Section 1	Explanation
All persons born or naturalized in the United States, and subject to the jurisdiction thereof, are citizens of the United States and of the State wherein they reside.	This was meant to define and grant citizenship to African Americans which had been denied by the Dred Scott ruling. It defined both National and State citizenship.
No State shall make or enforce any law which shall abridge the privileges or immunities of citizens of the United States;	First Additional State Restriction "State Privileges or Immunities Clause"
nor shall any State deprive any person of life, liberty, or property, without due process of law;	Second Additional State Restriction "State Due Process Clause"
nor deny to any person within its jurisdiction the equal protection of the laws.	Third Additional State Restriction "State Equal Protection Clause"

powerful Nationwide Privileges and Immunities that Chief Justice Taney had fought so hard to deny them in the *Dred Scott* case. By granting African Americans State citizenship too, the former Slave States couldn't try to reverse their approach from *Dred Scott* by hypothetically claiming that even though African Americans were United States citizens, that didn't automatically make them citizens of their State. This could have allowed them to try to keep and maintain the special laws and police regulations that they had used to deny free African Americans rights.

The second part of Section 1 of the 14th Amendment is the first of three additional State level restrictions intended to protect African Americans from legal abuse. This is known as the 14th Amendments Privileges or Immunities Clause. Figure 15 shows how this state restricting Privileges or Immunities Clause works with the primary Nationwide

Figure 15 - Additional State Protection for Privileges and Immunities

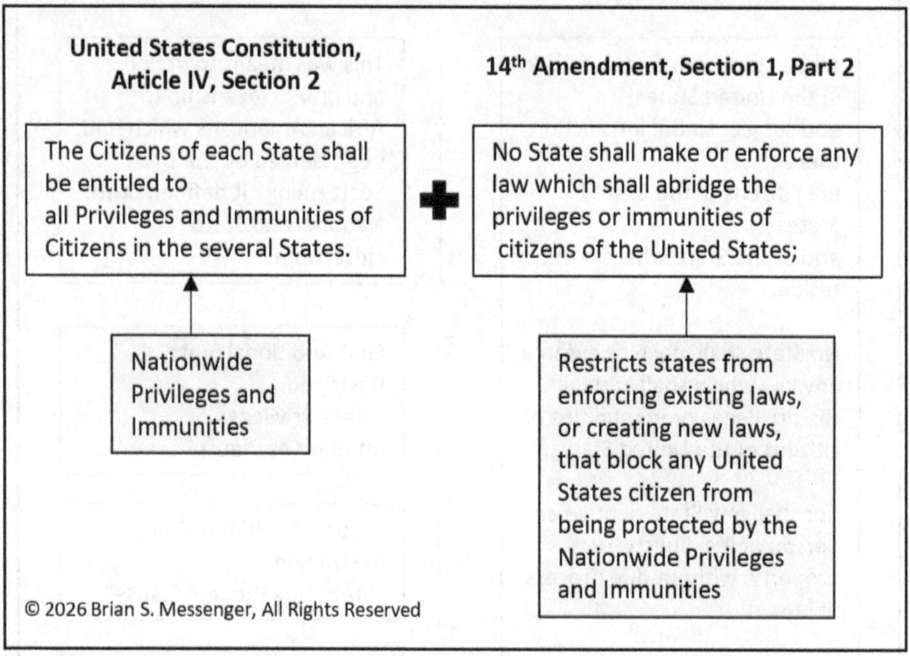

Privileges and Immunities Clause in the United States Constitution. The switch to "privileges or immunities" for the state level restriction provides enhanced protection against recalcitrant states and courts. Some state could try to claim that a right such as the "right to habeas corpus" was an immunity only. They might try to claim that the "right to travel between states without paying a tax" could be called a privilege only. Using this sort of distorted reasoning, a state or court could try to claim that since those examples are not both Privileges and Immunities, they are not protected. The country had just experienced the Civil War, which was partly a result of the *Dred Scott* decision and its contorted definitions of citizenship. The 14th Amendment change in language would protect against similar machinations by a future court.

The next two parts of Section 1 of the 14th Amendment are further restrictions on the state governments. Prior to the 13th Amendment, Slave States had been depriving slaves of their life, liberty and property. They had many discriminatory laws remaining on their books with regards to free African Americans. The previously discussed case of *Barron v. Baltimore(1833)* said that the *Bill of Rights* did not apply to State

Figure 16 - Additional State Level Protections for Due Process

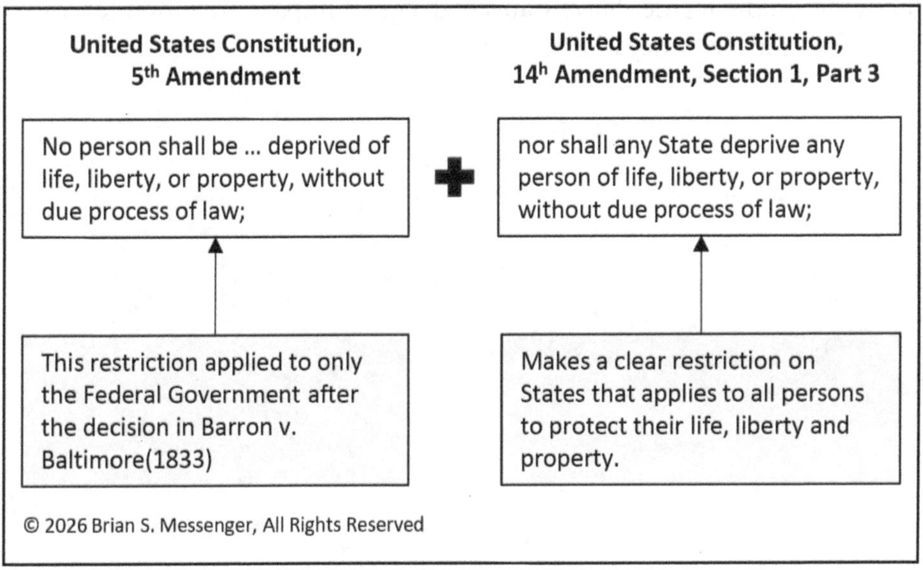

governments. Figure 16 shows how the Due Process clause of the 14th Amendment declared that States could no longer use these discriminatory laws.

The final part of the first section of the 14th Amendment is the Equal Protection Clause which states: "No State shall … deny to any person within its jurisdiction the equal protection of the laws.". To attempt to control former Slave States, so that they couldn't legally enforce their "special laws" and police regulations that discriminated against African Americans, the Equal Protection Clause provided a catch-all provision. The *Constitution* and the *Bill of Rights* did not have a specific "Equal Protection Clause", but the 14th Amendment created it. In the simplest reading, this clause would have incorporated the rights from the 4th, 5th and 6th Amendments against the states.

The history of the world has seen many cases where the pursuit of ambitious goals starts of with short-term successes, but then fall apart over time. With the ratification of the 14th Amendment, and the initial attempts at Reconstruction in the Southern States, things started out positively. The problem was that safety and security had to be provided by Federal troops. In the coming Chapter, we will see how when support for continued federal troops in the former Slave states waned, the South fell into an open state of violence by whites against former slaves. The activities in the former Slave states had a great impact on Supreme Court decisions for many decades to come.

CHAPTER 5

Frustration and Backsliding

(1868-1900 During and After Reconstruction)

If the United States history of African Americans were described in a movie series, it would have parallels to the original Star Wars trilogy. No analogy is perfect, but the following comparison provides a high-level perspective for the reader. The first movie in the series, *Star Wars(1974)*, has parallels to the battle to abolish slavery, victory by the Northern States in the Civil War, and the passage of the 14th Amendment. The second movie in the series, *The Empire Strikes Back(1980)*, has parallels to the collapse of Reconstruction, segregation, lynching and terrorizing of the African American community. The third movie in the series, *Return of the Jedi(1983)*, has parallels to the late 1900s that started with *Brown v. Board of Education(1954)*, the Civil Rights Acts of the 1960's, and finally the full integration of African Americans into American society that ultimately took over 100 years to achieve. This chapter is very dark, since it covers the period where the former slave "Empire" in the southern states struck back using all available resources.

The high-water mark of Reconstruction after the Civil War occurred somewhere around 1872. The American Battlefield Trust website provides[1] an excellent short overview of the Reconstruction era. Federal troops in southern states had restored order and were protecting African Americans and providing them with full civil rights. African Americans received full voting rights with the 15th Amendment passed

---

1American Battlefield Trust. (2026, Feb. 23).
https://www.battlefields.org/learn/articles/reconstruction-overview

in 1870. The State of Mississippi's legislature elected Blanche Bruce, a former slave, as a United States Senator in 1874. Many other African Americans were elected to Congress. A sequence of Civil Rights Acts that included the[2] *Enforcement Act of 1870* and the[3] *Civil Rights Act of 1875* became law, but their implementation was ultimately thwarted. Former confederates in the Southern States started to strike back.

Whites in the former Southern States, were now outnumbered in some instances by former slaves. The *Ku Klux Klan (KKK)* was one of the atrocious organizations that were formed to terrorize and murder former slaves in the south. In parallel with the social upheaval that proceeded, the United States Supreme Court became an unwitting accomplice to the denial of protection and civil rights for African Americans for decades to come. This does not appear to have been done intentionally, but was done out of a strong historical understanding of the rights of States to manage their own internal affairs without interference by the Federal government.

The ratification of the 14th Amendment initiated a slew of court cases over the following decades that attempted to define new Privileges and Immunities. Shortly after the 14th Amendment was ratified, three Supreme Court Cases helped to define the bounds of Nationwide Privileges and Immunities. These were *Paul v. Virginia(1869)*, *Ward v. Maryland(1870)*, and the *Slaughterhouse Cases(1873)*, and each of them will be discussed in detail. Many people consider the *Slaughterhouse Cases* to be the demise of the Privileges and Immunities Clause for all practical purposes. This case will be discussed to show how it heavily restricted the types of things that can be considered Nationwide Privileges and Immunities.

Between 1873-1899 the Supreme Court decided many cases that were related to Nationwide Privileges and Immunities in some form. Some of these cases have been forgotten, but they help to provide context as to what was happening in our country at that time. Many of them are related to the struggle for Civil Rights for African Americans and women, some involve rights found in the *Bill of Rights*, some involved businesses, and some are of a more mundane nature regarding various indi-

---

2 United States Senate. (2026, Feb. 23).
https://www.senate.gov/artandhistory/history/resources/pdf/EnforcementAct_1870.pdf

3 United States Senate. (2026, Feb. 23).
https://www.senate.gov/artandhistory/history/resources/pdf/Civil_Rights_Act_1875.pdf

vidual rights. Ultimately, there were very few instances that succeeded in identifying new Nationwide Privileges and Immunities. On a positive note, some of them provided clues and precedents for Nationwide Privileges and Immunities that are applicable today. Reflecting back on Article IV, Section 2 of the *United States Constitution* that stated "*The citizens of each state shall be entitled to all Privileges and Immunities of citizens in the several States*", the first question that would be answered by the Supreme Court was whether corporations are citizens as described therein.

Are Corporations Nationwide Citizens? - *Paul v. Virginia(1869)*

Four years after the end of the Civil War, the case of *Paul v. Virginia*[4] reached the United States Supreme Court. This case did not involve the 14th Amendment that granted African Americans and former slaves United States Citizenship. Instead, it revolved around a basic United States Constitutional question regarding corporations. Are corporations citizens that are protected by the Privileges and Immunities clause of the United States Constitution?

This defining case involved New York insurance companies that wanted to sell insurance policies (such as for fire) in the state of Virginia. Virginia passed a law in 1866 that required that insurance companies that were not incorporated in Virginia had to obtain a license. Part of the license requirements were to post a bond of between $30,000 and $50,000 with the treasurer of Virginia. Any company incorporated in Virginia did not have to post this bond. Samuel Paul was a Virginia citizen who represented a number of New York Insurance companies. He refused to deposit the required bonds for the New York companies he represented. His license was denied, but he sold insurance anyway. He was indicted, convicted, and fined $50 for his actions. He took this case all the way to the Supreme Court and lost.

The Supreme Court decided that corporations are artificial persons created by the legislature of a State. They are not natural persons, and therefore, are not entitled to the protection of the Privileges and Immunities Clause. Their key findings are shown[5] in Exhibit 20. The Supreme Court also provided an excellent logical analysis that explained

4 Paul v. Virginia, 75 U.S. 168 (1869)

5 Paul v. Virginia, 75 U.S. 168, 177-178 (1869)

Exhibit 20 - Corporations are not Nationwide Citizens, Paul v. Virginia

The answer which readily occurs to the objection founded upon the first clause consists in the fact that corporations are not citizens within its meaning. The term citizens as there used applies only to natural persons, members of the body politic, owing allegiance to the State, not to artificial persons created by the legislature, and possessing only the attributes which the legislature has prescribed. It is true that it has been held that where contracts or rights of property are to be enforced by or against corporations, the courts of the United States will, for the purpose of maintaining jurisdiction, consider the corporation as representing citizens of the State under the laws of which it is created, and to this extent will treat a corporation as a citizen within the clause of the Constitution extending the judicial power of the United States to controversies between citizens of different States.

the crazy results that would occur if corporations formed in one state had Nationwide Privileges and Immunities in every other state. Exhibit 21 shows[6] how States would lose all of their power over corporations from other states. For the purpose of determining the Nationwide Privileges and Immunities of citizens, Paul v. Virginia provided a number of new

6 Paul v. Virginia, 75 U.S. 168, 181-182 (1869)

Exhibit 21 - Problems with Alternative View, Paul v. Virginia

If, on the other hand, the provision of the Constitution could be construed to secure to citizens of each State in other States the peculiar privileges conferred by their laws, an extra-territorial operation would be given to local legislation utterly destructive of the independence and the harmony of the States. At the present day corporations are multiplied to an almost indefinite extent. There is scarcely a business pursued requiring the expenditure of large capital, or the union of large numbers, that is not carried on by corporations. It is not too much to say that the wealth and business of the country are to a great extent controlled by them. And if, when composed of citizens of one State, their corporate powers and franchises could be exercised in other States without restriction, it is easy to see that, with the advantages thus possessed, the most important business of those States would soon pass into their hands. The principal business of every State would, in fact, be controlled by corporations created by other States.

Exhibit 22 - Nationwide Privileges and Immunities, Paul v. Virginia

It was undoubtedly the object of the clause in question to place the citizens of each State upon the same footing with citizens of other States, so far as the advantages resulting from citizenship in those States are concerned. It relieves them from the disabilities of alienage in other States; it inhibits discriminating legislation against them by other States; it gives them the right of free ingress into other States, and egress from them; it insures to them in other States the same freedom possessed by the citizens of those States in the acquisition and enjoyment of property and in the pursuit of happiness; and it secures to them in other States the equal protection of their laws.

examples. These were described[7] in Exhibit 22 by Justice Field who wrote the Opinion of the Court. Using the description from Exhibit 22, the following new rights can be added to those that were already defined in the Dred Scott decision. SCP_PV_3 and SCP_PV_4 were both reclassified as State Privileges and Immunities with The *Slaughterhouse Cases(1873)* decision.

- SCP_PV_1 - *the right against discriminating legislation when in other States*
- *SCP_PV_2 - the right of free ingress into other States, and egress from other States.*
- [SCP_PV_3 – *the right to acquire and enjoy property in other States with the same freedom of the citizens of those states.*] Reclassified as State Privilege and Immunity by Slaughterhouse Cases(1873).
- [SCP_PV_4 – the right to pursue happiness in other States with the same freedoms of the citizens of those states.] Reclassified as State Privilege and Immunity by Slaughterhouse Cases(1873).
- SCP_PV_5 – *the right to equal protection of the laws when in other States.*

The *Slaughterhouse Cases(1873)* also corrected the State Level View description of Privileges and Immunities that could be implied by parts of Exhibit 22. It would clearly show that the Privileges and Immunities in the Constitution are Nationwide. Exhibit 22 was sometimes used to support the incorrect State Level View of Privileges and Immunities in later Supreme Court decisions. In Exhibit 23, *Paul v. Virginia* makes an interesting statement about Nationwide Privileges and Immunities by imply-

7 Paul v. Virginia, 75 U.S. 168, 180 (1869)

Exhibit 23 - State Privileges and Immunities Discussion, Paul v. Virginia

But the privileges and immunities secured to citizens of each State in the several States, by the provision in question, are those privileges and immunities which are common to the citizens in the latter States under their constitution and laws by virtue of their being citizens. Special privileges enjoyed by citizens in their own States are not secured in other States by this provision. It was not intended by the provision to give to the laws of one State any operation in other States. They can have no such operation, except by the permission, express or implied, of those States. The special privileges which they confer must, therefore, be enjoyed at home, unless the assent of other States to their enjoyment therein be given.

ing that they are "common" between citizens of different states instead of coming from a specific authority[8]. This too would be corrected.

Non Discriminatory Trade Rights - *Ward v. Maryland(1870)*

The Articles of Confederation discussion in Chapter 2 broke down the Non-Discriminatory Trade part of the Privileges and Immunities Clause in Figure 5. A key feature of Privileges and Immunities was that from a commerce perspective, citizens of one state, when in a different state, "*shall enjoy therein all the privileges of trade and commerce subject to the same duties, impositions and restrictions as the inhabitants thereof respectively*". The State of Maryland passed a law that required traders selling goods in the State to obtain a license. Residents of Maryland were required to pay between $12 and $150 for an annual license that relied on a sliding scale based upon the value of their supplies. Residents of other states automatically had to pay an annual license of $300.

Ward was a citizen of New Jersey who was selling horse harnesses in Baltimore, Maryland. He did not purchase a trader's license since he felt it violated his Privileges and Immunities, and he wanted to test that in court. Ward was indicted and convicted of violating the law of Maryland, and was fined $400 in the process. When his case reached the Supreme Court, the court declared[9] that it was "*unhesitatingly of the opinion that the statute in question is repugnant to the second section of the fourth ar-*

8 Paul v. Virginia, 75 U.S. 168, 180-181 (1869)

9 Ward v. Maryland, 79 U.S. 418, 429 (1870)

Exhibit 24- Commercial Privileges and Immunities, Ward v. Maryland

Attempt will not be made to define the words "privileges and immunities," or to specify the rights which they are intended to secure and protect, beyond what may be necessary to the decision of the case before the court. Beyond doubt those words are words of very comprehensive meaning, but it will be sufficient to say that the clause plainly and unmistakably secures and protects the right of a citizen of one State to pass into any other State of the Union for the purpose of engaging in lawful commerce, trade, or business without molestation; to acquire personal property; to take and hold real estate; to maintain actions in the courts of the State; and to be exempt from any higher taxes or excises than are imposed by the State upon its own citizens.

ticle of the Constitution, which provides that the citizens of each State shall be entitled to all privileges and immunities of citizens in the several States." To further explain its rationale, Exhibit 24 shows[10] how the Supreme Court viewed various Privileges and Immunities for Commerce. These Privileges and Immunities can be broken into Supreme Court precedents as shown below. SCP_WM_2, SCP_WM_3 and SCP_WM_4 were reclassified as State Privileges and Immunities in *The Slaughterhouse Cases(1873).*

- SCP_WM_1 - *the right of a citizen of one State to pass into any other State of the Union for the purpose of engaging in lawful commerce, trade, or business without molestation.*
- *[SCP_WM_2 – the right to acquire personal property in any other State.] Reclassified as State Privilege and Immunity by The Slaughterhouse Cases(1873).*
- *[SCP_WM_3 – the right to take and hold real estate in any other State.] Reclassified as State Privilege and Immunity by The Slaughterhouse Cases(1873).*
- *[SCP_WM_4 – the right to maintain actions in the courts of another State.] Reclassified as State Privilege and Immunity by The Slaughterhouse Cases(1873).*
- *SCP_WM_5 – the right to be exempt from any higher taxes or excises than are imposed by the State upon its own citizens.*

In Ward v. Maryland, the court also provided a logical argument as to

10 Ward v. Maryland, 79 U.S. 418, 423 (1870)

Exhibit 25 - Critical Commerce Discussion, Ward v. Maryland

Grant that the States may impose discriminating taxes against the citizens of other States, and it will soon be found that the power conferred upon Congress to regulate interstate commerce is of no value, as the unrestricted power of the States to tax will prove to be more efficacious to promote inequality than any regulations which Congress can pass to preserve the equality of right contemplated by the Constitution among the citizens of the several States. Excise taxes, it is everywhere conceded, may be imposed by the States, if not in any sense discriminating; but it should not be forgotten that the people of the several States live under one common Constitution, which was ordained to establish justice, and which, with the laws of Congress, and the treaties made by the proper authority, is the supreme law of the land; and that that supreme law requires equality of burden, and forbids discrimination in State taxation when the power is applied to the citizens of the other States. Inequality of burden, as well as the want of uniformity in commercial regulations, was one of the grievances of the citizens under the Confederation; and the new Constitution was adopted, among other things, to remedy those defects in the prior system.

how discriminatory taxes against out-of-state citizens would impinge upon Congress' right to regulate interstate commerce. This spoke directly to the court's decision, and is presented[11] in Exhibit 25.

The third major Privileges and Immunities case to be decided after the Civil War was the Supreme Court decision[12] in the *Slaughterhouse Cases(1873)* . This decision would have the greatest lasting impact on the American jurisprudence of the Privileges and Immunities clause. As with *Paul v. Virginia* and *Ward v. Maryland*, this decision would also revolve around the privileges and immunities of citizens to engage in businesses.

Categorizing Privileges and Immunities - *Slaughterhouse Cases(1873)*

From the founding of our country, the States were highly protective as to what their powers were. This was especially true in the former Slave States who wanted to defend and maintain their practice. It was generally understood from Supreme Court cases such as[13] *City of New York v. Miln(1837)* that States were responsible for

11 Ward v. Maryland, 79 U.S. 418, 430-431 (1870)

12 The Slaughterhouse Cases, 83 U.S. 36 (1873)

13 City of New York v. Miln, 36 U.S. 102 (1837)

their internal police and safety regulations. The Slaughterhouse Cases revolved around a health and safety law for the city of New Orleans.

New Orleans in the 1800's consisted of two narrow strips of land that bordered the Mississippi River, and a lot of swamplands beyond them. Land was at a premium. Thinking about life in New Orleans over 150 years ago, you can imagine how messy and potentially disease spreading, the slaughtering of animals would be in this sort of location. The State of Louisiana passed a law that gave to a corporation the exclusive right to land and slaughter cattle for a 25-year period. People and companies that had previously slaughtered animals sued the city over this monopoly that had been granted. They felt that the Privileges and Immunities Clause of the United States Constitution precluded the city from granting this monopoly.

Justice Samuel Miller was appointed to the Supreme Court by President Lincoln in 1862 at the height of the Civil War. Early in his life he had a medical degree and practiced medicine in Kentucky for 10 years. Reading from Justice Miller's "Opinion of the Court" in the Slaughterhouse Cases, the opinion bounces around. Analyzing the opinion has similarities to deciphering an old-fashioned Doctor's prescription that was written by hand. Ultimately, after surveying prior cases, Justice Miller reached the heart of the Privileges and Immunities matter by determining that most privileges and immunities are granted by states. He explained[14] why the general rights alluded to in *Corfield v. Collier* and *Ward v. Maryland* are "*rights belonging to the individual as a citizen of a State.*" As such, he found that they "have always been held to be the class of rights which the State governments were created to establish and secure." Relying on the decision of *Paul v. Virginia*, Justice Miller explained[15] that States were obligated to not discriminate against citizens of other states with regard to these general rights (Exhibit 26). He also starts to consider what rights might be Nationwide Privileges and Immunities using some obvious examples from the United States Constitution.

At the bottom of Exhibit 26, Justice Miller starts to consider Nationwide Privileges and Immunities. As shown in Chapter 4, the only Pre-Civil War case that delineated privileges and immunities as a critical part of the rationale for the decision was the *Dred Scott* case. Justice Miller

14 Slaughterhouse Cases, 83 U.S. 36, 76 (1873)

15 Slaughterhouse Cases, 83 U.S. 36, 77 (1873)

Exhibit 26 - Function of State Specific Rights vs. Nationwide Rights

> The constitutional provision there alluded to did not create those rights, which it called privileges and immunities of citizens of the States. It threw around them in that clause no security for the citizen of the State in which they were claimed or exercised. Nor did it profess to control the power of the State governments over the rights of its own citizens. ...
>
> It would be the vainest show of learning to attempt to prove by citations of authority, that up to the adoption of the recent amendments, no claim or pretence was set up that those rights depended on the Federal government for their existence or protection, beyond the very few express limitations which the Federal Constitution imposed upon the States--such, for instance, as the prohibition against ex post facto laws, bills of attainder, and laws impairing the obligation of contracts. But with the exception of these and a few other restrictions, the entire domain of the privileges and immunities of citizens of the States, as above defined, lay within the constitutional and legislative power of the States, and without that of the Federal government.

actually quoted that decision twice[16] in the *Slaughterhouse Cases* with respect to citizenship for African Americans. He then seems to have come to an epiphany that the prior right he described in *Crandall v. Nevada* was a Nationwide Privilege and Immunity. That right was a close sibling to the Privileges and Immunities listed and described by Chief Justice Taney in *Dred Scott*. Justice Miller describes[17] his revelation in Exhibit 27.

---

16 Slaughterhouse Cases, 83 U.S. 36, 73 (1873) Justice Miller's Opinion of the Court: "But it had been held by this court, in the celebrated Dred Scott case, only a few years before the outbreak of the civil war, that a man of African descent, whether a slave or not, was not and could not be a citizen of a State or of the United States. This decision, while it met the condemnation of some of the ablest statesmen and constitutional lawyers of the country, had never been overruled;"
When referring to the 14th Amendment Justice Miller said: "It declares that persons may be citizens of the United States without regard to their citizenship of a particular State, and it overturns the Dred Scott decision by making all persons born within the United States and subject to its jurisdiction citizens of the United States."

17 Slaughterhouse Cases, 83 U.S. 36,78 (1873) – This exhibit is prefaced with the paragraph "Having shown that the privileges and immunities relied on in the argument are those which belong to citizens of the States as such, and that they are left to the State governments for security and protection, and not by this article placed under the special care of the Federal government, we may hold ourselves excused from defining the privileges and immunities of citizens of the United States which no State can abridge, until some case involving those privileges may make it necessary to do so."

Exhibit 27 - A Revelation regarding Crandall v. State of Nevada

But lest it should be said that no such privileges and immunities are to be found if those we have been considering are excluded, we venture to suggest some which owe their existence to the Federal government, its National character, its Constitution, or its laws. One of these is well described in the case of Crandall v. Nevada.* It is said to be the right of the citizen of this great country, protected by implied guarantees of its Constitution, "to come to the seat of government to assert any claim he may have upon that government, to transact any business he may have with it, to seek its protection, to share its offices, to engage in administering its functions. He has the right of free access to its seaports, through which all operations of foreign commerce are conducted, to the subtreasuries, land offices, and courts of justice in the several States."

At this point, Justice Miller makes a very mysterious quotation. Supreme Court opinions are virtually always written to precisely reference prior decisions. Instead of doing that, Justice Miller references "another case" when describing a quote from Chief Justice Taney. The full quote is shown[18] in Exhibit 28. There is no way to know for sure why Justice Miller did this, but there is a very plausible reason why he might have done so. First, let's dispense with the claim that he really didn't know where the quote came from. The quote in Exhibit 28 is from Chief Justice Taney's dissenting opinion in the Passenger Cases that was discussed in Chapter 4. In the case of *Crandall v. Nevada*, which was also discussed in Chapter 4, Justice Miller's Opinion of the Court discussed in depth the *Passenger Cases*. In *Crandall v. Nevada*, Justice Miller specifically described Chief Justice Taney's dissenting opinion in the *Passenger Cases* in two places . In the second instance he directly quoted a version of the phrase from Exhibit 28 (Exhibit 28 replaced "formed" with "established ",

18 Slaughterhouse Cases, 83 U.S. 36, 79 (1873)

Exhibit 28 - Justice Miller's Mysterious Quotation

And quoting from the language of Chief Justice Taney in another case, it is said "that for all the great purposes for which the Federal government was established, we are one people, with one common country, we are all citizens of the United States;" and it is, as such citizens, that their rights are supported in this court in Crandall v., Nevada.

and combined two sentences into one)[19].

By referring to "*Chief Justice Taney in another case*", Justice Miller might have been leaving a "breadcrumb" for people to review *Dred Scott*. After the trauma of the Civil War, he might not have wanted to quote it directly; while still giving Chief Justice Taney credit. This breadcrumb would push readers to review *Dred Scott*, *Crandall v. Nevada*, and the *Passenger Cases*, which all spoke to nationwide rights in detail. Since the privileges and immunities described in *Crandall v. Nevada* were so similar to the privileges and immunities described in *Dred Scott*, this seems very plausible.

Nationwide Privileges and Immunities, The Slaughterhouse Cases

After the revelation that the right Justice Miller had described in *Crandall v. Nevada* was a privilege and immunity, he went on to identify a number of other nationwide privileges and immunities. Table 11

19 Crandall v. Nevada, 73 U.S. 35, 39-40 (1868) First Quotation: "We shall have occasion to refer hereafter somewhat in detail, to the opinions of the judges of this court in The Passenger Cases,* in which there were wide differences on several points involved in the case before us....Chief Justice Taney, while he differed from the majority of the court, and held the law to be valid, said of the tax levied by the analogous statute of Massachusetts, that "its payment is the condition upon which the State permits the alien passenger to come on shore and mingle with its citizens, and to reside among them...."

Crandall v. Nevada, 73 U.S. 35, 48-49 (1868) Second quotation where Justice Miller is describing Chief Justice Taney's dissenting opinion in the Passenger Cases: "But the principles here laid down may be found more clearly stated in the dissenting opinion of the Chief Justice in those cases, and with more direct pertinency to the case now before us than anywhere else. After expressing his views fully in favor of the validity of the tax, which he said had exclusive reference to foreigners, so far as those cases were concerned, he proceeds to say, for the purpose of preventing misapprehension, that so far as the tax affected American citizens it could not in his opinion be maintained, He then adds: "Living as we do under a common government, charged with the great concerns of the whole Union, every citizen of the United States from the most remote States or territories, is entitled to free access, not only to the principal departments established at Washington, but also to its judicial tribunals and public offices in every State in the Union ....For all the great purposes for which the Federal government was formed we are one people, with one common country. We are all citizens of the United States, and as members of the same community must have the right to pass and repass through every part of it without interruption, as freely as in our own States...."

lists these while also identifying the source. These are based on Justice Miller's test from Exhibit 27 that they must owe their existence to the Federal government, its National character, its Constitution, or its laws. There are a number of observations that can be made about Table 11. The first observation is that after the first 10 rights listed, Justice Miller said "*To these may be added the rights secured by the thirteenth and fifteenth articles of amendment, and by the other clause of the fourteenth, next to be considered.*" Generally, those rights would be protected by Congress through Section 2 of the 13th Amendment, through Section 5 of the 14th Amendment, and through Section 2 of the 15th Amendment. If those protections are insufficient, then Justice Miller indicates that the Amendments also create nationwide privileges and immunities.

The second observation is that Justice Miller violates the standard put in place by Chief Justice Marshall in *Barron v. Baltimore* in a number of places. In Chapter 3, that case was discussed where Chief Justice Marshall indicated that the *Bill of Rights* did not apply to the States since the Amendments did not specifically exclude the States from doing these things. In his text descriptions, Justice Miller indicated that both the "privilege of the writ of habeas corpus" and the "right to peaceably assemble and petition for redress of grievances" came from the Constitution. The Constitution does not specifically block the states from violating these rights, so by Chief Justice Marshall's logic these rights were only

Table 11 - Nationwide Privileges and Immunities, Slaughterhouse Cases

Identifier	Nationwide Privilege and Immunity	Reference	Source[1]
SCP_SH_1	prohibition against ex post facto laws	83 U.S. 36, 77	Constitution
SCP_SH_2	prohibition against … bills of attainder	83 U.S. 36, 77	Constitution
SCP_SH_3	prohibition against … laws impairing the obligation of contracts	83 U.S. 36, 77	Constitution

1 Using "Federal Government", "National Character", "Constitution", or "Laws" as described in Exhibit 27

Identifier	Nationwide Privilege and Immunity	Reference	Source[1]
SCP_SH_4	the right ... to come to the seat of government to assert any claim he may have upon that government, to transact any business he may have with it, to seek its protection, to share its offices, to engage in administering its functions...."	83 U.S. 36, 78	Federal Government & National Character
SCP_SH_5	The right ... of free access to its seaports, through which all operations of foreign commerce are conducted, to the subtreasuries, land offices, and courts of justice in the several States.	83 U.S. 36, 78	Federal Government & National Character
SCP_SH_6	to demand the care and protection of the Federal government over his life, liberty, and property when on the high seas or within the jurisdiction of a foreign government.	83 U.S. 36, 79	Federal Government & National Character
SCP_SH_7	The right to peaceably assemble and petition for redress of grievances,	83 U.S. 36, 79	Constitution & National Character
SCP_SH_8	the privilege of the writ of habeas corpus	83 U.S. 36, 79	Constitution & National Character
SCP_SH_9	The right to use the navigable waters of the United States, however they may penetrate the territory of the several States	83 U.S. 36, 79	Federal Government & National Character
SCP_SH_10	all rights secured to our citizens by treaties with foreign nations	83 U.S. 36, 79	Federal Government & National Character
SCP_SH_11	Neither slavery nor involuntary servitude, except as a punishment for crime whereof the party shall have been duly convicted, shall exist within the United States, or any place subject to their jurisdiction.	83 U.S. 36, 80	Constitution 13th Amendment

Identifier	Nationwide Privilege and Immunity	Reference	Source[1]
SCP_SH_12	a citizen of the United States can, of his own volition, become a citizen of any State of the Union by a bona fide residence therein, with the same rights as other citizens of that State.	83 U.S. 36, 80	Constitution 14th Amendment
SCP_SH_13	The right of citizens of the United States to vote shall not be denied or abridged by the United States or by any State on account of race, color, or previous condition of servitude.	83 U.S. 36, 80	Constitution 15th Amendment

protected with respect to the Federal government. Fortunately, these nationwide privileges and immunities happen to have far preceded the Constitution. Interspersed with his analysis of privileges and immunities, Justice Miller looked at the other parts of the 14th Amendment to determine their applicability to the *Slaughterhouse Cases.*

A Contemporary View of the Purposes for the 14th Amendment

The Slaughterhouse decision came only a few short years after the passage of the 14th Amendment. The Opinion of the Court considered all four of the Clauses in the first section of the 14th Amendment (See Figure 14) in order to determine whether Constitutional rights were being violated by Louisiana's Slaughterhouse law. Since these views were the Supreme Courts contemporary impression of the meanings of this Amendment, they provide us with excellent historical context. First, the Court viewed[20] that the Amendment came from Congress' determination that "*something more was necessary in the way of constitutional protection to the unfortunate race who had suffered so much.*" To achieve these new protections against the former Slave states, Congress refused[21] to allow the former Confederate States "*their full participation in the government of the Union ... until they ratified that article by a formal vote of their legislative bodies.*"

20 Slaughterhouse Cases, 83 U.S. 36, 70 (1873)

21 Slaughterhouse Cases, 83 U.S. 36, 70-71 (1873)

These contemporary Supreme Court views remain very important to this day. There still remain significant arguments regarding the purposes of the 14th Amendment. For instance, the *Slaughterhouse Cases* clearly did not believe in birthright citizenship for children born to citizens or subjects of foreign States. The *Slaughterhouse Cases* clearly saw the Due Process Clause as incorporating the 5th Amendment against the States only. Finally, it saw the Equal Protection Clause as a means to keep States from using the "Special Laws and Police Regulations" (described in Chapter 4) against the newly emancipated African Americans.

The 14th Amendment gave three powerful new abilities to protect the rights of Americans. In shorthand, they are known as the Privileges and Immunities Clause, the Due Process Clause, and the Equal Protection Clause. As seen in Table 12, each of these had their own intention to help protect the rights of the recently freed slaves who had now been granted full United States citizenship as well as citizenship in the states where they resided. While the rights of African Americans were advancing, women were frustrated with their position in society.

Table 12 - Contemporary View of the 14th Amendment Clauses

These contemporary Supreme Court views remain very import

14th Amendment Clause	Reference	Opinion Text
All persons born or naturalized in the United States, and subject to the jurisdiction thereof, are citizens of the United States and of the State wherein they reside.	83 U.S. 36, 73	That its main purpose was to establish the citizenship of the negro can admit of no doubt. The phrase, "subject to its jurisdiction" was intended to exclude from its operation children of ministers, consuls, and citizens or subjects of foreign States born within the United States.

14th Amendment Clause	Reference	Opinion Text
No State shall make or enforce any law which shall abridge the privileges or immunities of citizens of the United States;	83 U.S. 36, 74	It is a little remarkable, if this clause was intended as a protection to the citizen of a State against the legislative power of his own State, that the word citizen of the State should be left out when it is so carefully used, and used in contradistinction to citizens of the United States, in the very sentence which precedes it. Of the privileges and immunities of the citizen of the United States, and of the privileges and immunities of the citizen of the State, and what they respectively are, we will presently consider; but we wish to state here that it is only the former which are placed by this clause under the protection of the Federal Constitution, and that the latter, whatever they may be, are not intended to have any additional protection by this paragraph of the amendment.
nor shall any State deprive any person of life, liberty, or property, without due process of law;	83 U.S. 36, 80	…has been in the Constitution since the adoption of the fifth amendment, as a restraint upon the Federal power. It is also to be found in some form of expression in the constitutions of nearly all the States, as a restraint upon the power of the States. This law, then, has practically been the same as it now is during the existence of the government, except so far as the present amendment may place the restraining power over the States in this matter in the hands of the Federal government.
nor deny to any person within its jurisdiction the equal protection of the laws.	83 U.S. 36, 81	In the light of the history of these amendments, and the pervading purpose of them, which we have already discussed, it is not difficult to give a meaning to this clause. The existence of laws in the States where the newly emancipated negroes resided, which discriminated with gross injustice and hardship against them as a class, was the evil to be remedied by this clause, and by it such laws are forbidden.

Women's Rights Delayed

While the 14th Amendment (1868) brought new citizenship rights to African Americans, and the 15th Amendment (1870) provided them voting rights, nothing had changed for women. After the Slaughterhouse Cases decision, two of the first three Supreme Court cases addressing Privileges and Immunities related to women's rights. The case of *Bradwell v. State(1873)* involved the right for a woman to practice law in a state court. The United States Supreme Court ruled[22] that this was not a privilege and immunity that belongs to citizens of the United States. A more interesting case was *Minor v. Happersett(1874)*. In this case, Mrs. Minor of Missouri argued that the new 14th Amendment granted her the right to vote. Exhibit 29 shows the argument[23] that Mrs. Minor made.

Unfortunately, for Mrs. Minor, and the women of the United States, it would take another 56 years for women to receive the right to vote. This happened with the adoption of the 19th Amendment in 1920. In the meantime, the United States Supreme Court ruled that the 14th Amendment did not change Mrs. Minor's citizenship status and her rights as shown in Exhibit 30. Since women had not had the right to vote at the beginning of the nation's history, this was clearly[24] not a Nationwide Privilege and Immunity of citizens of the United States.

22 Bradwell v. State, 83 U.S. 130, 139 (1873) "... there are privileges and immunities belonging to citizens of the United States, in that relation and character, and that it is these and these alone which a State is forbidden to abridge. But the right to admission to practice in the courts of a State is not one of them. This right in no sense depends on citizenship of the United States."

23 Minor v. Happersett, 88 U.S. 162, 165 (1874)

24 Minor v. Happersett, 88 U.S. 162, 170 (1874)

Exhibit 29 - Argument for Women's Right to Vote, Minor v. Happersett

It is contended that the provisions of the constitution and laws of the State of Missouri which confine the right of suffrage and registration therefor to men, are in violation of the Constitution of the United States, and therefore void. The argument is, that as a woman, born or naturalized in the United States and subject to the jurisdiction thereof, is a citizen of the United States and of the State in which she resides, she has the right of suffrage as one of the privileges and immunities of her citizenship, which the State cannot by its laws or constitution abridge.

Exhibit 30 - Rejection of a Women's Right to Vote, Minor v. Happersett

The fourteenth amendment did not affect the citizenship of women any more than it did of men. In this particular, therefore, the rights of Mrs. Minor do not depend upon the amendment. She has always been a citizen from her birth, and entitled to all the privileges and immunities of citizenship. The amendment prohibited the State, of which she is a citizen, from abridging any of her privileges and immunities as a citizen of the United States; but it did not confer citizenship on her. That she had before its adoption.

In the *Slaughterhouse Cases*, Justice Miller had acknowledged[25] that the 15th Amendment to the Constitution had created a new Nationwide Privilege and Immunity. This was further explained in the Supreme Court Case of *United States v. Reese(1876)*. In this case, two election inspectors in Kentucky refused to count the vote of an African American citizen named William Garner. His case reached the Supreme Court. While they ruled that the right to vote could not be abridged due to race as shown[26] in Exhibit 31, they found the law that Congress had written unconstitutional since it covered issues other than discrimination on account of race. The case was thrown out, but the Nationwide Privilege and

25 Slaughterhouse Cases, 83 U.S. 36, 80 (1873)

26 United States v. Reese, 92 U.S. 214, 217-218 (1876)

Exhibit 31 - Discrimination by Race in Voting, United States v. Reese

The Fifteenth Amendment does not confer the right of suffrage upon any one. It prevents the States, or the United States, however, from giving preference, in this particular, to one citizen of the United States over another on account of race, color, or previous condition of servitude. Before its adoption, this could be done. It was as much within the power of a State to exclude citizens of the United States from voting on account of race, &c., as it was on account of age, property, or education. Now it is not. If citizens of one race having certain qualifications are permitted by law to vote, those of another having the same qualifications must be. Previous to this amendment, there was no constitutional guaranty against this discrimination: now there is. It follows that the amendment has invested the citizens of the United States with a new constitutional right which is within the protecting power of Congress. That right is exemption from discrimination in the exercise of the elective franchise on account of race, color, or previous condition of servitude.

Immunity to vote without discrimination based on race was reinforced. Eight years later, in *Ex Parte Yarbrough(1884)*, Justice Miller used[27] this Nationwide Privilege and Immunity to maintain the incarceration of four defendants who "*beat, bruised, wounded and otherwise maltreated*" an African American named Barry Saunders.

The Decline of Reconstruction - *United States v. Cruikshank(1876)*

The 14th Amendment was primarily adopted to provide the full rights of citizenship to African Americans. In the 21st century, it is extremely frustrating to review the post-Civil War history. Things started off well with Reconstruction, but that came to a halt with the Compromise of 1877. That compromise resolved the Presidential election for Republican Rutherford B. Hayes in exchange for ending Reconstruction. In parallel with the end of Reconstruction, the Supreme Court took an extremely conservative view on protecting rights. In some instances, they provided hints and guidance that did not seem to be followed.

The "shiny new" 14th Amendment distracted people from focusing on the Privileges and Immunities Clause in Article IV of the Constitution. Other plaintiffs kept "banging their heads against the wall" by trying to effectively re-litigate *Barron v. Baltimore.* Instead of changing tacts, they continued to proclaim that the *Bill of Rights* applied to the states. Cases that reached the Supreme Court did not seem to address key facts that might have resulted in positive outcomes. This gave the Southern States carte-blanche to implement Jim Crow Laws and to segregate, subjugate and terrorize the newly freed African Americans for decades. To understand the key civil rights issues of the time, the three "unsuccessful" Supreme Court cases of *United States v. Cruikshank(1876), The Civil Rights Cases (1883)*, and *Plessy v. Ferguson (1896)* are analyzed in detail.

The 1876 *United States v. Cruikshank* Supreme Court decision[28] related to an awful slaughter of over 50 African Americans near Colfax, Louisiana by a group of whites. The circumstances, and the Supreme

27 Ex Parte Yarbrough, 110 U.S. 651, 657 (1884)

28 United States v. Cruikshank, 92 U.S. 542 (1876)

Court case are described in detail[29] in "*The Day Freedom Died*" by Charles Lane . It is easy for people who believe that Supreme Court decisions should correct every wrong in our country to argue that the Court should have ruled differently in the Cruikshank case. The reality is that the Supreme Court's role is to interpret the laws passed by Congress based on the United States Constitution and prior court precedents. There were many deficiencies in the case that resulted in the Supreme Court's decision and the ultimate release of the accused killers. Most importantly, this included the fact that racism was not part of the indictments.

Ultimately, to convict the killers in the Cruikshank case would have required the Federal government to take over local police powers. Since the founding of our republic, it has been the States' responsibility to manage crimes between individuals such as murder, robbery, and false imprisonment. In the case of *City of New York v. Miln(1837)*, the Supreme Court had decided[30] : "*That all those powers which relate to merely municipal legislation, or what may perhaps, more properly be called internal police, are not thus surrendered or restrained; and that, consequently, in relation to these, the authority of a state is complete, unqualified, and exclusive.*"

Before going into the details of the Cruikshank decision, reviewing the actions of the Supreme Court are very reminiscent of a joke from the mid-1990s. Since the target of the joke is a company whose products most people have used, and who was worth over three trillion dollars 30 years later, it is likely that the criticism helped them to correct a problem. The joke went something like this: '*a pilot was flying a vintage plane over the Seattle metropolitan area in poor visibility when all of his navigation and communications went out. He saw some people on the roof of a building and shouted to them: "where am I?". Their response was "in a plane". He quickly navigated directly to the airport. When he landed, his friends asked "how did you know where to go?". His answer was "I knew I must have been flying over Microsoft Technical Support, since the answer they gave me was 100% correct but totally useless"*'.

The Cruikshank Opinion of the Court was written by Chief Jus-

29 Lane, Charles. *The Day Freedom Died – The Colfax Massacre, the Supreme Court, and the Betrayal of Reconstruction.* Henry Holt and Company, LLC., 2008, New York, New York. - This provides a detailed analysis of the Colfax Massacre of April 13, 1873 and the Supreme Court decision in United States v. Cruikshank.

30 City of New York v. Miln, 36 U.S. 102, 139 (1837)

tice Waite. He provided a master class in providing truthful but unhelpful conclusions in his opinion. The opinion must be understood in the context of Reconstruction and states rights. By April 13, 1873 (Easter Day) when the Colfax massacre happened, Louisiana was in chaos. Federal troops had been removed from the State. Elsewhere, only South Carolina and Mississippi remained under total Republican control. The nation was tiring of Reconstruction and having Federal Troops in Southern states. Republican President Grant had taken significant criticism for his fight against the *KKK* in the South which was losing popular support. Table 13 was generated by summarizing the Opinion of the Court's description for each indictment count, followed by a summary of the Court's corresponding conclusion regarding the count. Appendix 24 contains the specific Supreme Court text used to generate these summaries.

Reviewing the sequence in which Chief Justice Waite disposed of the various counts of the Cruikshank indictment, a number of patterns can be observed. First, he declared that freedom of assembly and the right to bear arms were not rights granted by the Constitution. His argument was that these rights long preceded the Constitution. Chapter 1 showed how the rights to peaceably assemble and to bear arms far proceeded the founding of the United States. Initially, they were protected by the Privileges and Immunities clause in the Articles of Confederation and later by the equivalent clause in the Constitution. In Chapter 4 it was shown that these were recognized[31] in the *Dred Scott* decision as being rights that all American citizens had . The Supreme Court had determined that the *Bill of Rights* did not apply to State action in the[32] *Barron v. Baltimore* case described in Chapter 3. Using this background regarding the *Bill of Rights*, Chief Justice Waite made the argument that these rights were not "granted" by the Constitution. Therefore, he determined that the Federal government did not have the power to enforce them.

As a counterexample, to describe a right that the Federal government could enforce, Chief Justice Waite referred to the right to assemble to petition Congress for a redress of grievances. Exhibit 32 shows[33] this explanation from the Cruikshank decision. This right is very similar to

31 Dred Scott v. Sandford, 60 U.S. 393, 417 (1857)

32 Barron v. Mayor and City Council of Baltimore, 32 U.S. 243 (1833)

33 United States v. Cruikshank, 92 U.S. 542, 552-553 (1876)

Table 13 - Truthful buy Unhelpful Conclusions, United States v. Cruikshank

Counts	Summary of Indictment Count(s)	Opinion of the Court Decision Summary
1, 9	Violation of Right to Peaceably Assemble	This right existed long before the Constitution, and therefore is not a right granted to the people by the Constitution.
2, 10	Violation of Right to Bear Arms for a Lawful Purpose	This is not a right granted by the Constitution, and is not dependent on the Constitution for its existence.
3, 11	Violation of Right to Due Process	This is nothing else than alleging a conspiracy to falsely imprison or murder citizens of the United States. Protection of this right rests with the States.
4, 12	Violation of Right to Equal Protection of the Laws	There is no allegation that this was done because of the race or color.
6, 14	Violation of Right to Vote	The right to vote is decided by the States. The right against discrimination based on race comes from the United States. The indictment does not show that the defendants were trying to interfere with the right to vote based on discrimination. Indictment charges must be clearly stated, and cannot be inferred.
7, 15	Conspiracy to intimidate citizens from voting	The indictment does not indicate the conspiracy was based on race. The violation is nothing more than a conspiracy to breach peace in a State. States are responsible for protecting their citizens against domestic violence. The United States can only help protect against domestic violence when requested by the State.
5, 8, 13, 16	Preventing African American citizens from exercising their Nationwide and State level Privileges and Immunities	The indictment counts are too vague and general. They lack the certainty and precision required by the established rules of criminal pleading.

Exhibit 32 - Federal Assembly Right, United States v. Cruikshank

The right of the people peaceably to assemble for the purpose of petitioning Congress for a redress of grievances, or for any thing else connected with the powers or the duties of the national government, is an attribute of national citizenship, and, as such, under the protection of, and guaranteed by, the United States. The very idea of a government, republican in form, implies a right on the part of its citizens to meet peaceably for consultation in respect to public affairs and to petition for a redress of grievances. If it had been alleged in these counts that the object of the defendants was to prevent a meeting for such a purpose, the case would have been within the statute, and within the scope of the sovereignty of the United States. Such, however, is not the case. The offence, as stated in the indictment, will be made out, if it be shown that the object of the conspiracy was to prevent a meeting for any lawful purpose whatever.

the privilege and immunity from[34] *Crandall v. Nevada* that was re-characterized by Justice Miller in the *Slaughterhouse Cases.* It is closely related to the Nationwide privileges and immunities described in the *Dred Scott* decision.

After disposing of the indictment counts related to 1st and 2nd Amendment rights, Chief Justice Waite turned to the Due Process Clause and the Equal Protection Clause of the 14th Amendment. In these cases, the indictment counts were deemed to be the responsibility of the State of Louisiana. The deficiency in the indictments of not claiming that the actions were a result of race was also used against the United States government. Next, the issue of violating voting rights was addressed. Again, these claims were disposed of by claiming that the indictments did not claim that this was done on the basis of race. Finally, Chief Justice Waite addressed the violation of privileges and immunities. Since many of the actions violated nationwide privileges and immunities, the Chief Justice found another way to dispose of them. He turned to the fact that[35] "*these counts are too vague and general. They lack the certainty and precision required by the established rules of criminal proceedings.*" Basically, the key parts of the case were thrown out on a technicality.

As the saying goes, "hindsight is 20/20". There were a lot of problems with the Cruikshank case. First and foremost, the indictments were

34 Crandall v. State of Nevada, 73, U.S. 35, 43 (1868)

35 United States v. Cruikshank, 92 U.S. 542, 559 (1876)

poorly written. Secondly, the United States Supreme Court was in a no-win situation. If the Supreme Court had ruled differently, they would have dramatically shifted the burden for police powers from the states to the federal government. The nation was in a depression, and Northerners were tired of the fight over Civil Rights. Supreme Court justices are humans with feelings just like the rest of us. An interesting anecdote regarding Supreme Court Justice Miller after the Cruikshank decision was told by Charles Lane[36] to help explain Justice Miller's mood. It is shown in Exhibit 33. The reference to section 6 refers to the The Enforcement Act which was adopted[37] in 1870. This civil rights legislation, and the following amendments to it, attempted to provide African Americans with civil rights equal to those of whites. The key section of the Enforcement Act of 1870 is shown in Exhibit 34. With the findings in the Cruikshank decision, cases now required a high standard of showing that the motivation of any conspiracy had a racist intent.

Following the Cruikshank decision, life for African Americans went from bad to worse. The disputed 1876 Presidential election resulted in the Compromise of 1877 and President Rutherford B. Hayes' inauguration. He had promised to remove the Federal troops that remained in the South that were protecting the rights of African Americans. A year later, members of Congress from the former Confederate States were in-

36 Lane, Charles. *The Day Freedom Died – The Colfax Massacre, the Supreme Court, and the Betrayal of Reconstruction.* Henry Holt and Company, LLC, 2008, New York, New York, page 247

37 United States Senate. (2026, Feb. 23). https://www.senate.gov/artandhistory/history/resources/pdf/EnforcementAct_1870.pdf

Exhibit 33 - Justice Miller's Mood Post Cruikshank told by Charles Lane

For all his Republican loyalty and sympathy for the Negro, Miller was not immune to the general disenchantment with Reconstruction; he still nursed hurt feelings against Grant about being passed over for chief justice; and Slaughterhouse had committed him to a narrow view of federal power. Apparently, he and the Grant appointees could accept gutting section 6, as long as the Court did not explicitly strike it down. "I am losing interest in these matters," he confided to a friend in December 1875. "I will do my duty but will fight no more."

Exhibit 34 - 1870 Enforcement Act, Section 6

And be it further enacted, That if two or more persons shall band or conspire together, or go in disguise upon the public highway, or upon the premises of another, with intent to violate any provision of this act, or to injure, oppress, threaten, or intimidate any citizens with intent to prevent or hinder his free exercise and enjoyment of any right or privilege granted or secured to him by the Constitution or laws of the United States, or because of his having exercised the same, such person shall be held guilty of felony, and, on conviction thereof, shall be fined or imprisoned, or both, at the discretion of the court, -- the fine not to exceed five thousand dollars, and the imprisonment not to exceed ten years, -- and shall, moreover, be thereafter ineligible to, and disabled from holding any office or place of honor, profit, or trust created by the Constitution or laws of the United States.

strumental in the passage of the *Posse Comitatus Act*. This law severely restricts when Presidents can deploy troops to American states or cities to enforce Federal laws such as the Civil Rights Acts of the 1870s. In keeping with the approach of leaving police powers to the states, the United States Supreme Court struck down[38] the Federal government's ability to prosecute private groups and individuals, such as the KKK, in *United States v. Harris(1883).*

The *Civil Rights Cases(1883)* Reach the Supreme Court

The Civil Rights Cases[39] involved the Civil Rights Act of 1875's provisions that provided African Americans with equal civil rights on trains, at hotels and in theaters. In a devastating blow for civil rights, the Supreme Court ruled that only State action[40] was restricted by the 14th Amendment. Their key findings are shown in Exhibit 35. The result was that individuals were permitted to continue with the racist exclusion of African Americans.

In his book "The Great Dissenter", Peter Canellos describes the life of Supreme Court Justice John Marshall Harlan. In his famous Civil

38 United States v. Harris, 106 U.S. 629 (1883)

39 Civil Rights Cases, 109 U.S. 3 (1883)

40 Civil Rights Cases, 109 U.S. 3, 13 (1883)- Opinion of the Court

Exhibit 35 - 14th Amendment Limits State Actions, Civil Rights Cases

> And so in the present case, until some State law has been passed, or some State action through its officers or agents has been taken, adverse to the rights of citizens sought to be protected by the Fourteenth Amendment, no legislation of the United States under said amendment, nor any proceeding under such legislation, can be called into activity: for the prohibitions of the amendment are against State laws and acts done under State authority.

Rights Cases dissent, Justice John Marshall Harlan excoriated the Opinion of the Court. Peter Canellos described the mood of the nation after the court's decision as[41] *"igniting celebrations in many white precincts of the South and almost funereal convergences in Black neighborhoods of cities and towns across the country. Denunciations of the court's ruling by Black speakers were usually paired with reverential praise for Harlan"*. Among many problems he saw with the Supreme court opinion, Justice Harlan analyzed Nationwide Privileges and Immunities. He provided an excellent roadmap for potential legal challenges. Exhibit 36 shows a key part[42] of Justice Harlan's dissent.

Justice Harlan is posing this example as a straw-man to highlight one of the most egregious problems with the Opinion of the Court. More importantly, he is referring to Nationwide Privileges and Immunities that

41 Canellos, Peter S. *The Great Dissenter – The Story of John Marshall Harlan, America's Judicial Hero.* Simon and Schuster, 2021, New York, New York, page 267

42 Civil Rights Cases, 109 U.S. 3, 47-48 (1883) Harlan Dissent

Exhibit 36 - Justice Harlan's Roadmap for the Future, Civil Rights Cases

> ...no State can sustain her denial to colored citizens of other States, while within her limits; of privileges or immunities, fundamental in republican citizenship, upon the ground that she accords such privileges and immunities only to her white citizens and withholds them from her colored citizens. The colored citizens of other States, within the jurisdiction of that State, could claim, in virtue of section 2 of article 4 of the Constitution, every privilege and immunity which that State secures to her white citizens. Otherwise, it would be in the power of any State, by discriminating class legislation against its own citizens of a particular race or color, to withhold from citizens of other States, belonging to that proscribed race, when within her limits, privileges and immunities of the character regarded by all courts as fundamental in citizenship;

Chief Justice Taney was keeping out of the hands of African Americans through the Dred Scott decision. In the Dred Scott decision, Chief Justice Taney described "*the right to enter every other State whenever they pleased, singly or in companies, without pass or passport, and without obstruction, to sojourn there as long as they pleased, to go where they pleased at every hour of the day or night without molestation, unless they committed some violation of law for which a white man would be punished;*" This Nationwide Privilege and Immunity is "fundamental in citizenship" as Justice Harlan described. Additionally, Chief Justice Taney had described Nationwide Privileges and Immunities as including "*the full liberty of speech in public and in private upon all subjects upon which its own citizens might speak; to hold public meetings upon political affairs, and to keep and carry arms wherever they went*". These are critical rights of all citizens that Justice Harlan refers to as being "*fundamental in republican citizenship*".

The Opinion of the Court in the Civil Rights Cases attempted to make a strong distinction between discrimination by the State and discrimination by an individual. This allowed a decision that claimed that Congress cannot control discrimination by individuals since the 14th Amendment only applied to States. Justice Harlan's dissent described some of the variations between these two extremes with his comment[43] that: "*I am of the opinion that such discrimination practised by corporations and individuals in the exercise of their public or quasi-public functions is a badge of servitude the imposition of which Congress may prevent under its power*". The most interesting of the public or quasi-public functions that Justice Harlan described were likely done by corporations. With some exceptions, the financing required to develop large hotels, theaters, and amusement parks would generally require multiple investors and a corporation to do so. The Supreme Court case of *Paul v. Virginia* had established important limitations on corporations.

In *Paul v. Virginia*, the Supreme Court had ruled that corporations were not entitled to the Privileges and Immunities of citizens in Article IV of the Constitution. The Opinion of the Court said[44] that "*The term citizens as there used applies only to natural persons, members of the body politic, owing allegiance to the State, not to artificial persons created by the*

43 Civil Rights Cases (1883), 109 U.S. 3, 43 Harlan Dissent

44 Paul v. Virginia (1869), 75 U.S. 168, 177

legislature, and possessing only the attributes which the legislature has prescribed." Since the Supreme Court had ruled that corporations are "*created by the legislature*", and only possessed the rights that "*the legislature has prescribed*", Justice Harlan's position was extremely strong against Corporations. Referring back to Exhibit 35, the Opinion of the Court in the Civil Rights Cases said: "*for the prohibitions of the amendment are against State laws and acts done under State authority.*" Large corporations and facilities are subject to significant State authority. This can include state-mandated inspections, annual registration with the state, and various state taxes and fees. If State created corporations violate the privileges and immunities of citizens of the United States, is the State enforcing a law that does so?

Unfortunately, this question did not reach the Supreme Court in the aftermath of the Civil Rights decision. In hindsight, the assassination of Republican President James Garfield in 1881 removed a President who might have responded to the Supreme Court's Civil Rights Cases decision. Prior to becoming President, Garfield had been in the House of Representatives since 1863. This came after his time as a Major General from Ohio in the Civil War. He had voted on the 13th, 14th, and 15th Amendments as well as all of the Civil Rights Acts. His strong pro African American civil rights views, and experience in the House of Representatives would have provided him strong motivation to find a way to work around the Supreme Court's decision. Tragically, President Garfield was assassinated two years before the Supreme Court decision, and during the beginning of his first term. In her book "*Destiny of the Republic: A Tale of Madness, Medicine and the Murder of a President*", Candace Millard provides[45] an excellent history of President Garfield's life and his terribly shortened presidency.

In his short time in office, President Garfield appointed a former slave and United States Senator from Mississippi, Blanche Bruce, as Register of the Treasury. Blanche Bruce's signature appeared on all United States paper currency. President Garfield also appointed former slave Fredrick Douglas as the Registrar of Deeds for the District of Columbia. Fredrick Douglas was probably the most famous champion of African American civil rights in the 1800's. Over 15 years earlier, Douglas had visited President Abraham Lincoln at the White

45 Millard, Candice. *Destiny of the Republic: A Tale of Madness, Medicine and the Murder of a President.* Doubleday, 2011, New York, New York.

House twice. Lincoln's son Robert Todd Lincoln, who lived in the White House at that time, was President Garfield's Secretary of War. Can you imagine President Garfield, Blanche Bruce, Fredrick Douglas and Robert Todd Lincoln traveling together through the South to evaluate civil rights for African Americans? In Justice Harlan's dissent, shown in Exhibit 36, he discussed a similar sort of scenario.

Picture President Garfield's party, with protection by a detachment of army troops, traveling by rail through the Southern states. They could try to sit together in the "whites only" rail cars, and they could go to the finest hotels, theaters and restaurants that claimed to be "whites only". Can you imagine Blanche Bruce showing a proprietor his signature on a piece of currency? If Blanche Bruce and Fredrick Douglas were refused service, there would have been a tremendous setup for a Supreme Court case. In satisfying the nationwide privilege and immunity recognized[46] in the Cruikshank decision , they could announce that their purpose was to assemble and work together to develop a petition for a redress of grievances. If Blanche Bruce and Fredrick Douglas were permitted service, then the event could have been documented in photographs. Future customers would then be able to argue an Equal Protection violation against state-created corporations. How could it be argued that an African American is only allowed in the facility when accompanied by the President?

Congress has the right to protect Nationwide Privileges and Immunities that are protected by Article IV, Section 2 of the *Constitution*. They can do this using the Necessary and Proper Clause in Article I, Section 8 of the *Constitution*[47]. It also has the right to enforce the 14th Amendment through enabling legislation. The United States, or any citizen, could have brought a federal case directly based on a violation of the Privileges and Immunities Clause. It is possible that this could have been

---

46 United States v. Cruikshank, 92 U.S. 542, 552-553 (1876) – "The very idea of a government, republican in form, implies a right on the part of its citizens to meet peaceably for consultation in respect to public affairs and to petition for a redress of grievances. If it had been alleged in these counts that the object of the defendants was to prevent a meeting for such a purpose, the case would have been within the statute, and within the scope of the sovereignty of the United States."

47 United States Constitution, Article I, Section 8 - "Congress shall have Power … To make all Laws which shall be necessary and proper for carrying into Execution the foregoing Powers, and all other Powers vested by this Constitution in the Government of the United States, or in any Department or Officer thereof."

brought against either a state, or a state-created corporation. Justice Harlan also provided a roadmap for Congress to regulate Interstate Commerce as a means to enforce Civil Rights. This would finally happen 81 years later with the Civil Rights Act of 1964. Before that happened, things got even worse with the Supreme Court decision in *Plessy v. Ferguson (1896).*

The Doctrine of "Separate but Equal" - *Plessy v. Ferguson(1896)*

As the lone dissenting opinion in the Supreme Court case of *Plessy v. Ferguson(1896)*, Justice Harlan had amazing foresight. He predicted[48] that: "*In my opinion, the judgment this day rendered will, in time, prove to be quite as pernicious as the decision made by this tribunal in the Dred Scott case.*" The case revolved around a Louisiana law that provided for separate railroad cars for African Americans. The decision resulted in decades of segregation in the South as a result of permitting the doctrine of "Separate but Equal". The callous justification[49] for this egregious practice is captured in Exhibit 37 which comes from the Opinion of the Court.

When the decision was read, Peter Canellos described how[50]: "*If Zeus had hurled a lightning bolt into the Old Senate Chamber that Monday, May 18, he could not have rained more fire on the Supreme Court's majority than John Harlan did.*" Justice Harlan felt that the case violated all of the rights for African Americans that had been created and protected by the 13th, 14th, and 15th Amendments to the Constitution. Exhibit 38 shows a key part of Justice Harlan's dissent.

---

48 Plessy v. Ferguson, 163 U.S. 537. 559 (1896)

49 Plessy v. Ferguson, 163 U.S. 537. 551 (1896)

50 Canellos, Peter S. *The Great Dissenter – The Story of John Marshall Harlan, America's Judicial Hero.* Simon and Schuster, 2021, New York, New York, page 345

Exhibit 37 - Opinion of the Court's Justification, Plessy v. Ferguson

We consider the underlying fallacy of the plaintiff's argument to consist in the assumption that the enforced separation of the two races stamps the colored race with a badge of inferiority. If this be so, it is not by reason of anything found in the act, but solely because the colored race chooses to put that construction upon it.

Exhibit 38 - Justice Harlan Predictions in Dissent, Plessy v. Ferguson

The present decision, it may well be apprehended, will not only stimulate aggressions, more or less brutal and irritating, upon the admitted rights of colored citizens, but will encourage the belief that it is possible, by means of state enactments, to defeat the beneficent purposes which the people of the United States had in view when they adopted the recent amendments of the Constitution, by one of which the blacks of this country were made citizens of the United States and of the States in which they respectively reside, and whose privileges and immunities, as citizens, the States are forbidden to abridge.

As in his Opinion in the Civil Rights Cases, Justice Harlan clearly saw the "Separate but Equal" doctrine as violating the privileges and immunities of African Americans citizens. The simple Nationwide Privileges and Immunities of citizens recognized by Chief Justice Taney in the *Dred Scott* decision were now being kept from African Americans once they had been granted citizenship by the 14th Amendment. In the Statement of the Case for the Supreme Court, the description[51] contained: "*That petitioner was a citizen of the United States and a resident of the State of Louisiana, of mixed descent, in the proportion of seven eighths Caucasian and one eighth African blood; that the mixture of colored blood was not discernible in him, and that he was entitled to every recognition, right, privilege and immunity secured to the citizens of the United States of the white race by its Constitution and laws;*". As in the *Civil Rights Cases(1883)*, the *Plessy v. Ferguson* suit was written in a very general way. By not focusing on specific Nationwide privileges and immunities that were violated, the Opinion of the Court came down to permitting a State to exercise its inherent police powers to maintain order. Poorly written questions posed to the Supreme Court were a perennial problem that can be seen by reviewing all of the Supreme Court cases until 1900.

Summary of Cases from 1873-1899

Appendix 25 shows Supreme Court decisions between the Slaughterhouse Cases and 1900 that are related to Privileges and Immunities in some manner. Legal references and key pieces of the opinion text are shown in the Appendix. The proposed Nationwide Privilege and Immu-

51 Plessy v. Ferguson, 163 U.S. 537. 538 (1896) - Statement of the Case

nity is an interpretation based upon the Statement of the Case. Shockingly, out of the 31 cases shown in Table 14, only the two cases of *Ex Parte Yarbrough(1884)*, and *Blake v. McClung(1899)* were positively decided based upon Nationwide Privileges and Immunities. Other cases helped to refine the Supreme Court's views of Privileges and Immunities. Still others, such as *Strauder v. West Virginia(1880)*, provided the right for African Americans to be on juries using the Equal Protection Clause of the 14th Amendment. In the next chapter, we shall see that the success rate for suits based on violations of privilege and immunities were similarly stark after 1900.

Table 14 - Summary of Supreme Court Decisions, 1873-1899 (Appx. 25)

Supreme Court Case	Year	Nationwide right discussed in the Opinion	Opinion decision regarding Possible Privileges and Immunities Protection
Bradwell v. State	1873	Right for a woman to practice law in any state	Not a Nationwide Privilege and Immunity
Bartemeyer v. Iowa	1874	Right to sell liquor that was owned before 1860 even though Iowa outlawed sales in 1860	Not a Nationwide Privilege and Immunity
Minor v. Happersett	1874	Right for women citizens to vote	Not a Nationwide Privilege and Immunity. The 19th Amendment created a new Nationwide Privilege and Immunity
Walker v. Sauvinet	1876	Right to a trial by jury for civil suits in state courts	Not a Nationwide Privilege and Immunity
United States v. Reese	1876	Right for an African American to have his vote counted at the voting booth	Reaffirmed Nationwide Privilege and Immunity from Slaughterhouse Cases to be exempt from discrimination in voting on account of race.
United States v. Cruikshank	1876	Right for federal protection against heinous criminal acts performed by individuals	Reaffirmed Nationwide Privilege and Immunity for assembly and redress of grievances

Supreme Court Case	Year	Nationwide right discussed in the Opinion	Opinion decision regarding Possible Privileges and Immunities Protection
Hall v. DeCuir	1877	Right for African Americans to travel in the same ship cabins with white passengers	Interstate Commerce Clause based decision
Strauder v. West Virginia	1880	Right for African Americans to be on juries	Right Acknowledged based on Equal Protection Terms
Kirtland v. Hotchkiss	1880	Right for a resident of one state to avoid paying taxes upon a debt from a person of another state, and specifically upon real estate located in another state.	Not a Nationwide Privilege and Immunity
United States v. Harris	1883	Right to federal protection against criminal acts performed by individuals	Not a Nationwide Privilege and Immunity
The Civil Rights Cases	1883	Right for African Americans to be customers of all hotels, theatres and railroads on the same terms as white customers	Missed opportunity to determine based on the Nationwide Privilege and Immunities
Hurtado v. California	1884	Right to require indictment by a grand jury for state murder charges	Could have been decided as being a Nationwide Privilege and Immunity to require grand jury indictments for murder. (Discussion in Chapter 6)
Ex Parte Yarbrough	1884	Right for an African American to vote for a member of Congress without being attacked to stop him from voting	Nationwide Privilege and Immunity against discrimination from voting on account of race upheld
Presser v. Illinois	1886	Right to parade and drill non state sponsored militia units	Not a Nationwide Privilege and Immunity

Supreme Court Case	Year	Nationwide right discussed in the Opinion	Opinion decision regarding Possible Privileges and Immunities Protection
Mahon v. Justice	1888	Right for a fugitive not to be abducted from one state and removed to another state that has an indictment for them, unless it is done through a writ of habeas corpus.	Not a Nationwide Privilege and Immunity
Cole v. Cunningham	1890	Right to file suits in other states to assert legal rights for a bankruptcy and have those decisions respected in your state	Right Acknowledged based on Full Faith and Credit Clause of Constitution
In re. Kemmler	1890	Right not to be executed in the electric chair since it is cruel and unusual punishment	Not a Nationwide Privilege and Immunity
Crowley v. Christensen	1890	Right to a liquor license to sell alcohol	Not a Nationwide Privilege and Immunity
McElvaine v. Brush	1891	Right not to be held in solitary confinement when waiting for execution	Not a Nationwide Privilege and Immunity
O'Neil v. Vermont	1892	Right against cruel and unusual punishment	Could have been decided based upon Nationwide Privilege and Immunity against cruel and unusual punishment (Discussion in Chapter 6)
McPherson v. Blacker	1892	Right to choose Presidential electors by popular vote	Not a Nationwide Privilege and Immunity
Giozza v. Tiernan	1893	Right to sell intoxicating liquors	Not a Nationwide Privilege and Immunity
Duncan v. Missouri	1894	Right for the United States Supreme Court to rule that a State's Constitutional Amendment changing the structure of the States Supreme Court is an Ex Post Facto violation.	Thrown out on procedural grounds

Supreme Court Case	Year	Nationwide right discussed in the Opinion	Opinion decision regarding Possible Privileges and Immunities Protection
Miller v. Texas	1894	{Desperate final appeal after a murder conviction that argued 2nd, 4th, 5th and 14th Amendment violations during the arrest for the first time. The arguments were not made in the trial court for Supreme Court review}	Thrown out on procedural grounds
In re Lockwood	1894	Right for a woman to be considered a person under Virginia law which would permit her to practice law in the state of Virginia.	Left to states to determine the meaning of "person"
Iowa Central Ry. v. Iowa	1896	Right to specific legal processes in state courts	Not a Nationwide Privilege and Immunity
Plessy v. Ferguson	1896	Right for an African American to travel in any railcar that whites can travel in	Missed opportunity to determine based on the Nationwide Privilege and Immunities
Holden v. Hardy	1898	Right to work longer hours in an underground mine than state law allows	Not a Nationwide Privilege and Immunity
Blake v. McClung	1899	Right for out-of-state creditors of a bankrupt company to be treated equally with in-state creditors	Right Upheld based on Nationwide Privilege and Immunity
Orient Insurance Co. v. Daggs	1899	Right for an insurance company to limit its liability to actual damages caused by a fire	Corporations are not entitled to Nationwide Privileges and Immunities
Cumming v. Board of Education	1899	Right to have equal education spending for African American kids as for white kids	Not a Nationwide Privilege and Immunity

Chapter 6

Confusion and Forgetfulness

(1900-2025)

Have you ever seen a joke book with a title regarding a serious subject, and then every page of the book is left blank? This sort of a novelty book could almost be used to describe the history of the Privileges and Immunities Clause over the last 125 years. Chief Justice Rehnquist referred to[1] "*the previously dormant Privileges or Immunities Clause of the Fourteenth Amendment*" in his dissent in *Saenz v. Roe(1999)*. In the same case, Justice Thomas in his dissent said[2]: *"I believe that the demise of the Privileges or Immunities Clause has contributed in no small part to the current disarray of our Fourteenth Amendment jurisprudence"*. The views of Chief Justice Rehnquist and Justice Thomas are very reasonable when only the final results of Supreme Court cases are analyzed. Interestingly though, there are valuable nuggets of information in various decisions that can help to resurrect the correct usage of this key Constitutional provision.

Protection of Key Legal Rights for Criminal Prosecutions

Late in the 1800's and early in the 1900's, a group of four Supreme Court cases discussed whether key legal Constitutional criminal protections in the *Bill of Rights* applied to the states. After the case of *Barron v. Baltimore*(1833), the default position of the Supreme Court became

1 Saenz v. Roe, 526 U.S. 489, 511 (1999) – Chief Justice Rehnquist Dissent

2 Saenz v. Roe, 526 U.S. 489, 527-528 (1999) – Justice Thomas Dissent

that none of the *Bill of Rights* applied to the states. Remembering back to Chapter 3, half of the states didn't think any Constitutional Amendments were necessary during the Constitutional ratification process. States had been strong and virtually sovereign nations under the Articles of Confederation. Those who were not requesting Constitutional amendments could have been confident that their own states would never impinge upon their fundamental rights. With the years of experience under the Articles of Confederation, they could also be confident that the Privileges and Immunities clause of the Constitution would protect them when traveling to other states.

Reflecting back on Chapter 3, there were many more recommended Constitutional Amendments than were accepted. The most successful states were Virginia with 55% accepted and New Hampshire with 50% accepted. The least successful states were South Carolina with 25% and New York with 25% accepted. This shows a high level of discernment by all of the States when approving the *Bill of Rights*. Many of the protections in the *Bill of Rights* had been kingdom wide rules under the English monarchy. They had been extracted from English Monarchs through the *Magna Carta*, the *Petition of Right*, the *Habeus Corpus Act,* and the *English Bill of Rights.* These were discussed in detail in Chapter 1, and in Appendices 1-4. In fairness to the Supreme Court of over a century ago, it is possible that they did not have easy access to the English rights that existed over 100 years prior to their time when our country was formed. Table 15 shows the four decisions that will be described in more detail. These include the author of the key dissent in each case that discusses Privileges and Immunities. The final case of *Twining v. New Jersey(1908)* had the loosest connection to a prior English right, but if will be shown that the Supreme Court's decision to exclude this right had many other problems.

The first of the four cases was *Hurtado v. California(1884)* that pertained to the right to be indicted by a Grand Jury for murder charges. The *Petition of Right* has extensive discussions about Due Process of Law as shown in Appendix 2. Remembering back to Chapter 3, it was discussed how the risk of a traveler or merchant being charged with a crime, and especially a capital crime, was very dangerous. If a single individual could do that, the risk of abuse by an authoritarian could destroy an innocent man's life. With respect to Grand Jury's, the grievance text asso-

Table 15 - Key Criminal Prosecution Supreme Court Decisions (1880-1910)

Supreme Court Case	Year	Fundamental Right	Key Dissent	Prior Historical Privileges and Immunity Reference
Hurtado v. California	1884	right to be indicted by a Grand Jury for state murder charges	Harlan	Petition of Rights - PR2, PR4 described in Chapter 1 and Appx. 2
O'Neil v. Vermont	1892	right against cruel and unusual pun-ishment by state charges	Field	English Bill of Rights - EBR12, EBR13 described in Chapter 1 and Appx. 4.
Maxwell v. Dow	1900	right to be tried by a jury of 12 people in state trials	Harlan	English Bill of Rights - EBR10, described in Chapter 1 and Appx. 4
Twining v. New Jersey	1908	right against self-in-crimination in state trials	Harlan	English Common Law (according to the Opinion of the Court)

ciated with the Petition of Right (PR2 in Appendix 2) can be said to imply a Grand Jury for murder charges when it said "*That no Freeman may be taken or imprisoned or be disseised of his Freehold or Liberties or his free Customs or be outlawed or exiled or in any manner destroyed, but by the lawful Judgment of his Peers or by the Law of the Land.*" The fact that the sentence says that "*no Freeman may be taken or imprisoned... but by the lawful Judgement of his Peers*" implies the operation of a Grand Jury; especially for murder charges.

In a shocking explanation in the Opinion of the Court for why this right should not apply to states, Justice Matthews said[3] : "*But to hold that such a characteristic is essential to due process of law, would be to deny every quality of the law but its age, and to render it incapable of progress or improvement.*" Justice Matthews is saying that we shouldn't recognize this as a Constitutional right because it would be too difficult to change later. He then goes on to describe a practice in England from the 1100's where the punishment could involve losing your foot or your hand

3 Hurtado v. California110 U.S. 516, 529 (1884), Opinion of the Court

Exhibit 39 - Justice Harlan's Grand Jury Dissent, Hurtado v. California

So that the court, in this ease, while conceding that the requirement of due process of law protects the fundamental principles of liberty and justice, adjudges, in effect, that an immunity or right, recognized at the common law to be essential to personal security, jealously guarded by our national Constitution against violation by any tribunal or body exercising authority under the general government, and expressly or impliedly recognized, when the Fourteenth Amendment was adopted, in the Bill of Rights or Constitution of every State in the Union, is, yet, not a fundamental principle in governments established, as those of the States of the Union are, to secure to the citizen liberty and justice...

as a justification for wanting a flexible law[4] . It appears very contorted to argue that since extreme punishments existed over 800 years before, that justifies eliminating a key protection for a criminal defendant. Justice Harlan described this feeling in his dissent that is shown[5] in Exhibit 39. The issue of cruel punishments that Justice Matthews worried about in *Hurtado v. California* would be the concern of one justice in another case revolving around selling alcohol across state lines.

A Nationwide Privilege and Immunity regarding Cruel and Unusual Punishment was discussed by Justice Field in *O'Neil v. Vermont(1884).* He could not believe that the State Courts in Vermont, including its Supreme Court, had approved a sentence of almost 80 years for a New York man charged with illegally selling and shipping alcohol into Vermont. Reading the Supreme Court case, the issue was that the man was convicted of 457 distinct offenses. His punishment was then calculated based upon that fact. Justice Field expressed his disdain for the Opinion of the Court in his Dissent shown[6] in Exhibit 40.

---

4 Hurtado v. California110 U.S. 516, 529 (1884), Justice Matthews Opinion of the Court related the following English Law from 1176 - "if any one is accused before the justices of our Lord the King of murder, or theft, or robbery, or of harbouring persons committing those crimes, or of forgery or arson, by the oath-of twelve knights of the hundred, or, if there are no knights, by the oath of twelve free and lawful men, and by the oath of four men from each township of the hundred, let him go to the ordeal of water, and, if he fails, let him lose one foot. And at Northampton it was added, for greater strictness of justice (pro rigore justitice), that he shall lose his right hand at the same time with his foot, and abjure the realm and exile himself from the realm within forty days."

5 Hurtado v. California, 110 U.S. 516, 557-558 (1884), Justice Harlan Dissent

6 O'Neil v. Vermont, 144 U.S. 323, 338 (1892), Justice Field Dissent

Exhibit 40 - Justice Field's Punishment Dissent, O'Neil v. Vermont

The punishment imposed was one exceeding in severity, considering the offences of which the defendant was convicted, … he was convicted of four hundred and fifty-seven distinct offences, and sentenced to pay to the treasurer of the State a fine of $9140 and the costs of prosecution taxed at $472.96, and be confined at hard labor in the house of correction in the county of Rutland for one month, and, in case the fine and costs should not be paid on or before the expiration of this month's imprisonment, to be confined there at hard labor for the further term of twenty-eight thousand eight hundred and thirty-six days, to be computed from the expiration of the month's imprisonment. This was more than seventy-nine years for selling, furnishing and giving away, as alleged, intoxicating liquor, which took place in New York, to be delivered in Vermont.

The protection against Cruel and Unusual Punishment had been recognized in the *English Bill of Rights* in 1688. In Appendix 4, EBR11-EBR13 protect against excessive bail, excessive fines, and cruel and unusual punishment. These Nationwide English rights preceded the United States Constitution by over 100 years. They should have been automatically recognized by the Supreme Court as being Nationwide Privileges and Immunities. The right of States to manage their own affairs has limits, as further re-emphasized by the Privileges and Immunities clause of the 14th Amendment.

The next case regarding criminal prosecution was *Maxwell v. Dow(1900)*. The state of Utah had achieved statehood only four years earlier in 1896. In criminal cases including murder, Utah chose to use a jury of 8 jurors instead of 12. The *English Bill of Rights* (Appx. 4 -EBR10) described the grievance that: "*And whereas of late years Partial, Corrupt and Unqualified Persons have been returned and served on Juries in Trials and particularly diverse Jurors in Trials for High Treason which were not Freeholders,*" . It is hard to explain the use of "Partial" in this sentence without meaning that a partial jury was empaneled. These Nationwide English Rights preceded the United States Constitution by over 100 years, and the United States of America had already existed for over 100 years when this case arose. When a young state is setting up its legal system, this is the perfect time for the United States Supreme Court to correct any issues. Instead of acknowledging a Privilege and Immunity that had existed for hundreds of years, the United States Supreme Court focused on the 14th Amendment and the Due Process Clause. In his dissent in

Exhibit 41 - Justice Harlan Dissent on Jury Sizes, Maxwell v. Dow

For if prior to the adoption of the Fourteenth Amendment it was one of the privileges or immunities of citizens of the United States that they should not be tried for crime in any court organized or existing under National authority except by a jury composed of twelve persons, how can it be that a citizen of the United States may be now tried in a state court for crime, particularly for an infamous crime, by eight jurors, when that amendment expressly declares that "no State shall make or enforce any law which shall abridge the privileges or immunities of citizens of the United States"? It does not meet the case to say that a trial by eight jurors is as much a trial by jury as if there were twelve jurors; for if a citizen charged with crime can be subjected to trial by a less number of jurors than that prescribed by the Constitution, the number may be reduced to three.

the case, Justice Harlan explained the slippery slope that would happen if this were permitted. As Justice Harlan said[7] in Exhibit 41, once you allow 8 jurors, then why not three?

The final case in this quartet of Supreme Court decisions was *Twining v. New Jersey(1908).* This case involved self-incrimination, or what most people think of as "pleading the fifth amendment". At the time of the case, according to the Opinion of the Court, one question was whether this was part of "due process" that was now protected by the 14th Amendment against state infringement. The court took an extremely conservative approach by declaring that since the specific phrase "*nor shall be compelled in any criminal case to be a witness against himself*" was not copied over from the 5th Amendment to the 14th Amendment's Due Process Clause, it was presumed to be intentionally left out. Then, Justice Moody makes a Catch-22 declaration shown[8] in Exhibit 42 in the Opinion of the Court. He is saying that since this Nationwide Privilege was not listed in the original Constitution prior to the *Bill of Rights*, it was not a Nationwide Privilege. Chapter 1 and a myriad of Supreme Court Cases have explained the rationale for not listing Nationwide Privileges and Immunities explicitly.

In another shocking declaration in Justice Moody's Opinion of the Court, he confirms that this was settled in English law, but that did

7 Maxwell v. Dow, 176 U.S. 581, 612 (1900) – Justice Harlan Dissent

8 Twining v. New Jersey, 211 U.S. 78, 92 (1908) - Justice Moody Opinion of the Court

Exhibit 42 - Historical Analysis by Justice Moody, Twining v. New Jersey

The privilege was not included in the Federal Constitution as originally adopted, but was placed in one of the ten Amendments which were recommended to the States by the first Congress, and by them adopted. Since then all the States of the Union have, from time to time, with varying form but uniform meaning, included the privilege in their constitutions, except the States of New Jersey and Iowa, and in those States it is held to be part of the existing law.

not make it an essential part of due process of law. He then goes on to declare[9] that to if that were done, it would put a straitjacket on American jurisprudence in Exhibit 43.

Even worse, was Justice Moody's discussion of the founding[10] of the Constitution. He noted that only four of the seven states that recommended amendments to the Constitution included the right against self-incrimination. These were discussed in Chapter 3, and the actual proposals are included in Appendices 11-17. Absence of a proposed amendment is meaningless if the states thought that the right was already covered by the Privileges and Immunities clause. Justice Moody used the fact that only four of thirteen colonies requested an amendment regarding self-incrimination to justify not applying this privilege to the states. Continuing his reputation as a dissenter, Justice Harlan made a commonsense argument regarding this privilege. Exhibit 44 shows how he reflected back upon how a courtroom at the time of the American

9 Twining v. New Jersey, 211 U.S. 78, 101 (1908) – Justice Moody Opinion of the Court

10 Twining v. New Jersey, 211 U.S. 78, 109 (1908) – Opinion of the Court, Justice Moody, "Thus it appears that four only of the thirteen original States insisted upon incorporating the privilege in the Constitution, and they separately and simultaneously with the requirement of due process of law, and that three States proposing amendments were silent upon this subject."

Exhibit 43 - Extreme Limitation by Justice Moody, Twining v. New Jersey

It does not follow, however, that a procedure settled in English law at the time of the emigration, and brought to this country and practiced by our ancestors, is an essential element of due process of law. If that were so the procedure of the first half of the seventeenth century would be fastened upon the American jurisprudence like a straightjacket, only to be unloosed by constitutional amendment.

Exhibit 44 - Justice Harlan's Dissent, Twining v. New Jersey

> Can there be any doubt that at the opening of the War of Independence the people of the colonies claimed as one of their birthrights the privilege of immunity from self-incrimination? This question can be answered in but one way. If at the beginning of the Revolutionary War any lawyer had claimed that one accused of crime, could lawfully be compelled to testify against himself, he would have been laughed at by his brethren of the bar, both in England and America.

Revolution would have viewed this question.

As opposed to the missed opportunities that the Supreme Court had to clarify Nationwide Privileges and Immunities in the criminal cases above, it managed to discover novel rights in the years to come. Switching from the realm of criminal law to taxation, the Supreme Court went on to identify a taxation right as a Nationwide Privilege and Immunity. The following description of the case of *Colgate v. Harvey(1935)* will explain how this error was quickly overruled five years later in *Madden v. Kentucky(1940)*. Even in the case of such an opinion and its overturning, there are important facts that can be learned.

Privilege and Immunity Misidentification, *Colgate v. Harvey(1935)*

In the middle of the Great Depression, people were looking for any way to generate income. The same could be said for the states. In the case of *Colgate v. Harvey(1935)*, Justice Sutherland "discovered" a Nationwide Privilege and Immunity. This Supreme Court case was decided by a 6-3 vote. The case revolved around a state's ability to tax its citizens. The complaint was that the state of Vermont charged different taxes on interest earned from out-of-state investments versus in-state investments. Justice Sutherland determined that this discriminatory tax violated Nationwide Privileges and Immunities as shown[11] in Exhibit 45.

In his dissent, Justice Stone summarized why this should not be considered a Nationwide Privilege and Immunity. Many of the cases that reached the Supreme Court charged violations of multiple parts of the 14th Amendment including the Privileges and Immunity Clause. This

---

11 Colgate v. Harvey, 296 U.S. 404, 433 (1935) – Justice Sutherland Opinion of the Court

Exhibit 45 - Justice Sutherland's Discriminatory Taxes, Colgate v. Harvey

The statute, as here applied, says that if a citizen resident in Vermont loan his money at 5% or less in another state, he must pay a tax upon the income; but if he loan money in Vermont at the same rate, no tax whatever shall be imposed. The power to tax income here asserted by Vermont is, in the final analysis, the power to tax so heavily as to preclude loans outside the state altogether. It reasonably is not open to doubt that the discriminatory tax here imposed abridges the privilege of a citizen of the United States to loan his money and make contracts with respect thereto in any part of the United States.

Exhibit 46 - Justice Stone's Dissenting Argument, Colgate v. Harvey

We are thus returned to the point of beginning, to a discussion of the question whether the exemption in the present tax is so unreasonable, so without support of a permissible state policy, as to infringe constitutional limitations. If the exemption does not merit condemnation as a denial of the equal protection which the Fourteenth Amendment extends to every person, nothing can be added to the vehemence or effectiveness of the denunciation by invoking the command of the privileges and immunities clause.

was the case as described[12] by Justice Stone in Exhibit 46.

Only five years after the *Colgate v. Harvey(1935)* decision, it was overturned in *Madden v. Kentucky(1940)*. That decision explained the same concepts of State Level Privileges and Immunities that had been originally declared in the *Slaughterhouse Cases(1873)*. In that case, Justice Miller had ruled that States had a large amount of power over trade and business. The Opinion of the Court in *Madden v. Kentucky* explains this concept very well as shown[13] in Exhibit 47.

While the Supreme Court was cleaning up the case of Colgate v. Harvey(1935), it missed major opportunities to acknowledge Nationwide Privileges and Immunities that had preceded the founding of the country. Those rights involved assembly, speech, the press, and the right to hand out literature. A major issue that confronted the Supreme Court was that Privileges and Immunities only apply to citizens.

---

12 Colgate v. Harvey, 296 U.S. 404, 450 (1935) – Justice Stone dissent

13 Madden v. Kentucky, 309 U.S. 83, 92-93 (1940) - Opinion of the Court

Exhibit 47 - State Privileges and Immunities, Madden v. Kentucky

...We think it quite clear that the right to carry out an incident to a trade, business or calling such as the deposit of money in banks is not a privilege of national citizenship.

In the states, there reposes the sovereignty to manage their own affairs except only as the requirements of the Constitution otherwise provide. Within these constitutional limits the power of the state over taxation is plenary. An interpretation of the privileges and immunities clause which restricts the power of the states to manage their own fiscal affairs is a matter of gravest concern to them. It is only the emphatic requirements of the Constitution which properly may lead the federal courts to such a conclusion.

Privileges and Immunities based on Legal Status in the United States

For self-preservation and safety reasons, the United States has a strong impetus to protect its form of government and its citizens. The Constitution vests Congress with the power "*To establish an uniform Rule of Naturalization*" in Article I, Section 8. This corrected a serious problem with the Articles of Confederation where each state created its own immigration policies. Over the centuries, Congress has passed various immigration and naturalization laws to describe how non-citizens could become lawful permanent residents of our country and then have the chance to become citizens.

According to the US Citizenship and Information Services website[14], in 1940, the *Alien Registration Act* required all aliens to register with the United States government. Starting in 1951, aliens who could prove their legal permanent residence in the United States were provided with what colloquially become known as a "Green Card". Permanent Resident Green Card holders have the ability to move towards citizenship; but they have a number of requirements that they must scrupulously follow. Permanent Residents are "*Required to obey all laws of the United States and localities;*". They are "*Required to file your income tax returns*". They are "*Expected to support the democratic form of government*".

14 United States Department of Homeland Security, U.S. Citizenship and Immigration Services, *The Colorful History of the Green Card.* (2026, Feb. 23). https://www.uscis.gov/about-us/our-history/stories-from-the-archives/the-colorful-history-of-the-green-card

Finally, the are "*Required to register with the Selective Service, if you are a male age 18 through 25*".

As long as Permanent Residents follow those rules, they are entitled to "*Live permanently in the United States provided you do not commit any actions that would make you removable under Immigration law*". They are also allowed to "*Work in the United States at any legal work of your qualification and choosing.*" Finally, they will "*Be protected by all laws of the United States, your state of residence and local jurisdictions*". While Permanent Residents are permitted to contribute to federal election campaigns, they are not able to vote in federal, state or local elections. People who are on temporary work visas, or who have other immigration statuses, have much fewer rights than Permanent Residents. They can be issued a final removal order by an Immigration Judge for violating their Visa terms, or as a result of their immigration status.

Another question of rights pertains to corporations. In Chapter 5, the Paul v. Virginia(1869) case clearly established that corporations do not have the privileges and immunities of citizens. Corporations are established under the laws of a state where they are incorporated. They have limitations on election campaign financing and obviously do not have the right to vote. While corporations do not have all of the rights of United States citizens, they are not subject to deportation to another country. Figure 17 provides a comparative diagram of the relative rights for people and corporations in the United States. The differences in rights

Figure 17 - Relative Rights of People and Corporations in the United States

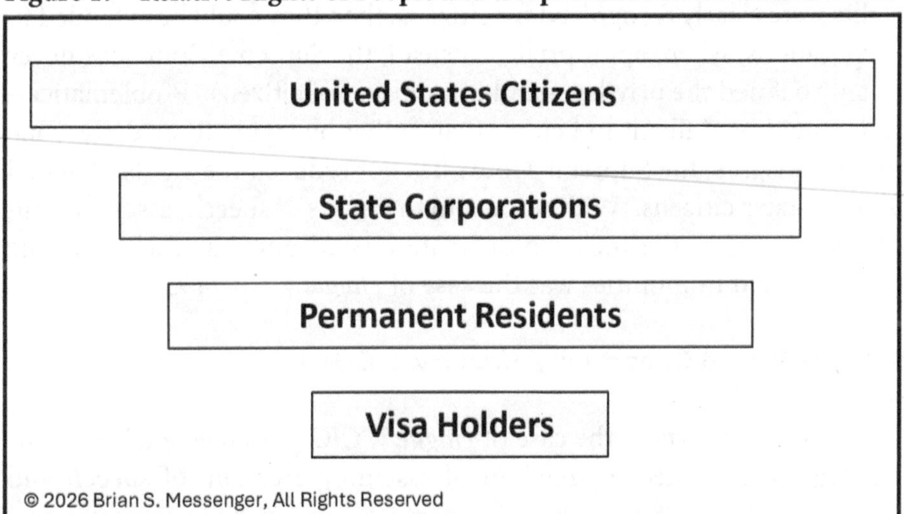

shown in Figure 17 have contributed to the 3rd Butterfly Affect for the Privileges and Immunities Clause.

The Third Privileges and Immunities Butterfly Effect

In the world of Real Estate, the famous maxim is that the three most important criteria are location, location and location. The positioning of the Privileges or Immunities Clause in the 14th Amendment was literally front and center. Due to this prime location, most lawsuits that reached the Supreme Court over the decades after the 14th Amendment included privileges and immunity claims in addition to due process violation claims and/or equal protection violation claims. In a perverse sense, this prime location created a multitude of confused and frivolous claims that have virtually destroyed the understanding and usage of our Nationwide Privileges and Immunities.

The second part of this butterfly effect is that privileges and immunities only apply to United States citizens. Many lawsuits that reach the Supreme Court are by corporations, and in order to garner them similar rights as those possessed by citizens, either the due process clause or the equal protection clause were employed by the Supreme Court. In hindsight, the Supreme Court could have started with the privileges and immunities of citizens as being the "gold standard" of rights. If laws targeted individuals, everyone would benefit if they were struck down since they infringed on the privileges and immunities of citizens. Once rights were clearly recognized for citizens, then they could be extended to corporations, where appropriate. Instead, the Supreme Court has never cleanly defined the privileges and immunities of citizens. Problematically, it would be difficult to believe that in that by trying to give everyone the same rights, the Supreme Court has not reduced the rights of actual United States citizens. With respect to the rights of speech, assembly and the press, one of the most unfortunate missed opportunities to define privileges and immunities was the case of *Hague v. CIO(1939).*

A Major Missed Opportunity, *Hague v. CIO(1939)*

On the surface, the case of *Hague v. CIO* presented a fairly clean-cut argument related to freedom of assembly, freedom of speech and freedom of the press. The CIO (Committee for Industrial Organization) was a powerful federation of labor unions in the 1930s, and is presently part of the AFL-CIO which is the largest federation of labor unions in our country. Justice Owen Roberts described in his Opinion how the CIO wanted to have peaceful assemblies in Jersey City, New Jersey to speak and handout literature to discuss the National Labor Relations Act. The Mayor, named Hague, was enforcing a city law that banned handing out printed material and holding public meetings without permits on streets or in other public places. The problem was that the city could refuse permits if they didn't like the organization. After determining that some of the litigants were individual citizens, and not the CIO itself, Justice Owen Roberts proposed that the law was a clear violation of their privileges and immunities. Table 16 shows the breakdown of the Opinions in this case.

Justices Roberts and Black believed that the city regulation was a clear violation of Nationwide Privileges and Immunities. Justice Roberts

Table 16 - Justices Positions in Hague v. CIO

Supreme Court Justice	Opinion	Notes
Owen Roberts	Roberts	Opinion that this was a Privileges and Immunities Violation
Hugo Black	Roberts	Opinion that this was a Privileges and Immunities Violation
Harlan Stone	Stone	Opinion that the Best Precedent was a Due Process Clause Violation of 14th Amendment
Stanley Reed	Stone	Opinion that the Best Precedent was a Due Process Clause Violation of 14th Amendment
Charles Hughes	Roberts/ Stone	Opinion that this was a Privileges and Immunities Violation but the record was not clear enough to decide on those grounds.
James McReynolds	McReynolds	Dissent arguing that this should have progressed through state courts first.
Pierce Butler	Butler	Dissent arguing that the local ordinance was not unconstitutional.
Felix Frankfurter		Did not Participate
William Douglas		Did not Participate

Exhibit 48 - Justice Roberts' Privileges and Immunities, Hague v. CIO

Wherever the title of streets and parks may rest, they have immemorially been held in trust for the use of the public and, time out of mind, have been used for purposes of assembly, communicating thoughts between citizens, and discussing public questions. Such use of the streets and public places has, from ancient times, been a part of the privileges, immunities, rights, and liberties of citizens. The privilege of a citizen of the United States to use the streets and parks for communication of views on national questions may be regulated in the interest of all; it is not absolute, but relative, and must be exercised in subordination to the general comfort and convenience, and in consonance with peace and good order; but it must not, in the guise of regulation, be abridged or denied.

described[15] how both the *Slaughterhouse Cases* and the *United States v. Cruikshank* decision supported the privilege to peaceably assemble and petition for a redress of grievances[16]. Justice Roberts' Opinion identified that this was a clear violation of Nationwide Privileges and Immunities in[17] Exhibit 48.

Chief Justice Hughes felt that the case was a clear violation of Nationwide Privileges and Immunities, but that the record was not clear enough[18]. Justice Stone and Justice Reed felt that the path of least resistance was to use the Due Process Clause of the 14th Amendment, as had

---

15 Hague v. CIO, 307 U.S. 496, 513 (1939) – Opinion of Justice Owen Roberts describing precedents: "In the Slaughter-House Cases it was said, 16 Wall. 79: "The right to peaceably assemble and petition for redress of grievances, the privilege of the writ of habeas corpus, are rights of the citizen guaranteed by the Federal Constitution."

16 Hague v. CIO, 307 U.S. 496, 516 (1939), Opinion of Justice Owen Roberts describing the problem with refusing permits: "It enables the Director of Safety to refuse a permit on his mere opinion that such refusal will prevent "riots, disturbances or disorderly assemblage." It can thus, as the record discloses, be made the instrument of arbitrary suppression of free expression of views on national affairs, for the prohibition of all speaking will undoubtedly "prevent" such eventualities."

17 Hague v. CIO, 307 U.S. 496, 519 (1939), Opinion of Justice Owen Roberts

18 Hague v. CIO, 307 U.S. 496, 532 (1939) – Chief Justice Hughes Concurrence – "With respect to the merits I agree with the opinion of MR. JUSTICE ROBERTS and in the affirmance of the judgment as modified. With respect to the point as to jurisdiction I agree with what is said in the opinion of MR. JUSTICE ROBERTS as to the right to discuss the National Labor Relations Act being a privilege of a citizen of the United States, but I am not satisfied that the record adequately supports the resting of jurisdiction upon that ground. As to that matter, I concur in the opinion of MR. JUSTICE STONE.

Exhibit 49 - Justice Stone's Due Process Clause Fallback, Hague v. CIO

It has been explicitly and repeatedly affirmed by this Court, without a dissenting voice, that freedom of speech and of assembly for any lawful purpose are rights of personal liberty secured to all persons, without regard to citizenship, by the due process clause of the Fourteenth Amendment. Gitlow v. New York, 268 U. S. 652; Whitney v. California, 274 U. S. 357; Fiske v. Kansas, 274 U. S. 380; Stromberg v. California, 283 U. S. 359; Near v. Minnesota, 283 U. S. 697; Grosjean v. American Press Co., 297 U. S. 233; De Jonge v. Oregon, 299 U. S. 353; Herndon v. Lowry, 301 U. S. 242; Lovell v. Griffin, 303 U. S. 444.

been done in a series of cases. Justice Stone's Opinion discussed the lack of precedent[19] for the Privileges and Immunities Clause. Unfortunately, he did not address the precedents of *Dred Scott*, the *Slaughterhouse Cases*, and *United States v. Cruikshank* that all provided prior descriptions of these rights. Exhibit 49 shows[20] the cases that Justice Stone relied upon for his decision based on the Due Process Clause.

Reviewing Justice Stone's precedents, the first is the case of *Gitlow v. New York(1925)*. This case revolved around a person who[21] "*had advocated, advised and taught the duty, necessity and propriety of overthrowing and overturning organized government by force, violence and unlawful means,*". The defendants were members[22] of the Left Wing Section of the Socialist Party. This was a classic case where the question presented to the Supreme Court limited its opinion. The Opinion of the Court described[23] how "*The precise question presented, and the only question which we can consider under this writ of error, then is, whether the statute, as construed and applied in this case by the state courts, deprived the*

19 Hague v. CIO, 307 U.S. 496, 519 (1939) – Justice Stone's Opinion – "It has never been held that either is a privilege or immunity peculiar to citizenship of the United States, to which alone the privileges and immunities clause refers, Slaughter-House Cases, 16 Wall. 36; Duncan v. Missouri, 152 U. S. 377, 382; Twining v. New Jersey, 211 U. S. 78, 97; Maxwell v. Bugbee, 250 U. S. 525, 538; Hamilton v. Regents, 293 U. S. 245, 261, and neither can be brought within the protection of that clause without enlarging the category of privileges and immunities of United States citizenship as it has hitherto been defined.

20 Hague v. CIO, 307 U.S. 496, 519 (1939) – Justice Stone's Opinion

21 Gitlow v. New York, 268 U.S. 652, 655 (1925), Opinion of the Court

22 Gitlow v. New York, 268 U.S. 652, 655 (1925), Opinion of the Court

23 Gitlow v. New York, 268 U.S. 652, 664 (1925), Opinion of the Court

defendant of his liberty of expression in violation of the due process clause of the Fourteenth Amendment." This forced the Supreme Court's hand to analyze the Due Process Clause of the 14th Amendment. Exhibit 50 shows[24] how declarations and assumptions that the Supreme Court made ended up producing a precedent that lasts to this day.

The Supreme Court's assumption in Exhibit 50 helped to lead to the usage of the Due Process Clause of the 14th Amendment in later cases. Ironically, the law at issue in the case of *Gitlow v. New York* was found to be unconstitutional or misapplied in the case. One of the cases that *Gitlow v. New York* relied upon to describe the "liberty" portion of the Due Process Clause of the 14th Amendment was *Meyer v. Nebraska (1923)* where a key description is shown[25] in Exhibit 51.

The Supreme Court's approach is reminiscent of the saying that "if all you have is a hammer, everything looks like a nail". Appendix 26 shows Supreme Court cases from 1900 to the present that are related in some way to Privileges and Immunities. In the Criminal cases described earlier in this chapter, the Supreme Court was extremely parsimonious in identifying Nationwide Privileges and Immunities This was even in the presence of tremendous historical evidence. The only non-criminal case where it found a Nationwide Privilege and Immunity (Colgate v. Harvey) was overruled five years later.

The Due Process Clause of the 14th Amendment became the obvious means to protect specific rights. The problem is that its use in this

24 Gitlow v. New York, 268 U.S. 652, 666 (1925), Opinion of the Court

25 Meyer v. Nebraska, 262 U.S. 390, 399 (1923), Opinion of the Court

Exhibit 50 - Due Process Clause Protection, Gitlow v. New York

For present purposes we may and do assume that freedom of speech and of the press-which are protected by the First Amendment from abridgment by Congress are among the fundamental personal rights and "liberties" protected by the due process clause of the Fourteenth Amendment from impairment by the States. ...

It is a fundamental principle, long established, that the freedom of speech and of the press which is secured by the Constitution, does not confer an absolute right to speak or publish, without responsibility, whatever one may choose, or an unrestricted and unbridled license that gives immunity for every possible use of language and prevents the punishment of those who abuse this freedom.

Exhibit 51 - Due Process Liberty Definitions, Meyer v. Nebraska

While this Court has not attempted to define with exactness the liberty thus guaranteed, the term has received much consideration and some of the included things have been definitely stated. Without doubt, it denotes not merely freedom from bodily restraint but also the right of the individual to contract, to engage in any of the common occupations of life, to acquire useful knowledge, to marry, establish a home and bring up children, to worship God according to the dictates of his own conscience, and generally to enjoy those privileges long recognized at common law as essential to the orderly pursuit of happiness by free men.

manner is oxymoronic and circular in its reasoning. Virtually every law deprives citizens of liberty. When a law deprives a certain liberty, as long as the law is administered fairly, and the legal process is followed correctly, liberty is not being deprived without due process of law. More worrisomely, this approach allows a majority of the Supreme Court to ordain whatever "liberty" they want to protect at any given time. Instead, the Privileges and Immunities Clause should have been used to protect appropriate rights. Unfortunately, it was relegated to cases involving the right to travel between states. This was first seen in the case of *Edwards v. California*(1941) that involved transporting indigent people across state lines.

Freedom to Move Between States, *Edwards v. California(1941)*

The case of Edwards v. California required a review of the Articles of Confederation Privileges and Immunities Clause that was discussed in Chapter 2. The issue revolved around who was entitled to privileges and immunities. There had been an exception for "paupers, vagabonds, and fugitives from justice" that States who joined the Articles of Confederation did not want to be required to accept from other states. Over 150 years later, the United States had gone through a Great Depression in the 1930s, and unemployment was extremely high. It is only natural for workers, who may lose their jobs, to try to migrate to other states that may offer greater employment opportunities. California had a law[26] that made it a misdemeanor for anyone "*that brings or assists in bringing into the State any indigent person who is not a resident of the State, knowing*

26 Edwards v. California, 314 U.S. 160, 171 (1941), Opinion of the Court

him to be an indigent person,".

The situation that faced Edwards should be relatable to most married men. He drove from California to Texas to pick up his wife's brother to bring him back to California. When he got to Texas, he found that his brother-in-law was no longer working and had $20 left to his name. Arriving back in California with his brother-in-law, Edwards was charged and convicted of breaking the California law regarding transporting indigents. He was sentenced to six months in jail, and thankfully, the sentence was suspended[27] . When Edwards' case reached the Supreme Court, the Interstate Commerce Clause from Article 1, Section 8 of the Constitution was evaluated. Readers may be interested to know that[28] according to the Supreme Court: "*And it is settled beyond question that the transportation of persons is 'commerce,' within the meaning of that provision.*". The states powers according to the Opinion of the Court are explained as[29]: "*It is nevertheless true, that the States are not wholly precluded from exercising their police power in matters of local concern even though they may thereby affect interstate commerce*". Ultimately, the Supreme Court ruled that California's law violated the Interstate Commerce Clause with the statement[30]: "*The issue presented in this case, therefore, is whether the prohibition embodied in § 2615 against the 'bringing' or transportation of indigent persons into California is within the police power of that State. We think that it is not, and hold that it is an unconstitutional barrier to interstate commerce*".

After the Supreme Court disposed of the law using the Interstate Commerce Clause, it went on to evaluate the "paupers" exception. It reviewed a series of cases including the *Passenger Cases* that was discussed in Chapter 3. Ultimately, the Opinion of the Court by Justice Byrnes declared[31] : "*In none of these cases, however, was the power of a State to exclude 'paupers' actually involved. Whether an able-bodied but unemployed person like Duncan is a 'pauper' within the historical meaning of the term is open to considerable doubt.*" Supreme Court Justice William Douglas

---

27 Edwards v. California, 314 U.S. 160, 170-171 (1941) – Opinion of the Court description of the case.

28 Edwards v. California, 314 U.S. 160, 172 (1941) – Opinion of the Court

29 Edwards v. California, 314 U.S. 160, 172-173 (1941)– Opinion of the Court

30 Edwards v. California, 314 U.S. 160, 173 (1941) – Opinion of the Court

31 Edwards v. California, 314 U.S. 160, 177 (1941) – Opinion of the Court

wrote a concurring opinion that was joined by Justice Hugo Black and Justice Frank Murphy. It strongly argued that the right of free movement is a right of national citizenship and that it is unfair to stigmatize paupers since it would make them second class citizens. His feelings are shown[32] in Exhibit 52, and are similar to another concurring opinion by Justice Robert Jackson.

The case of Edwards v. California(1941) is important to provide perspective for two cases that would come later in the 1900's. In 1941, a majority of the court was not prepared to upend 164 years of legal precedent that indicated that "paupers" did not have the automatic privilege and immunity to move between states. States had police powers and budget concerns that provided reasonable concerns regarding being flooded with people who could not support themselves. By resolving this case using the Interstate Commerce Clause, the Supreme Court kicked the can down the road to the case of *Shapiro v. Thompson(1969).* In the intervening decades the Supreme Court and the country were busy with

32 Edwards v. California, 314 U.S. 160, 181 (1941) – Justice Douglas concurrence joined by Justice Black and Justice Murphy expressing National Privilege and Immunity to travel without "pauper" exclusion.

Exhibit 52 - Justice Douglas' Travel Privileges, Edwards v. California

The conclusion that the right of free movement is a right of national citizenship stands on firm historical ground. If a state tax on that movement, as in the CrandalI case, is invalid, a fortiori a state statute which obstructs or in substance prevents that movement must fall. That result necessarily follows unless perchance a State can curtail the right of free movement of those who are poor or destitute. But to allow such an exception to be engrafted on the rights of national citizenship would be to contravene every conception of national unity. It would also introduce a caste system utterly incompatible with the spirit of our system of government. It would permit those who were stigmatized by a State as indigents, paupers, or vagabonds to be relegated to an inferior class of citizenship. It would prevent a citizen because he was poor from seeking new horizons in other States. It might thus withhold from large segments of our people that mobility which is basic to any guarantee of freedom of opportunity. The result would be a substantial dilution of the rights of national citizenship, a serious impairment. of the principles of equality. Since the state statute here challenged involves such consequences, it runs afoul of the privileges and immunities clause of the Fourteenth Amendment.

helping to provide African Americans with full Civil Rights. This arduous process reversed the decades old decisions in the *Civil Rights Cases(1883)* and *Plessy v. Ferguson(1896)* amongst others.

Brown v. Board of Education(1954) and Key Decisions that followed

The unanimous decision in *Brown v. Board of Education(1954)* started a multi-decade long process to integrate schools throughout our country. In this case, the Equal Protection Clause of the 14th Amendment was used to highlight that[33] "*Separate educational facilities are inherently unequal*". Later, the Commerce Clause in Article 1, Section 8 of the Constitution was used with success in *Boynton v. Virginia(1960)* and *Hearts of Atlanta Motel v. United States(1964)* to start integrating restaurants and hotels with a tie to interstate commerce. The Supreme Court decision in *Katzenbach v. McClung(1964)* found that the Civil Rights Act of 1964 was Constitutional under Congress' powers under the Commerce Clause. Almost 100 years after Congress had unsuccessfully tried to regulate the behavior of Southern States in the Civil Rights Acts of the 1860s and 1870s, they were finally able to use alternative means to achieve the goal of full racial integration.

The *United States v. Cruikshank(1876)* case had left the federal government fairly powerless to protect African Americans in the south. This was due to the fact that police powers are inherently provided at the state level. In *United States v. Price(1966)*, also known as the "Mississippi Burning" case, the Supreme Court correctly ruled on a violation of the Due Process Clause of the 14th Amendment. The movie *Mississippi Burning(1988)* tells the awful story of the murder of the three civil rights activists addressed in this case. The victims were killed as a result of a conspiracy between local law enforcement and private individuals. Their lives were deprived due to an actual failure of due process of law. In the same year, the case of *United States v. Guest(1966)* declared that it was a violation of the Equal Protection Clause of the 14th Amendment to falsely arrest and harass African Americans by claiming that they had committed crimes.

The subject of this book is Nationwide Privileges and Immunities, and it is not meant to provide a complete history of the Civil Rights

33 Brown v. Board of Education, 347 U.S. 483, 495 (1957)

era. Reflecting back upon Justice Harlan's dissents in the *Civil Rights Cases(1883)* and *Plessy v. Ferguson(1896)*, it is frustrating that the Privileges and Immunities Clause was not used to recognize the right for all American citizens to assemble together in public places operating under the authority, control, and power of the states; especially after the passage of the 14th Amendment. To add insult to injury, the Privileges and Immunities Clause usage was relegated to topics regarding welfare grants to people moving between states.

Privileges and Immunities and Welfare, *Shapiro v. Thompson(1969)*

In 1969, the case of Shapiro v. Thompson reached the Supreme Court. The United States had long recovered from the Great Depression and World War II. The economy was doing well, and the federal government and the states started to enhance the "safety net" for struggling Americans. The most altruistic and giving-minded states were at risk of creating a magnet that would attract poor people from other states. In order to cut down on this "magnetic attraction", Connecticut, Pennsylvania and the District of Columbia established a one-year waiting period to collect welfare benefits. Their waiting periods were allowed by Congressional legislation that helped to set up the joint federal and state implementation of benefits for the poor. In a very surprising 6-3 decision, the Supreme Court justified overturning these waiting periods. A major part of their justification involved the "right to travel" that originated with the Articles of Confederation discussed in Chapter 2. The Supreme Court's Opinion of the Court claimed that these laws discouraged the "right to travel" and were therefore unconstitutional as shown[34] in Exhibit 53.

Justice John Marshall Harlan (1899-1971) wrote a passionate dissent in this case, much like his grandfather's dissents in the *Civil Rights Cases(1883)* and *Plessy v. Ferguson(1896)*. He dissected the basis for the right to travel and how welfare residency did not significantly impact on this right. Exhibit 54 shows the key findings[35] of his dissent.

The Supreme Court decision in *Shapiro v. Thompson* indirectly relied upon the Privileges and Immunities Clause of the Constitution through the right to travel between states. It was very creative in applying

34 Shapiro v. Thompson, 383 U.S. 618, 629 (1969) – Opinion of the Court

35 Shapiro v. Thompson, 383 U.S. 618, 676 (1969) – Justice Harlan Dissent

Exhibit 53 - Right to Collect Welfare Benefits, Shapiro v. Thompson

We do not doubt that the one-year waiting-period device is well suited to discourage the influx of poor families in need of assistance. An indigent who desires to migrate, resettle, find a new job, and start a new life will doubtless hesitate if he knows that he must risk making the move without the possibility of falling back on state welfare assistance during his first year of residence, when his need may be most acute. But the purpose of inhibiting migration by needy persons into the State is constitutionally impermissible.

This Court long ago recognized that the nature of our Federal Union and our constitutional concepts of personal liberty unite to require that all citizens be free to travel throughout the length and breadth of our land uninhibited by statutes, rules, or regulations which unreasonably burden or restrict this movement.

Exhibit 54 - Justice Harlan's Dissent in Shapiro v. Thompson

Taking all of these competing considerations into account, I believe that the balance definitely favors constitutionality. In reaching that conclusion, I do not minimize the importance of the right to travel interstate. However, the impact of residence conditions upon that right is indirect and apparently quite insubstantial. On the other hand, the governmental purposes served by the requirements are legitimate and real, and the residence requirements are clearly suited to their accomplishment. To abolish residence requirements might well discourage highly worthwhile experimentation in the welfare field. The statutes come to us clothed with the authority of Congress and attended by a correspondingly heavy presumption of constitutionality.

the Equal Protection Clause of the 14th Amendment to Connecticut and Pennsylvania, but that wouldn't work for the District of Columbia which was not a state. The Opinion of the Court stated[36] that "*the Due Process Clause of the Fifth Amendment prohibits Congress from denying public assistance to poor persons otherwise eligible solely on the ground that they have not been residents of the District of Columbia for one year at the time their applications are filed.*" The Supreme Court relied upon the *Bolling v. Sharpe(1954)* decision that was released on the same day as *Brown v. Board of Education(1954)*. To deal with racial segregation in District of Columbia schools, Chief Justice Warren had made the declaration[37] in Exhibit 55.

---

36 Shapiro v. Thompson, 383 U.S. 618, 642 (1969) – Opinion of the Court

37 Bolling v. Sharpe, 347 U.S. 497, 499 (1954) - Opinion of the Court

Exhibit 55 - Discrimination and Due Process, Bolling v. Sharpe

The Fifth Amendment, which is applicable in the District of Columbia, does not contain an equal protection clause as does the Fourteenth Amendment which applies only to the states. But the concepts of equal protection and due process, both stemming from our American ideal of fairness, are not mutually exclusive. The "equal protection of the laws" is a more explicit safeguard of prohibited unfairness than "due process of law," and, therefore, we do not imply that the two are always interchangeable phrases. But, as this Court has recognized, discrimination may be so unjustifiable as to be violative of due process.

The fact that racially discriminatory laws could violate due process is very different than a law that is applied to all people equally. Even Chief Justice Warren, who had written the Opinion of the Court in *Bolling v. Sharpe*, did not agree with the usage in *Shapiro v. Thompson*. In his dissenting opinion, Chief Justice Warren politely said [38]: "*If this is the import of the Court's opinion, then it seems to have departed from our precedents.*" After the *Shapiro v. Thompson* case, the Privileges and Immunities Clause would go into hibernation for another 30 years. At that point, much like a cicada, it would reappear in another case related to reducing the attraction for people to move to other states to collect higher welfare payments.

Welfare Payment Adjustments, *Saenz v. Roe(1999)*

After the *Shapiro v. Thompson* case ruled that waiting periods for benefits for people moving into a state were unconstitutional, California took a different approach to reduce the attraction. It passed a law that said if you came to California from another state, you would receive the benefits that your original state provided for the first year. After that point, you could receive the higher benefits that California provided. This reached the Supreme Court as the case of *Saenz v. Roe(1999)*.

In the Opinion of the Court, *Justice Stevens* works like a magician. The last sentence[39] in Exhibit 56 is true with respect to Nationwide Privileges and Immunities that all citizens possess wherever they are in the country. The creation of welfare type programs started in the 1930's

38 Shapiro v. Thompson, 383 U.S. 618, 652 (1969) – Chief Justice Warren Dissent

39 Saenz v. Roe, 526 U.S. 489, 504-505 (1999) – Opinion of the Court, Justice Stevens

Exhibit 56 - Justice Stevens' Sleight of Hand, Saenz v. Roe

Because this case involves discrimination against citizens who have completed their interstate travel, the State's argument that its welfare scheme affects the right to travel only "incidentally" is beside the point. Were we concerned solely with actual deterrence to migration, we might be persuaded that a partial withholding of benefits constitutes a lesser incursion on the right to travel than an outright denial of all benefits. See Dunn v. Blumstein, 405 U. S. 330, 339 (1972). But since the right to travel embraces the citizen's right to be treated equally in her new State of residence, the discriminatory classification is itself a penalty.

during the Great Depression, which was over 150 years after the founding of the country. Therefore, in the absence of a Constitutional Amendment guaranteeing welfare, it is impossible that welfare is a historic Nationwide Privilege and Immunity protected by the Article IV, Section 2 of the Constitution or the 14th Amendment's Privileges and Immunities Clause.

The next sleight of hand that Justice Stevens performed was the use of "treated equally" and "discriminatory" in the last sentence of Exhibit 56. Figure 3 in Chapter 2 showed how the Articles of Confederation had a non-discriminatory trade rights clause that applied to citizens from other states. This applied to trade, and not to other activities. State Level Privileges and Immunities have always been recognized, and they can include residency requirements. By claiming that unless citizens are treated equally or it is discriminatory, Justice Stevens is creating a new right that is not founded upon Nationwide Privileges and Immunities which include the right to travel. Using this newly ordained right, Justice Stevens ruled California's law unconstitutional. Chief Justice Rehnquist dissented and made the statement that[40]: "*In unearthing from its tomb the right to become a state citizen and to be treated equally in the new State of residence, however, the Court ignores a State's need to assure that only persons who establish a bona fide residence receive the benefits provided to current residents of the State.*"

In another dissent, Justice Thomas made a very important observation regarding the sudden appearance of the Privileges and Immunities Clause shown[41] in Exhibit 57. Justice Thomas was worried that the Privileges and Immunity Clause would just become another mechanism

---

40 Saenz v. Roe, 526 U.S. 489, 516 (1999) - Dissent of Chief Justice Rehnquist

41 Saenz v. Roe, 526 U.S. 489, 527-528 (1999) – Dissent of Justice Thomas

Exhibit 57 - Justice Thomas' Concerns in Dissent, Saenz v. Roe

Because I believe that the demise of the Privileges or Immunities Clause has contributed in no small part to the current disarray of our Fourteenth Amendment jurisprudence, I would be open to reevaluating its meaning in an appropriate case. Before invoking the Clause, however, we should endeavor to understand what the Framers of the Fourteenth Amendment thought that it meant. We should also consider whether the Clause should displace, rather than augment, portions of our equal protection and substantive due process jurisprudence. The majority's failure to consider these important questions raises the specter that the Privileges or Immunities Clause will become yet another convenient tool for inventing new rights, limited solely by the "predilections of those who happen at the time to be Members of this Court." Moore v. East Cleveland, 431 U. S. 494, 502 (1977).

to invent new rights after what he observed in *Saenz v. Roe.* He noted the a real understanding of the Privileges and Immunities Clause should precede its use in future cases. Justice Thomas' fear of the invention of new rights would soon be overshadowed by the risk of the destruction of rights that Americans had possessed since prior to the creation of our country.

Gun Rights - *DC v. Heller(2008)* and *McDonald v. Chicago(2010)*

In 2008, the District of Columbia had one of the most draconian gun laws in the country. They virtually outlawed handguns for protection in the home. Various other states tried to regulate gun purchases, usage, and storage in this recently conceived anti-gun drive. Private gun ownership and usage throughout the nation's history had been so ubiquitous that there was very little court precedent for these types of laws that impinged upon fundamental rights[42]. There was an interesting predicament for the Supreme Court regarding what gun rights case to take first. By selecting one from the District of Columbia, only the 2nd Amendment was involved since the district is under the control of the Federal government. The 14th Amendment and State Laws were ostensibly not involved in the case of *District of Columbia v. Heller* (2008).

The regularly overlooked Privileges and Immunities Clause of the Constitution operates in tandem with the 2nd Amendment since it protects the rights of citizens anywhere in the country. But, as in many Supreme Court cases, the Privileges and Immunities Clause was not part of the question asked of the court. In a sense, Justice Scalia, in his powerful Opinion of the Court, alluded to Nationwide Privileges and Immunities with his statement shown[43] in Exhibit 58.

Justice Stevens' dissent in *DC v. Heller* had a multitude of problems. The Opinion of the Court calls many of them out[44], but they are

42 The English Bill of Rights of 1688 enshrined a long standing right to self defense as discussed in Chapter 1. State recommended amendments to the Constitution that became the 2nd Amendment strongly supported this right as shown in Chapter 3. State Constitutional Amendments regarding dueling showed that individuals unaffiliated with militias could have pistols, and there was very little states could do to stop them from dueling other than not allowing them to hold state offices. Large migrations through the country, such as during the Gold Rush, highlighted the right for citizens to "carry arms wherever they went". This was recognized as a Nationwide Privilege and Immunity in Dred Scott as described in Chapter 4. The Supreme Court decisions of United States v. Cruikshank(1876) and Presser v. Illinois(1886) reinforced the right by showing that it was not exclusive to the 2nd Amendment and had pre-dated the Constitution.

43 District of Columbia v. Heller, 554 U.S. 570 (2008)

44 District of Columbia v. Heller, 554 U.S. 570, 573-636 (2008), Opinion of the Court

Exhibit 58 - Pre Existing Gun Rights - Opinion of the Court, DC v. Heller

Putting all of these textual elements together, we find that they guarantee the individual right to possess and carry weapons in case of confrontation. This meaning is strongly confirmed by the historical background of the Second Amendment. We look to this because it has always been widely understood that the Second Amendment, like the First and Fourth Amendments, codified a pre-existing right. The very text of the Second Amendment implicitly recognizes the pre-existence of the right and declares only that it "shall not be infringed."

almost too numerous to count. An additional problem in Justice Stevens' dissent is an understanding of punctuation. In the State Recommended Constitutional Amendments that were used to generate the 2nd Amendment, a semi-colon was used to separate independent clauses as was shown in Figure 10 in Chapter 3. The right to keep and bear arms was an independent clause separate from other clauses describing the needs for a militia and the desire to avoid the need for a standing army. Another major problem was Justice Stevens' disregard for the part of the *Presser v. Illinois(1884)* opinion that strongly alluded to the Nationwide Privilege and Immunity to keep and bear arms as shown[45] in Exhibit 59. In this exhibit, the "*constitutional provision in question*" is the 2nd Amendment, and the "*sections under consideration*" refer to people associating together in non-approved military organizations[46].

Thankfully, Justice Scalia's Opinion of the Court prevailed. Otherwise, the country could have been thrown into turmoil. The elimination of the fundamental right to bear arms would have dramatically reduced the rights of approximately 300 Million Americans. In some ways it would have been seen as orders of magnitude worse than the *Dred Scott* decision. That decision took away the right to bear arms from hundreds of thousands of free African Americans as described in Chapter 4. Given what transpired after the *Dred Scott* decision, we can only shudder to

45 Presser v. Illinois, 116 U.S. 252, 265-266 (1884), Opinion of the Court

46 Presser v. Illinois, 116 U.S. 252, 264-265 (1884), "We think it clear that the sections under consideration, which only forbid bodies of men to associate together as military organizations, or to drill or parade with Arms in cities and towns unless authorized by law, do not infringe the right of the people to keep and bear arms."

Exhibit 59 - Reserve Force of All Citizens, Presser v. Illinios(1884)

It is undoubtedly true that all citizens capable of bearing arms constitute the reserved military force or reserve militia of the United States as well as of the States, and, in view of this prerogative of the general government, as well as of its general powers, the States cannot, even laying the constitutional provision in question out of view, prohibit the people from keeping and bearing arms, so as to deprive the United States of their rightful resource for maintaining the public security, and disable the people from performing their duty to the general government. But, as already stated, we think it clear that the sections under consideration do not have this effect.

think about what might have happened if a fifth justice had joined with Justice Stevens' dissent in *District of Columbia v. Heller.*

The Supreme Court case of *McDonald v. Chicago(2010)* was the next case to address the right to keep and bear arms for personal protection. It confirmed that this right applied to the states. It might have been much simpler and stronger to do this using the Privileges and Immunities clause. The Nationwide Privileges and Immunity regarding bearing arms had already been identified in many cases; but most descriptively in *Dred Scott(1857)* as explained in Chapter 4. In his concurring opinion in *McDonald v. Chicago*, Justice Thomas proposed such an alternative. He raised a number of issues, but did not have a complete historical and legal analysis to flesh out his opinion. One issue with Justice Thomas' Opinion was that it relied upon the Privileges or Immunities Clause of the 14th Amendment as opposed to the Nationwide Privileges and Immunity Clause in Article IV, Section 2 of the Constitution. This book was written with the intent to identify missing historical proof, legal explanations, and prior Supreme Court precedents to help bring the Privileges and Immunities Clause of the Constitution back to life.

In *McDonald v. Chicago*, Justice Stevens quoted a concern by Judge Wilkinson from a 1989 article to claim a hazard with using the Privileges or Immunities Clause. Judge Wilkinson's quote repeated by Justice Stevens was[47] "*For the very reason that it has so long remained a clean slate, a revitalized Privileges or Immunities Clause holds special hazards for judges who are mindful that their proper task is not to write their personal views of appropriate public policy into the Constitution.*" This book has delineated the Nationwide Privileges and Immunities from our founding, that are a function of our national character, and are protected by our Constitution. This picture is virtually complete; as opposed to a clean slate. Not only that, but the next chapter will provide a table of standing Supreme Court privileges and immunities precedent for many of these identified rights.

Before moving on to look at the future, a final evaluation of Supreme Court cases from 1900-2025 is necessary. Table 17 shows a summary of all of cases that are more thoroughly reviewed in Appendix 26. A universal statement that can be made is that the Supreme Court has frequently failed to recognize Nationwide Privileges and Immunities where it could have done so. Years later, it resorted to finding contorted

47 McDonald v. Chicago, 561 U.S. 742, 860 (2010) - Justice Stevens Dissent

and imaginative means to achieve the same goal. Unfortunately, in the last two cases where the Supreme Court directly considered the Privileges and Immunities Clause (*Shapiro v. Thompson* and *Saenz v. Roe*) the meaning of the clause was improperly construed. The next chapter will evaluate existing court precedents for actual Nationwide Privileges and Immunities, and how they are applicable to this day.

Table 17 - Summary of Supreme Court Decisions, 1900-2025 (Appx. 26)

Supreme Court Case	Year	Nationwide right discussed in the opinion	Possible Privileges and Immunities Protection
Maxwell v. Dow	1900	Right to be tried by a jury of 12 people	Could have been decided as being a Nationwide Privilege and Immunity
Williams v. Fears	1900	Right to not have a tax collected on labor that could be used interstate	Not a Nationwide Privilege and Immunity
Orr v. Gilman	1902	Right not to have a state estate tax charged	Not a Nationwide Privilege and Immunity
Board of Education v. Illinois	1906	Right not to pay inheritance tax on charitable donations made to out of state charities	Not a Nationwide Privilege and Immunity
Ballard v. Hunter	1907	Right to have equal tax summons service times for in state and out-of-state residents	Not a Nationwide Privilege and Immunity
Western Turf Assn. v. Greenberg	1907	Right to publish a horse racing chart at an establishment where the association has sold the right to another company	Corporations are not Citizens having Nationwide Privileges and Immunities
Halter v. Nebraska	1907	Right to use the United States flag in advertising	Not a Nationwide Privilege and Immunity
Wilmington Star Mining Co. v. Fulton	1907	Right to operate mining property without employing licensed managers and following other requirements	Not a Nationwide Privilege and Immunity
Twining v. New Jersey	1908	Right against self-incrimination	Could have been decided as being a Nationwide Privilege and Immunity
Graham v. West Virginia	1912	Right not to have increased penalties for repeat offenders	Not a Nationwide Privilege and Immunity
Selover, Bates & Co. v. Walsh	1912	Interstate land contract dispute	Corporations are not Citizens having Nationwide Privileges and Immunities

Supreme Court Case	Year	Nationwide right discussed in the opinion	Possible Privileges and Immunities Protection
Rosenthal v. New York	1912	Right to accept junk metal that might be stolen property without checking on the source	Not a Nationwide Privilege and Immunity
Waugh v. Board of Trustees of the University of Mississippi	1915	Right to be in a fraternity when a student at the University of Mississippi	Not a Nationwide Privilege and Immunity
Crane v. Campbell	1917	Right to carry a bottle of whiskey on your person in a prohibition district	Not a Nationwide Privilege and Immunity
Armour & Co. v. Virginia	1918	Right for there not to be tax breaks for manufacturers who offer for sale at the place of manufacture	Not a Nationwide Privilege and Immunity
Omaechevarria v. Idaho	1918	Right for sheep owners to use the public lands equally with cattle ranchers	Not a Nationwide Privilege and Immunity
Maxwell v. Bugbee	1919	Right not to pay an inheritance tax since you are not a resident of the state where the person dies.	Not a Nationwide Privilege and Immunity
United States v. Wheeler	1920	Right to reside and remain in a state and to be immune from unlawful deportation from that state by a conspiracy of individuals	Not a Nationwide Privilege and Immunity
Ferry v. Spokane, P. & S. R. Co	1921	Right to dowry rights for a widow who is living in another state to inherit property in a different state	Not a Nationwide Privilege and Immunity
Prudential Ins. Co. v. Cheek	1922	Right to refuse to provide a letter describing a former employee's service with a company	Not a Nationwide Privilege and Immunity
New York ex rel. Bryant v. Zimmerman	1928	Right not to file an organization's Constitution, By-laws and membership lists for secret organizations such as the Ku Klux Klan	Not a Nationwide Privilege and Immunity

Supreme Court Case	Year	Nationwide right discussed in the opinion	Possible Privileges and Immunities Protection
Helson and Randolph v. Kentucky	1929	Right to import gasoline into a state without being taxed by the state on the importation	Properly Regulated as Interstate Commerce
Hamilton v. Regents	1934	Right to refuse to take a required military science class at the University of California which is a land-grant University	Not a Nationwide Privilege and Immunity
Colgate v. Harvey	1935	Right not to be taxed at a higher rate on out-of-state dividends or interest for state tax purposes	Incorrectly determined to be a Nationwide Privilege and Immunity
Whitfield v. Ohio	1936	Right to sell prison made goods from one state in another state	Ruled not to be a Constitutional conflict as long as in state and out-of-state people are treated equivalently
Breedlove v. Suttles	1937	Right not to pay a poll tax to vote	Not a Nationwide Privilege and Immunity, but later made one by the 24th Amendment to the Constitution
Palko v. Connecticut	1937	Right not to be retried by a state as a result of a state appeal to correct and error, and then to receive a greater sentence: in this case death versus life imprisonment	Not a Nationwide Privilege and Immunity
United States v. Miller	1939	Right to carry an unregistered sawed-off shotgun	National Firearms Act of 1934 ruled not to violate the 2nd Amendment.
Hague v. Committee for Industrial Organization	1939	Right to assemble in public parks and streets to discuss the National Labor Relations Act	Could have been decided based on the Nationwide Privilege and Immunity for citizens to assemble, speak and write about issues related to the government
Madden v. Kentucky	1940	Right not to pay higher state taxes on interest from out-of-state banks	Not a Nationwide Privilege and Immunity. (Overruled Colgate v. Harvey)
Edwards v. California	1941	Right to transport indigent people across state lines	Nationwide Privilege and Immunity with reasonable interpretation of "pauper" exception for people wanting to work
Henderson v. United States	1950	Right for an African American to dine at a table with white passengers on a train	Missed opportunity in the 1800s to determine based on the Nationwide Privilege and Immunities

Supreme Court Case	Year	Nationwide right discussed in the opinion	Possible Privileges and Immunities Protection
Brown v. Board of Education	1954	Right for African American children to attend schools with white children	Missed opportunity in the 1800s to determine based on the Nationwide Privilege and Immunities
Kent v. Dulles	1958	Right for a Communist to obtain a passport	Decided on Due Process grounds
Boynton v. Virginia	1960	Right for an African American bus passenger to eat in a restaurant at a stop that serves interstate customers.	Missed opportunity in the 1800s to determine based on the Nationwide Privilege and Immunities
Aptheker v. Secretary of State	1964	Right for a member of the Communist party to receive a passport.	Decided on Due Process Grounds
Hearts of Atlanta Motel v. United States	1964	Right for African Americans to use a hotel that advertises along interstate highways and is used for interstate commerce.	Missed opportunity in the 1800s to determine based on the Nationwide Privilege and Immunities
Katzenbach v. McClung	1964	Right for African Americans to eat in a restaurant that serves interstate travelers and gets significant food from outside the state	Missed opportunity in the 1800s to determine based on the Nationwide Privilege and Immunities
Zemel v. Rusk	1965	Right to travel to Cuba when the State Department has banned it	Not a Nationwide Privilege and Immunity
United States v. Guest	1966	Right for African Americans to equally use public facilities without being falsely arrested	Violation of the Equal Protection Clause of the 14th Amendment
United States v. Price	1966	Right to protection against a conspiracy between local law enforcement and private individuals	Violation of the Due Process Clause of the 14th Amendment
Shapiro v. Thompson	1969	Right to collect welfare benefits without needing to meet residency requirements.	Improperly relied on the Privileges and Immunities clause
Saenz v. Roe	1999	Right to collect higher welfare benefits that you would have been entitled to in your previous state for the first year of residence in a new state	Improperly relied on the Privileges and Immunities clause

Supreme Court Case	Year	Nationwide right discussed in the opinion	Possible Privileges and Immunities Protection
District of Columbia v. Heller	2008	Right to bear arms for self-defense within the home in the District of Columbia	The Privileges and Immunities Clause should have been used in partnership with the 2nd Amendment to provide additional rights.
McDonald v. Chicago	2010	Right to bear arms in the states	The Privileges and Immunities Clause should be used to provide the best protection against state laws that infringe on this fundamental right

Chapter 7

The Path to Resurrect Our Rights

(2026 and Beyond)

The present status of the Privileges and Immunities Clause remains dormant as Chief Justice Rehnquist described[1] it in 1999. There are many similarities between what has happened to the Privileges and Immunities Clause and the movie *The Wizard of Oz (1939)*. The three "*Butterfly Effects*" described in this book can be compared to the tornado at the beginning of the movie. They sent litigants and the Supreme Court spinning through a dreamland parallel universe. Justice Harlan's(1833-1911) key dissents showed how Privileges and Immunities should have been used in the *Civil Rights Cases(1883)* and *Plessy v. Ferguson(1896)*. These can be compared to the Good Witch of the North who worked to lead Dorothy to the Wizard of Oz by telling her to follow the yellow brick road. In his dissenting opinion in *Saenz v. Roe(1999)*, and in his concurring opinion in *McDonald v. Chicago(2010)*, Justice Thomas was providing guidance to the court to review the Privileges and Immunities Clause. This can be compared to the Good Witch of the South telling Dorothy how she can easily return to Kansas. Now, all that is missing, is for the Supreme Court to "*click their shoes together three times*" while saying "*there are no rights as powerful as the Privileges and Immunities of American citizens.*" That would allow the Privileges and Immunities Clause to awaken from this slumber. The Supreme Court just has to recognize, reaffirm, and strengthen its prior findings to bring our rights back to life. This Chapter will describe many ways that existing precedents can be used to do just that.

1 Saenz v. Roe, 526 U.S. 489, 511 (1999), Chief Justice Rehnquist Dissent

Safety and Security in our Nation

In the *Slaughterhouse Cases(1873)*, the Supreme Court recognized the Nationwide Privilege and Immunity[2] "*to demand the care and protection of the Federal government over his life, liberty, and property when on the high seas or within the jurisdiction of a foreign government.*" If our federal government is supposed to protect us from foreigners who might attack, rob or injure us on the high seas, or in a foreign country, there is an obvious and even stronger corollary right here at home. That corollary is that we have the right to have the federal government protect us from foreigners who might attack, rob or injure us that are within the bounds of our own country.

Under the Articles of Confederation government discussed in Chapter 2, each individual state had a high degree of sovereignty. Each state controlled their own immigration and naturalization. When the states agreed to our present Constitution, they handed over all rights to control immigration and naturalization to the newly established federal government. States that are trying to revert to the old approach using what they call "*Sanctuary Cities*" or "*Sanctuary States*" are violating the Constitution. It is a Nationwide Privilege and Immunity for all Americans to be protected from dangerous foreigners in our country. It is unconscionable that states and localities will not cooperate with the federal government to remove anyone illegally in our country who is convicted of a crime. When states or cities try to play a game of "*cat and mouse*" with federal authorities to hide people illegally in our country, they are violating the 14th Amendment's clause that "*No State shall make or enforce any law which shall abridge the privileges or immunities of citizens of the United States*". Any "*Sanctuary*" law is violating this requirement.

Sanctuary laws are also endangering citizens through such actions as providing standard and commercial driver's licenses to people that are not legally in our country. This results in danger to citizens on our roadways nationwide. The resulting scarcity of limited resources such as hospitals, schools, and homes due to Sanctuary policies increases costs, and restricts availability, for tax paying citizens. Sanctuary laws create an affordability crisis for all Americans.

---

2 Slaughterhouse Cases, 83 U.S. 36, 79 (1873), Opinion of the Court

Safety and Security of our Persons

This book has provided extensive discussions regarding gun rights that have existed in our country for well over 150 years before its founding. These rights are fundamental and have been instrumental in shaping the discovery, settlement and defense of our nation. Supreme Court cases such as *District of Columbia v. Heller(2008), McDonald v. Chicago(2010)* and *New York State Rifle & Pistol Association, Inc. v. Bruen (2022)*[3] have focused on affirming the individual's rights to bear arms either at home or on their person.

Throughout our nation's history, citizens have been free to move between the states with their firearms. Whether they were moving their household in a covered wagon in the 1700's and 1800's, or utilizing a moving van in the 1900's and 2000's, Americans have always enjoyed the right to freely move between states. Due to this right, states and cities that a person travels through cannot make firearms that are legal in one state suddenly illegal in another. This violates the Nationwide Privilege and Immunity that Chief Justice Taney recognized in Dred Scott, and worked so hard to keep out of the hands of African Americans. That right was described as[4] "*the right to enter every other state whenever they please, and to keep and carry arms wherever they went*".

"Assault Weapons Bans" only make life more dangerous and difficult for law-abiding citizens. These legislators hope that they can limit gun magazine sizes, while somehow believing that in an event where a gun owner's life is being threatened, the gun owner will have the skill, courage and accuracy of *James Bond*(Sean Connery) *in Goldfinger(1964).* These legislators feel that they can remove gun features that improve accuracy such as pistol grips, while not considering that they are artificially hindering senior citizens and handicapped individuals whose physical abilities are more limited. They turn their law-abiding citizens into second class citizens, while we all know that criminals will evade their laws. Beyond these bans on certain guns and their components, state laws regarding transport of guns are another issue that violate Nationwide Privileges and Immunities.

---

3 20-843 New York State Rifle & Pistol Assn., Inc. v. Bruen (06/23/2022)

4 Dred Scott, 60 U.S. 393, 417 (1857), Chief Justice Taney's Opinion of the Court

As an example, California has an approximately 600-mile-long border with the state of Nevada. Two Interstate Highways (80 and 15) cross this border along with a myriad of other roads. At various points along the border, hiking trails such as the Tahoe Rim Trail cross between the states. Mountain Lions, Black Bears and other dangers exist for those hiking these trails; especially if they are hiking alone. Lake Tahoe also has boat taxis that take people across the lake between the states. When it comes to driving, Reno, Nevada is only a two hours drive from Sacramento, California in good weather. The problem is that in the winter, storms such as the one that trapped the Donner Party in 1846, can trap vehicles for days until snowplows can get to them. A citizen of Nevada, with a pistol having a 15 or 17 bullet magazine, would be violating California State Law[5] if they carried their gun in their car, backpack, boat or on their person into California. State and local gun laws of these types clearly violate the Privileges and Immunities of citizens from other states. Importantly, these also violate the Privileges and Immunities of Californians returning from another state. Everyone in our nation is entitled to defend themselves with federally legal guns, and no state should be able to turn their citizens into second class Americans. Americans have an inherent right to protect themselves so that they can survive to pass on life and knowledge to new generations of Americans.

Birthright Citizenship, *Wong Kim Ark(1898)*

Whether it was the birth of Jesus Christ, or the birth of any mortal child, birth is the culmination of approximately nine months of the development of an infant in the womb. An interesting question is: "At what point does the infant possess the privileges and immunities of citizens?". Looking back to the times before the American Revolution, William Blackstone in his Commentaries on the Laws of England provided excellent context and perspective shown[6] in Exhibit 60.

Blackstone's summary of English law describes the act of quickening which generally occurs between 16 and 20 weeks after conception.

5 California Office of Attorney General. (2026, Feb. 23). https://www.oag.ca.gov/ogvp/fed-assault-weapons-ban

6 Blackstone, William. *Commentaries on the Laws of England Book I: The Rights of Persons, Chapter 1 – Of the Absolute Rights of Individuals*

Exhibit 60 - Blackstone Summary of English Law for Pre-Born Infants

> Life is the immediate gift of God, a right inherent by nature in every individual; and it begins in contemplation of the law as soon as an infant is able to stir in the mother's womb. For if a woman is quick with child, and by a potion, or otherwise kills it in her womb; or if any one beat her, whereby the child dies in her body, and she is delivered of a dead child; this though not murder was by the ancient law homicide or manslaughter. But at present it is not looked upon in quite so atrocious a light, though it remains a very heinous misdemeanor.
>
> An infant in ventre sa mere, or in the mother's womb, is supposed in law to be born for many purposes. It is capable of having a legacy, or a surrender of a copyhold estate made to it. It may have a guardian assigned to it; and it is enabled to have an estate limited to its use, and to take afterwards by such limitation, as if it were then actually born. And in this point the civil law agrees with ours.

This is when the mother first feels the baby stirring in her womb. If you can imagine life in the 1700's, it was not possible to go to a *neighborhood* pharmacy to purchase a pregnancy test. Disease was rampant, and might mask the signs of pregnancy. Especially in the case of first-time mothers, they might not realize they were pregnant until they felt quickening. At this point, English law was very clear with regards to the responsibility of the mother. Using poison or other means to kill the infant in the womb had been considered murder by ancient law. At the time of our nation's founding, it was considered a very heinous misdemeanor.

These principles regarding the sanctity of unborn infants are protected in the laws of most states. They recognize that killing a pregnant woman also kills her unborn child. In these states, killing a pregnant woman equates to two homicides. The National Right to Life organization provides details[7] of "*State Homicide Laws that Recognize Unborn Victims*". These laws follow in the moral and legal tradition of protecting the rights of unborn victims that originated centuries before our nation's founding. As Blackstone referenced, these pre-born infants are supposed "*to be born for many purposes*". In our country, these pre-born infants are about to inherit the amazing privileges and immunities of citizenship.

Powerful rights are not to be given away like candy at Halloween. Our nation fought a brutal Civil War to provide these rights to African Americans. This was done after the Dred Scott decision attempted to

7 National Right to Life. (2026, Feb. 23). https://nrlc.org/federal/unbornvictims/statehomicidelaws092302/

keep Nationwide Privileges and Immunities away from African Americans in order to protect the institution of slavery. Which children born in our country deserve these powerful rights? We have the contemporary Supreme Court opinion in the *Slaughterhouse Cases(1873)*, that described the purposes of the 14th Amendment clause regarding citizenship. It said[8]: "*That its main purpose was to establish the citizenship of the negro can admit of no doubt. The phrase, 'subject to its jurisdiction' was intended to exclude from its operation children of ministers, consuls, and citizens or subjects of foreign States born within the United States.* " The last phrase in the Slaughterhouse Cases sentence is the most applicable to questions arising regarding Birthright citizenship in 2026. Justice Miller was stating that the phrase "*subject to its jurisdiction*" was meant to exclude children who were born to "*citizens or subjects of foreign States born within the United States*".

Citizens or subjects of foreign states are always subject to deportation if they violate their rules for remaining in the United States. Figure 17 in Chapter 6 showed how even persons in the United States as Permanent Residents have significantly less rights than Americans; not the least of which is that they can be deported to their home country for breaking the law or the rules of their residency. Persons in the United States on temporary visas have even fewer rights, and their situation is all the more transitory. In their case, it would be extremely humane to decide that they would have the 18-year life of their child for one or both of the parents to become American citizens. In this proposed approach, once one of both of the parents became citizens, then the child could become a naturalized United States citizen. Otherwise, if the parents and child return to their home country, how does it make sense that the child has the full Privileges and Immunities of American citizenship while having no ties to the country?

The Supreme Court case of *Wong Kim Ark(1898)* provides valuable insight into the issue of birthright citizenship. Wong Kim Ark was born in 1873. His parents were Chinese and operated a business in San Francisco. His parents were not permitted to become citizens[9] , but were

8 Slaughterhouse Cases, 83 U.S. 36, 73 (1873)

9 Wong Kim Ark, 169 U.S. 649, 701 (1898) – Opinion of the Court – "It is true that Chinese persons born in China cannot be naturalized, like other aliens, by proceedings under the naturalization laws."

long-time permanent residents. In 1890, when Wong Kim Ark was 17, his parents returned to China to live. He traveled to China (probably with his parents though not stated in the Statement of the Case). He returned to the United States in the summer of 1890 by himself, and was allowed back into the United States. In 1894, as an adult, Wong Kim Ark made another visit to China. According to the Statement of the Case, there is no mention that he had a Passport or a Certificate of Residence. Returning to the United States as a 21-year-old adult, he would have fallen under the *Chinese Exclusion Act*[10]. That act had passed in 1880 to protect American workers, and was followed up by the *Geary Act* in 1892. According to the *Geary Act*[11], Wong Kim Ark should have had a Certificate of Residence that would have permitted him to be in the country when he returned. Instead, he was rejected[12] as not being a citizen. Wong Kim Ark was permitted to stay in the country while he appealed his case all the way up to the Supreme Court.

The Wong Kim Ark Opinion of the Court provides an excellent seven-part history lesson regarding birthright citizenship. Appendix 27 shows the key quotes from each section. Section 2 analyzed the principle of English nationality at birth according to the English Common Law. It described how[13] "*The principle embraced all persons born within the King's allegiance and subject to his protection. Such allegiance and protection were mutual...and were not restricted to natural-born subjects and naturalized subjects, or to those who had taken an oath of allegiance; but were predicable of aliens in amity, so long as they were within the kingdom. Children, born in England, of such aliens, were therefore natural-born subjects.*" The key factors for the common law were that allegiance and protection

---

10 United States National Archives and Records Administration. (2026, Feb. 22). https://www.archives.gov/milestone-documents/chinese-exclusion-act

11 University of Texas, Austin, Dept. of History, Immigration History. (2026, Feb. 23). https://immigrationhistory.org/item/geary-act/

12 Wong Kim Ark, 169 U.S. 649, 651 (1898)– Statement of the Case
"That after his said return the said Wong Kim Ark remained in the United States, claiming to be a citizen thereof, until the year 1894, when he again departed for China upon a temporary visit, and with the intention of returning to the United States, and did return thereto in the month of August, 1895, and applied to the collector of customs to be permitted to land; and that such application was denied upon the sole ground that said Wong Kim Ark was not a citizen of the United States.

13 Wong Kim Ark, 169 U.S. 649, 655 (1898)– Opinion of the Court

were a mutual operation. Aliens who showed temporary allegiance by being in amity (friendship, peaceful harmony) with the Kingdom could assert (predicable) the right of birthright citizenship.

The 14th Amendment's citizenship clause states: "*All persons born or naturalized in the United States, and subject to the jurisdiction thereof, are citizens of the United States and of the State wherein they reside.*" The key qualification for this sentence is the phrase "*and subject to the jurisdiction thereof*". Confusion arises when people think that the phrase "*within the jurisdiction*" and the phrase "*and subject to the jurisdiction thereof*" are the same thing. They are clearly not the same, and the Wong Kim Ark analyzed numerous exceptions in detail.

Section 5 of the Wong Kim Ark Opinion of the Court referred back to Chief Justice Marshall's Opinion in The *Schooner Exchange v. McFadden(1812)*[14] to identify a variety of exceptions to being "*subject to the jurisdiction thereof*". These included exceptions for foreign heads of state, ambassadors, friendly foreign troops, and friendly foreign naval vessels. In addition, the Wong Kim Ark Opinion referred to the Supreme Court's opinion in *Elk v. Wilkins(1884)* that showed that American Indians born within the territory of the United States were not American citizens since their members:[15] "*owed immediate allegiance to their several tribes, and were not part of the people of the United States; that the alien and dependent condition of the members of one of these tribes could not be put off at their own will, without the action or assent of the United States;*". To permit American Indians to become citizens required an act of Congress. They could not just unilaterally separate from their tribes, take up residence amongst United States citizens, and then claim citizenship. In 1924, the *Indian Citizenship Act* granted American Indians full United States citizenship rights. Figure 18 shows exceptions described in Wong Kim Ark to being "*subject to the jurisdiction thereof*".

One possible way to think about the phrase "subject to the jurisdiction thereof" is to consider what would happen in the outbreak of a

14 The Schooner Exchange v. McFadden, 11 U.S. 116 (1812), Chief Justice Marshall's Opinion of the Court

15 Elk v. Wilkins, 112 U.S. 94, 99-100 (1884)

Figure 18 - "subject to the jurisdiction thereof", Wong Kim Ark

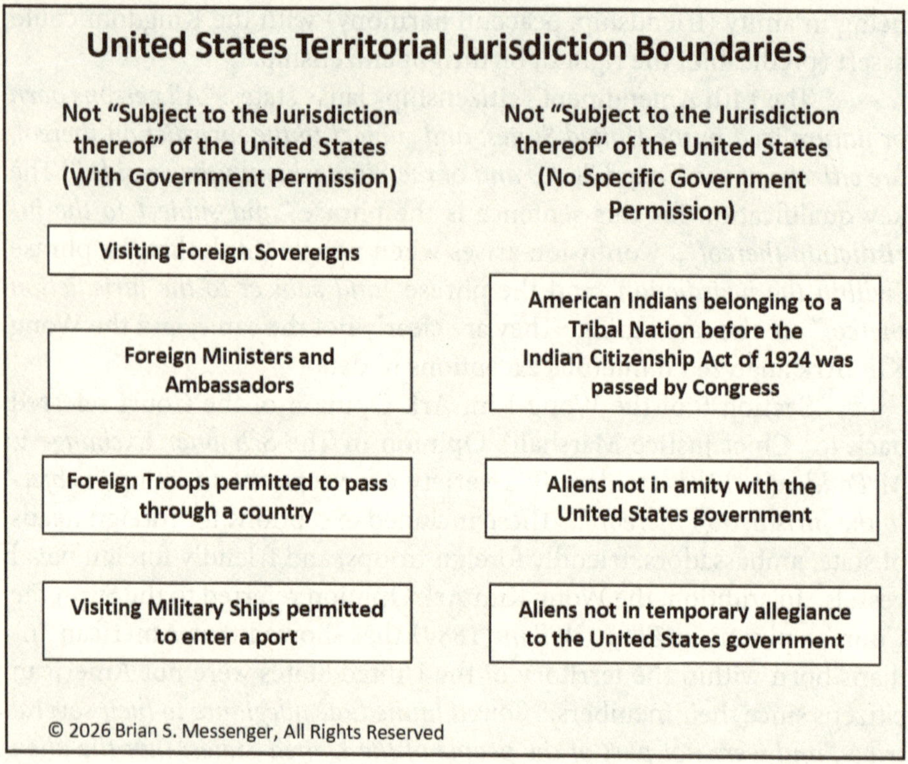

war. A permanent resident is:[16] "*Required to register with the Selective Service, if you are a male age 18 through 25.*" This means that permanent residents are required to fight, and potentially die, to protect the United States. They are also required to obey all laws, file income tax returns, and support the democratic form of government. All of these factors make them "*subject to the jurisdiction thereof*" and permit the immigrant to pursue a "trial-run" to become a citizen of our country. Do immigrants who are on temporary visas show that they "*owe allegiance to the United States*" while they continue to be subject to the jurisdiction of the country of their citizenship? In case of war, especially one with their country of citizenship, who do they owe allegiance to? They are literally subjects of the enemy country.

16 United States Department of Homeland Security, U.S. Citizenship and Immigration Services. (2026, Feb. 23).
https://www.uscis.gov/green-card/after-we-grant-your-green-card/rights-and-responsibilities-of-a-green-card-holder-permanent-resident

The Supreme Court had already ruled that Congress' use of the *Chinese Exclusion Act* was Constitutional, and that it was a right of the United States to expel permanent residents from China, for reasons applicable to all aliens, even if they had a commercial business[17]. Figure 19[18] breaks down the complex sentence in Section 6 of the Wong Kim Ark

17 Wong Kim Ark, 169 U.S. 649, 699 (1898) – Opinion of the Court, "The acts of Congress, known as the Chinese Exclusion Acts, the earliest of which was passed some fourteen years after the adoption of the Constitutional Amendment, cannot control its meaning, or impair its effect, but must be construed and executed in subordination to its provisions. And the right of the United States, as exercised by and under those acts, to exclude or to expel from the country persons of the Chinese race, born in China, and continuing to be subjects of the Emperor of China, though having acquired a commercial domicil in the United States, has been upheld by this court, for reasons applicable to all aliens alike, and inapplicable to citizens, of whatever race or color."

18 Wong Kim Ark, 169 U.S. 649, 694, Opinion of the Court

Figure 19 - Complex Sentence Breakdown, Wong Kim Ark

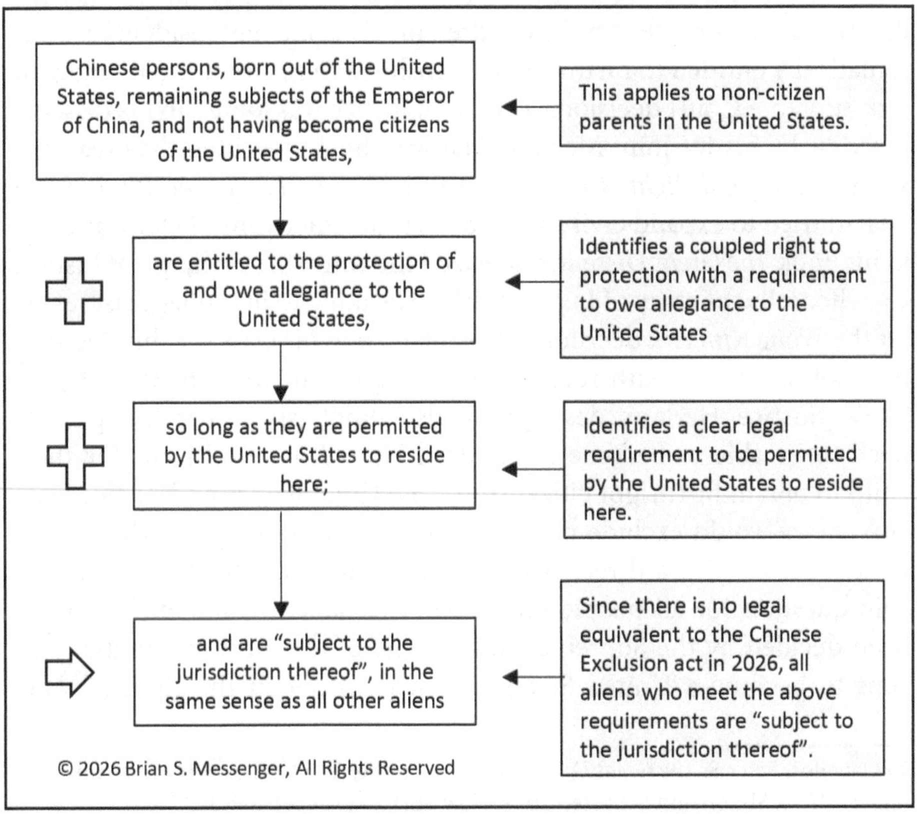

Opinion of the Court that justified granting Wong Kim Ark citizenship. The sections of this sentence tie back directly to the English Common Law. Owing allegiance to the United States is coupled with receiving protection from the United States. Receiving permission from the United States to continue residing in the country was a clear prerequisite for Wong Kim Ark's parents. The last part of Figure 18 uses the phrase "*in the same sense as all other aliens*". Due to the *Chinese Exclusion Acts*, this is putting Chinese parents on the same playing field as parents who are citizens of other countries. It is clearly not referring to every alien in the country, but refers to similarly situated aliens from countries whose parents could become citizens. Based upon those factors, the court determined that Wong Kim Ark was a citizen through the action of the 14th Amendment.

The decision in Wong Kim Ark was by a vote of 6-2. Chief Justice Fuller wrote a detailed dissent where he stated that children born of permanent residents who cannot become citizens of the United States are not citizens. Since there are no equivalents to the *Chinese Exclusion Acts* today, there is no debate that the children of all permanent residents are automatically entitled to birthright citizenship as a result of the Wong Kim Ark Supreme Court decision. The Chief Justice was joined in his dissenting view by Justice John Marshall Harlan who had written the great dissents in the *Civil Rights Cases(1883)* and *Plessy v. Ferguson(1896)* where he had tried to expand civil rights to African Americans. Peter Canellos, in his book *The Great Dissenter* analyzed the entire life of this great Justice. Canellos tells the story of Justice Harlan speaking to his college classes after the *Wong Kim Ark* decision. He explained to his class that his decision had nothing to do with race by providing the analogy in Exhibit 61[19].

Justice Harlan's description also emphasizes that the parents need to be able to become naturalized United States citizens for their child to obtain birthright citizenship. The Chief Justice and Justice Harlan's views would exclude people of all races who are not living in the United States with a direct path to citizenship. The birthright citizenship question for all people other than permanent residents has never been decided by the Supreme Court. One of the most substantial reasons to become a United States citizen is to obtain the right to vote.

---

19 Canellos, Peter S. *The Great Dissenter – The Story of John Marshall Harlan, America's Judicial Hero.* Simon and Schuster, 2021, New York, NY, pages 369-370

Exhibit 61 - Justice Harlan's Discussion regarding Wong Kim Ark Decision

After the court's decision in United States v. Wong Kim Ark, John discussed the case with his students at Columbian University. According to George Johannes's notes, the justice posited the example of an English couple, loyal to the British crown, who "went down to Hot Springs [Arkansas] to get rid of the gout" and had a child before returning to England. "Is this child a citizen of the United States, born to the jurisdiction thereof, by the mere accident of his birth?" Harlan asked rhetorically. In answering no, Harlan was signaling that his objection to Wong's citizenship would apply equally to a white European whose parents remained subjects of a monarch.

"My belief [was that the Fourteenth Amendment] was never intended to embrace everybody in our citizenship if he was the child of parents who cannot under the law become naturalized in the United States," John declared in his lecture to the students, referring to the Wong case. But he added, as was his custom, "I was one of the minority, and of course I was wrong."

Citizen Voting Rights

In Chapter 5, the right against discrimination in voting due to race was discussed as it was created by the *15th Amendment(1870)*[20] to the Constitution. In a virtually identical amendment form, women received the right to vote by the *19th Amendment(1920)*[21] . Finally, during the Vietnam War, it was acknowledged that it was unfair for men to be drafted and risk their lives in the military at age 18, but not be allowed to vote on whether the country should go to war until age 21. To deal with this issue, the *26th Amendment(1971)*[22] was ratified. Each of these Constitutional Amendments created corresponding privileges and immunities for United States citizens.

With respect to voting rights, a key statement in each of these

20 United States Constitution, 15th Amendment, Section 1 – "The right of citizens of the United States to vote shall not be denied or abridged by the United States or by any State on account of race, color, or previous condition of servitude—",

21 United States Constitution, 19th Amendment, Section 1 – "The right of citizens of the United States to vote shall not be denied or abridged by the United States or by any State on account of sex.",

22 United States Constitution, 26th Amendment, Section 1 – "The right of citizens of the United States, who are eighteen years of age or older, to vote shall not be denied or abridged by the United States or by any State on account of age.",

Constitutional Amendments is that the rights of citizens shall not be "abridged". Any dilution of citizen's votes by non-citizens will automatically abridge the rights of all citizens. Additionally, no matter the mixture of sex or race of non-citizen voters, they will be abridging the rights of some portion of the electorate. As a simple example, if the citizen population is 50% female, but the non-citizen population is only 30% female (since a large number of single men of working age are in the city or state), the rights of all females are being abridged on account of their sex by allowing non-citizens to vote. Similarly, no matter what the racial percentages are in a given population of citizens, the non-citizen population will never be an exact match. If there are 10% African Americans in the citizen population, but only 2% African Americans in the non-citizen population, then African American citizens are having their voting rights abridged on account of race by allowing non-citizens to vote. The Nationwide Privileges and Immunities created by the 15th and 19th Amendments are being violated when localities, cities or states permit non-citizen voting. In the case of underage voting, it abridges the rights of all citizens over 18 as protected by the 26th Amendment. The right to vote has been a key motivator for people to become citizens, and to take part in making the decisions that affect our country. It should never be given to those who remain subjects of another country.

In Chapter 4, the issue of slavery was covered in depth. At the Constitutional Convention, there were serious debates regarding Congressional representation for slaves. These debates led to the 3/5 compromise where even though slaves had no chance to vote, their states received credit for 3/5 of a person for each slave in their territory. Luther Martin of Maryland predicted[23] that the 3/5 apportionment for representation would encourage the slave trade. He was clearly proven right as shown by comparing state populations in 1790 (Appendix 21) and state populations in 1860 (Appendix 22). Oh, how doth history repeat!

Over the last century, the United States has become a greater and greater magnet for immigrants who are primarily seeking economic opportunity. Many of these people violate our Immigration law the minute they step into our country. These immigrant's view is that the reward

---

23 The Anti-Federalist Papers and the [Constitutional Convention Debates], Signet Classics, 1986, pages 153, Madison's notes for MR. L. MARTIN. (Luther Martin of Maryland) "as five slaves are to be counted as 3 free men in the apportionment of Representatives; such a clause would leave an encouragement to this traffic."

greatly outweighs the risk. Unfortunately, their illegal behavior is encouraged by "*drunk on power*" politicians who appreciate their low-cost labor and the additional political power that they provide. Some of the states in our country encourage this behavior due to the political reward of receiving full (1=5/5) apportionment for each person illegally in the country. They have conjured up a deal that is more egregious than the slaveholders who received 3/5 apportionment for each slave that they legally had in the country. This "system" provides citizens in certain states with greater voting power since fewer actual citizens live in each congressional district balanced by population. More importantly, it abridges the voting rights of every citizen in states that do not participate and hence lose congressional representation.

The United States census should count both citizens and permanent residents. Since permanent residents have the opportunity to become citizens, it is likely that most of them will become voting citizens in the following decade. State congressional representation, as well as the balancing of congressional districts by population, should be done using the total numbers of citizens and permanent residents. All other people in the country on temporary visas, or having another status, should not be counted with regards to voting. This is obvious, since they have no long-term right to remain in the country. In keeping with the wisdom of Luther Martin's observation from almost 240 years ago, this method would remove a major encouragement to this abuse.

Speech, Press and Assembly Rights

Tyrants and authoritarians always try to suppress the speech and writings of their opponents. In a functional republic, each citizen must be able to speak and write clearly about their thoughts regarding the government and how it functions. This implied Nationwide Privilege and Immunity comes to us from our founding and the *Declaration of Independence*. Specific rights were covered in D1, D2 and D16 of Appendix 5. Fundamentally, if "*Governments are instituted among Men, deriving their just powers from the consent of the governed*", the government should never be able to silence citizens from speaking their minds about either government officials, laws, or policies.

No person in government has the power, like an ancient king, to say that their thoughts or policies cannot be questioned. No person who believes in science, and the scientific method, can claim that their beliefs cannot be questioned. The constant expansion of scientific knowledge demands the exact opposite. Everything can legitimately be questioned, and scientists should be prepared to provide answers based on repeatable and convincing data. Otherwise, the should be required to identify appropriate experiments to prove their hypothesis. It is the responsibility of the government to show such strong and universally accepted proof that doubters will fade away. It is not the right of government to claim that alternative views are some sort of "disinformation" as was done during COVID-19.

In the centuries preceding our nation's founding, freedom of speech and of the press were in their infancy in Europe. Our powerful Nationwide Privilege and Immunity to[24] "*enter every other state whenever they pleased, and ... [to have] the full liberty of speech in public and private upon all subjects which its own citizens might speak;*" was recognized in the *Dred Scott* decision. In the modern world, this covers almost all speech with possible exceptions for speech inciting government overthrow, speech that is lewd, and speech promoting imminent violent actions. These sorts of "corner cases" are just the types of decisions that our lawmakers and the Supreme Court should consider. *Freedom of Speech* does not remove the responsibility and liability for the speaker with respect to slandering others.

Even prior to the founding of our country, the truth was considered as a defense against libel charges for something that a citizen published. Like *Freedom of Speech*, *Freedom of the Press* comes with responsibilities and liability for libel. *Freedom of the Press* is an integral part of people's ability to speak their minds about government officials, laws and policies. It has been an integral part of our Nationwide Privileges and Immunities since the Declaration of Independence. In the modern world, this right covers most topics with similar corner case exceptions as for speech.

The Nationwide Privilege and Immunity for assembly was strongly recognized in *Dred Scott*, The *Slaughterhouse Cases*, and *United States v. Cruikshank*. It is another fundamental right that is critical to the proper functioning of a republic. *Dred Scott* recognized "*the right to enter*

24 Dred Scott, 60 U.S. 393, 417 (1857) – Opinion of the Court

every other state whenever they pleased, singly or in companies", and to "*hold public meetings upon political affairs*". The Slaughterhouse Cases and United States v. Cruikshank focused on the right to assemble for a redress of grievances against the Federal government as being a Nationwide Privilege and Immunity. The actions of states and cities blocking citizens from attending church services during COVID-19 were especially egregious violations of people's rights to assemble. To cover all of their bases, churches could have started their service with a list of their grievances against the lockdowns and the government, and then prayed that their public leaders would follow God's will and allow them to meet together in person without interruption. As identified in *United States v. Cruikshank*, the *Freedom to Assemble* was not created by the Constitution, and did not depend on it for its existence. The right to assemble is most powerful when addressing grievances associated with the government[25] . Since it is a Nationwide Privilege and Immunity, the states and local governments cannot abridge it through their laws as emphasized by the 14th Amendment.

Reclaiming Our Nationwide Privileges and Immunities

Using the analysis and the Supreme Court precedents provided in this book, it is possible to generate a list of our existing Nationwide Privileges and Immunities. It is the author's hope that this list (Table 18) can be used by citizens across our country to augment the rights from the *Bill of Rights* that they normally think of. This book has strived to provide a complete understanding of the history of the Privileges and Immunities Clause that Justice Thomas alluded to in his decisions. Critically, it has provided three "butterfly effects" that have resulted in confusion and a loss of interest in privileges and immunities. Understanding these factors, it is hoped that the Supreme Court can take full advantage of these rediscovered rights to empower American citizens nationwide.

165 years ago, our nation fought a terrible Civil War. Over 600,000 Americans died in the battle to save our republic and to rid our nation of slavery once and for all. The 14th Amendment was approved to

25 Peacefully protesting an improperly run election, with apparently nonsensical results, would seem to have the highest level of protection from the Nationwide Privilege and Immunity to assemble and demand a redress of grievances.

Table 18 - Privileges and Immunities of United States Citizens

Category	Identified Right[1]	Supreme Court Precedent
Freedoms to freely move about within the United States	The right of free access to the seaports of the United States, through which all operations of foreign commerce are conducted, to the sub-treasuries, land offices, and courts of justice in the several States	Crandall v. Nevada via the Slaughter-House Cases, 83 U.S. 36, 79 (1873)
	The right to use the navigable waters of the United States, however they may penetrate the territory of the several States	Slaughter-House Cases, 83 U.S. 36, 79 (1873)
	The right to enter every other State whenever you please, singly or in companies, without pass or passport, and without obstruction, to sojourn there as long as you please, to go where you please at every hour of the day or night without molestation, unless you commit some violation of the law.	Dred Scott, 60 U.S. 393, 417 (1857)
	The right to enter every other State whenever you please, and to keep and carry arms wherever you go.	Dred Scott, 60 U.S. 393, 417 (1857)
	The right to come to the seat of government to assert any claim you may have upon the government, to transact any business you may have with it, to seek its protection, to share its offices, to engage in administering its functions.	Crandall v. Nevada via the Slaughter-House Cases, 83 U.S. 36, 79 (1873)
	The right, on your own volition, to become a citizen of any State of the Union by a bona fide residence therein, with the same rights as other citizens of that state.	US Const. 14th Amendment interpretation in Slaughter-House Cases, 83 U.S. 36, 80 (1873)

1 Phrasing taken directly from binding Supreme Court precedent, accounting for multiple clauses, obvious verb tense changes, and replacing "he" with" you")

Category	Identified Right[1]	Supreme Court Precedent
Freedoms outside the United States	The right to demand the care and protection of the Federal government over your life, liberty, and property when on the high seas or within the jurisdiction of a foreign government.	Slaughter-House Cases, 83 U.S. 36, 79 (1873)
	All rights secured to our citizens by treaties with foreign nations.	Slaughter-House Cases, 83 U.S. 36, 79 (1873)
Freedoms of Expression in the United States	The right to enter every other State whenever you please, [with] the full liberty of speech in public and in private upon all subjects upon which its own citizens might speak.	Dred Scott, 60 U.S. 393, 417 (1857)
	The right to enter every other State whenever you please, to hold public meetings upon political affairs	Dred Scott, 60 U.S. 393, 417 (1857)
	The right to peaceably assemble	Slaughter-House Cases, 83 U.S. 36, 79 (1873)
	The right of the people peaceably to assemble for the purpose of petitioning Congress for a redress of grievances, or for anything else connected with the powers or the duties of the national government	United States v. Cruikshank, 92 U.S. 542, 552 (1876) and Slaugh-ter-House Cases, 83 U.S. 36, 79 (1873)
	The right of citizens of the United States to vote shall not be denied or abridged by the United States or by any State on account of race, color, previous condition of servitude, sex or age	US Const. 15th Amendment via Slaughter-House Cases, 83 U.S. 36, 80 (1873) and US Const. 19th and 26th Amend-ments
Freedoms of trade and commerce	The prohibition against laws impairing the obligation of contracts	US Const. Article 1, Section 10 via Slaugh-ter-House Cases 83 U.S. 36, 77 (1873),

Category	Identified Right[1]	Supreme Court Precedent
Freedoms associated with Legal Processes	The privilege of the writ of habeas corpus shall not be suspended unless when in Cases of Rebellion or Invasion the public Safety may require it.	US Const. Article 1, Section 9, via Slaughter-House Cases, 83 U.S. 36, 77 (1873)
	The prohibition against ex post facto laws and bills of attainder	US Const. Article 1, Section 9 via Slaughter-House Cases, 83 U.S. 36, 77 (1873)
	All persons born or naturalized in the United States, and subject to the jurisdiction thereof, are citizens of the United States and of the State wherein they reside	US Const. 14th Amendment via Slaughter-House Cases 83 U.S. 36, 80 (1873)
	Nor shall any State deprive any person of life, liberty or property, without due process of law; nor deny to any person within its jurisdiction the equal protection of the laws	US Const. 14th Amendment via Slaughter-House Cases 83 U.S. 36, 80 (1873)
	Neither slavery nor involuntary servitude, except as punishment for crime whereof the party shall have been duly convicted, shall exist within the United States, or any place subject to their jurisdiction	US Const. 13th Amendment via Slaughter-House Cases 83 U.S. 36, 80 (1873)

provide the freed slaves with the full rights of American citizenship that the *Dred Scott* decision had denied them. It is difficult to believe that the Supreme Court would want to be more restrictive of citizens than Chief Justice Taney was in *Dred Scott*. That would imply that since we gave African Americans the rights of citizenship, we had to reduce the rights of all other citizens.

In our three branches of the federal government, we pay the salaries for a total of 546 primary level servants for the citizens of the United States of America. In the legislative branch, these include 100 members of United States Senate and 435 members of the United States House of Representatives. In the executive branch, these include the President and the Vice President. Finally, in the judicial branch, this includes 9 members of the United States Supreme Court. Between the Legislative and Executive branches, we pay for a total of 537 primary level politicians. Is it too much to ask that the nine members of the United States Supreme Court be non-political?

The problem with Supreme Court justices being political is that it can lead to legally irrational and societally destructive decisions. When justices allow their feelings to overrule the original meaning of the Constitution, and our nation's laws and history, they can stumble into writing atrocious decisions such as *Dred Scott*(see Chapter 4). To support their political wishes, they can also be forced to write factually incorrect and distorted decisions such as the primary dissent in *District of Columbia v. Heller*(See Chapter 6). If a justice is not happy with how a case needs to be decided based on the Constitution and our laws, their duty should be to write a dissent describing what needs to be done to change the outcome. At the extreme, this could involve the need for a Constitutional Amendment. More often, it would require Congress to actually implement or change a law.

American citizens are those who have implemented and funded the government of the United States of America. When we read "*We the People of the United States*" in the preamble of the United States Constitution, it is American citizens that are being described. Anyone else is legally part of the "people" of another country. The rights of American citizens (their privileges and immunities) should be the gold standard of rights. The Supreme Court should work to protect and enshrine them; instead of reducing them by trying to make everyone in our country's rights be the same. People should be proud of their American citizenship and the resulting benefits. There is no place for the Supreme Court to be apologetic for the differences in rights between citizens and non-citizens.

With regards to our Nationwide Privileges and Immunities, it is understandable that people with longstanding perspectives may have a difficult time accepting change. That is why this book has endeavored to show overwhelming evidence. It shows an almost thousand year history to show what has happened. Most importantly, it has identified three "Butterfly" effects that explain the causes of confusion. If a reader thinks that one of the pieces of the puzzle is out of place or incorrect, a sincere discussion of the facts should be able to discern the truth. Ultimately, it is hoped that this analysis will be used by the United States Supreme Court to help to resurrect our Nationwide Privileges and Immunities.

Acknowledgments

First and foremost, as a Christian, I would like to thank God for providing me with the inspiration, perseverance, and ability to research, develop, and write this book. Next, I would like to thank my amazing wife Cathy, who has been married to me for over 36 years and counting. She has been at my side through both good times and bad. She has always been willing to provide her advice and opinions, and has thoroughly supported me throughout my effort to research and write this book.

Reading Supreme Court Opinions over the years, I have been intrigued for over a decade with the mystery of the demise of the Privileges and Immunities clause. Justice Clarence Thomas' writings inspired me to spend the time to delve into this topic to understand what went wrong. As someone who has always loved American History, the uncertainty around such an important subject was maddening. I felt an obligation to look at the problem from a new perspective; especially on the 250th Anniversary of our great country.

Next, I would like to thank my friend Tim for inviting me to join the *Books and Brews* book club that meets monthly at different craft brewerys throughout Silicon Valley. I would like to acknowledge the spirited discussions with Tim over our opposing opinions on topics of the day. As a constructive outlet for my thoughts, I started to write and publish articles with the American Thinker website. Later, when my writings became too complex for their article length limits, I reached out to the Intellectual Conservative website. I truly want to thank Rachel Alexander for allowing me to post in depth studies on the intellectualconservative.com website. After reading an in depth study of mine on the Privileges and Immunities Clause, a dear friend Mariel suggested I write a book. I realized that this topic was way too complex to continue to try to explain in articles, and that was the genesis of this effort.

Having lived my entire life in California for the last 64 years, I have been sorely disappointed by the direction of the state this Millennium. I want to acknowledge the actions of NIAID Director Dr. Anthony Fauci, California Governor Gavin Newsom and Santa Clara County Health Director, Dr. Sara Cody during the COVID-19 pandemic. Without the extreme nature of their actions, I might not have found it necessary to write this book.

On a positive note, I want to thank our founding fathers for setting up a Constitutional Republic that provides every American citizen with the right to express their opinions. I especially want to thank those who have given their lives to protect our rights throughout our nation's history. These include my great-great-great-great-great Grandfather Benoni Messenger(1718-1777) who fought in the Revolutionary War at the Battle of Bennington, Vermont. He was already a third generation Messenger born in what is now the United States. They originally settled in the 1630's in Connecticut Colony. Benoni lost his two eldest sons fighting for the British in the French and Indian Wars in Quebec in 1759. At the age of 59, he rode over 50 miles on horseback from his home in Becket, Massachusetts to Bennington, Vermont where our Revolutionary Army defeated the British in a major battle. He wasn't killed in the battle, but died approximately a month later after the arduous effort.

In the coming generations, my Messenger relatives were early settlers in Ohio. My great-great grandfather William B. Messenger fought for the Union Army during the end of the Civil War at the age of 39. He was in Georgia and Tennessee as the war ended. He was protecting the newly freed slaves, and maintaining order with the returning Confederate soldiers. His letters from the war describe the sorrow of hearing of President Lincoln's assassination. Ultimately, disease killed over 50 members of his Ohio 186th Infantry unit. He passed away just hours before his wife arrived from Ohio to comfort him. William left behind three children, including my four year old great-grandfather. This book is written in memory of my relatives who died protecting the rights of Americans, as well as my many relatives who served in the Armed forces.

Finally, I want to acknowledge my father Miles and my mother Frances who are no longer with us. They both worked very hard to provide a loving household with a powerful focus on education. They provided me with a strong moral compass and the life skills that helped to shape me into the person that I am today.

Other Publications by the Author

American Thinker, May 25, 2019
California Liberals Can Beat Climate Change by Stopping Illegal Immigration

Climate change and illegal immigration are the two biggest crises that we hear about on the news today. What may come as a surprise is that there is a significant link between these two. This article shows how California could dramatically help the greenhouse gas problem in the short term. Using revenue generated from those improvements, this article then shows how California can help move the world towards energy security and a greenhouse gas emission free future...

American Thinker, June 7, 2019
How a Post-Civil War Supreme Court Decision Dismantles Sanctuary Cities

Shortly after the Civil War and the passage of the 14th Amendment, the US Supreme Court decided the Slaughter-House cases. Historically, many people have looked at these decisions as severely limiting the ability of the federal government and federal courts from interfering with state government functions by using the Privileges and Immunities clause of the 14th Amendment. Regardless of your position on that debate, this article looks at how the decision by Justice Miller in 1873 actually provides a strong precedent for using the Privileges and Immunities clause of the 14th Amendment against all sanctuary states, counties, and cities....

American Thinker, June 21, 2019

Liberals' National Popular Vote Scheme Is Unconstitutional and Dangerous

As of now, fourteen states have passed the National Popular Vote Interstate Compact (NPVIC), which attempts to eliminate the Electoral College as set forth in the United States Constitution. There have been many good articles written about the legality of interstate compacts to achieve the desired National Popular Vote goals. The author does not need to rehash all of those problems but believes that there are three additional ways that the NPVIC is both unconstitutional and dangerous....

Intellectual Conservative, 03/29/2021

Washington, D.C. Statehood is the Wrong Solution for America's Federal District

My first of many visits to Washington, D.C. was in the summer of 1969. I was eight and my family drove across the country from California. That family visit made me excited and proud to be an American. I distinctly remember visiting the US Capitol, where there was tremendous anticipation in the Senate gallery that Vice President Agnew could be coming into the Senate for a tie-breaking vote. I also remember touring the White House and being amazed by its size and that the president got to live there. During the 1960s, as today, the issue of Washington, D.C. Representation was in the forefront of many resident's minds. This paper compares three possible plans for Washington, D.C. representation: the status quo, Maryland retrocession, and statehood. It uses the lenses of history, size, equity, and the Constitution to arrive at conclusions....

Intellectual Conservative, 04/27/2021

Does my State have to accept Gold or Silver Coins for my State Income Tax Payments?

As a resident of California, with the highest state Income tax rates in the country, this question is especially applicable to the 40 Million people in my state. This article shows how the wisdom of the founders could help halt the destruction of the US Dollar by out-of-control Federal spending. The use of gold and silver as currency has been around for over 5,000 years. Until 1971, United States Federal Reserve Notes were backed by gold. This article proposes that the removal of the US from the Gold Standard did not remove the obligation of the states to accept gold and silver coins as legal tender.

This article describes with a concise example how the requirement that states accept gold and silver coins in the US Constitution creates a financial arbitrage opportunity. It then shows how this situation could result in the states applying pressure on the Federal Government to control spending to stabilize the dollar. Since this is a novel proposal, a series of possible arguments against the approach are described with proposed rebuttals. Ultimately, this is a theoretical question, and the practical and legal answer can only be determined by state taxing authorities and the courts....

Intellectual Conservative, 08/24/24

Reclaiming our American Privileges and Immunities Inheritance

United States Supreme Court Justice Clarence Thomas has been on a 25+ year mission to resurrect the Privileges and Immunities clause of the United States Constitution. His opinions in cases including Saenz v. Roe(1999), Timbs v. Indiana(2019), and McDonald v. Chicago(2010) inspired the author to research this topic. The author was searching for historical perspective when he came across a very obscure and detailed Supreme Court precedent that describes the rights of travel, assembly, speech, and carrying arms. Justice Thomas obliquely referenced this text in McDonald v. Chicago with regards to gun rights, but he appeared to hit a roadblock and was able to move on to other historical examples to make his point....

This essay provides additional historical information and perspective to help counteract the roadblock that Justice Thomas faced. It uses graphics with Supreme Court text in white boxes and adjacent helpful information in shaded boxes to explain complex topics and sentence structures. This essay explains how Privileges and Immunities can, and should, be more powerful in protecting our freedoms than even the 1st and 2nd Amendments in the Bill of Rights. More details can be found in Appendix 1 which provides a formal list of Privileges and Immunities and their associated Supreme Court precedents, as well as Appendix 2 which shows a timeline of key Supreme Court precedents....

Intellectual Conservative, 10/23/24

The Kamala Harris Environmental Disaster

This article presents a detailed analysis that describes the massive hypocrisy of Kamala Harris and other Democrats with respect to their proclaimed fight against Climate Change. It uses their own metrics to show that in their own words "they have created an environmental disaster". This disaster is a direct result of the tsunami of migrants that they have both allowed and brought into our country over the last 3 ½ years.

Prior to the COVID pandemic, Gallup reported that over 750 Million people would like to migrate worldwide. By 2021, this had increased to almost 900 Million people. The root cause of virtually all human migration is a desire for a better life, and the belief that the risks of migrating are exceeded by the expected rewards of that better life. The Biden-Harris reversals of approximately 50 common-sense executive orders to enforce our border has created a giant attraction to migrating to our country. Instead of forcing unvetted and predominately unqualified asylum seekers to wait in the first safe country they enter while their claims are reviewed, the Biden-Harris administration allows them to live and work in the United States for many years before their claims are even heard. Instead of having our Border Patrol Agents spending their time stopping illegal border crossings of people and drugs, the Biden-Harris administration has them spending their time as a concierge service for migrants.

Over the last 7 years, no person has had more power over migration and climate change than Kamala Harris. As a United States Senator from California from 2017-2021, she co-sponsored the Green New Deal while she fought President Trump's border wall proposals. As Vice President, she has been the tie breaking vote on the oxymoronically named "Inflation Reduction Act" which helped to bring about the highest inflation in over 40 years to American citizens. As the media ordained "Border Czar", in charge of finding and addressing the root causes of immigration, she failed to quickly acknowledge and correct the fact that the Biden-Harris administration's actions were the root cause of the problem.

Appendix 1 - Magna Carta (1215)

ID[1]	Translation of the Magna Carta Paragraphs by Professor Nicholas Vincent, Copyright Sotheby's Inc.[2]	Simplified Description of Right[3]
	[The National Archives provides a translation of the Magna Carta from 1297. King Edward I reigned in 1297, and he is referring to his father King Henry III whose reign lasted from 1216-1272. King John had approved the original Magna Carta a year before his father's reign in 1215] Edward by the grace of God King of England, lord of Ireland and duke of Aquitaine sends greetings to all to whom the present letters come. We have inspected the great charter of the lord Henry, late King of England, our father, concerning the liberties of England in these words: Henry by the grace of God King of England, lord of Ireland, duke of Normandy and Aquitaine and count of Anjou sends greetings to his archbishops, bishops, abbots, priors, earls, barons, sheriffs, reeves, ministers and all his bailiffs and faithful men inspecting the present charter. Know that we, at the prompting of God and for the health of our soul and the souls of our ancestors and successors, for the glory of holy Church and the improvement of our realm, freely and out of our good will have given and granted to the archbishops, bishops, abbots, priors, earls, barons and all of our realm these liberties written below to hold in our realm of England in perpetuity.	
MC1	[Section 1 explains that these rights are perpetual] In the first place we grant to God and confirm by this our present charter for ourselves and our heirs in perpetuity that the English Church is to be free and to have all its rights fully and its liberties entirely. We furthermore grant and give to all the freemen of our realm for ourselves and our heirs in perpetuity the liberties written below to have and to hold to them and their heirs from us and our heirs in perpetuity.	Right for the Church of England to be free with full rights and liberties.

1 ID values provided by the Author for internal referencing purposes. They reference the paragraph number from the Translation.

2 United States National Archives and Records Administration. (2026, Feb. 22). https://www.archives.gov/exhibits/featured-documents/magna-carta/translation.html Comments in "[ ]" are provided by the author to provide additional perspective.

3 Simplified Description of Right is generated by the author.

ID[1]	Translation of the Magna Carta Paragraphs by Professor Nicholas Vincent, Copyright Sotheby's Inc.[2]	Simplified Description of Right[3]
MC2	[Section 2 pertains to inheritance for earls and barons who die in military service]	Not directly applicable to the United States of America
MC3	[Defines additional inheritance conditions from MC2 for heirs who are under age]	Not directly applicable to the United States of America
MC4	[Defines additional inheritance conditions to MC2 and MC3]	Not directly applicable to the United States of America
MC5	[Defines additional inheritance conditions to MC2-MC4]	Not directly applicable to the United States of America
MC6	Heirs are to be married without disparagement.	Right to inherit an estate and then not to be disparaged in getting married.
MC7	A widow, after the death of her husband, is immediately and without any difficulty to have her marriage portion and her inheritance, nor is she to pay anything for her dower or her marriage portion or for her inheritance which her husband and she held on the day of her husband's death, and she shall remain in the chief dwelling place of her husband for forty days after her husband's death, within which time dower will be assigned her if it has not already been assigned, unless that house is a castle, and if it is a castle which she leaves, then a suitable house will immediately be provided for her in which she may properly dwell until her dower is assigned to her in accordance with what is aforesaid, and in the meantime she is to have her reasonable necessities (estoverium) from the common property. As dower she will be assigned the third part of all the lands of her husband which were his during his lifetime, save when she was dowered with less at the church door. No widow shall be distrained to marry for so long as she wishes to live without a husband, provided that she gives surety that she will not marry without our assent if she holds of us, or without the assent of her lord, if she holds of another.	Rights for widows to inherit their husband's estates and the right to a formal process to do so.
MC8	Neither we nor our bailiffs will seize any land or rent for any debt, as long as the existing chattels of the debtor suffice for the payment of the debt and as long as the debtor is ready to pay the debt, nor will the debtor's guarantors be distrained for so long as the principal debtor is able to pay the debt; and should the principal debtor default in his payment of the debt, not having the means to repay it, or should he refuse to pay it despite being able to do so, the guarantors will answer for the debt and, if they wish, they are to have the lands and rents of the debtor until they are repaid the debt that previously they paid on behalf of the debtor, unless the principal debtor can show that he is quit in respect to these guarantors.	Right to due process by the government in collection of debts.
MC9	[Defines rights for the city of London and English Ports]	Not directly applicable to the United States of America
MC10	No-one is to be distrained to do more service for a knight's fee or for any other free tenement than is due from it.	Right to due process in the collection of fees.

ID[1]	Translation of the Magna Carta Paragraphs by Professor Nicholas Vincent, Copyright Sotheby's Inc.[2]	Simplified Description of Right[3]
MC11	Common pleas are not to follow our court but are to be held in a certain fixed place	Right to have judicial proceedings in fixed locations.
MC12	[Assizes refers to sessions of court proceedings. In ancient England, these were handled by traveling judges] Recognisances of novel disseisin and of mort d'ancestor are not to be taken save in their particular counties and in the following way. We or, should we be outside the realm, our chief justiciar, will send our justices once a year to each county, so that, together with the knights of the counties, that may take the aforesaid assizes in the counties; and those assizes which cannot be completed in that visitation of the county by our aforesaid justices assigned to take the said assizes are to be completed elsewhere by the justices in their visitation; and those which cannot be completed by them on account of the difficulty of various articles (of law) are to be referred to our justices of the Bench and completed there.	Right to have judicial proceedings in each county at least once per year. Difficult cases can be moved to a central location.
MC13	[Continuation of requirement for handling specific judicial cases]	Not directly applicable to the United States of America
MC14	[Amerced refers to being fined by amounts that are not established in law] A freeman is not to be amerced for a small offence save in accordance with the manner of the offence, and for a major offence according to its magnitude, saving his sufficiency (salvo contenemento suo), and a merchant likewise, saving his merchandise, and any villain other than one of our own is to be amerced in the same way, saving his necessity (salvo waynagio) should he fall into our mercy, and none of the aforesaid amercements is to be imposed save by the oath of honest and law-worthy men of the neighbourhood. Earls and barons are not to be amerced save by their peers and only in accordance with the manner of their offence.	Right to due process in collection of fines for breaking the law.
MC15	[Refers to forced labor to build bridges and river banks]	Not directly applicable to the United States of America
MC16	[Additional qualification on maintenance of river banks]	Not directly applicable to the United States of America
MC17	No sheriff, constable, coroner or any other of our bailiffs is to hold pleas of our crown.	Right to due process in who can run trials.

ID[1]	Translation of the Magna Carta Paragraphs by Professor Nicholas Vincent, Copyright Sotheby's Inc.[2]	Simplified Description of Right[3]
MC18	If anyone holding a lay fee from us should die, and our sheriff or bailiff shows our letters patent containing our summons for a debt that the dead man owed us, our sheriff or bailiff is permitted to attach and enroll all the goods and chattels of the dead man found in lay fee, to the value of the said debt, by view of law-worthy men, so that nothing is to be removed thence until the debt that remains is paid to us, and the remainder is to be released to the executors to discharge the will of the dead man, and if nothing is owed to us from such a person, all the chattels are to pass to the (use of) the dead man, saving to the dead man's wife and children their reasonable portion.	Right to due process in collection of fees owed to the government when a person dies.
MC19	No constable or his bailiff is to take corn or other chattels from anyone who not themselves of a vill where a castle is built, unless the constable or his bailiff immediately offers money in payment of obtains a respite by the wish of the seller. If the person whose corn or chattels are taken is of such a vill, then the constable or his bailiff is to pay the purchase price within forty days.	Right not to have the government seize property without fair payment.
MC20	[Pertains to fulfilling of castle guard duty]	Not directly applicable to the United States of America
MC21	No sheriff or bailiff of ours or of anyone else is to take anyone's horses or carts to make carriage, unless he renders the payment customarily due, namely for a two-horse cart ten pence per day, and for a three-horse cart fourteen pence per day. No demesne cart belonging to any churchman or knight or any other lady (sic) is to be taken by our bailiffs, nor will we or our bailiffs or anyone else take someone else's timber for a castle or any other of our business save by the will of he to whom the timber belongs.	Right not to have the government seize property without fair payment.
MC22	We shall not hold the lands of those convicted of felony save for a year and a day, whereafter such land is to be restored to the lords of the fees.	Right to due process in handling the land of people convicted of a felony.
MC23	[Pertains to fish weirs in England]	Not directly applicable to the United States of America
MC24	[A 'writ of praecipe' commands you to do something or to appear in court] The writ called 'praecipe' is not to be issued to anyone in respect to any free tenement in such a way that a free man might lose his court	Right to due process regarding requirement to appear in court.
MC25	There is to be a single measure for wine throughout our realm, and a single measure for ale, and a single measure for Corn, that is to say the London quarter, and a single breadth for dyed cloth, russets, and haberjects, that is to say two yards within the lists. And it shall be the same for weights as for measures.	Right to uniform weights and measures.
MC26	Henceforth there is to be nothing given for a writ of inquest from the person seeking an inquest of life or member, but such a writ is to be given freely and is not to be denied.	Right to a free inquest for someone who has died.

ID[1]	Translation of the Magna Carta Paragraphs by Professor Nicholas Vincent, Copyright Sotheby's Inc.[2]	Simplified Description of Right[3]
MC27	[Specific requirements for payments for knight service]	Not directly applicable to the United States of America
MC28	No bailiff is henceforth to put any man on his open law or on oath simply by virtue of his spoken word, without reliable witnesses being produced for the same.	Right to bail with reliable witnesses
MC29	No freeman is to be taken or imprisoned or disseised of his free tenement or of his liberties or free customs, or outlawed or exiled or in any way ruined, nor will we go against such a man or send against him save by lawful judgement of his peers or by the law of the land. To no-one will we sell or deny of delay right or justice.	Right to trial by jury. Right to speedy trial.
MC30	All merchants, unless they have been previously and publicly forbidden, are to have safe and secure conduct in leaving and coming to England and in staying and going through England both by land and by water to buy and to sell, without any evil exactions, according to the ancient and right customs, save in time of war, and if they should be from a land at war against us and be found in our land at the beginning of the war, they are to be attached without damage to their bodies or goods until it is established by us or our chief justiciar in what way the merchants of our land are treated who at such a time are found in the land that is at war with us, and if our merchants are safe there, the other merchants are to be safe in our land.	Discussed in Chapter 1 Not directly applicable to the United States of America
MC31	[Discussed specific inheritance rights in England]	Not directly applicable to the United States of America
MC32	[English restriction on land sales when having debts to the lord of the fee]	Not directly applicable to the United States of America
MC33	[English rights of possession of abbeys]	Not directly applicable to the United States of America
MC34	No-one is to be taken or imprisoned on the appeal of woman for the death of anyone save for the death of that woman's husband.	[This restricts a woman's ability to request the arrest of a killer unless they killed her husband]
MC35	No county court is to be held save from month to month, and where the greater term used to be held, so will it be in future, nor will any sheriff or his bailiff make his tourn through the hundred save for twice a year and only in the place that is due and customary, namely once after Easter and again after Michaelmas, and the view of frankpledge is to be taken at the Michaelmas term without exception, in such a way that every man is to have his liberties which he had or used to have in the time of King H(enry II) my grandfather or which he has acquired since. The view of frankpledge is to be taken so that our peace be held and so that the tithing is to be held entire as it used to be, and so that the sheriff does not seek exceptions but remains content with that which the sheriff used to have in taking the view in the time of King H(enry) our grandfather.	Right to due process in collection of taxes.

ID[1]	Translation of the Magna Carta Paragraphs by Professor Nicholas Vincent, Copyright Sotheby's Inc.[2]	Simplified Description of Right[3]
MC36	Nor is it permitted to anyone to give his land to a religious house in such a way that he receives it back from such a house to hold, nor is it permitted to any religious house to accept the land of anyone in such way that the land is restored to the person from whom it was received to hold. If anyone henceforth gives his land in such a way to any religious house and is convicted of the same, the gift is to be entirely quashed and such land is to revert to the lord of that fee.	[This restricts the ability to donate land to a church and receive some benefit back for donating it.]
MC37	Scutage furthermore is to be taken as it used to be in the time of King H(enry) our grandfather, and all liberties and free customs shall be preserved to archbishops, bishops, abbots, priors, Templars, Hospitallers, earls, barons and all others, both ecclesiastical and secular persons, just as they formerly had.	Discussed in Chapter 1. Not directly applicable to the United States of America

Appendix 2 - Petition of Right (1627)

ID[1]	Petitioned Right Text[2]	Grievance Text[3]	Simplified Description of Right[4]
PR1	that no man hereafter be compelled to make or yield any Gift, Loan, Benevolence, Tax or such like Charge without common consent by Act of Parliament And that none be called to make answer or take such Oath or to give attendance or be confined or otherwise molested or disquieted concerning the same or for refusal thereof.	That whereas it is declared and enacted by a Statute made in the time of the reign of King Edward I commonly called "Statutum de Tallagio non concedendo", That no Tallage or Aid should be laid or levied by the King or his heirs in this realm without the good will and assent of the Archbishops, Bishops, Earles, Barons, Knights, Burgesses and other the Freemen of the commonality of this realm, And by Authority of the Parliament held in the 25th year of the reign of King Edward III it is declared and enacted, That from thenceforth no person should be compelled to make any Loans to the King against his will because such Loans were against reason and the franchise of the Land, And by other Laws of this Realm it is provided that none should be charged by any charge or Imposition called a Benevolence nor by such like Charge by which the Statutes before mentioned and other the good Laws and Statutes of this Realm your Subjects have inherited this Freedom That they should not be compelled to contribute to any Tax, Tallage, Aid or other like Charge not set by common consent in Parliament. [CONTINUED]	Right not to be taxed without legislative approval

1 ID values provided by the Author for internal referencing purposes

2 United Kingdom National Archives. (2026, Feb. 22). Petition of Right. https://www.legislation.gov.uk/aep/Cha1/3/1/enacted
Conversion to modern American spelling for ease of reading.

3 Ibid. Conversion to modern American spelling for ease of reading.

4 Simplified Description of Right is generated by the author to describe the Petitioned Right in light of the Grievance.

ID[1]	Petitioned Right Text[2]	Grievance Text[3]	Simplified Description of Right[4]
PR1		[CONTINUED] Yet nevertheless of late diverse Commissions directed to sundry Commissioners in several Counties with Instructions have issued, by means whereof your people have been in diverse places assembled and required to lend certain sums of money unto your Majestie, and many of them upon their refusal so to do have had an Oath administered unto them not warrantable by the Laws or Statutes of this Realm and have been constrained to become bound to make appearance and give attendance before your Privy Council and in other places; and others of them have been therefore imprisoned confined and sundry other ways molested and disquieted And diverse other charges have been laid and levied upon your people in several Counties by Lord Lieutenants, Deputy Lieutenants, Commissioners for Musters, Justices of Peace, and others by Command or Direction from your Majestie or your Privy Council against the Laws and free Customs of the Realm.	
PR2	And that no freeman in any such manner as is before mentioned be imprisoned or detained.	And where also by the Statute called The great Charter of the Liberties of England, It is declared and enacted, That no Freeman may be taken or imprisoned or be disseised of his Freehold or Liberties or his free Customs or be outlawed or exiled or in any manner destroyed, but by the lawful Judgment of his Peers or by the Law of the Land. And in the 28th year of the reign of King Edward III it was declared and enacted by authority of Parliament, that no man of what estate or condition that he be, should be put out of his Land or Tenements, nor taken, nor imprisoned, nor disinherited, nor put to death, without being brought to answer by due process of Law. [CONTINUED]	Right to being formally charged with a crime, and to due process, before being imprisoned

ID[1]	Petitioned Right Text[2]	Grievance Text[3]	Simplified Description of Right[4]
PR2		[CONTINUED] Nevertheless against the tenor of the said Statutes and other the good Laws and Statutes of your Realm to that end provided, diverse of your Subjects have of late been imprisoned without any cause showed: And when for their deliverance they were brought before your Justices by your Majesties Writs of Habeas Corpus there to undergo and receive as the Court should order, and their Keepers commanded to certify the causes of their detainer, no cause was certified, but that they were detained by your Majesties special command signified by the Lords of your Privy Council, and yet were returned back to several prisons without being charged with anything to which they might make answer according to the Law.	
PR3	And that your Majestie would be pleased to remove the said Soldiers and Mariners and that your people may not be so burdened in time to come.	And whereas of late great Companies of Soldiers and Mariners have been dispersed into diverse Counties of the Realm, and the inhabitants against their wills have been compelled to receive them into their houses, and there to suffer them to sojourn against the Laws and Customs of this Realm and to the great grievance and vexation of the people.	Right not to have soldiers or sailors quartered in your home
PR4	And that the aforesaid Commissions for proceeding by Martial Law may be revoked and annulled. And that hereafter no Commissions of like nature may issue forth to any person or persons whatsoever to be executed as aforesaid, lest by color of them any of your Majesties Subjects be destroyed or put to death contrary to the Laws and Franchise of the Land.	and that Commissions have issued under the Great Seal for Proceedings according to Martial Law. And whereas also by authority of Parliament in the 25th year of the Reign of King Edward III it is declared and enacted that no man should be forejudged of life or limb against the form of the Great Charter and the Law of the Land, And by the said Great Charter, and other the Laws and Statutes of this your Realm no man ought to be adjudged to death but by the Laws established in this your Realm, either by the customs of the same Realm or by Acts of Parliament. And whereas no offender of what kind soever is exempted from the proceedings to be used and punishments to be inflicted by the Lawes and Statutes of this your Realm, [CONTINUED]	Right not to be tried and executed under martial law that is not approved by the legislature

ID[1]	Petitioned Right Text[2]	Grievance Text[3]	Simplified Description of Right[4]
PR4		[CONTINUED] Nevertheless of late time diverse Commissions under your Majesties great Seal have issued forth, by which certain persons have been assigned and appointed Commissioners with power and authority to proceed within the land according to the Justice of Martial Law against such Soldiers or Mariners or other dissolute persons joining with them as should commit any murder, robbery, felony, mutiny, or other outrage or misdemeanor whatsoever, and by such summary course and order as is agreeable to Martial Law and as is used in Armies in time of war to proceed to the trial and condemnation of such offenders, and them to cause to be executed and put to death according to the Law Martial. By pretext whereof some of your Majesties Subjects have been by some of the said Commissioners put to death, when and where, if by the Laws and Statutes of the land they had deserved death, by the same Laws and Statutes also they might and by no other ought to have been judged and executed. And also sundry grievous offenders by color thereof claiming an exemption have escaped the punishments due to them by the Laws and Statutes of this your Realm, by reason that diverse of your Officers and ministers of Justice have unjustly refused or forborne to proceed against such Offenders according to the same Laws and Statutes upon pretense that the said offenders were punishable only by Martial law and by authority of such Commissions as aforesaid. Which Commissions and all other of like nature are wholly and directly contrary to the said Lawes and Statutes of this your Realm.	

Appendix 3 - Habeus Corpus Act (1679)

ID[1]	Petitioned Right Text[2]	Grievance Text[3]	Simplified Description of Right[4]
HC1	For the prevention whereof, and the more speedy relief of all persons imprisoned for any such criminal or supposed criminal matters; be it enacted by the King's most excellent majesty, by and with the advice and consent of the lords spiritual and temporal, and Commons, in this present Parliament assembled, and by the authority thereof. That whensoever any person or persons shall bring any habeas corpus directed unto any sheriff or sheriffs, jailer, minister or other person whatsoever, for any person in his or their custody, and the said writ shall be served upon the said officer, or left at the jail or prison with any of the under-officers, under-keepers, or deputy of the said officers or keepers, that the said officer or officers, his or their under-officers, under-keepers or deputies, shall, within three days after the service thereof as aforesaid, (unless the commitment aforesaid were for treason or felony, plainly and specially expressed in the warrant of commitment), upon payment or tender of the charges of bringing the said prisoner, to be ascertained by the Judge or Court that awarded the same…	WHEREAS great Delays have been used by Sheriffs, Jailers and other Officers to whose Custody any of the Kings Subjects have been committed for criminal or supposed criminal Matters in making Returns of Writs of Habeas Corpus to them directed by standing out an Alias and Pluries Habeas Corpus and sometimes more and by other shifts to avoid their yielding Obedience to such Writs contrary to their Duty and the known Laws of the Land whereby many of the Kings Subjects have been and hereafter may be long detained in Prison in such Cases where by Law they are bailable to their great charge and vexation.	Right to Habeus Corpus

1 ID values provided by the Author for internal referencing purposes

2 United Kingdom National Archives. (2026, Feb. 22). Habeus Corpus Act. https://www.legislation.gov.uk/aep/Cha2/31/2
Conversion to modern American spelling for ease of reading. The word "gaol" has been replaced with "jail".

3 Ibid. Conversion to modern American spelling for ease of reading. The word "gaol" has been replaced with "jail".

4 Simplified Description of Right is generated by the author to describe the Petitioned Right in light of the Grievance.

ID[1]	Petitioned Right Text[2]	Grievance Text[3]	Simplified Description of Right[4]
HC2	And, for preventing illegal imprisonments in prisons beyond the seas, be it further enacted by the authorities aforesaid that no subject of this realm that now is, or hereafter shall be an inhabitant or resident of this Kingdom of England, dominion of Wales, or town of Berwick upon Tweed, shall or may be sent prisoner		Right not to be imprisoned overseas or far from home

Appendix 4 - [English] Bill of Rights (1688)

ID[1]	Declared Right in the Bill of Rights text[2]	Corresponding Grievance in the Bill of Rights text[3]	Simplified Description of Right[4]
	[In front of each declared right, the following sentence should be read] "And thereupon the said Lords Spiritual and Temporal and Commons pursuant to their respective Letters and Elections being now assembled in a full and free Representative of this Nation taking into their most serious Consideration the best means for attaining the Ends aforesaid Doe in the first place (as their Ancestors in like Case have usually done) for the Vindicating and Asserting their ancient Rights and Liberties, Declare"	**[In front of each grievance, the following sentence should be read]** "Whereas the late King James the Second by the Assistance of diverse evil Counselors, Judges and Ministers employed by him did endeavor to subvert and extirpate the Protestant Religion and the Laws and Liberties of this Kingdom"	
	[After each declared right, the following sentence should be read] "And they do Claim, Demand, and Insist upon all and singular the Premises as their undoubted Rights and Liberties and that no Declarations, Judgements, Doings or Proceedings to the Prejudice of the People in any of the said Premises ought in any wise to be drawn hereafter into Consequence or Example."	**[After each grievance, the following sentence should be read]** "All which are utterly and directly contrary to the known Laws and Statutes and Freedom of this Realm."	

1 ID values provided by the Author for internal referencing purposes

2 United Kingdom National Archives. (2026, Feb. 22). [English] Bill of Rights. https://www.legislation.gov.uk/aep/WillandMarSess2/1/2/introduction/enacted
Comments in "[ ]" are provided by the author to provide additional perspective. Conversion to modern American spelling for ease of reading.

3 Ibid.
Comments in "[ ]" are provided by the author to provide additional perspective. Conversion to modern American spelling for ease of reading.

4 Simplified Description of Right is generated by the author to describe the Petitioned Right in light of the Grievance.

ID[1]	Declared Right in the Bill of Rights text[2]	Corresponding Grievance in the Bill of Rights text[3]	Simplified Description of Right[4]
EBR1	That the pretended Power of Suspending of Laws or the Execution of Laws by Regal Authority without Consent of Parliament is illegal.	By Assuming and Exercising a Power of Dispensing with and Suspending of Laws and the Execution of Laws without Consent of Parliament.	Right not to have laws suspended without legislature's approval
EBR2	That the pretended Power of Suspending of Laws or the Execution of Laws by Regal Authority as it hath been assumed and exercised of late is illegal.	By Committing and Prosecuting diverse Worthy Prelates for humbly Petitioning to be excused from Concurring to the said Assumed Power.	Right not to be prosecuted for petitioning to be excused from laws
EBR3	That the Commission for erecting the late Court of Commissioners for Ecclesiastical Causes and all other Commissions and Courts of like nature are Illegal and Pernicious.	By issuing and causing to be executed a Commission under the Great Seal for Erecting a Court called The Court of Commissioners for Ecclesiastical Causes.	Right not to be prosecuted by an Ecclesiastical Court
EBR4	That levying Money for or to the Use of the Crowne by pretense of Prerogative without Grant of Parliament for longer time or in other manner then the same is or shall be granted is Illegal.	By Levying Money for and to the Use of the Crowne by pretense of Prerogative for other time and in other manner then the same was granted by Parliament.	Right not to have the government spend money not approved by the legislature
EBR5	That it is the Right of the Subjects to petition the King and all Commitments and Prosecutions for such Petitioning are Illegal.		Right to petition the government for a redress of grievances
EBR6	That the raising or keeping a standing Army within the Kingdome in time of Peace unless it be with Consent of Parliament is against Law.	By raising and keeping a Standing Army within this Kingdome in time of Peace without Consent of Parliament and Quartering Soldiers contrary to Law.	Right not to have a standing army without the approval of the legislature
EBR7	That the Subjects which are Protestants may have Arms for their Defense suitable to their Conditions and as allowed by Law.	By causing several good Subjects being Protestants to be disarmed at the same time when Papists were both Armed and Employed contrary to Law.	Right for citizens to have arms for their personal defense
EBR8	That Election of Members of Parliament ought to be free.	By Violating the Freedom of Election of Members to serve in Parliament.	Right to have free elections
EBR9	That the Freedom of Speech and Debates or Proceedings in Parliament ought not to be impeached or questioned in any Court or Place out of Parliament.	By Prosecutions in the Court of Kings Bench for Matters and Causes cognizable only in Parliament and by diverse other Arbitrary and Illegal Courses.	Right for members of the legislature to speak and debate freely

ID[1]	Declared Right in the Bill of Rights text[2]	Corresponding Grievance in the Bill of Rights text[3]	Simplified Description of Right[4]
EBR10	That Jurors ought to be duly impaneled and returned and Jurors which passe upon Men in Trials for High Treason ought to be Freeholders.	And whereas of late years Partial, Corrupt and Unqualified Persons have been returned and served on Juries in Trials and particularly diverse Jurors in Trials for High Treason which were not Freeholders,	Right to have only qualified jurors seated for trials
EBR11	That excessive Bail ought not to be required	And excessive Baile hath been required of Persons committed in Criminal Cases to elude the Benefit of the Lawes made for the Liberty of the Subjects.	Right to not have excessive bail required
EBR12	…nor excessive Fines imposed	And excessive Fines have been imposed.	Right to not have excessive fines imposed
EBR13	…nor cruel and unusual Punishments inflicted	And illegal and cruel Punishments inflicted.	Right to not have cruel or unusual punishments inflicted
EBR14	That all Grants and Promises of Fines and Forfeitures of particular persons before Conviction are illegal and void.	And several Grants and Promises made of Fines and Forfeitures before any Conviction or Judgement against the Persons upon whom the same were to be levied.	Right against pre-conviction fines and forfeitures
EBR15	And that for Redress of all Grievances and for the amending strengthening and preserving of the Laws Parliaments ought to be held frequently.		Right to have frequent meetings of the legislature
	[At the end of the description of the Declaration required for new Kings or Queens to be made prior to the Coronation Oath.] "All which Their Majesties are contented and pleased shall be declared enacted and established by authority of this present Parliament and shall stand remain and be the Law of this Realm forever …		

Appendix 5 - Declaration of Independence Rights (1776)

ID[1]	Opening Paragraphs to the Declaration of Independence[2]	Simplified Description of Implied Right[3]
	We hold these truths to be self-evident, that all men are created equal, that they are endowed by their Creator with certain unalienable Rights, that among these are Life, Liberty and the pursuit of Happiness.--That to secure these rights, Governments are instituted among Men, deriving their just powers from the consent of the governed,	Since the government is instituted by men, and it derives its power from the men who institute it, it is implied that all men have the:
D1	**[From Above]**	The right to speak and write about issues associated with the government (including regarding laws, policies, and members of the government)
D2	**[From Above]**	The right to assemble to support or protest the actions of the government
D3	That whenever any Form of Government becomes destructive of these ends, it is the Right of the People to alter or to abolish it, and to institute new Government, laying its foundation on such principles and organizing its powers in such form, as to them shall seem most likely to effect their Safety and Happiness.	The right to alter or abolish destructive governments

ID	List of Grievance(s) against King George III of England	Simplified Description of Implied Right
D4	He has refused his Assent to Laws, the most wholesome and necessary for the public good. He has forbidden his Governors to pass Laws of immediate and pressing importance, unless suspended in their operation till his Assent should be obtained; and when so suspended, he has utterly neglected to attend to them. [CONTINUED]	The right to have a representative government that is responsive to the citizen's needs

1 ID values are provided by the Author for internal referencing purposes

2 United States National Archives and Records Administration. (2026, Feb. 22). https://www.archives.gov/founding-docs/declaration-transcript

3 Simplified Description of Implied Right is generated by the author based on the context of the description and/or in light of the grievance.

ID	List of Grievance(s) against King George III of England	Simplified Description of Implied Right
D4	[CONTINUED] He has refused to pass other Laws for the accommodation of large districts of people, unless those people would relinquish the right of Representation in the Legislature, a right inestimable to them and formidable to tyrants only. He has dissolved Representative Houses repeatedly, for opposing with manly firmness his invasions on the rights of the people. He has refused for a long time, after such dissolutions, to cause others to be elected; whereby the Legislative powers, incapable of Annihilation, have returned to the People at large for their exercise; the State remaining in the mean time exposed to all the dangers of invasion from without, and convulsions within. He has endeavoured to prevent the population of these States; for that purpose obstructing the Laws for Naturalization of Foreigners; refusing to pass others to encourage their migrations hither, and raising the conditions of new Appropriations of Lands. He has combined with others to subject us to a jurisdiction foreign to our constitution, and unacknowledged by our laws; giving his Assent to their Acts of pretended Legislation: For imposing Taxes on us without our Consent: For taking away our Charters, abolishing our most valuable Laws, and altering fundamentally the Forms of our Governments: For suspending our own Legislatures, and declaring themselves invested with power to legislate for us in all cases whatsoever.	
D5	He has called together legislative bodies at places unusual, uncomfortable, and distant from the depository of their public Records, for the sole purpose of fatiguing them into compliance with his measures.	The right to have public records conveniently available for legislative use
D6	He has obstructed the Administration of Justice, by refusing his Assent to Laws for establishing Judiciary powers. He has made Judges dependent on his Will alone, for the tenure of their offices, and the amount and payment of their salaries.	The right to an independent judiciary
D7	He has erected a multitude of New Offices, and sent hither swarms of Officers to harrass our people, and eat out their substance.	The right not to have targeted financial harassment from government officers and authorities
D8	He has kept among us, in times of peace, Standing Armies without the Consent of our legislatures.	The right not to have standing armies without legislative approval

ID	List of Grievance(s) against King George III of England	Simplified Description of Implied Right
D9	He has affected to render the Military independent of and superior to the Civil power. For protecting [quartered armed troops] them, by a mock Trial, from punishment for any Murders which they should commit on inhabitants of these States:	The right to have civilian control of the military
D10	For Quartering large bodies of armed troops among us:	The right not to have troops quartered in your home
D11	For cutting off our Trade with all parts of the world:	The right not to have complete trade embargoes with all other countries
D12	For depriving us in many cases, of the benefits of Trial by Jury:	The right to a trial by jury
D13	For transporting us beyond Seas to be tried for pretended offences:	The right to be tried near where a crime allegedly occurred
D14	For abolishing the free System of English Laws in a neighbouring Province, establishing therein an Arbitrary government, and enlarging its Boundaries so as to render it at once an example and fit instrument for introducing the same absolute rule into these Colonies:	The right to the existing System of English Laws
D15	He has abdicated Government here, by declaring us out of his Protection and waging War against us. He has plundered our seas, ravaged our Coasts, burnt our towns, and destroyed the lives of our people. He is at this time transporting large Armies of foreign Mercenaries to compleat the works of death, desolation and tyranny, already begun with circumstances of Cruelty & perfidy scarcely paralleled in the most barbarous ages, and totally unworthy the Head of a civilized nation. He has constrained our fellow Citizens taken Captive on the high Seas to bear Arms against their Country, to become the executioners of their friends and Brethren, or to fall themselves by their Hands. He has excited domestic insurrections amongst us, and has endeavoured to bring on the inhabitants of our frontiers, the merciless Indian Savages, whose known rule of warfare, is an undistinguished destruction of all ages, sexes and conditions.	The right not to have the government waging war against its citizens

ID	Closing Paragraphs to the Declaration of Independence	Simplified Description of Implied Right
D16	In every stage of these Oppressions We have Petitioned for Redress in the most humble terms: Our repeated Petitions have been answered only by repeated injury.	The right to petition government for a redress of grievances

Appendix 6 - Articles of Confederation Rights (1777)

ID[1]	Source in Articles of Confederation[2]	Simplified Description of Implied Right[3]
AC1	Article IV – "and the people of each state shall have free ingress and regress to and from any other state" "paupers, vagabonds, and fugitives from justice excluded"	The right to freely travel between states; paupers, vagabonds, and fugitives from justice excluded.
AC2	Article IV - "and shall enjoy therein all the privileges of trade and commerce, subject to the same duties, impositions and restrictions as the inhabitants thereof respectively," "paupers, vagabonds, and fugitives from justice excluded"	The right to non-discriminatory trade and commerce when in other states; paupers, vagabonds, and fugitives from justice excluded.
AC3	Article IV – "provided that such restrictions shall not extend so far as to prevent the removal of property imported into any state, to any other State of which the owner is an inhabitant" "paupers, vagabonds, and fugitives from justice excluded"	The right to take property out of a state that you brought into the state; paupers, vagabonds, and fugitives from justice excluded.

1 ID values are provided by the Author for internal referencing purposes

2 United States National Archives and Records Administration. (2026, Feb. 22). https://www.archives.gov/milestone-documents/articles-of-confederation#transcript

3 Simplified Description of Implied Right is generated by the author based on the context of the description.

Appendix 7 - State Constitutional Speech, Press, Redress and Assembly RIghts (prior to United States Constitution)

State	Month/ Year[1]	Freedom of Speech	Freedom of the Press	Redress of Grievances	Freedom of Assembly
New Hampshire	Jan. 1776			Have taken into our serious consideration the unhappy circumstances, into which this colony is involved by means of many grievous and oppressive acts of the British Parliament, depriving us of our natural and constitutional rights and privileges; ...[2]	
South Carolina	Mar. 1776			... harmony between Great Britain and America, ardently desired by the latter, would be thereby immediately restored, and that the colonists confided in the magnanimity and justice of the King and Parliament for redress of the many other grievances under which they labored.[3]	

1 Embedded Dates are used, if they exist in the document, to provide added context

2 Yale Law School, Lillian Goldman Law Library, *The Avalon Project.* (2026, Feb. 23) https://avalon.law.yale.edu/18th_century/nh09.asp

3 Yale Law School, Lillian Goldman Law Library, *The Avalon Project.* (2026, Feb. 23) https://avalon.law.yale.edu/18th_century/sc01.asp#1

State	Month/ Year[1]	Freedom of Speech	Freedom of the Press	Redress of Grievances	Freedom of Assembly
Virginia	Jun. 1776		[Section 12 – Declaration of Rights] That the freedom of the press is one of the great bulwarks of liberty, and can never be restrained but by despotic governments.[4]	WHEREAS George the Third, King of Great Britain … by answering our repeated Petitions for Redress with a Repetition of Injuries;[5]	
New Jersey[6]	Jul. 1776				
Maryland[7]	Aug. 1776		XXXVIII. That the liberty of the press ought to be inviolably preserved.	X. That, for redress of grievances, and for amending, strengthening and preserving the laws, the Legislature ought to be frequently convened. XI. That every man hath a right to petition the Legislature, for the redress of grievances, in a peaceable and orderly manner.	

4 United States National Archives and Records Administration. (2026, Feb. 23). https://www.archives.gov/founding-docs/virginia-declaration-of-rights

5 Virginia Humanities, Encyclopedia Virginia. (2026, Feb. 23). https://encyclopediavirginia.org/primary-documents/the-constitution-of-virginia-1776/

6 New Jersey, Department of State, New Jersey State Archives. (2026, Feb. 23). https://www.nj.gov/state/archives/docconst76.html

7 Yale Law School, Lillian Goldman Law Library, *The Avalon Project*. (2026, Feb. 23). https://avalon.law.yale.edu/17th_century/ma02.asp

State	Month/ Year[1]	Freedom of Speech	Freedom of the Press	Redress of Grievances	Freedom of Assembly
Pennsylvania[8]	Sep, 1776	XII. That the people have a right to freedom of speech,	XII. That the people have a right to … writing, and publishing their sentiments; therefore the freedom of the press ought not to be restrained. SECT. 35. The printing presses shall be free to every person who undertakes to examine the proceedings of the legislature, or any part of government.	XVI. That the people have a right … to apply to the legislature for redress of grievances, by address, petition, or remonstrance.	XVI. That the people have a right to assemble together, to consult for their common good …
Delaware[9]	Sep. 1776				
North Carolina[10]	Dec. 1776		XV. That the freedom of the press is one of the great bulwarks of liberty, and therefore ought never to he restrained.	XVIII. That the people have a right to ... apply to the Legislature, for redress of grievances. XX. That, for redress of grievances, and for amending and strengthening the laws, elections ought to be often held.	XVIII. That the people have a right to assemble together, to consult for their common good…
Georgia[11]	Feb. 1777		ART. LXI. Freedom of the press … to remain inviolate forever.		

8 Yale Law School, Lillian Goldman Law Library, *The Avalon Project.* (2026, Feb. 23). https://avalon.law.yale.edu/18th_century/pa08.asp

9 Yale Law School, Lillian Goldman Law Library, *The Avalon Project.* (2026, Feb. 23). https://avalon.law.yale.edu/18th_century/de02.asp

10 Yale Law School, Lillian Goldman Law Library, *The Avalon Project.* (2026, Feb. 23). https://avalon.law.yale.edu/18th_century/nc07.asp#1

11 Yale Law School, Lillian Goldman Law Library, *The Avalon Project.* (2026, Feb. 23). https://avalon.law.yale.edu/18th_century/ga02.asp

State	Month/ Year[1]	Freedom of Speech	Freedom of the Press	Redress of Grievances	Freedom of Assembly
New York[12]	Apr. 1777			… and whereas no answers whatever to the humble petition of the colonies for redress of grievances and reconciliation with Great Britain has been, or is likely to be, given, but the whole force of that kingdom, aided by foreign mercenaries, is to be exerted for the destruction of the good people of these colonies; … In every stage of these oppressions, we have petitioned for redress in the most humble terms. Our repeated petitions have been answered only by repeated injury.	
Vermont Republic[13]	Jul. 1777	XIV. That the people have a right to freedom of speech…	XIV. That the people have a right to … writing and publishing their sentiments; therefore, the freedom of the press ought not be restrained.		XVIII. That the people have a right to assemble together, to consult for their common good-to instruct their representatives, and to apply to the legislature for redress of grievances, by address, petition or remonstrance.

12 New York, Historical Society of the New York Courts. (2026, Feb. 23). https://history.nycourts.gov/wp-content/uploads/2019/01/Publications_1777-NY-Constitution-compressed.pdf

13 Yale Law School, Lillian Goldman Law Library, *The Avalon Project.* (2026, Feb. 23). https://avalon.law.yale.edu/18th_century/vt01.asp

Appendix 7 - State Constitutional Speech, Press, Redress and Assembly RIghts (prior to the United States Constitution)

State	Month/ Year[1]	Freedom of Speech	Freedom of the Press	Redress of Grievances	Freedom of Assembly
South Carolina[14]	Mar. 1778		XLIII. That the liberty of the press be inviolably preserved.		
Massachusetts[15]	Jun. 1780	Article XVI. The right of free speech shall not be abridged.	Article XVI. The liberty of the press is essential to the security of freedom in a state: it ought not, therefore, to be restrained in this commonwealth.	Article XIX. The people have a right, in an orderly and peaceable manner, to ... give instructions to their representatives, and to request of the legislative body, by the way of addresses, petitions, or remonstrances, redress of the wrongs done them, and of the grievances they suffer.	Article XIX. The people have a right, in an orderly and peaceable manner, to assemble to consult upon the common good;
New Hampshire (Bill of Rights)[16]	Oct. 1783		XXII. The Liberty of the Press is essential to the security of freedom in a state; it ought, therefore, to be inviolably preserved.	XXXII. The people have a right in an orderly and peaceable manner, to ... give instructions to their representatives; and to request of the legislative body, by way of petition or remonstrance, redress of the wrongs done them, and of the grievances they suffer.	XXXII. The people have a right in an orderly and peaceable manner, to assemble and consult upon the common good ...

14 Yale Law School, Lillian Goldman Law Library, *The Avalon Project*. (2026, Feb. 23). https://avalon.law.yale.edu/18th_century/sc02.asp#1

15 The 194th General Court of the Commonwealth of Massachusetts. (2026, Feb. 23). https://malegislature.gov/Laws/Constitution

16 Teaching American History. (2026, Feb. 23). https://teachingamericanhistory.org/document/new-hampshire-bill-of-rights/

State	Month/ Year[1]	Freedom of Speech	Freedom of the Press	Redress of Grievances	Freedom of Assembly
New York (Bill of Rights)[17]				Tenth That it is the right of the citizens of this State to Petition the person administering the government of this State for the time being, or either house of the legislature and all commitments and prosecutions for such petitioning are illegal.	

17 New York, Historical Society of the New York Courts. (2026, Feb. 23). https://history.nycourts.gov/wp-content/uploads/2019/01/Publications_NY-Bill-Rights-compressed.pdf

Appendix 8 - State Constitutional Right to Bear Arms and Militia Structure (prior to the United States Constitution)

State	Month/ Year[1]	Right to Bear Arms	Military & Militia Structure
New Hamp-shire[2]	Jan. 1776		That general and field officers of the militia, on any vacancy, be appointed by the two houses, and all inferior officers be chosen by the respective companies. That all officers of the Army be appointed by the two houses, except they should direct otherwise in case of any emergency.
South Carolina[3]	Mar. 1776	...The colonists were therefore driven to the necessity of taking up arms, to repel force by force, and to defend themselves and their properties against lawless invasions and depredations.[4]	XXIII. That all field-officers in the army, and all captains in the navy, shall be, by the general assembly and legislative council, chosen jointly by ballot, and commissioned by the president and commander-in-chief, and that all other officers in the army or navy shall be commissioned by the president and commander-in-chief XXV. That the president and commander-in-chief, with the advice and consent of the privy council, may appoint during pleasure, until otherwise directed by resolution of the general assembly and legislative council, all other necessary officers, except such as are by law directed to be otherwise chosen. XXVI. That the president and commander-in-chief shall have no power to make war or peace, or enter into any final treaty,- without the consent of the general assembly and legislative council. XXX. That the executive authority be vested in the president and commander-in-chief, limited and restrained as aforesaid.

1 If Embedded Dates exist in the document, tbey are used for added context

2 Yale Law School, Lillian Goldman Law Library, *The Avalon Project.* (2026, Feb. 23) https://avalon.law.yale.edu/18th_century/nh09.asp

3 Yale Law School, Lillian Goldman Law Library, *The Avalon Project.* (2026, Feb. 23) https://avalon.law.yale.edu/18th_century/sc01.asp#1

4 Includes many of the grievances from the Declaration of Independence in an earlier and more detailed form. This corresponds to part of Item D14 in Appendix 5.

State	Month/ Year[1]	Right to Bear Arms	Military & Militia Structure
Virginia[5]	June 1776	Sec. 13. That a well-regulated militia, composed of the body of the people, trained to arms, is the proper, natural, and safe defence of a free State;	Sec. 13. That a well-regulated militia, composed of the body of the people, trained to arms, is the proper, natural, and safe defence of a free State; that standing armies, in time of peace, should be avoided, as dangerous to liberty; and that in all cases the military should be under strict subordination to, and governed by, the civil power. THE present Militia Officers shall be continued, and Vacancies supplied by appointment of the Governour, with the advice of the Privy , on recommendations from the respective County Courts; but the Governour and Council shall have a power of suspending any Officer, and ordering a Court-Martial on Complaint for misbehaviour or inability, or to supply Vacancies of Officers happening when in actual Service. The Governour may embody the Militia, with the advice of the privy Council; and, when embodied, shall alone have the direction of the Militia, under the laws of the Country. [6]
New Jersey[7]	Jul. 1776		8. That the Governor, or, in his Absence, the Vice-President of the Council shall have the Supreme executive Power, be Chancellor of the Colony, and act as Captain-General &Commander in Chief of all the Militia, & other military Force in this Colony; 10. That Captains, & all other inferior Officers of the Militia, shall be chosen by the Companies in the respective Counties; but Field & General Officers by the Council & Assembly.

5 United States National Archives and Records Administration. (2026, Feb. 23). https://www.archives.gov/founding-docs/virginia-declaration-of-rights

6 Virginia Humanities, Encyclopedia Virginia. (2026, Feb. 23). https://encyclopediavirginia.org/primary-documents/the-constitution-of-virginia-1776/

7 New Jersey, Department of State, New Jersey State Archives. (2026, Feb. 23). https://www.nj.gov/state/archives/docconst76.html

State	Month/ Year[1]	Right to Bear Arms	Military & Militia Structure
Maryland[8]	Aug. 1776		XXV. That a well-regulated militia is the proper and natural defence of a free government. XXVI. That standing armies are dangerous to liberty, and ought not to be raised or kept up, without consent of the Legislature. XXVII. That in all cases, and at all times, the military ought to be under strict subordination to and control of the civil power.
Pennsylvania[9]	Sep. 1776	XIII. That the people have a right to bear arms for the defence of themselves and the state; SECT. 43. The inhabitants of this state shall have liberty to fowl and hunt in seasonable times on the lands they hold, and on all other lands therein not inclosed;	VIII. That every member of society hath a right to be protected in the enjoyment of life, liberty and property, and therefore is bound to contribute his proportion towards the expence of that protection, and yield his personal service when necessary, or an equivalent thereto: But no part of a man's property can be justly taken from him, or applied to public uses, without his own consent, or that of his legal representatives: Nor can any man who is conscientiously scrupulous of bearing arms, be justly compelled thereto, if he will pay such equivalent, nor are the people bound by any laws, but such as they have in like manner assented to, for their common good. XIII. ...standing armies in the time of peace are dangerous to liberty, they ought not to be kept up; And that the military should be kept under strict subordination to, and governed by, the civil power. SECT. 20. The president , and in his absence the vice-president, with the council, five of whom shall be a quorum, shall have power to appoint and commissionate judges, naval officers, judge of the admiralty, attorney general and all other officers, civil and military,... The president shall be commander in chief of the forces of the state, but shall not command in person, except advised thereto by the council, and then only so long as they shall approve thereof.

8 Yale Law School, Lillian Goldman Law Library, *The Avalon Project.* (2026, Feb. 23). https://avalon.law.yale.edu/17th_century/ma02.asp

9 Yale Law School, Lillian Goldman Law Library, *The Avalon Project.* (2026, Feb. 23). https://avalon.law.yale.edu/18th_century/pa08.asp

State	Month/ Year[1]	Right to Bear Arms	Military & Militia Structure
Delaware[10]	Sep. 1776	ART. 28. To prevent any violence or force being used at the said elections, no person shall come armed to any of them, and no muster of the militia shall be made on that day; nor shall any battalion or company give in their votes immediately succeeding each other, if any other voter, who offers to vote, objects thereto; nor shall any battalion or company, in the pay of the continent, or of this or any other State, be suffered to remain at the time and place of holding the said elections, nor within one mile of the said places respectively, for twenty-four hours before the opening said elections, nor within twenty-four hours after the same are closed, so as in any manner to impede the freely and conveniently carying on the said election: Provided always, That every elector may, in a peaceable and orderly manner, give in his vote on the said day of election.	ART. 9. The president[11] , with the advice and consent of the privy council, may embody the militia, and act as captain-general and commander-in-chief of them, and the other military force of this State, under the laws of the same. ART. 16. The general assembly, by joint ballots shall appoint the generals and field-officers, and all other officers in the army or navy of this State; and the president may appoint, during pleasure, until otherwise directed by the legislature, all necessary civil officers not hereinbefore mentioned.
North Carolina[12]	Dec. 1776	XVII. That the people have a right to bear arms, for the defence of the State	XVII. … as standing armies, in time of peace, are dangerous to liberty, they ought not to be kept up; and that the military should be kept under strict subordination to, and governed by, the civil power.

10 Yale Law School, Lillian Goldman Law Library, *The Avalon Project.* (2026, Feb. 23). https://avalon.law.yale.edu/18th_century/de02.asp

11 Initially, the state of Delaware had a president instead of a governor.

12 Yale Law School, Lillian Goldman Law Library, *The Avalon Project.* (2026, Feb. 23). https://avalon.law.yale.edu/18th_century/nc07.asp#1

State	Month/ Year[1]	Right to Bear Arms	Military & Militia Structure
Georgia[13]	Feb. 1777	ART. X. No officer whatever shall serve any process, or give any other hinderances to any person entitled to vote, either in going to the place of election' or during the time of the said election, or on their returning home from such election; nor shall any military officer, or soldier, appear at any election in a military character, to the intent that all elections may be free and open.	ART. XVII. No person bearing any post of profit under this State, or any person bearing any military commission under this or any other State or States, except officers of the militia, shall be elected a representative. ART. XXI. The governor, with the advice of the executive council shall fill up all intermediate vacancies that shall happen in offices till the next general election; and all commissions, civil and military, shall be issued by the governor, under his hand and the great seal of the State. ART. XXXV. Every county in this State that has, or hereafter may have, two hundred and fifty men, and upwards, liable to bear arms, shall be formed into a battalion; and when they become too numerous for one battalion, they shall be formed into more, by bill of the legislature; and those counties that have a less number than two hundred and fifty shall be formed into independent companies.

13 Yale Law School, Lillian Goldman Law Library, *The Avalon Project.* (2026, Feb. 23). https://avalon.law.yale.edu/18th_century/ga02.asp

State	Month/ Year[1]	Right to Bear Arms	Military & Militia Structure
New York[14]	Apr, 1777	XL. And whereas it is of the utmost importance to the safety of every State that it should always be in a condition of defence; and it is the duty of every man who enjoys the protection of society to be prepared and willing to defend it;	XVIII. That the governor shall continue in office three years, and shall, by virtue of his office, be general and commander-in-chief of all the militia, and admiral of the navy of this State; XXIV. That all military officers be appointed during pleasure; that all commissioned officers, civil and military, be commissioned by the governor; … XL. …this convention therefore, in the name and by the authority of the good people of this State, doth ordain, determine, and declare that the militia of this State, at all times here-after, as well in peace as in war, shall be armed and disciplined, and in readiness for service. That all such of the inhabitants of this State being of the people called Quakers as, from scruples of conscience, may be averse to the bearing of arms, be therefrom excused by the legislature; and do pay to the State such sums of money, in lieu of their personal service, as the same may, in the judgment of the legislature, be worth. And that a proper magazine of warlike stores, proportionate to the number of inhabitants, be, forever hereafter, at the expense of this State, and by acts of the legislature, established, maintained, and continued in every county in this State.

14 New York, Historical Society of the New York Courts. (2026, Feb. 23). https://history.nycourts.gov/wp-content/uploads/2019/01/Publications_1777-NY-Constitution-compressed.pdf

State	Month/ Year[1]	Right to Bear Arms	Military & Militia Structure
Vermont Republic[15]	Jul. 1977	XV. That the people have a right to bear arms for the defence of themselves and the State; and, as standing armies, in the time of peace, are dangerous to liberty, they ought not to be kept up; and that the military should be kept under strict subordination to, and governed by, the civil power. SECTION XXXIX. That the inhabitants of this State, shall have liberty to hunt and fowl, in seasonable times, on the lands they hold, and on other lands (not enclosed;)	IX. That every member of society hath a right to be protected in the enjoyment of life, liberty and property, and therefore, is bound to contribute his proportion towards the expense of that protection, and yield his personal service, when necessary, or an equivalent thereto; but no part of a man's property can be justly taken from him, or applied to public uses, without his own consent, or that of his legal representatives; nor can any man who is conscientiously scrupulous of bearing arms, be justly compelled thereto, if he will pay such equivalent; nor are the people bound by any law' but such as they have, in like manner, assented to, for their common good. SECTION V. The freemen of this Commonwealth, and their sons, shall be trained and armed for its defence, under such regulations, restrictions and exceptions, as the general assembly shall, by law, direct; preserving always to the people, the right of choosing their colonels of militia, and all commissioned officers under that rank, in such manner, and as often, as by the said laws shall be directed. SECTION XVIII. The Governor, and in his absence, the Lieutenant or Deputy Governor, with the Council-seven of whom shall be a quorum-shall have power to appoint and commissionate all officers, (except those who are appointed by the General Assembly,) agreeable to this frame of government, and the laws that may be made hereafter; and shall supply every vacancy in any office, occasioned by death, resignation, removal or disqualification, until the office can be filled, in the time and manner directed by law or this constitution. SECTION XLII. All field and staff officers, and commissioned officers of the army, and all general officers of the militia, shall be chosen by the General Assembly.

15 Yale Law School, Lillian Goldman Law Library, *The Avalon Project.* (2026, Feb. 23). https://avalon.law.yale.edu/18th_century/vt01.asp

State	Month/ Year[1]	Right to Bear Arms	Military & Militia Structure
South Carolina[16]	Mar. 1778		XI. That the executive authority be vested in the governor and commander-in-chief, in manner herein mentioned XXX. That all the officers in the army and navy of this State, of and above the rank of captain, shall be chosen by the senate and house of representatives jointly, by ballot in the house of representatives, and commissioned by the governor and commander-in-chief, and that all other officers in the army and navy of this State shall be commissioned by the governor and commander-in-chief. XXXI. That in case of vacancy in any of the offices above directed to be filled by the senate and house of representatives, the governor and commander-in-chief, with the advice and consent of the privy council, may appoint others in their stead, until there shall be an election by the senate and house of representatives to fill those vacancies respectively XXXII. That the governor and commander-in-chief, with the advice and consent of the privy council, may appoint during pleasure, until otherwise directed by law, all other necessary officers, except such as are now by law directed to be otherwise chosen. XXXIII. That the governor and commander-in-chief shall have no power to commence war, or conclude peace, or enter into any final treaty without the consent of the senate and house of representatives. XLII. That the military be subordinate to the civil power of the State.

16 Yale Law School, Lillian Goldman Law Library, *The Avalon Project.* (2026, Feb. 23). https://avalon.law.yale.edu/18th_century/sc02.asp#1

State	Month/ Year[1]	Right to Bear Arms	Military & Militia Structure
Massachusetts[17]	Jun. 1780	Part of the First Article XVII. The people have a right to keep and to bear arms for the common defence	Part of the First Article X. Each individual of the society has a right to be protected by it in the enjoyment of his life, liberty and property, according to standing laws. He is obliged, consequently, to contribute his share to the expense of this protection; to give his personal service, or an equivalent, when necessary: Article XVII. … And as, in time of peace, armies are dangerous to liberty, they ought not to be maintained without the consent of the legislature; and the military power shall always be held in an exact subordination to the civil authority, and be governed by it. Article XXVIII. No person can in any case be subject to law-martial, or to any penalties or pains, by virtue of that law, except those employed in the army or navy, and except the militia in actual service, but by authority of the legislature. Section 2 Article VII. The governor of this commonwealth for the time being, shall be the commander in chief of the army and navy, and of all the military forces of the state, by sea and land, and shall have full power by himself, or by any commander, or other officer or officers, from time to time, to train, instruct, exercise and govern the militia and navy;... Article X. ... The governor, with advice of council, shall appoint all officers of the continental army, whom by the confederation of the United States it is provided that this commonwealth shall appoint, as also all officers of forts and garrisons. The divisions of the militia into brigades, regiments and companies, made in pursuance of the militia laws now in force, shall be considered as the proper divisions of the militia of this commonwealth, until the same shall be altered in pursuance of some future law

17 The 194th General Court of the Commonwealth of Massachusetts. (2026, Feb. 23). https://malegislature.gov/Laws/Constitution

State	Month/ Year[1]	Right to Bear Arms	Military & Militia Structure
New Hampshire (Bill of Rights)[18]	Oct. 1783	XII. Every member of the community has a right to be protected by it in the enjoyment of his life, liberty and property; he is therefore bound to contribute his share in the expence of such protection, and to yield his personal service when necessary, or an equivalent.	XIII. No person who is conscientiously scrupulous about the lawfulness of bearing arms, shall be compelled thereto, provided he will pay an equivalent. XXIV. A well regulated militia is the proper, natural, and sure defence of a state. XXV. Standing armies are dangerous to liberty, and ought not to be raised or kept up without the consent of the legislature. XXVI. In all cases, and at all times, the military ought to be under strict subordination to, and governed by the civil power.
New York (Bill of Rights)[19]	Jan. 1787	Ninth That all elections shall be free and that no person by force of arms nor by malice or menacing or otherwise presume to disturb or hinder any citizen of this State to make free election upon pain of fine and imprisonment and treble damages to the party grieved.	

18 Teaching American History. (2026, Feb. 23). https://teachingamericanhistory.org/document/new-hampshire-bill-of-rights/

19 New York, Historical Society of the New York Courts. (2026, Feb. 23). https://history.nycourts.gov/wp-content/uploads/2019/01/Publications_NY-Bill-Rights-compressed.pdf

Appendix 9 - State Constitutional Religious Provisions (prior to the United States Constitution)

State	Month/ Year[1]	Religious Worship and Individual Rights	Government Restrictions
New Hamp-shire[2]	Jan. 1776		
South Carolina[3]	Mar. 1776	... the English laws and a free government, to which the inhabitants of Quebec were entitled by the King's royal proclamation, are abolished and French laws are restored; the Roman Catholic religion (although before tolerated and freely exercised there) and an absolute government are established in that province, and its limits extended through a vast tract of country so as to border on the free Protestant English settlements, with design of using a whole people differing in religious principles from the neighboring colonies, and subject to arbitrary power, as fit instruments to overawe and subdue the colonies.	

1 Embedded Dates are used, if they exist in the document, to provide added context

2 Yale Law School, Lillian Goldman Law Library, *The Avalon Project.* (2026, Feb. 23). https://avalon.law.yale.edu/18th_century/nh09.asp

3 Yale Law School, Lillian Goldman Law Library, *The Avalon Project.* (2026, Feb. 23). https://avalon.law.yale.edu/18th_century/sc01.asp#1

State	Month/ Year[1]	Religious Worship and Individual Rights	Government Restrictions
Virginia[4]	Jun. 1776	Declaration of Rights, Section 16 That religion, or the duty which we owe to our Creator, and the manner of discharging it, can be directed only by reason and conviction, not by force or violence; and therefore all men are equally entitled to the free exercise of religion, according to the dictates of conscience; and that it is the mutual duty of all to practise Christian forbearance, love, and charity toward each other. Declaration of Rights, Section 15 That no free government, or the blessings of liberty, can be preserved to any people but by a firm adherence to justice, moderation, temperance, frugality, and virtue and by frequent recurrence to fundamental principles.	
New Jersey[5]	Jul. 1776	18. That no Person shall ever within this Colony be deprived of the inestimable Privilege of worshipping Almighty God in a Manner agreeable to the Dictates of his own Conscience; nor under any Pretence whatsoever compelled to attend any Place of Worship, contrary to his own Faith and Judgment; nor shall any Person within this Colony ever be obliged to pay Tithes, Taxes, or any other Rates, for the Purpose of building or repairing any Church or Churches, Place or Places of Worship, or for the Maintenance of any Minister or Ministry, contrary to what he believes to be right, or has deliberately or voluntarily engaged himself to perform.	19. That there shall be no Establishment of any one religious Sect in this Province in Preference to another; and that no Protestant Inhabitant of this Colony shall be denied the Enjoyment of any civil Right merely on Account of his religious Principles; but that all Persons, professing a Belief in the Faith of any Protestant Sect, who shall demean themselves peaceably under the Government as hereby established, shall be capable of being elected into any Office of Profit or Trust, or being a Member of either Branch of the Legislature, & shall fully & freely enjoy every Privilege & Immunity enjoyed by others their Fellow-Subjects.

4 United States National Archives and Records Administration. (2026, Feb. 23). https://www.archives.gov/founding-docs/virginia-declaration-of-rights

5 New Jersey, Department of State, New Jersey State Archives. (2026, Feb. 23). https://www.nj.gov/state/archives/docconst76.html

State	Month/ Year[1]	Religious Worship and Individual Rights	Government Restrictions
Maryland[6]	Aug. 1776	XXXIII. That, as it is the duty of every man to worship God in such manner as he thinks most acceptable to him; all persons, professing the Christian religion, are equally entitled to protection in their religious liberty; wherefore no person ought by any law to be molested in his person or estate on account of his religious persuasion or profession, or for his religious practice; unless, under colour of religion, any man shall disturb the good order, peace or safety of the State, or shall infringe the laws of morality, or injure others, in their natural, civil, or religious rights; nor ought any person to be compelled to frequent or maintain, or contribute, unless on contract, to maintain any particular place of worship, or any particular ministry; XXXIV. That every gift, sale, or devise of lands, to any minister, public teacher, or preacher of the gospel, as such, or to any religious sect, order or denomination, or to or for the support, use or benefit of, or in trust for, any minister, public teacher, or preacher of the gospel, as such, or any religious sect, order or denomination-and every gift or sale of good-e, or chattels, to go in succession, or to take place after the death of the seller or donor, or to or for such support, use or benefit-and also every devise of goods or chattels to or for the support, use or benefit of any minister, public teacher, or preacher of the gospel, as such, or any religious sect, order, or denomination, without the leave of the Legislature, shall be void;	XXXIII. ... yet the Legislature may, in their discretion, lay a general and equal tax for the support of the Christian religion; leaving to each individual the power of appointing the payment over of the money, collected from him, to the support of any particular place of worship or minister, or for the benefit of the poor of his own denomination, or the poor in general of any particular county: but the churches, chapels, globes, and all other property now belonging to the church of England, ought to remain to the church of England forever. ... XXXV. That no other test or qualification ought to be required, on admission to any office of trust or profit, than such oath of support and fidelity to this State, and such oath of office, as shall be directed by this Convention or the Legislature of this State, and a declaration of a belief in the Christian religion. XXXVI. That the manner of administering an oath to any person, ought to be such, as those of the religious persuasion, profession, or denomination, of which such person is one, generally esteem the most effectual confirmation, by the attestation of the Divine Being. And that the people called Quakers, those called Dunkers, and those called Menonists, holding it unlawful to take an oath on any occasion, ought to be allowed to make their solemn affirmation, in the manner that Quakers have been heretofore allowed to affirm; and to be of the same avail as an oath, in all such cases, as the affirmation of Quakers hath been allowed and accepted within this State, instead of an oath ...

6 Yale Law School, Lillian Goldman Law Library, *The Avalon Project.* (2026, Feb. 23). https://avalon.law.yale.edu/17th_century/ma02.asp

State	Month/ Year[1]	Religious Worship and Individual Rights	Government Restrictions
Pennsylvania[7]	Sep. 1776	II. That all men have a natural and unalienable right to worship Almighty God according to the dictates of their own consciences and understanding: And that no man ought or of right can be compelled to attend any religious worship, or erect or support any place of worship, or maintain any ministry, contrary to, or against, his own free will and consent: Nor can any man, who acknowledges the being of a God, be justly deprived or abridged of any civil right as a citizen, on account of his religious sentiments or peculiar mode of religious worship: And that no authority can or ought to be vested in, or assumed by any power whatever, that shall in any case interfere with, or in any manner controul, the right of conscience in the free exercise of religious worship. XIV. That a frequent recurrence to fundamental principles, and a firm adherence to justice, moderation, temperance, industry, and frugality are absolutely necessary to preserve the blessings of liberty, and keep a government free: The people ought therefore to pay particular attention to these points in the choice of officers and representatives, and have a right to exact a due and constant regard to them, from their legislatures and magistrates, in the making and executing such laws as are necessary for the good government of the state.	SECT. 10. … And each member, before he takes his seat, shall make and subscribe the following declaration, viz: I do believe in one God, the creator and governor of the universe, the rewarder of the good and the punisher of the wicked. And I do acknowledge the Scriptures of the Old and New Testament to be given by Divine inspiration. And no further or other religious test shall ever hereafter be required of any civil officer or magistrate in this State. SECT. 45. Laws for the encouragement of virtue, and prevention of vice and immorality, shall be made and constantly kept in force, and provision shall be made for their due execution: And all religious societies or bodies of men heretofore united or incorporated for the advancement of religion or learning, or for other pious and charitable purposes, shall be encouraged and protected in the enjoyment of the privileges, immunities and estates which they were accustomed to enjoy, or could of right have enjoyed, under the laws and former constitution of this state.

7 Yale Law School, Lillian Goldman Law Library, *The Avalon Project.* (2026, Feb. 23). https://avalon.law.yale.edu/18th_century/pa08.asp

State	Month/ Year[1]	Religious Worship and Individual Rights	Government Restrictions
Delaware[8]	Sep. 1776		ART. 29. There shall be no establishment of any one religious sect in this State in preference to another; and no clergyman or preacher of the gospel, of any denomination, shall be capable of holding any civil once in this State, or of being a member of either of the branches of the legislature, while they continue in the exercise of the pastorial function. ART. 22. Every person who shall be chosen a member of either house, or appointed to any office or place of trust, before taking his seat, or entering upon the execution of his office, shall take the following oath, or affirmation, if conscientiously scrupulous of taking an oath, to wit: " I, A B. will bear true allegiance to the Delaware State, submit to its constitution and laws, and do no act wittingly whereby the freedom thereof may be prejudiced." And also make and subscribe the following declaration, to wit: " I, A B. do profess faith in God the Father, and in Jesus Christ His only Son, and in the Holy Ghost, one God, blessed for evermore; and I do acknowledge the holy scriptures of the Old and New Testament to be given by divine inspiration." And all officers shall also take an oath of office.

8 Yale Law School, Lillian Goldman Law Library, *The Avalon Project.* (2026, Feb. 23). https://avalon.law.yale.edu/18th_century/de02.asp

State	Month/ Year[1]	Religious Worship and Individual Rights	Government Restrictions
North Carolina[9]	Dec. 1776	Declaration of Rights XIX. That all men have a natural and unalienable right to worship Almighty God according to the dictates of their own consciences.	XXXI. That no clergyman, or preacher of the gospels of any denomination, shall be capable of being a member of either the Senate, House of Commons, or Council of State, while he continues in the exercise of the pastoral function. XXXII. That no person, who shall deny the being of God or the truth of the Protestant religion, or the divine authority either of the Old or New Testaments, or who shall hold religious principles incompatible with the freedom and safety of the State, shall be capable of holding any office or place of trust or profit in the civil department within this State. XXXIV. That there shall be no establishment of any one religious church or denomination in this State, in preference to any other; neither shall any person, on any presence whatsoever, be compelled to attend any place of worship contrary to his own faith or judgment, nor be obliged to pay, for the purchase of any glebe, or the building of any house of worship, or for the maintenance of any minister or ministry, contrary to what he believes right, of has voluntarily and personally engaged to perform; but all persons shall be at liberty to exercise their own mode of worship: -- Provided, That nothing herein contained shall be construed to exempt preachers of treasonable or seditious discourses, from legal trial and punishment.

9 Yale Law School, Lillian Goldman Law Library, *The Avalon Project.* (2026, Feb. 23). https://avalon.law.yale.edu/18th_century/nc07.asp#1

Appendix 9 - State Constitutional Religious Provisions (prior to the United States Constitution)

State	Month/ Year[1]	Religious Worship and Individual Rights	Government Restrictions
Georgia[10]	Feb. 1777	ART. LVI. All persons whatever shall have the free exercise of their religion; provided it be not repugnant to the peace and safety of the State; and shall not, unless by consent, support any teacher or teachers except those of their own profession.	ART. VI. The representatives shall be chosen out of the residents in each county, who... shall be of the Protestent religion, and of the age of twenty-one years, and shall be possessed in their own right of two hundred and fifty acres of land, or some property to the amount of two hundred and fifty pounds. ART. LXII. No clergyman of any denomination shall be allowed a seat in the legislature.
New York[11]	Apr. 1777	XXXVIII. And whereas we are required, by the benevolent principles of rational liberty, not only to expel civil tyranny, but also to guard against that spiritual oppression and intolerance wherewith the bigotry and ambition of weak and wicked priests and princes have scourged mankind, this convention doth further, in the name and by the authority of the good people of this State, ordain, determine, and declare, that the free exercise and enjoyment of religious profession and worship, without discrimination or preference, shall forever hereafter be allowed, within this State, to all mankind: Provided, That the liberty of conscience, hereby granted, shall not be so construed as to excuse acts of licentiousness, or justify practices inconsistent with the peace or safety of this State.	XXXV ...That all such parts of the said common law, and all such of the said statutes and acts aforesaid, or parts thereof as may be construed to establish or maintain any particular denomination of Christians or their ministers, or concern the allegiance heretofore yielded to, and the supremacy, sovereignty, government, or prerogatives claimed or exercised by, the King of Great Britain and his predecessors, over the colony of New York and its inhabitants, or are repugnant to this constitution, be, and they hereby are, abrogated and rejected. XXXIX. And whereas the ministers of the gospel are, by their profession, dedicated to the service of God and the care of souls, and ought not to be diverted from the great duties of their function; therefore, no minister of the gospel, or priest of any denomination whatsoever, shall, at any time hereafter, under any pretence or description whatever, be eligible to, or capable of holding, any civil or military office or place within this State.

10 Yale Law School, Lillian Goldman Law Library, *The Avalon Project*. (2026, Feb. 23). https://avalon.law.yale.edu/18th_century/ga02.asp

11 New York, Historical Society of the New York Courts. (2026, Feb. 23). https://history.nycourts.gov/wp-content/uploads/2019/01/Publications_1777-NY-Constitution-compressed.pdf

State	Month/ Year[1]	Religious Worship and Individual Rights	Government Restrictions
Vermont Republic[12]	Jul. 1777	III. That all men have a natural and unalienable right to worship ALMIGHTY GOD, according to the dictates of their own consciences and understanding, regulated by the word of GOD; and that no man ought, or of right can be compelled to attend any religious worship, or erect, or support any place of worship, or maintain any minister, contrary to the dictates of his conscience; nor can any man who professes the protestant religion, be justly deprived or abridged of any civil right, as a citizen, on account of his religious sentiment, or peculiar mode of religious worship, and that no authority can, or ought to be vested in, or assumed by, any power whatsoever, that shall, in any case, interfere with, or in any manner controul, the rights of conscience, in the free exercise of religious worship: nevertheless, every sect or denomination of people ought to observe the Sabbath, or the Lord's day, and keep up, and support, some sort of religious worship, which to them shall seem most agreeable to the revealed will of GOD.	SECTION IX. A quorum of the house of representatives shall consist of two-thirds of the whole number of members elected; and having met and chosen their speaker, shall, each of them, before they proceed to business, take and subscribe, as well the oath of fidelity and allegiance herein after directed, as the following oath or affirmation, viz. " I ____ do solemnly swear, by the ever living God, (or, I do solemnly affirm in the presence of Almighty God) that as a member of this assembly, I will not propose or assent to any bill, vote, or resolution, which shall appear to me injurious to the people; nor do or consent to any act or thing whatever, that shall have a tendency to lessen or abridge their rights and privileges, as declared in the Constitution of this State; but will, in all things' conduct myself as a faithful, honest representative and guardian of the people, according to the best of my judgment and abilities." And each member, before he takes his seat, shall make and subscribe the following declaration, viz. " I ____ do believe in one God, the Creator and Governor of the Diverse, the rewarder of the good and punisher of the wicked. And I do acknowledge the scriptures of the old and new testament to be given by divine inspiration, and own and profess the protestant religion." And no further or other religious test shall ever, hereafter, be required of any civil officer or magistrate in this State.

12 Yale Law School, Lillian Goldman Law Library, *The Avalon Project.* (2026, Feb. 23). https://avalon.law.yale.edu/18th_century/vt01.asp

State	Month/ Year[1]	Religious Worship and Individual Rights	Government Restrictions
			SECTION XLI. Laws for the encouragement of virtue and prevention of vice and immorality, shall be made and constantly kept in force; and provision shall be made for their due execution; and all religious societies or bodies of men, that have or may be hereafter united and incorporated, for the advancement of religion and learning, or for other pious and charitable purposes, shall be encouraged and protected in the enjoyment of the privileges, immunities and estates which they, in justice, ought to enjoy, under such regulations; as the General Assembly of this State shall direct.
South Carolina[13]	Mar. 1778	XXXVIII. That all persons and religious societies who acknowledge that there is one God, and a future state of rewards and punishments, and that God is publicly to be worshipped, shall be freely tolerated. The Christian Protestant religion shall be deemed, and is hereby constituted and declared to be, the established religion of this State. That all denominations of Christian Protestants in this State, demeaning themselves peaceably and faithfully, shall enjoy equal religious and civil privileges. To accomplish this desirable purpose without injury to the religious property of those societies of Christians which are by law already incorporated for the purpose of religious worship, and to put it fully into the power of every other society of Christian Protestants, either already formed or hereafter to be formed, to obtain the like incorporation, it is hereby constituted, appointed, and declared that the respective societies of the Church of England that are already formed in this State for the purpose of religious worship shall still continue incorporate and hold the religious property now in their possession.	III. That as soon as may be after the first meeting of the senate and house of representatives, and at every first meeting of the senate and house of representatives thereafter, to be elected by virtue of this constitution, they shall jointly in the house of representatives choose by ballot from among themselves or from the people at large a governor and commander-in-chief, a lieutenant-governor, both to continue for two years, and a privy council, all of the Protestant religion, and till such choice shall be made the former president or governor and commander-in-chief, and vice-president or lieutenant-governor, as the case may be, and privy council, shall continue to act as such. XII. … and that no person shall be eligible to a seat in the said senate unless he be of the Protestant religion, and hath attained the age of thirty years, and hath been a resident in this State at least five years.

13 Yale Law School, Lillian Goldman Law Library, *The Avalon Project.* (2026, Feb. 23). https://avalon.law.yale.edu/18th_century/sc02.asp#1

State	Month/ Year[1]	Religious Worship and Individual Rights	Government Restrictions
South Carolina [CONT.]	Mar. 1778	And that whenever fifteen or more male persons, not under twenty-one years of age, professing the Christian Protestant religion, and agreeing to unite themselves In a society for the purposes of religious worship, they shall, (on complying with the terms hereinafter mentioned,) be, and be constituted a church, and be esteemed and regarded in law as of the established religion of the State, and on a petition to the legislature shall be entitled to be incorporated and to enjoy equal privileges. That every society of Christians so formed shall give themselves a name or denomination by which they shall be called and known in law, and all that associate with them for the purposes of worship shall be esteemed as belonging to the society so called. But that previous to the establishment and incorporation of the respective societies of every denomination as aforesaid, and in order to entitle them thereto, each society so petitioning shall have agreed to and subscribed in a book the following five articles, without which no agreement fir union of men upon presence of religion shall entitle them to be incorporated and esteemed as a church of the established religion of this State: 1st. That there is one eternal God, and a future state of rewards and punishments. 2d. That God is publicly to be worshipped. 3d. That the Christian religion is the true religion 4th. That the holy scriptures of the Old and New Testaments are of divine inspiration, and are the rule of faith and practice. 5th. That it is lawful and the duty of every man being thereunto called by those that govern, to bear witness to the truth.	XIII. … No person shall be eligible to sit in the house of representatives unless he be of the Protestant religion, and hath been a resident in this State for three years previous to his election. XXI. And whereas the ministers of the gospel are by their profession dedicated to the service of God and the cure of souls, and ought not to be diverted from the great duties of their function, therefore no minister of the gospel or public preacher of any religious persuasion, while he continues in the exercise of his pastoral function, and for two years after, shall be eligible either as governor, lieutenant-governor, a member of the senate, house of representatives, or privy council in this State.

State	Month/ Year[1]	Religious Worship and Individual Rights	Government Restrictions
South Carolina [CONT.]	Mar. 1778	And that every inhabitant of this State, when called to make an appeal to God as a witness to truth, shall be permitted to do it in that way which is most agreeable to the dictates of his own conscience. And that the people of this State may forever enjoy the right of electing their own pastors or clergy, and at the same time that the State may have sufficient security for the due discharge of the pastoral office, by those who shall be admitted to be clergymen, no person shall officiate as minister of any established church who shall not have been chosen by a majority of the society to which he shall minister, or by persons appointed by the said majority, to choose and procure a minister for them; nor until the minister so chosen and appointed shall have made and subscribed to the following declaration, over and above the aforesaid five articles, viz: "That he is determined by God's grace out of the holy scriptures, to instruct the people committed to his charge, and to teach nothing as required of necessity to eternal salvation but that which he shall be persuaded may be concluded and proved from the scripture; that he will use both public and private admonitions, as well to the sick as to the whole within his cure, as need shall require and occasion shall be given, and that he will be diligent in prayers, and in reading of the same; that he will be diligent to frame and fashion his own self and his family according to the doctrine of Christ, and to make both himself and them, as much as in him lieth, wholesome examples and patterns to the flock of Christ; that he will maintain and set forwards, as much as he can, quietness, peace, and love among all people, and especially among those that are or shall be committed to lids charge.	

State	Month/ Year[1]	Religious Worship and Individual Rights	Government Restrictions
South Carolina [CONT.]	Mar. 1778	No person shall disturb or molest any religious assembly; nor shall use any reproachful, reviling, or abusive language against any church, that being the certain way of disturbing the peace, and of hindering the conversion of any to the truth, by engaging them in quarrels and animosities, to the hatred of the professors, and that profession which otherwise they might be brought to assent to. To person whatsoever shall speak anything in their religious assembly irreverently or seditiously of the government of this State. No person shall, by law, be obliged to pay towards the maintenance and support of a religious worship that he does not freely join in, or has not voluntarily engaged to support. But the churches, chapels, parsonages, globes, and all other property now belonging to any societies of the Church of England, or any other religious societies, shall remain and be secured to them forever. The poor shall be supported, and elections managed in the accustomed manner, until laws shall be provided to adjust those matters in the most equitable way.	
Massachusetts[14]	Jun. 1780	Article II. It is the right as well as the duty of all men in society, publicly, and at stated seasons to worship the Supreme Being, the great Creator and Preserver of the universe. And no subject shall be hurt, molested, or restrained, in his person, liberty, or estate, for worshipping God in the manner and season most agreeable to the dictates of his own conscience; or for his religious profession or sentiments; provided he doth not disturb the public peace, or obstruct others in their religious worship.	Chapter II, Article II. The governor shall be chosen [annually]; and no person shall be eligible to this office, unless at the time of his election, he shall have been an inhabitant of this commonwealth for seven years next preceding; and unless he shall at the same time, be seised in his own right, of a freehold within the commonwealth of the value of one thousand pounds; and unless he shall declare himself to be of the Christian religion.

14 The 194th General Court of the Commonwealth of Massachusetts. (2026, Feb. 23). https://malegislature.gov/Laws/Constitution

State	Month/ Year[1]	Religious Worship and Individual Rights	Government Restrictions
Massachusetts [CONT.]	Jun. 1780		Chapter V, Article I. Whereas our wise and pious ancestors, so early as the year one thousand six hundred and thirty-six, laid the foundation of Harvard College, in which university many persons of great eminence have, by the blessing of God, been initiated in those arts and sciences, which qualified them for public employments, both in church and state: and whereas the encouragement of arts and sciences, and all good literature, tends to the honor of God, the advantage of the Christian religion, and the great benefit of this and the other United States of America Chapter VI, Article I. Any person chosen governor, lieutenant governor, councillor, senator or representative, and accepting the trust, shall before he proceed to execute the duties of his place or office, make and subscribe the following declaration, viz.-- "I, A. B., do declare, that I believe the Christian religion, and have a firm persuasion of its truth; and that I am seised and possessed, in my own right, of the property required by the constitution as one qualification for the office or place to which I am elected."

State	Month/ Year[1]	Religious Worship and Individual Rights	Government Restrictions
Massachusetts [CONT.]	Jun. 1780		Article III. As the happiness of a people, and the good order and preservation of civil government, essentially depend upon piety, religion and morality; and as these cannot be generally diffused through a community, but by the institution of the public worship of God, and of public instructions in piety, religion and morality: Therefore, to promote their happiness and to secure the good order and preservation of their government, the people of this commonwealth have a right to invest their legislature with power to authorize and require, and the legislature shall, from time to time, authorize and require, the several towns, parishes, precincts, and other bodies politic, or religious societies, to make suitable provision, at their own expense, for the institution of the public worship of God, and for the support and maintenance of public Protestant teachers of piety, religion and morality, in all cases where such provision shall not be made voluntarily. And the people of this commonwealth have also a right to, and do, invest their legislature with authority to enjoin upon all the subjects an attendance upon the instructions of the public teachers aforesaid, at stated times and seasons, if there be any on whose instructions they can conscientiously and conveniently attend. Provided, notwithstanding, that the several towns, parishes, precincts, and other bodies politic, or religious societies, shall, at all times, have the exclusive right of electing their public teachers, and of contracting with them for their support and maintenance.

State	Month/ Year[1]	Religious Worship and Individual Rights	Government Restrictions
Massachusetts [CONT.]	Jun. 1780		And all moneys paid by the subject to the support of public worship, and of the public teachers aforesaid, shall, if he require it, be uniformly applied to the support of the public teacher or teachers of his own religious sect or denomination, provided there be any on whose instructions he attends; otherwise it may be paid towards the support of the teacher or teachers of the parish or precinct in which the said moneys are raised. Any every denomination of Christians, demeaning themselves peaceably, and as good subjects of the commonwealth, shall be equally under the protection of the law: and no subordination of any one sect or denomination to another shall ever be established by law.
New Hampshire[15] (Bill of Rights)	Jun. 1780	V. Every individual has a natural and unalienable right to worship God according to the dictates of his own conscience, and reason; and no subject shall be hurt, molested, or restrained in his person, liberty or estate for worshipping God, in the manner and season most agreeable to the dictates of his own conscience, or for his religious profession, sentiments or persuasion; provided he doth not disturb the public peace, or disturb others, in their religious worship.	VI. As morality and piety, rightly grounded on evangelical principles, will give the best and greatest security to government, and will lay in the hearts of men the strongest obligations to due subjection; and as the knowledge of these, is most likely to be propagated through a society by the institution of the public worship of the Deity, and of public instruction in morality and religion; therefore, to promote those important purposes, the people of this state have a right to impower, and do hereby fully impower the legislature to authorize from time to time, the several towns, parishes, bodies-corporate, or religious societies within this state, to make adequate provision at their own expence, for the support and maintenance of public protestant teachers of piety, religion and morality:

15 Teaching American History. (2026, Feb. 23). https://teachingamericanhistory.org/document/new-hampshire-bill-of-rights/

State	Month/ Year[1]	Religious Worship and Individual Rights	Government Restrictions
New Hampshire (Bill of Rights) [CONT.]	Oct. 1783		Provided notwithstanding, That the several towns, parishes, bodies-corporate, or religious societies, shall at all times have the exclusive right of electing their own public teachers, and of contracting with them for their support and maintenance. And no portion of any one particular religious sect or denomination, shall ever be compelled to pay towards the support of the teacher or teachers of another persuasion, sect or denomination. And every denomination of christians demeaning themselves quietly, and as good subjects of the state, shall be equally under the protection of the law: and no subordination of any one sect or denomination to another, shall ever be established by law. And nothing herein shall be understood to affect any former contracts made for the support of the ministry; but all such contracts shall remain, and be in the same state as if this constitution had not been made. Every member of the house of representatives shall be chosen by ballot; and for two years at least next preceding his election, shall have been an inhabitant of this state, shall have an estate within the town, parish, or place which he may be chosen to represent, of the value of one hundred pounds, one half of which to be a freehold, whereof he is seized in his own right; shall be at the time of his election, an inhabitant of the town, parish, or place he may be chosen to represent; shall be of the protestant religion, and shall cease to represent such town, parish, or place immediately on his ceasing to be qualified as aforesaid.

Appendix 9 - State Constitutional Religious Provisions (prior to the United States Constitution)

State	Month/ Year[1]	Religious Worship and Individual Rights	Government Restrictions
New Hamp- shire (Bill of Rights) [CONT.]	Jun. 1780		Provided nevertheless, That no person shall be capable of being elected a senator, who is not of the protestant religion, and seized of a freehold estate in his own right of the value of two hundred pounds, lying within this state, who is not of the age of thirty years, and who shall not have been an inhabitant of this state for seven years immediately preceding his election; and at the time thereof he shall be an inhabitant of the district for which he shall be chosen. There shall be a supreme executive magistrate, who shall be stiled, The President of the State of New-Hampshire; and whose title shall be His Excellency. The President shall be chosen annually; and no person shall be eligible to this office, unless at the time of his election, he shall have been an inhabitant of this state for seven years next preceding, and unless he shall be of the age of thirty years; and unless he shall, at the same time, have an estate of the value of five hundred pounds, one half of which shall consist of a freehold, in his own right, within the state; and unless he shall be of the Protestant religion.
New York[16] (Bill of Rights)	Jan. 1787		

16 New York, Historical Society of the New York Courts. (2026, Feb. 23). https://history.nycourts.gov/wp-content/uploads/2019/01/Publications_NY-Bill-Rights-compressed.pdf

Appendix 10 - United States Constitution Rights (1787)

Nationwide Rights created in the Constitution

ID[1]	Source in the Constitution	Constitutional Text[2]	Simplified Description of Implied Nationwide Rights[3]
C1	Article I, Section 9 Article I, Section 10	No Bill of Attainder … shall be passed. No State shall … pass any Bill of Attainder	Right against bills of attainder.
C2	Article I, Section 9 Article I, Section 10	No … ex post facto Law shall be passed. No State shall … pass any ex post facto Law	Right against ex post facto laws.
C3	Article IV, Section 4	The United States shall guarantee to every State in this Union a Republican Form of Government	Right to have a republican form of government for your state
C4	Article IV, Section 4	The United States … shall protect each of them against Invasion	Right to have your state protected against invasion

1 ID values are provided by the Author for internal referencing purposes

2 United States National Archives and Records Administration. (2026, Feb. 23). https://www.archives.gov/founding-docs/constitution-transcript

3 Simplified descriptions are provided by the author

Rights Restricting the Federal Government Only

ID	Source in the Constitution	Constitutional Text	Simplified Protection against Federal Government
CFG1	Article I, Section 9	The Privilege of the Writ of Habeas Corpus shall not be suspended, unless when in Cases of Rebellion or Invasion the public Safety may require it.	Right to habeas corpus unless during rebellion, invasion, or if required for public safety
CFG2	Article VI	but no religious Test shall ever be required as a Qualification to any Office or public Trust under the United States.	Right against being required to pass a religious test to work for the United States government

Rights Restricting State Governments Only

ID	Source in the Constitution	Constitutional Text	Simplified Protection against State Government
CSG1	Article I, Section 10	No State shall … pass any … Law impairing the Obligation of Contracts	Right not to have your obligation of contracts impaired by state law”

Appendix 11 - Massachusetts Recommendatory Amendments

ID[1]	Text from the State Constitutional Convention[2]	Simplified Purpose[3]	Disposition in the Bill of Rights
MRA1	That it be explicitly declared that all Powers not expressly delegated by the aforesaid Constitution are reserved to the several States to be by them exercised.	To keep all unenumerated powers for State governments	Incorporated in the 10th Amendment
MRA2	That there shall be one representative to every thirty thousand persons according to the Census mentioned in the Constitution until the whole number of the Representatives amounts to Two hundred.	To limit the size of the House of Representatives to 200 members	Proposed by Congress as part of initial 12 Amendments but failed Constitutional Ratification
MRA3	That Congress do not exercise the powers vested in them by the fourth Section of the first article, but in cases when a State shall neglect or refuse to make the regulations therein mentioned or shall make regulations subversive of the rights of the People to a free & equal representation in Congress agreeably to the Constitution	To restrict Congress from setting election laws unless a state failed to do so, or a state did not provide for free and equal representation in Congress.	Dropped
MRA4	That Congress do not lay direct Taxes but when the Monies arising from the Impost & Excise are insufficient for the Publick exigencies nor then until Congress shall have first made a requisition upon the States to assess levy & pay their respective proportions of such Requisition agreeably to the Census fixed in the said Constitution, in such way & manner as the Legislature of the States shall think best, & in such case if any State shall neglect or refuse to pay its proportion pursuant to such requisition then Congress may assess & levy such State's proportion together with interest thereon at the rate of Six per cent per annum from the time of payment prescribed in such requisition.	That when Impost and Excise taxes are not enough for Congress' expenses, they shall make requisitions of the states based on the census.	Dropped

1 ID values provided by the Author for internal referencing purposes

2 University of Wisconsin-Madison, Department of History, Center for the Study of the American Constitution. (2026, Feb. 24). https://csac.history.wisc.edu/wp-content/uploads/sites/281/2024/04/DC3-08-09-02_Mass.-Form-of-Ratification_6-7Feb88.pdf

3 Simplified Purpose is generated by the Author

ID[1]	Text from the State Constitutional Convention[2]	Simplified Purpose[3]	Disposition in the Bill of Rights
MRA5	That Congress erect no Company of Merchants with exclusive advantages of Commerce.	To keep Congress from providing exclusive arrangements for specific merchants	Dropped
MRA6	That no person shall be tried for any Crime by which he may incur an infamous punishment or loss of life until he be first indicted by a Grand Jury, except in such cases as may arise in the Government & regulation of the Land & Naval forces	To require a Grand Jury Indictment for capital crimes	Incorporated in the 5th Amendment
MRA7	The Supreme Judicial Federal Court shall have no jurisdiction of Causes between Citizens of different States unless the matter in dispute whether it concerns the realty or personalty be of the value of Three thousand dollars at the least nor shall the Federal Judicial Powers extend to any actions between Citizens of different States where the matter in dispute whether it concerns the Realty or Personalty is not of the value of Fifteen hundred dollars at the least.	To keep the Supreme Court from hearing cases between Citizens of different states unless the real and/or personal property has a value of at least $3,000.	Dropped
MRA8	In civil actions between Citizens of different States every issue of fact arising in Actions at common law shall be tried by a Jury if the parties or either of them request it.	To create a right to jury trial for civil cases between Citizens of different states in Federal Courts.	Incorporated in the 7th Amendment
MRA9	Congress shall at no time consent that any Person holding an office of trust or profit under the United States shall accept of a title of Nobility or any other title or office from any King, Prince or Foreign State.	To keep government officials from having dual allegiance to a foreign country.	Dropped

Appendix 12 - South Carolina Recommendatory Amendments

ID[1]	Text from the State Constitutional Convention[2]	(Prior Source)[3] and Simplified Purpose[4]	Disposition in the Bill of Rights
SCRA1	And Whereas it is essential to the preservation of the rights reserved to the several states, and the freedom of the people under the operations of a General government that the right of prescribing the manner time and places of holding the Elections to the Federal Legislature, should be for ever inseparably annexed to the sovereignty of the several States. This convention doth declare that the same ought to remain to all posterity a perpetual and fundamental right in the local, exclusive of the interference of the General Government except in cases where the Legislatures of the States, shall refuse or neglect to perform and fulfil the same according to the tenor of the said Constitution.	(Enhanced version of Massachusetts' recommended amendment MRA3 in Appendix 11)	Dropped
SCRA2	This Convention doth also declare that no Section or paragraph of the said Constitution warrants a Construction that the states do not retain every power not expressly relinquished by them and vested in the General Government of the Union.	(Modified version of Massachusetts' recommended amendment MRA1 in Appendix 11)	Incorporated in the 10th Amendment

1 ID values provided by the Author for internal referencing purposes

2 University of Wisconsin-Madison, Department of History, Center for the Study of the American Constitution. (2026, Feb. 24). https://csac.history.wisc.edu/wp-content/uploads/sites/281/2024/04/DC3-08-09-04_S.C.-Recommendatory-Amendments_23May88.pdf

3 The travel time between Massachusetts and South Carolina by sea would permit results from the February 7 Massachusetts Constitutional convention to reach South Carolina by May 23.

4 Simplified Purpose is generated by the Author

ID[1]	Text from the State Constitutional Convention[2]	(Prior Source)[3] and Simplified Purpose[4]	Disposition in the Bill of Rights
SCRA3	Resolved that the general Government of the United States ought never to impose direct taxes, but where the monies arising from the duties, imposts, and excise are insufficient for the public exigencies nor then until Congress shall have made a requisition upon the states to assess levy and pay their respective proportions of such requisitions and in case any State shall neglect or refuse to pay its proportion pursuant to such requisition then Congress may assess and levy such state's proportion together with Interest thereon at the rate of Six per centum per annum from the time of payment prescribed by such requisition.	(Modified version of Massachusetts' recommended amendment MRA4 in Appendix 11) That when Impost and Excise taxes are not enough for Congress' expenses, they shall make requisitions of the states based on the census. If states did not pay their requisition, then their debt would have a 6% annual interest rate.	Dropped
SCRA4	Resolved that the third Section of the Sixth Article ought to be amended by inserting the word "other" between the words "no" and "religious"	Article VI, Section 3 of the Constitution: "The Senators and Representatives before mentioned, and the Members of the several State Legislatures, and all executive and judicial Officers, both of the United States and of the several States, shall be bound by Oath or Affirmation, to support this Constitution; but no religious Test shall ever be required as a Qualification to any Office or public Trust under the United States.". South Carolina wanted the final clause to read "but no other religious Test shall ever be required ...". This indicates that they viewed the Oath to the Constitution as a religious test.	Dropped

Appendix 13 - New Hampshire Recommendatory Amendments

ID[1]	Text from the State Constitutional Convention[2]	(Prior Source)[3] and Simplified Purpose[4]	Disposition in the Bill of Rights
NHRA1	That it be explicitly declared, that all powers not expressly and particularly delegated by the aforesaid Constitution, are reserved to the several states, to be by them exercised.	(Copied Massachusetts' recommended amendment MRA1 in Appendix 11) To keep all unenumerated powers for State governments	Incorporated in the 10th Amendment
NHRA2	That there shall be one representative to every 30,000 persons, according to the census mentioned in the Constitution, until the whole number of the representatives amounts to 200.	(Small text changes to Massachusetts' recommended amendment MRA2 in Appendix 11) To limit the size of the House of Representatives to 200 members	Proposed by Congress as part of initial 12 Amendments but failed Constitutional Ratification
NHRA3	That Congress do not exercise the powers vested in them by the 4th section of the first article, but in cases when a state shall neglect or refuse to make the regulations therein mentioned, or shall make regulations contrary to a free and equal representation.	(Small text changes to Massachusetts' recommended amendment MRA3 in Appendix 11) To restrict Congress from setting election laws unless a state failed to do so, or a state did not provide for free and equal representation in Congress.	Dropped

1 ID values provided by the Author for internal referencing purposes

2 University of Wisconsin-Madison, Department of History, Center for the Study of the American Constitution. (2026, Feb. 24). https://csac.history.wisc.edu/wp-content/uploads/sites/281/2024/04/DC3-08-09-05_N.H.-Recommendatory-Amendments_21Jun88.pdf

3 The travel time between South Carolina and New Hampshire by sea likely would have not allowed South Carolina's amendments to reach New Hampshire for their convention. This would have been less than a month (May 23 to June 21). The Massachusetts results from their constitutional convention would have reached New Hampshire months in advance (February 7 to June 21) since the two states are neighbors.

4 Simplified Purpose is generated by the Author

ID[1]	Text from the State Constitutional Convention[2]	(Prior Source)[3] and Simplified Purpose[4]	Disposition in the Bill of Rights
NHRA4	That Congress do not lay direct taxes, but when the money arising from the Impost, Excise, and their other resources are insufficient for the public exigencies; nor then, until proportions of such requisition, agreeably to the census fixed in the said constitution, in such way and manner as the legislature of the state shall think best; and in such case if any state shall neglect or refuse to pay its proportion, pursuant to such requisition, then Congress may assess and levy such state's proportion – together with interest thereon at the rate of 6 per cent. Per annum, from the time of payment prescribed in such requisition.	(Slight modifications to Massachusetts' recommended amendment MRA4 in Appendix 11) That when Impost and Excise taxes are not enough for Congress' expenses, they shall make requisitions of the states based on the census. If states did not pay their requisition, then their debt would have a 6% annual interest rate.	Dropped
NHRA5	That Congress erect no company of merchants, with exclusive advantages of commerce.	(Small text changes to Massachusetts' recommended amendment MRA5 in Appendix 11) To keep Congress from providing exclusive arrangements for specific merchants	Dropped
NHRA6	That no person shall be tried for any crime by which he may incur an infamous punishment, or loss of life, until he be first indicted by a grand jury; except in such cases as may arise in the government and regulation of the land and naval forces.	(Small text changes to Massachusetts' recommended amendment MRA6 in Appendix 11) To require a Grand Jury Indictment for capital crimes	Incorporated in the 5th Amendment
NHRA7	All common law causes between citizens of different states shall be commenced in the common law courts of the respective states – and no appeal shall be allowed to the federal court in such cases, unless the sum or value of the thing in controversy amount to 3000 dollars.	(Reduced and simplified version of Massachusetts' recommended amendment MRA7 in Appendix 11) To start all civil trials between people of different states in state courts and not to allow appeals to federal courts unless the controversy is at least 3000 dollars.	Dropped

ID[1]	Text from the State Constitutional Convention[2]	(Prior Source)[3] and Simplified Purpose[4]	Disposition in the Bill of Rights
NHRA8	In civil actions between citizens of different states, every issue of fact arising in actions at common law, shall be tried by jury, if the parties or either of them request it.	(Small text changes to Massachusetts' recommended amendment MRA8 in Appendix 11) To create a right to jury trial for civil cases between Citizens of different states.	Incorporated in the 7th Amendment
NHRA9	Congress shall at no time consent that any person holding an office of trust or profit under the United States, shall accept of a title of nobility, or any other title or office from any king, prince or foreign state.	(Small text changes to Massachusetts' recommended amendment MRA9 in Appendix 11) To keep government officials from having dual allegiance to a foreign country.	Dropped
NHRA10	That no standing army shall be kept up in time of peace, unless with the consent of three-quarters of the members of each branch of Congress – nor shall soldiers in time of peace be quartered upon private houses, without the consent of the owner.	To require ¾ votes in Congress to approve a standing army. To keep soldiers from being quartered in people's homes during peacetime.	Dropped Incorporated in the 3rd Amendment
NHRA11	Congress shall make no laws touching religion, or to infringe the rights of conscience.	To protect the "right to conscience" and to keep Congress from making any religious laws.	Incorporated in the 1st Amendment
NHRA12	Congress shall never disarm any citizen, unless such as are or have been in actual rebellion.	To protect the "right to bear arms"	Incorporated in the 2nd Amendment

Appendix 14 - Virginia Recommendatory Amendments

ID[1]	Text from the State Constitutional Convention[2]	(Prior Source)[3] and Simplified Purpose[4]	Disposition in the Bill of Rights
VRA1	That there are certain natural rights, of which men, when they form a social compact, cannot deprive or divest their posterity: among which are the enjoyment of life and liberty, with the means of acquiring, possessing, and protecting property, and pursuing and obtaining happiness and safety.	To recognize that natural rights cannot be taken away by the government.	Dropped
VRA2	That all power is naturally invested in, and consequently derived from, the people; that magistrates therefore are their trustees and agents, at all times amenable to them.	To recognize that the power of government comes from the people.	Dropped
VRA3	That government ought to be instituted for the common benefit, protection, and security of the people; and that the doctrine of non-resistance against arbitrary power and oppression is absurd, slavish, and destructive to the good and happiness of mankind.	To declare that arbitrary and oppressive government actions can be resisted.	Dropped

1 ID values provided by the Author for internal referencing purposes

2 University of Wisconsin-Madison, Department of History, Center for the Study of the American Constitution. (2026, Feb. 24). https://csac.history.wisc.edu/wp-content/uploads/sites/281/2024/04/DC3-08-09-06_Va.-Recommendatory-Amendments_27Jun88.pdf

3 The travel time by sea from Massachusetts to Virginia between February 7 and June 27 would permit the Massachusetts convention results (Appendix 11) to reach Virginia well before their convention. The travel time by sea from South Carolina to Virgina between May 23 and June 27 makes it probable that the South Carolina convention results (Appendix 12) reached Virginia before the convention. The travel time by sea from New Hampshire to Virginia between June 21 and June 27 makes it virtually impossible that the New Hampshire convention results (Appendix 13) reached Virginia before the convention. This means that similarities with New Hampshire's recommended amendments must have come from an earlier source.

4 Simplified Purpose is generated by the Author

ID[1]	Text from the State Constitutional Convention[2]	(Prior Source)[3] and Simplified Purpose[4]	Disposition in the Bill of Rights
VRA4	That no man or set of men are entitled to separate or exclusive public emoluments or privileges from the community, but in consideration of public services, which not being descendible, neither ought the officers of magistrate, legislator, or judge, or any other public office, to be hereditary.	To declare that no government offices can be hereditary	Dropped
VRA5	That the legislative, executive, and judicial powers of government should be separate and distinct; and that the members of the two first may be restrained from oppression by feeling and participating the public burdens, they should, at fixed periods, be reduced to a private station, return into the mass of the people, and the vacancies be supplied by certain and regular elections, in which all or any part of the former members to be eligible or ineligible, as the rules of the Constitution of government, and the laws, shall direct.	To declare a need for fixed terms of office for people in the legislative and executive branches and to recognize Constitutional or legal limits on their ability to run for election again.	Dropped
VRA6	That the elections of representatives in the legislature ought to be free and frequent, and all men having sufficient evidence of permanent common interest with, and attachment to, the community, ought to have the right of suffrage; and no aid, charge, tax, or fee, can be set, rated or levied, upon the people without their own consent, or that of their representatives, so elected; nor can they be bound by any law to which they have not, in like manner, assented, for the public good.	To recognize a right to vote for all men with ties to the community. To declare that no taxes or fees can be charged without approval by the people or their representatives.	Dropped
VRA7	That all power of suspending laws, or the execution of laws, by any authority, without the consent of the representatives of the people in the legislature, is injurious to their rights, and ought not to be exercised.	To declare that suspension of laws can only be done with legislative approval.	Dropped

ID[1]	Text from the State Constitutional Convention[2]	(Prior Source)[3] and Simplified Purpose[4]	Disposition in the Bill of Rights
VRA8	That, in all criminal and capital prosecutions, a man hath a right to demand the cause and nature of his accusation, to be confronted with the accusers and witnesses, to call for evidence, and to be allowed counsel in his favor, and to a fair and speedy trial by an impartial jury of his vicinage, without whose unanimous consent he cannot be found guilty (except in the government of the land and naval forces), nor can he be compelled to give evidence against himself.	To guarantee legal protection including: 1) The right to confront your accuser 2) The ability to request and present evidence 3) The right to defense counsel 4) The right to a speedy trial with an impartial jury 5) Unanimous jury necessary for conviction 6)The right not to testify against yourself	Incorporated in the 5th and 6th Amendments
VRA9	That no freeman ought to be taken, imprisoned, or dis-seized of his freehold, liberties, privileges, or franchise, or outlawed, or exiled, or in any manner destroyed or deprived of his life, liberty, or property, but by the law of the land.	To guarantee due process of law before anyone can be deprived of their life, liberty or property.	Incorporated in the 5th Amendment
VRA10	That every freeman restrained of his liberty is entitled to a remedy, to inquire into the lawfulness thereof, and to remove the same, if unlawful, and that such remedy ought not to be denied or delayed.	To guarantee the writ of habeas corpus	Dropped
VRA11	That, in controversies respecting property, and in suits between man and man, the ancient trial by jury is on of the greatest securities to the rights of the people, and to remain sacred and inviolable.	To require jury trials for civil suits	Incorporated in the 7th Amendment
VRA12	That every freeman ought to find a certain remedy, by recourse to the laws, for all injuries and wrongs he may receive in his person, property, or character. He ought to obtain right and justice freely, without sale, completely and without denial, promptly and without delay; and that all establishments or regulations contravening these rights are oppressive and unjust.	To recognize a legal right to recourse for wrongs	Partially incorporated in the last clause of the 5th Amendment
VRA13	That excessive bail ought not to be required, nor excessive fines imposed, nor cruel and unusual punishments inflicted.	To prohibit excessive bail or fines, or cruel and unusual punishment	Incorporated in the 8th Amendment

ID[1]	Text from the State Constitutional Convention[2]	(Prior Source)[3] and Simplified Purpose[4]	Disposition in the Bill of Rights
VRA14	That every freeman has a right to be secure from all unreasonable searches and seizures of his person, his papers, and property; all warrants, therefore, to search suspected places or seize any freeman, his papers, or property, without information on oath (or affirmation of a person religiously scrupulous of taking and oath) of legal and sufficient cause, are grievous and oppressive; and all general warrants to search suspected places, or to apprehend any suspected person, without specially naming or describing the place or person, are dangerous, and ought not to be granted.	To declare strong requirements to obtain search warrants, and to outlaw general warrants	Incorporated in the 5th Amendment
VRA15	That the people have a right peaceably to assemble together to consult for the common good, or to instruct their representatives: and that every freeman has a right to petition or apply to the legislature for redress of grievances	To recognize a "right to peaceably assemble" To recognize a "right to petition the legislature for a redress of grievances"	Incorporated in the 1st Amendment
VRA16	That the people have a right to freedom of speech, and of writing and publishing their sentiments; that the freedom of the press is one of the greatest bulwarks of liberty, and out not to be violated.	To recognize a "right to freedom of speech" To recognize a "right to freedom of the press"	Incorporated in the 1st Amendment
VRA17	That the people have a right to keep and bear arms; that a well regulated militia, composed of the body of the people trained to arms, is the proper, natural, and safe defence of a free state; that standing armies, in times of peace, are dangerous to liberty, and therefore ought to be avoided, as far as the circumstances and protection of the community will admit; and that, in all cases, the military should be under strict subordination to, and governed by, the civil power.	(Similar to New Hampshire's recommended amendment NHRA12 combined with New Hampshire's recommended amendment NHRA10 in Appendix 13) To recognize a "right to keep and bear arms" To declare the desire to avoid standing armies, and to always have civilian control of the military.	Incorporated in the 2nd Amendment
VRA18	That no soldier in time of peace ought to be quartered in any house without the consent of the owner, and in time of war in such manner only as the law directs.	(Similar to a subset of New Hampshire's recommended amendments NHRA10 in Appendix 13) To recognize a "right against having soldiers quartered in your home"	Incorporated in the 3rd Amendment

ID[1]	Text from the State Constitutional Convention[2]	(Prior Source)[3] and Simplified Purpose[4]	Disposition in the Bill of Rights
VRA19	That any person religiously scrupulous of bearing arms ought to be exempted, upon payment of an equivalent to employ another to bear arms in his stead	To declare a "right for religious people with strict moral convictions against bearing arms to pay for someone to take their place in the military"	Dropped
VRA20	That religion, or the duty which we owe to our Creator, and the manner of discharging it, can be directed only by reason and conviction, not by force or violence; and therefore all men have an equal, natural, and unalienable right to the free exercise of religion, according to the dictates of conscience, and that no particular religious sect or society ought to be favored or established, by law, in preference to others.	To recognize a "right of conscience to worship God as the individual sees fit." To restrict the government from favoring a particular religion in preference to others.	Incorporated in the 1st Amendment

Appendix 15 - New York Recommendatory Amendments

ID[1]	Text from the State Constitutional Convention[2]	(Prior Source)[3] and Simplified Purpose[4]	Disposition in the Bill of Rights
NYRA1	That all Power is originally vested in and consequently derived from the People, and that Government is instituted by them for their common Interest Protection and Security.	(Small text change from Virginia's recommended amendment VRA2 in Appendix 14) Declaration that government's power comes from the people	Dropped
NYRA2	That the enjoyment of Life, Liberty and the pursuit of Happiness are essential rights which every Government ought to respect and preserve.	Declaration that government should respect essential rights	Dropped

1 ID values provided by the Author for internal referencing purposes

2 University of Wisconsin-Madison, Department of History, Center for the Study of the American Constitution. (2026, Feb. 24). https://csac.history.wisc.edu/wp-content/uploads/sites/281/2024/04/DC3-08-09-07_N.Y.-Recommendatory-Amendments_26Jul88.pdf

3 Given its central location, the Massachusetts convention results from February 7 (Appendix 11), the South Carolina convention results from May 23 (Appendix 12), the New Hampshire convention results from June 21 (Appendix 13), and the Virginia convention results from June 27 (Appendix 14) all would have arrived in New York prior to its convention.

4 Simplified Purpose is generated by the Author

ID[1]	Text from the State Constitutional Convention[2]	(Prior Source)[3] and Simplified Purpose[4]	Disposition in the Bill of Rights
NYRA3	That the Powers of Government may be reassumed by the People, whensoever it shall become necessary to their Happiness; that every Power, Jurisdiction and right, which is not by the said Constitution clearly delegated to the Congress of the United States, or the departments of the Government thereof, remains to the People of the several States, or to their respective State Governments to whom they may have granted the same; And that those Clauses in the said Constitution, which declare, that Congress shall not have or exercise certain Powers, do not imply that Congress is entitled to any Powers not given by the said Constitution; but such Clauses are to be construed either as exceptions to certain specified Powers, or as inserted merely for greater Caution.	(Significant additions to Massachusetts' recommended amendment MRA1 in Appendix 11) To declare that arbitrary and oppressive government actions can be resisted. To keep all unenumerated powers for State governments	 Dropped Incorporated in the 10th Amendment
NYRA4	That the People have an equal, natural and unalienable right, freely and peaceably to Exercise their Religion according to the dictates of Conscience, and that no Religious Sect or Society ought to be favoured or established by Law in preference of others.	(Similarities to New Hampshire's recommended amendment NHRA11 in Appendix 13 and Virginia's recommended amendment VRA20 in Appendix 14) Declaration of "right of conscience" and that government should not favor any sect or religious society	Incorporated in the 1st Amendment
NYRA5	That the People have a right to keep and bear Arms; that a well regulated Militia, including the body of the People capable of bearing Arms, is the proper, natural and safe defence of a free State;	(Reduced version of Virginia's recommended amendment VRA17 in Appendix 14) Declaration of the "right to bear arms"	Incorporated in the 2nd Amendment

ID[1]	Text from the State Constitutional Convention[2]	(Prior Source)[3] and Simplified Purpose[4]	Disposition in the Bill of Rights
NYRA6	That the Militia should not be subject to Martial Law, except in time of War, Rebellion or Insurrection.	(Reduced version of Virginia's recommended amendment VRA17 in Appendix 14) Declaration that militia operates as a civilian function unless during war.	Dropped
NYRA7	That standing Armies in time of Peace are dangerous to Liberty, and ought not to be kept up, except in Cases of necessity; and that at all times, the Military should be under strict Subordination to the civil Power	(Reduced version of Virginia's recommended amendment VRA17 in Appendix 14) Declaration opposing standing armies and promoting civilian control of the military.	Dropped
NYRA8	That in time of Peace no Soldier ought to be quartered in any House without the consent of the Owner, and in time of War only by the civil Magistrate in such manner as the Laws may direct.	(Expanded version of Virginia's recommended amendment VRA18 in Appendix 14) Declaration of "the right not to have soldiers quartered in your house"	Incorporated in the 3rd Amendment
NYRA9	That no Person ought to be taken imprisoned, or disseised of his freehold, or be exiled or deprived of his Privileges Franchises, Life, Liberty or Property, but by due process of Law.	(Modified version of Virginia's recommended amendment VRA9 in Appendix 14) Declaration of the "right to Due Process"	Incorporated in the 5th Amendment
NYRA10	That no Person ought to be put twice in Jeopardy of Life or Limb for one and the same Offence, nor, unless in case of impeachment, be punished more than once for the same Offence	Declaration of the right not to be subject to "Double Jeopardy".	Incorporated in the 5th Amendment

ID[1]	Text from the State Constitutional Convention[2]	(Prior Source)[3] and Simplified Purpose[4]	Disposition in the Bill of Rights
NYRA11	That every Person restrained of his Liberty is entitled to an enquiry into the lawfulness of such restraint, and to a removal thereof if unlawful, and that such enquiry and removal ought not to be denied or delayed, except when on account of Public Danger the Congress shall suspend the privilege of the Writ of Habeas Corpus.	(Combination of Virginia's recommended amendments VRA9 and VRA10 in Appendix 14) Declaration of right to due process of law. Declaration that the writ of habeas corpus can only be suspended by Congress in emergencies	Incorporated in the 6th Amendment
NYRA12	That excessive Bail ought not to be required; nor excessive Fines imposed; nor Cruel or unusual Punishments inflicted.	(Small text changes to Virginia's recommended amendment VRA13 in Appendix 14) Declaration of the rights against excessive bail or fines or cruel and unusual punishment	Incorporated in the 8th Amendment
NYRA13	That (except in the Government of the Land and Naval Forces, and of the Militia when in actual Service, and in cases of Impeachment) a Presentment or Indictment by a Grand Jury ought to be observed as a necessary preliminary to the trial of all Crimes cognizable by the Judiciary of the United States, and such Trial should be speedy, public, and by an impartial Jury of the County where the Crime was committed; and that no person can be found Guilty without the unanimous consent of such Jury. But in cases of Crimes not committed within any County of any of the United States, and in Cases of Crimes committed within any County in which a general Insurrection may prevail, or which may be in the possession of a foreign Enemy, the enquiry and trial may be in such County as the Congress shall by Law direct; which County in the two Cases last mentioned should be as near as conveniently may be to that County in which the Crime may have been committed. And that in all Criminal Prosecutions, the Accused ought to be informed of the cause and nature of his Accusation, to be confronted with his accusers and the Witnesses against him, to have the means of producing his Witnesses, and the assistance of Council for his defence, and should not be compelled to give Evidence against himself	(Adds to Virginia's recommended amendment VRA8 in Appendix 14) Declaration of the right to presentment or indictment by a Grand Jury as happening before a trial. Declaration of the right to a speedy trial Declaration to the right of impartial jury Declaration of the requirement of unanimous jury verdict for conviction. Declaration of the right to be informed of the cause of the trial and to confront accusers. Declaration of the right to council for defense. Declaration of the right against self-incrimination.	Incorporated in the 5th and 6th Amendments

ID[1]	Text from the State Constitutional Convention[2]	(Prior Source)[3] and Simplified Purpose[4]	Disposition in the Bill of Rights
NYRA14	That the trial by Jury in the extent that it obtains by the Common Law of England is one of the greatest securities to the rights of a free People, and ought to remain inviolate.	(Small modifications to Virginia's recommended amendment VRA11 in Appendix 14) Declaration of the right to a trial by jury.	Incorporated in the 7th Amendment
NYRA15	That every Freeman has a right to be secure from all unreasonable searches and seizures of his person his papers or his property, and therefore, that all Warrants to search suspected places or seize any Freeman his papers or property, without information upon Oath or Affirmation of sufficient cause, are grievous and oppressive; and that all general Warrants (or such in which the place or person suspected are not particularly designated) are dangerous and ought not to be granted.	Declaration of freedom from unreasonable searches and seizures. Declaration of requirements for search warrants under oath. Declaration against general warrants.	Incorporated in the 4th Amendment
NYRA16	That the People have a right peaceably to assemble together to consult for their common good, or to instruct their Representatives; and that every person has a right to Petition or apply to the Legislature for redress of Grievances.	(Small text changes to Virginia's recommended amendment VRA15 in Appendix 14) Declaration of the right to assemble. Declaration of the right to petition the legislature for a redress of grievances	Incorporated in the 1st Amendment
NYRA17	That the Freedom of the Press ought not to be violated or restrained.	Declaration of the right to free press	Incorporated in the 1st Amendment
NYRA18	That there should be once in four years an Election of the President and Vice President, so that no Officer who may be appointed by the Congress to act as President in case of the removal, death, resignation or inability of the President and Vice President can in any case continue to act beyond the termination of the period for which the last President and Vice President were elected	Declaration of a requirement to elect the President and Vice President every 4 years	Dropped
NYRA19	That nothing contained in the said Constitution is to be construed to prevent the Legislature of any State from passing Laws at its discretion from time to time to divide such State into convenient Districts, and to apportion its Representatives to and amongst such Districts.	Declaration of state's right to apportion congressional districts.	Dropped

ID[1]	Text from the State Constitutional Convention[2]	(Prior Source)[3] and Simplified Purpose[4]	Disposition in the Bill of Rights
NYRA20	That the Prohibition contained in the said Constitution against ex post facto Laws, extends only to Laws concerning Crimes.	Concern about real estate issues and the restriction against ex post facto laws.	Dropped
NYRA21	That all Appeals in Causes determineable according to the course of the common Law, ought to be by Writ of Error and not otherwise.	Concern that appeals courts issue writs of error to evaluate lower court rulings	Dropped
NYRA22	That the Judicial Power of the United States in cases in which a State may be a party, does not extend to criminal Prosecutions, or to authorize any Suit by any Person against a State.	Proposed clarifications when a State is a party to a lawsuit	Dropped
NYRA23	That the Judicial Power of the United States as to Controversies between Citizens of the same State claiming Lands under Grants of different States is not to be construed to extend to any other Controversies between them, except those which relate to such Lands, so claimed under Grants of different States.	Proposal to exclude land suits between citizens of the same state from federal jurisdiction.	Dropped
NYRA24	That the Jurisdiction of the Supreme Court of the United States, or of any other Court to be instituted by the Congress, is not in any case to be encreased enlarged or extended by any Fiction Collusion or mere suggestion;	Proposal to limit the jurisdiction of the Supreme Court	Dropped
NYRA25	That no Treaty is to be construed so to operate as to alter the Constitution of any State	Declaration that no treaty should alter the workings of State Constitutions	Dropped
NYRA26	That there shall be one Representative for every thirty thousand Inhabitants, according to the enumeration or Census mentioned in the Constitution, until the whole number of Representatives amounts to two hundred; after which that number shall be continued or encreased but not diminished, as Congress shall direct, and according to such ratio as the Congress shall fix, in conformity to the rule prescribed for the Apportionment of Representatives and direct Taxes	(Addition to Massachusetts' recommended amendment MRA2 in Appendix 11) To limit the size of the House of Representatives to 200 members	Proposed by Congress as part of initial 12 Amendments but failed at state level
NYRA27	That the Congress do not impose any Excise on any Article (except Ardent Spirits) of the Growth production or Manufacture of the United States, or any of them.	Proposal to limit excise taxes to alcohol	Dropped

ID[1]	Text from the State Constitutional Convention[2]	(Prior Source)[3] and Simplified Purpose[4]	Disposition in the Bill of Rights
NYRA28	That Congress do not lay direct Taxes but when the Monies arising from the Impost and Excise shall be insufficient for the Public Exigencies, nor then until Congress shall first have made a Requisition upon the States to assess levy and pay their respective proportions of such Requisition, agreably to the Census fixed in the said Constitution, in such way and manner as the Legislatures of the respective States shall judge best; and in such Case, if any State shall neglect or refuse to pay its proportion pursuant to such Requisition, then Congress may assess and levy such States proportion, together with Interest at the rate of six per Centum per Annum, from the time of Payment prescribed in such Requisition.	(Slight modifications to Massachusetts' recommended amendment MRA4 in Appendix 11) That when Impost and Excise taxes are not enough for Congress' expenses, they shall make requisitions of the states based on the census. If states did not pay their requisition, then their debt would have a 6% annual interest rate.	Dropped
NYRA29	That the Congress shall not make or alter any Regulation in any State respecting the times places and manner of holding Elections for Senators or Representatives, unless the Legislature of such State shall neglect or refuse to make Laws or Regulations for the purpose, or from any circumstance be incapable of making the same, and then only until the Legislature of such State shall make provision in the premisses; provided that Congress may prescribe the time for the Election of Representatives.	(Modifications to Massachusetts' recommended amendment MRA3 in Appendix 11) Declaration that Congress should not be involved in State elections.	Dropped
NYRA30	That no Persons except natural born Citizens, or such as were Citizens on or before the fourth day of July one thousand seven hundred and seventy six, or such as held Commissions under the United States during the War, and have at any time since the fourth day of July one thousand seven hundred and seventy six become Citizens of one or other of the United States, and who shall be Freeholders, shall be eligible to the Places of President, Vice President, or Members of either House of the Congress of the United States.	Proposal for further restrictions on Presidential eligibility.	Dropped
NYRA31	That the Congress do not grant Monopolies or erect any Company with exclusive Advantages of Commerce	(Modification to Massachusetts' recommended amendment MRA5 in Appendix 11) To keep Congress from providing exclusive arrangements for specific merchants	Dropped

ID[1]	Text from the State Constitutional Convention[2]	(Prior Source)[3] and Simplified Purpose[4]	Disposition in the Bill of Rights
NYRA32	That no standing Army or regular Troops shall be raised or kept up in time of peace, without the consent of two-thirds of the Senators and Representatives present, in each House.	(Modification of New Hampshire's recommended amendment NHRA10 in Appendix 13) Declaration against Standing Armies and requiring a 2/3 vote to raise one.	Dropped
NYRA33	That no Money be borrowed on the Credit of the United States without the Assent of twothirds of the Senators and Representatives present in each House.	Declaration that Congress should have a 2/3 vote to borrow money.	Dropped
NYRA34	That the Congress shall not declare War without the concurrence of two-thirds of the Senators and Representatives present in each House.	Declaration that Congress should have a 2/3 vote to declare War.	Dropped
NYRA35	That the Privilege of the Habeas Corpus shall not by any Law be suspended for a longer term than six Months, or until twenty days after the Meeting of the Congress next following the passing of the Act for such suspension.	Proposal to limit suspensions of the Privilege of Habeas Corpus to 6 months.	Dropped
NYRA36	That the Right of the Congress to exercise exclusive Legislation over such District, not exceeding ten Miles square, as may by cession of a particular State, and the acceptance of Congress, become the Seat of the Government of the United States, shall not be so exercised, as to exempt the Inhabitants of such District from paying the like Taxes Imposts Duties and Excises, as shall be imposed on the other Inhabitants of the State in which such District may be; and that no person shall be privileged within the said District from Arrest for Crimes committed, or Debts contracted out of the said District.	Proposal that the residents of the District, what would become Washington D.C., would have to pay equivalent taxes as if they lived in the state where the land was taken from. Proposal that people could not flee to the District to avoid arrest for crimes or relief from debts from other states.	Dropped Dropped
NYRA37	That the Right of exclusive Legislation with respect to such places as may be purchased for the Erection of Forts, Magazines, Arsenals, Dock yards and other needful Buildings, shall not authorize the Congress to make any Law to prevent the Laws of the States respectively in which they may be, from extending to such places in all civil and Criminal Matters, except as to such Persons as shall be in the Service of the United States; nor to them with respect to Crimes committed without such Places	Proposal to restrict Congress' control over State Laws that impact all places of civil and criminal matters.	Dropped

ID[1]	Text from the State Constitutional Convention[2]	(Prior Source)[3] and Simplified Purpose[4]	Disposition in the Bill of Rights
NYRA38	That the Compensation for the Senators and Representatives be ascertained by standing Laws; and that no alteration of the existing rate of Compensation shall operate for the Benefit of the Representatives, until after a subsequent Election shall have been had.	Proposal to limit raises for Congress until after the next election.	27th Amendment Finally Approved in 1992 over 200 years after its proposal
NYRA39	That the Journals of the Congress shall be published at least once a year, with the exception of such parts relating to Treaties or Military operations, as in the Judgment of either House shall require Secrecy; and that both Houses of Congress shall always keep their Doors open during their Sessions, unless the Business may in their Opinion require Secrecy. That the yeas & nays shall be entered on the Journals whenever two Members in either House may require it.	Proposal to publish Congressional Journals	Dropped
NYRA40	That no Capitation Tax shall ever be laid by the Congress	Declaration that Congress should never create a Capitation Tax which is an equal tax per person.	Dropped
NYRA41	That no Person be eligible as a Senator for more than six years in any term of twelve years; and that the Legislatures of the respective States may recal their Senators or either of them, and elect others in their stead, to serve the remainder of the time for which the Senators so recalled were appointed.	Proposal to term limit Senators	Dropped
NYRA42	That no Senator or Representative shall during the time for which he was elected be appointed to any Office under the Authority of the United States	Proposal that Senators or Representatives cannot hold executive branch offices.	Dropped
NYRA43	That the Authority given to the Executives of the States to fill the vacancies of Senators be abolished, and that such vacancies be filled by the respective Legislatures.	Proposal to require vacant Senators to be filled by the State Legislatures.	Dropped
NYRA44	That the Power of Congress to pass uniform Laws concerning Bankruptcy shall only extend to Merchants and other Traders; and that the States respectively may pass Laws for the relief of other Insolvent Debtors.	Proposal to limit Congress' bankruptcy laws to merchants and traders only.	Dropped
NYRA45	That no Person shall be eligible to the Office of President of the United States a third time.	Proposal to limit President to 2 terms	Later implemented as the 22nd Amendment in 1951

ID[1]	Text from the State Constitutional Convention[2]	(Prior Source)[3] and Simplified Purpose[4]	Disposition in the Bill of Rights
NYRA46	That the Executive shall not grant Pardons for Treason, unless with the Consent of the Congress; but may at his discretion grant Reprieves to persons convicted of Treason, until their Cases can be laid before the Congress.	Proposal to limit the President's pardon to exclude Treason without Congressional approval	Dropped
NYRA47	That the President or person exercising his Powers for the time being, shall not command an Army in the Field in person, without the previous desire of the Congress.	Proposal that the President should not command the Army in battle without Congressional approval.	Dropped
NYRA48	That all Letters Patent, Commissions, Pardons, writs and process of the United States, shall run in the Name of the People of the United States, and be tested in the Name of the President of the United States, or the person exercising his powers for the time being, or the first Judge of the Court out of which the same shall issue, as the case may be.	Proposal for processing and defending letters, patents, commissions, pardons and writs in the name of the United States.	Dropped
NYRA49	That the Congress shall not constitute ordain or establish any Tribunals or Inferior Courts, with any other than Appellate Jurisdiction, except such as may be necessary for the Tryal of Causes of Admiralty and Maritime Jurisdiction, and for the Trial of piracies and Felonies committed on the High Seas; and in all other Cases to which the Judicial power of the United States extends, and in which the Supreme Court of the United States has not original Jurisdiction, the Causes shall be heard tried, and determined in some one of the State Courts, with the right of appeal to the Supreme Court of the United States, or other proper Tribunal to be established for that purpose by the Congress, with such exceptions, and under such regulations as the Congress shall make.	Restrictions on Article III courts to use State Courts in most cases.	Dropped

ID[1]	Text from the State Constitutional Convention[2]	(Prior Source)[3] and Simplified Purpose[4]	Disposition in the Bill of Rights
NYRA50	That the Court for the Trial of Impeachments shall consist of the Senate, the Judges of the Supreme Court of the United States, and the first or Senior Judge for the time being, of the highest Court of general and ordinary common Law Jurisdiction in each State;—that the Congress shall by standing Laws designate the Courts in the respective States answering this Description, and in States having no Courts exactly answering this Description, shall designate some other Court, preferring such if any there be, whose Judge or Judges may hold their places during good Behaviour—provided that no more than one Judge, other than Judges of the Supreme Court of the United States, shall come from one State—That the Congress be authorized to pass Laws for compensating the said Judges for such Services and for compelling their Attendance—and that a Majority at least of the said Judges shall be requisite to constitute the said Court—that no person impeached shall sit as a Member thereof. That each Member shall previous to the entering upon any Trial take an oath or Affirmation, honestly and impartially to hear and determine the Cause—and that a Majority of the Members present shall be necessary to a Conviction.	Proposal to change impeachment proceeding to include the entire United States Supreme Court and the Chief Justices of each State Supreme Court.	Dropped
NYRA51	That persons aggrieved by any Judgment, Sentence or Decree of the Supreme Court of the United States, in any Cause in which that Court has original Jurisdiction, with such exceptions and under such Regulations as the Congress shall make concerning the same, shall upon application, have a Commission to be issued by the President of the United States, to such Men learned in the Law as he shall nominate, and by and with the Advice and consent of the Senate appoint, not less than seven, authorizing such Commissioners, or any seven or more of them, to correct the Errors in such Judgment or to review such Sentence and Decree, as the case may be, and to do Justice to the parties in the Premisses.	Proposal to allow the President to appoint a Commission with Senate approval to review and potentially overturn Supreme Court decisions where the Supreme Court was operating under Original Jurisdiction.	Dropped
NYRA52	That no Judge of the Supreme Court of the United States shall hold any other Office under the United States, or any of them.	Proposal that Supreme Court Justices cannot hold executive branch offices.	Dropped

ID[1]	Text from the State Constitutional Convention[2]	(Prior Source)[3] and Simplified Purpose[4]	Disposition in the Bill of Rights
NYRA53	That the Judicial Power of the United States shall extend to no Controversies respecting Land, unless it relate to Claims of Territory or Jurisdiction between States, or to Claims of Lands between Individuals, or between States and Individuals under the Grants of different States.	Proposal to limit Article III Judiciary powers regarding land controversies.	Dropped
NYRA54	That the Militia of any State shall not be compelled to serve without the limits of the State for a longer term than six weeks, without the Consent of the Legislature thereof.	Proposal to limit State Militia service to six weeks per year without legislative approval.	Dropped
NYRA55	That the words without the Consent of the Congress in the seventh Clause of the ninth Section of the first Article of the Constitution, be expunged.	Proposal to eliminate Congress' ability to allow grants of nobility.	Dropped
NYRA56	That the Senators and Representatives and all Executive and Judicial officers of the United States shall be bound by Oath or Affirmation not to infringe or violate the Constitutions or Rights of the respective States.	Proposal that the oaths of the legislative and executive branch shall not infringe upon the Constitutions or rights of the States	Dropped
NYRA57	That the Legislatures of the respective States may make Provision by Law, that the Electors of the Election Districts to be by them appointed shall chuse a Citizen of the United States who shall have been an Inhabitant of such District for the Term of one year immediately preceeding the time of his Election, for one of the Representatives of such State	Proposal to allow the State Legislature to appoint one of the Representatives from each of the States.	Dropped

Appendix 16 - North Carolina Recommendatory Amendments Hillsborough and Fayetteville Conventions

ID[1]	Text from the State Constitutional Convention[2]	(Prior Source)[3] and Simplified Purpose[4]	Disposition in the Bill of Rights
NCHRA1-NCHRA20	North Carolina copied the text from Virginia's Proposed Amendments	Virginia's recommendatory amendments VRA1-VRA20 were copied directly by North Carolina at their Hillsborough Convention. (See VRA1-VRA20 in Appendix 14)	(See dispositions of recommended amendments in Appendix 14)
NCHRA21	That each state in the union shall, respectively, retain every power, jurisdiction and right, which is not by this constitution delegated to the Congress of the United States, or to the departments of the Federal Government.	(Similar to Massachusetts' recommended amendment MRA1 in Appendix 11) To keep all unenumerated powers for State governments	Incorporated in the 10th Amendment

1 ID values provided by the Author for internal referencing purposes

2 University of Wisconsin-Madison, Department of History, Center for the Study of the American Constitution. (2026, Feb. 24). https://csac.history.wisc.edu/wp-content/uploads/sites/281/2024/04/DC3-08-09-08_N.C.-Hillsborough-Conv.-Amendments_2Aug88.pdf

3 Given North Carolina's location, the Massachusetts convention results from February 7 (Appendix 11), the South Carolina convention results from May 23 (Appendix 12), the New Hampshire convention results from June 21 (Appendix 13), the Virginia convention results from June 27 (Appendix 14), the New York convention results from June 26 (Appendix 15) all would have arrived in North Carolina prior to its convention.

4 Simplified Purpose is generated by the Author

ID[1]	Text from the State Constitutional Convention[2]	(Prior Source)[3] and Simplified Purpose[4]	Disposition in the Bill of Rights
NCHRA22	That there shall be one representative for every 30,000, according to the enumeration or census, mentioned in the constitution, until the whole number of representatives amounts to two hundred; after which, that number shall be continued or increased, as Congress shall direct, upon the principles fixed in the constitution, by apportioning the representatives of each state to some greater number of people from time to time, as population encreases.	(Similar to New Hampshire's recommended amendment NHPCA2 in Appendix 13 and New York's recommended amendment NYRA26 in Appendix 15) To limit the size of the House of Representatives to 200 members	Proposed by Congress as part of initial 12 Amendments but failed at state level.
NCHRA23	When Congress shall lay direct taxes or excises, they shall immediately inform the executive power of each state, of the quota of such state, according to the census herein directed, which is proposed to be thereby raised: And if the legislature of any state shall pass a law, which shall be effectual for raising such quota at the time required by Congress, the taxes and excises laid by Congress shall not be collected in such state.	Proposed requirement for Congress to immediately notify States what their direct tax contributions will be.	Dropped
NCHRA24	That the members of the senate and house of representatives shall be ineligible to, and incapable of holding any civil office under the authority of the United States, during the time for which they shall, respectively, be elected.	(Slightly modified version of New York's recommended amendment NYRA42 in Appendix 15) Proposal that Senators or Representatives cannot hold executive branch offices.	Dropped
NCHRA25	That the journals of the proceedings of the senate and house of representatives shall be published at least once in every year, except such parts thereof relating to treaties, alliances, or military operations, as in their judgment require secrecy	(Reduced version of New York's recommended amendment NYRA39 in Appendix 15) Proposal to publish Congressional Journals	Dropped
NCHRA26	That a regular statement and account of the receipts and expenditures of the public money shall be published at least once in every year.	To require full government accounting for expenses once per year.	Dropped

ID[1]	Text from the State Constitutional Convention[2]	(Prior Source)[3] and Simplified Purpose[4]	Disposition in the Bill of Rights
NCHRA27	That no commercial treaty shall be ratified without the concurrence of two-thirds of the whole number of the members of the senate: And no treaty, ceding, contracting, or restraining or suspending the territorial rights or claims of the United States, or any of them or their, or any of their rights or claims to fishing in the American seas, or navigating the American rivers shall be made, but in cases of the most urgent and extreme necessity; nor shall any such treaty be ratified without the concurrence of three-fourths of the whole number of the members of both houses respectively.	To require a 2/3 vote in Congress for commercial treaties. To require a ¾ vote in Congress to cede land of the United States	Dropped Dropped
NCHRA28	That no navigation law, or law regulating commerce shall be passed without the consent of two-thirds of the members present in both houses.	To require a 2/3 vote of both houses of Congress for laws affecting navigation or commerce.	Dropped
NCHRA29	That no standing army or regular troops shall be raised or kept up in time of peace, without the consent of two thirds of the members present in both houses.	(Similar to New Hampshire's recommended amendment NHRA10 in Appendix 13, and New York's recommended amendment NYRA32 in Appendix 15) To require a 2/3 vote of both houses of Congress for maintain a standing army.	Dropped
NCHRA30	That no soldier shall be inlisted for any longer term than four years, except in time of war, and then for no longer term than the continuance of the war.	To limit military enlistments to four years except during war.	Dropped

ID[1]	Text from the State Constitutional Convention[2]	(Prior Source)[3] and Simplified Purpose[4]	Disposition in the Bill of Rights
NCHRA31	That each state, respectively, shall have the power to provide for organizing, arming and disciplining its own militia whensoever Congress shall omit or neglect to provide for the same. That the militia shall not be subject to martial law, except when in actual service in time of war, invasion or rebellion: And when not in the actual service of the United States, shall be subject only to such fines, penalties, and punishments as shall be directed or inflicted by the laws of its own state.	To provide for state control over the militia	Dropped
NCHRA32	That Congress shall not declare any state to be in rebellion without the consent of at least two-thirds of all the members present of both houses.	To require a 2/3 vote of both houses of Congress to declare a state in rebellion.	Dropped
NCHRA33	That the exclusive power of Legislation given to Congress over the federal town and its adjacent district, and other places, purchased or to be purchased by Congress, of any of the states, shall extend only to such regulations as respect the police and good government thereof.	To limit Congress' power over the District that would become Washington D.C. to only cover police and good government.	Dropped
NCHRA34	That no person shall be capable of being president of the United States for more than eight years in any term of sixteen years.	To limit the President to two terms every 16 years.	Dropped

ID[1]	Text from the State Constitutional Convention[2]	(Prior Source)[3] and Simplified Purpose[4]	Disposition in the Bill of Rights
NCHRA35	That the judicial power of the United States shall be vested in one supreme court, and in such courts of admiralty as Congress may from time to time ordain and establish in any of the different states. The judicial power shall extend to all cases in law and equity, arising under treaties made, or which shall be made under the authority of the United States; to all cases affecting ambassadors, other foreign ministers and consuls; to all cases of admiralty, and maritime jurisdiction; to controversies to which the United States shall be a party; to controversies between two or more states, and between parties claiming lands under the grants of different states. In all cases affecting ambassadors, other foreign ministers and consuls, and those in which a state shall be a party; the supreme court shall have original jurisdiction, in all other cases before mentioned; the supreme court shall have appelate jurisdiction as to matters of law only, except in cases of equity, and of admiralty and maritime jurisdiction, in which the supreme court shall have appelate jurisdiction both as to law and fact, with such exceptions, and under such regulations as the Congress shall make. But the judicial power of the United States shall extend to no case where the cause of action shall have originated before the ratification of this constitution, except in disputes between states about their territory; disputes between persons claiming lands under the grants of different states, and suits for debts due to the united states.	To more firmly establish limits on the Article III Judiciary powers.	Dropped
NCHRA36	That in criminal prosecutions, no man shall be restrained in the exercise of the usual and accustomed right of challenging or excepting to the jury.	Recognizes a right to challenge jurors in criminal prosecutions.	Dropped

ID[1]	Text from the State Constitutional Convention[2]	(Prior Source)[3] and Simplified Purpose[4]	Disposition in the Bill of Rights
NCHRA37	That Congress shall not alter, modify, or interfere in the times, places, or manner of holding elections for senators and representatives, or either of them, except when the legislature of any state shall neglect, refuse or be disabled by invasion or rebellion, to prescribe the same.	(Similar to Massachusetts' recommended amendment MRA3 in Appendix 11, and New Hampshire's recommended amendment NHRA3 in Appendix 13) To restrict Congress from setting State election laws.	Dropped
NCHRA38	That those clauses which declare that Congress shall not exercise certain powers, be not interpreted in any manner whatsoever to extend the powers of Congress; but that they be construed either as making exceptions to the specified powers where this shall be the case, or otherwise, as inserted merely for greater caution.	To declare that denying Congress powers should never be used to extend their powers.	Partially covered by the 10th Amendment
NCHRA39	That the laws ascertaining the compensation of senators and representatives for their services be pos[t]poned in their operation, until after the election of representatives immediately succeeding the passing thereof, that excepted, which shall first be passed on the subject.	(Similar to New York's recommended amendment NYRA38 in Appendix 15) To limit raises for Congress until after the next election.	(Similar to New York's recommended amendment NYRA38 in Appendix 15) To limit raises for Congress until after the next election.
NCHRA40	That some tribunal, other than the senate, be provided for trying impeachments of senators.	Senators should be impeached in a different forum.	Dropped
NCHRA41	That the salary of a judge shall not be increased or diminished during his continuance in office, otherwise than by general regulations of salary which may take place, on a revision of the subject at stated periods of not less than seven years, to commence from the time such salaries shall be first ascertained by Congress.	To limit judicial salaries so that they could not be increased or decreased more often than every seven years.	Dropped

ID[1]	Text from the State Constitutional Convention[2]	(Prior Source)[3] and Simplified Purpose[4]	Disposition in the Bill of Rights
NCHRA42	That Congress erect no company of merchants with exclusive advantages of commerce.	(Copied from Massachusetts' recommended amendment MRA5 in Appendix 11) To keep Congress from providing exclusive arrangements for specific merchants.	Dropped
NCHRA43	That no treaties which shall be directly opposed to the existing laws of the United States in Congress assembled, shall be valid until such laws shall be repealed, or made conformable to such treaty; nor shall any treaty be valid which is contradictory to the constitution of the United States.	To require Congress to repeal laws conflicting with treaties and to require that treaties do not conflict with the Constitution.	Dropped
NCHRA44	That the latter part of the fifth paragraph of the 9th section of the first article be altered to read thus,—Nor shall vessels bound to a particular state be obliged to enter or pay duties in any other; nor when bound from any one of the States be obliged to clear in another.	Wants to change "nor shall Vessels bound to, or from, one State, be obliged to enter, clear, or pay Duties in another."	Dropped
NCHRA45	That Congress shall not directly or indirectly, either by them selves or thro' the judiciary, interfere with any one of the states in the redemption of paper money already emitted and now in circulation, or in liquidating and discharging the public securities of any one of the states: But each and every state shall have the exclusive right of making such laws and regulations for the above purposes as they shall think proper.	To restrict Congress from limiting the states abilities to deal with paper money already in circulation.	Dropped
NCHRA46	That Congress shall not introduce foreign troops into the United States without the consent of two-thirds of the members present of both houses.	To require a 2/3 vote of both houses of Congress to allow foreign troops in the US.	Dropped

ID[1]	Text from the State Constitutional Convention[2]	(Prior Source)[3] and Simplified Purpose[4]	Disposition in the Bill of Rights
NCFRA1	That Congress shall not alter, modify, or interfere in the times, places and manner of holding elections for Senators and Representatives, or either of them, except when the Legislature of any state shall neglect, refuse, or be disabled by invasion or rebellion to prescribe the same, or in case when the provision made by the state is so imperfect as that no consequent election is had.	(Slight addition to North Carolina's recommended amendment NCHRA37 in Appendix 15) To further restrict Congress from setting State election laws.	Dropped
NCFRA2	That Congress shall not, directly or indirectly, either by themselves or through the Judiciary, interfere with any one of the states in the redemption of paper money already emitted and now in circulation, or in liquidating and discharging the public securities of any one of the states; but each and every state shall have the exclusive right of making such laws and regulations for the above purposes, as they shall think proper	(Textual cleanup of North Carolina's recommended amendment NCHRA45 in Appendix 15)	Dropped
NCFRA3	That the members of the Senate and House of Representatives shall be ineligible to, and incapable of holding any civil office under the authority of the United States, during the time for which they shall respectively be elected.	(Textual cleanup of North Carolina's recommended amendment NCHRA24 in Appendix 15)	Dropped
NCFRA4	That the journals of the proceedings of the Senate and House of Representatives shall be published at least once in every year, except such parts thereof, relating to treaties, alliances, or military operations, as in their judgment require secrecy.	(Textual cleanup of North Carolina's recommended Amendment NCHRA25 in Appendix 15)	Dropped

1 ID values provided by the Author for internal referencing purposes

2 University of Wisconsin-Madison, Department of History, Center for the Study of the American Constitution. (2026, Feb. 24). https://csac.history.wisc.edu/wp-content/uploads/sites/281/2024/04/DC3-08-09-09_N.C.-Fayetteville-Convention-Amendments_23Nov89.pdf

3 Given that this convention was over a year after all others, all prior Recommendatory Amendments would have been known.

4 Simplified Purpose is generated by the Author

ID[1]	Text from the State Constitutional Convention[2]	(Prior Source)[3] and Simplified Purpose[4]	Disposition in the Bill of Rights
NCFRA5	That a regular statement and account of the receipts and expenditures of all public monies, shall be published at least once in every year.	(Textual cleanup of North Carolina's recommended Amendment NCHRA26)	Dropped
NCFRA6	That no navigation law, or law regulating commerce, shall be passed, without the consent of two-thirds of the members present in both Houses	(Textual cleanup of North Carolina's recommended Amendment NCHRA28)	Dropped
NCFRA7	That no soldier shall be enlisted for any longer term than four years, except in time of war, and then for no longer term than the continuance of the war.	(Textual cleanup of North Carolina's recommended Amendment NCHRA30)	Dropped
NCFRA8	That some tribunal, other than the Senate, be provided for trying impeachments of Senators.	(Textual cleanup of North Carolina's recommended Amendment NCHRA40)	Dropped

Appendix 17 - Rhode Island Recommendatory Amendments

ID[1]	Text from the State Constitutional Convention[2]	(Prior Source)[3] and Simplified Purpose[4]	Disposition in the Bill of Rights
RIRA1	That there are certain natural rights, of which men when they form a social compact, cannot deprive or divest their posterity, among which are the enjoyment of Life and Liberty, with the means of acquiring, possessing and protecting Property, and pursuing and obtaining happiness and safety.	(Copied from Virginia's recommended amendment VRA1 in Appendix 14) To recognize that natural rights cannot be taken away by the government	Dropped
RIRA2	That all power is naturally vested in, and consequently derived from the people; that magistrates therefore are their trustees and agents, and at all times amenable to them.	(Copied from Virginia's recommended amendment VRA2 in Appendix 14) To recognize that the power of government comes from the people.	Dropped

1 ID values provided by the Author for internal referencing purposes

2 University of Wisconsin-Madison, Department of History, Center for the Study of the American Constitution. (2026, Feb. 24). https://csac.history.wisc.edu/wp-content/uploads/sites/281/2024/04/DC3-08-09-10_R.I.-Recommindatory-Amendments_29May90.pdf

3 Given that the last prior constitutional convention having been in November 1789, the results of all prior constitutional conventions should have been available to Rhode Island (Appendices 11-16).

4 Simplified Purpose is generated by the Author

ID[1]	Text from the State Constitutional Convention[2]	(Prior Source)[3] and Simplified Purpose[4]	Disposition in the Bill of Rights
RIRA3	That the powers of government may be reassumed by the people, whensoever it shall become necessary to their happiness.—That the rights of the States respectively, to nominate and appoint all state Officers, and every other power, jurisdiction and right, which is not by the said constitution clearly delegated to the Congress of the United States or to the departments of government thereof, remain to the people of the several states, or their respective State Governments to whom they may have granted the same, and that those clauses in the said constitution which declare that Congress shall not have or exercise certain powers, do not imply, that Congress is entitled to any powers not given by the said constitution, but such clauses are to be construed as exceptions to certain specified powers, or as inserted merely for greater caution.	(Combination of Virginia's recommended amendment VRA3 in Appendix 14 and Massachusetts' recommended amendments MRA1 in Appendix 11) To declare that arbitrary and oppressive government actions can be resisted. To keep all unenumerated powers for State governments	Partially incorporated in the 10th Amendment
RIRA4	That religion, or the duty which we owe to our Creator, and the manner of discharging it, can be directed only by reason and conviction, and not by force or violence, and therefore all men, have an equal, natural and unalienable right to the free exercise of religion, according to the dictates of conscience, and that no particular religious sect or society ought to be favoured, or established by law in preference to others.	(Copied from Virginia's recommended amendment VRA20 in Appendix 14) To recognize a "right of conscience to worship God as the individual sees fit." To restrict the government from favoring a particular religion in preference to others.	Incorporated in the 1st Amendment

ID[1]	Text from the State Constitutional Convention[2]	(Prior Source)[3] and Simplified Purpose[4]	Disposition in the Bill of Rights
RIRA5	That the legislative, executive and judiciary powers of government, should be separate and distinct, and that the members of the two first may be restrained from oppression, by feeling and participating the publick burthens, they should at fixed periods be reduced to a private station, return into the mass of the people, and the vacancies be supplied by certain and regular elections, in which all or any part of the former members, to be eligible or ineligible, as the rules of the constitution of government and the laws shall direct.	(Copied from Virginia's recommended amendment VRA5 in Appendix 14) To declare a need for fixed terms of office for people in the legislative and executive branches and to recognize Constitutional or legal limit on their ability to run for election again.	Dropped
RIRA6	That elections of representatives in legislature ought to be free and frequent, and all men having sufficient evidence of permanent common interest with, and attachment to the community ought to have the right of suffrage, and no aid, charge, tax or fee can be set, rated or levied upon the people without their own consent or that of their representatives so elected, nor can they be bound by any law, to which they have not in like manner assented for the publick good.	(Copied from Virginia's recommended amendment VRA6 in Appendix 14) To recognize a right to vote for all men with ties to the community.	Dropped
RIRA7	That all power of suspending laws or the execution of laws, by any authority without the consent of the representatives of the people in the legislature, is injurious to their rights, and ought not to be exercised.	(Copied from Virginia's recommended amendment VRA7 in Appendix 14) To declare that suspension of laws can only be done with legislative approval.	Dropped

ID[1]	Text from the State Constitutional Convention[2]	(Prior Source)[3] and Simplified Purpose[4]	Disposition in the Bill of Rights
RIRA8	That in all capital and criminal prosecutions, a man hath a right to demand the cause and nature of his accusation, to be confronted with the accusers and witnesses, to call for evidence and be allowed counsel in his favour, and to a fair and speedy trial by an impartial jury of his vicinage, without whose unanimous consent he cannot be found guilty, (except in the government of the land and naval forces) nor can he be compelled to give evidence against himself.	Copied from Virginia's recommended amendment VRA8 in Appendix 14) To guarantee legal protection including: 1) The right to confront your accuser 2) The ability to request and present evidence 3) The right to defense counsel 4) The right to a speedy trial with an impartial jury 5) Unanimous jury necessary for	Incorporated in the 5th and 6th Amendments
RIRA9	That no freeman ought to be taken, imprisoned or disseized of his freehold, liberties, privileges, or franchises, or outlawed, or exiled, or in any manner destroyed or deprived of his life, liberty or property but by the trial by jury, or by the law of the land.	(Copied from Virginia's recommended amendment VRA9 in Appendix 14) To guarantee due process of law before anyone can be deprived of their life, liberty or property.	Incorporated in the 5th Amendment
RIRA10	That every freeman restrained of his liberty, is intitled to a remedy, to enquire into the lawfulness thereof, and to remove the same if unlawful, and that such remedy ought not to be denied or delayed.	(Copied from Virginia's recommended amendment VRA10 in Appendix 14) To guarantee the writ of habeas corpus	Dropped
RIRA11	That in controversies respecting property, and in suits between man and man the antient trial by jury, as hath been exercised by us and our ancestors, from the time whereof the memory of man is not to the contrary, is one of the greatest securities to the rights of the people, and ought to remain sacred and inviolate.	(Added language to Virginia's recommended amendment VRA11 in Appendix 14) To require jury trials for civil suits	Incorporated in the 7th Amendment

ID[1]	Text from the State Constitutional Convention[2]	(Prior Source)[3] and Simplified Purpose[4]	Disposition in the Bill of Rights
RIRA12	That every freeman ought to obtain right and justice, freely and without sale, completely and without denial, promptly and without delay, and that all establishments or regulations contravening these rights, are oppressive and unjust.	(Modified version of Virginia's recommended amendment VRA12 in Appendix 14) To recognize a legal right to recourse for wrongs.	Partially incorporated in the last clause of the 5th Amendment
RIRA13	That excessive bail ought not to be required, nor excessive fines imposed, nor cruel or unusual punishment inflicted.	(Copied from Virginia's recommended amendment VRA13 in Appendix 14) To prohibit excessive bail or fines, or cruel or unusual punishment.	Incorporated in the 8th Amendment
RIRA14	That every person has a right to be secure from all unreasonable searches and seizures of his person, his papers or his property, and therefore that all warrants to search suspected places or seize any person, his papers or his property, without information upon oath, or affirmation of sufficient cause, are grievous and oppressive, and that all general warrants (or such in which the place or person suspected, are not particularly designated,) are dangerous, and ought not to be granted.	(Copied from Virginia's recommended amendment VRA14) To declare strong requirements to obtain search warrants, and to outlaw general warrants	Incorporated in the 5th Amendment
RIRA15	That the people have a right peaceably to assemble together, to consult for their common good, or to instruct their representatives, and that every person has a right to petition or apply to the legislature for redress of grievances.	(Small textual changes to Virginia's recommended amendment VRA15 in Appendix 14) To recognize a "right to peaceably assemble" To recognize a "right to petition the legislature for a redress of grievances"	Incorporated in the 1st Amendment
RIRA16	That the people have a right to freedom of speech and of writing, and publishing their sentiments, that freedom of the press is one of the greatest bulwarks of liberty, and ought not to be violated.	(Small textual changes to Virginia's recommended amendment VRA16 in Appendix 14) To recognize a "right to freedom of speech" To recognize a "right to freedom of the press"	Incorporated in the 1st Amendment

ID[1]	Text from the State Constitutional Convention[2]	(Prior Source)[3] and Simplified Purpose[4]	Disposition in the Bill of Rights
RIRA17	That the people have a right to keep and bear arms, that a well regulated militia, including the body of the people capable of bearing arms, is the proper, natural and safe defence of a free state; that the militia shall not be subject to martial law except in time of war, rebellion or insurrection; that standing armies in time of peace are dangerous to liberty, and ought not to be kept up, except in cases of necessity, and that at all times the military should be under strict subordination to the civil power; that in time of peace no soldier ought to be quartered in any house, without the consent of the owner, and in time of war, only by the civil magistrate, in such manner as the law directs	(Small textual changes to Virginia's recommended amendment VRA17 and addition of Virginia's recommended amendment VRA18 in Appendix 14) To recognize a "right to keep and bear arms" To declare the desire to avoid standing armies, and to always have civilian control of the military. To recognize a "right against having soldiers quartered in your home"	Incorporated in the 2nd Amendment and the 3rd Amendment
RIRA18	That any person religiously scrupulous of bearing arms, ought to be exempted, upon payment of an equivalent, to employ another to bear arms in his stead.	(Small textual change to Virginia's recommended amendment VRA19 in Appendix 14) To declare a "right for religious people with strict moral convictions against bearing arms to pay for someone to take their place in the military"	Dropped
RIRA19	The United States shall guarantee to each State its sovereignty, freedom and independence, and every power, jurisdiction and right which is not by this constitution expressly delegated to the United States.	(Additions to Massachusetts' recommended amendment MRA1 in Appendix 11) To keep all unenumerated powers for State government.	Incorporated in the 10th Amendment

ID[1]	Text from the State Constitutional Convention[2]	(Prior Source)[3] and Simplified Purpose[4]	Disposition in the Bill of Rights
RIRA20	That Congress shall not alter, modify or interfere in the times, places or manner of holding elections for Senators and Representatives or either of them, except when the legislature of any state shall neglect, refuse or be disabled by invasion or rebellion to prescribe the same; or in case when the provision made by the states, is so imperfect as that no consequent election is had, and then only until the legislature of such state, shall make provision in the premises.	(Additions to New York's recommended amendment NYRA29 in Appendix 15) To restrict Congress from interfering with state election laws.	Dropped
RIRA21	It is declared by the Convention, that the judicial power of the United States in cases in which a state may be a party, does not extend to criminal prosecutions, or to authorize any suit by any person against a state; but to remove all doubts or controversies respecting the same, that it be especially expressed as a part of the constitution of the United States, that Congress shall not directly or indirectly, either by themselves or through the judiciary, interfere with any one of the states, in the redemption of paper money already emitted and now in circulation, or in liquidating or discharging the publick securities of any one state, that each and every state shall have the exclusive right of making such laws and regulations for the before mentioned purpose, as they shall think proper.	(Addition to New York's recommended amendment NYRA22 in Appendix 15 and North Carolina's recommended amendment NCHRA45 in Appendix 16) Proposed clarification as to when a State is a party to a lawsuit. To restrict Congress from limiting the states abilities to deal with paper money already in circulation.	Incorporated in the 11th Amendment in 1795.
RIRA22	That no amendments to the constitution of the United States hereafter to be made, pursuant to the fifth article, shall take effect, or become a part of the constitution of the United States after the year one thousand seven hundred and ninety three, without the consent of eleven of the states heretofore united under one confederation.	To increase the requirement for Constitutional Amendments so that 11/13 states had to agree after 1793.	Dropped

ID[1]	Text from the State Constitutional Convention[2]	(Prior Source)[3] and Simplified Purpose[4]	Disposition in the Bill of Rights
RIRA23	That the judicial powers of the United States shall extend to no possible case, where the cause of action shall have originated before the ratification of this constitution, except in disputes between states about their territory, disputes between persons claiming lands under grants of different states, and debts due to the United States.	(Part of North Carolina's recommended amendment NCHRA35 in Appendix 16) To more firmly establish limits on the Article III Judiciary powers.	Dropped
RIRA24	That no person shall be compelled to do military duty, otherwise than by voluntary enlistment, except in cases of general invasion, any thing in the second paragraph of the sixth article of the constitution, or any law made under the constitution to the contrary notwithstanding	To proclaim an all-volunteer army except cases of invasion. To claim that it is the right of the states to determine rules for military duty.	Dropped
RIRA25	That no capitation or poll-tax shall ever be laid by Congress	(Addition to New York's recommended amendment NYRA40 in Appendix 15 to include prohibitions on poll-taxes) To prohibit capitation (per person) taxes. To prohibit poll-taxes.	Poll Taxes were outlawed by the 24th Amendment passed in 1964
RIRA26	In cases of direct taxes, Congress shall first make requisitions on the several states to assess, levy and pay their respective proportions of such requisitions, in such way and manner, as the legislatures of the several states shall judge best; and in case any state shall neglect or refuse to pay its proportion pursuant to such requisition, then Congress may assess and levy such state's proportion, together with interest at the rate of six per cent. per annum, from the time prescribed in such requisition.	(Modification of Massachusetts' recommended amendment MRA4 in Appendix 11) That when direct taxes are not enough for Congress' expenses, the states need to tax their citizens their share. States that do not pay their requisition will be charged 6% annual interest on their debt.	Dropped
RIRA27	That Congress shall lay no direct taxes, without the consent of the legislatures of three fourths of the states in the Union.	To require ¾ of the state legislatures to approve any direct taxes.	Dropped

ID[1]	Text from the State Constitutional Convention[2]	(Prior Source)[3] and Simplified Purpose[4]	Disposition in the Bill of Rights
RIRA28	That the journals of the proceedings of the Senate and house of Representatives shall be published as soon as conveniently may be, at least once in every year, except such parts thereof relating to treaties, alliances or military operations, as in their judgment require secrecy.	(Modification of North Carolina's recommended amendment NCHRA25 in Appendix 16) Proposal to publish Congressional journals at least once per year.	Dropped
RIRA29	That regular statements of the receipts and expenditures of all publick monies, shall be published at least once a year.	(Modification of North Carolina's recommended amendment NCHRA26 in Appendix 16) To require full government accounting for expenses once per year.	Dropped
RIRA30	As standing armies in time of peace are dangerous to liberty and ought not to be kept up, except in cases of necessity; and as at all times the military should be under strict subordination to the civil power, that therefore no standing army, or regular troops shall be raised, or kept up in time of peace.	(Combination of New York's recommended amendments NYRA7 and NYRA6 in Appendix 15) Declaration opposing standing armies and promoting civilian control of the military.	Dropped
RIRA31	That no monies be borrowed on the credit of the United States without the assent of two thirds of the Senators and Representatives present in each house	(Modified version of New York's recommended amendment NYRA33 in Appendix 15) Requires a 2/3 vote of both houses of Congress to borrow money.	Dropped
RIRA32	That the Congress shall not declare war, without the concurrence of two thirds of the Senators and Representatives present in each house.	(Copied from New York's recommended amendment NYRA34 in Appendix 15) Requires a 2/3 vote of both houses of Congress to declare war.	Dropped

ID[1]	Text from the State Constitutional Convention[2]	(Prior Source)[3] and Simplified Purpose[4]	Disposition in the Bill of Rights
RIRA33	That the words "without the consent of Congress" in the seventh clause in the ninth section of the first article of the constitution be expunged.	(Modification from New York's recommended amendment NYRA55 in Appendix 15) Proposal to eliminate Congress' ability to allow grants of nobility.	Dropped
RIRA34	That no judge of the supreme court of the United States, shall hold any other office under the United States, or any of them, nor shall any officer appointed by Congress, or by the President and Senate of the United States, be permitted to hold any office under the appointment of any of the states.	(Addition to New York's recommended amendment NYRA52 in Appendix 15) Proposal that Supreme Court Justices cannot hold executive branch offices or offices under any state. Proposal that Executive branch members hold offices under any state.	Dropped
RIRA35	As a traffick tending to establish or continue the slavery of any part of the human species, is disgraceful to the cause of liberty and humanity, that Congress shall, as soon as may be, promote and establish such laws and regulations, as may effectually prevent the importation of slaves of every description into the United States.	Declaration regarding slavery as being disgraceful and imploring Congress to prevent the importation of slaves.	Dropped
RIRA36	That the State Legislatures have power to recall, when they think it expedient, their federal senators, and to send others in their stead.	Proposal that States can recall United States Senators and replace them.	Dropped
RIRA37	That Congress have power to establish a uniform rule of inhabitancy, or settlement of the poor of the different States throughout the United States.	Proposal that Congress can settle the poor around the states using a uniform rule.	Dropped
RIRA38	That Congress erect no company with exclusive advantages of commerce	(Copied from Massachusetts' recommended amendment MRA5 in Appendix 11) To keep Congress from providing exclusive arrangements for specific merchants.	Dropped

ID[1]	Text from the State Constitutional Convention[2]	(Prior Source)[3] and Simplified Purpose[4]	Disposition in the Bill of Rights
RIRA39	That when two members shall move or call for the ayes and nays on any question, they shall be entered on the journals of the houses respectively.	To require roll call votes to be recorded if requested by two members in a house of Congress.	Dropped.

Appendix 18 - Bill of Rights Crossover with Privileges and Immunities

Source in the Bill of Rights	Constitutional Text	Privilege and Immunity Precedents from the Magna Carta, the Petition of Right, the Habeus Corpus Act, the [English] Bill of Rights and the Declaration of Independence	Explanation and reasoning for importance as a Privilege and Immunity[1] for Travelers
1st Amendment	Congress shall make no law respecting an establishment of religion, or prohibiting the free exercise thereof;		Typical travelers may not be able to find their specific church for worship, but as long as their ability to pray and practice their religion are not impeded, this is a low priority for them. For the exception case of traveling ministers, or religious people, who want to promote their religion, this has a greater impact.
1st Amendment	Congress shall make no law … abridging the freedom of speech	Declaration of Independence (D1 in Appendix 5)	With the exception of speaking immorally, slanderously, or promoting violence or the overthrow of the government, travelers expect to be able to discuss issues of importance to them. Merchants may need to discuss government operations and regulations that apply to their business and expect to do so freely. Merchants are likely to speak to a more diverse set of the population and should not fear arrest.
1st Amendment	Congress shall make no law … abridging the freedom of ... the press;	Declaration of Independence (D1 in Appendix 5)	Merchants might be selling books, or passing out marketing material, and would expect to do so freely.

1 Explanation contains the reasons the author used to generate the level of importance.

Source in the Bill of Rights	Constitutional Text	Privilege and Immunity Precedents from the Magna Carta, the Petition of Right, the Habeus Corpus Act, the [English] Bill of Rights and the Declaration of Independence	Explanation and reasoning for importance as a Privilege and Immunity[1] for Travelers
1st Amendment	Congress shall make no law … abridging … the right of the people to peaceably assemble,	Declaration of Independence (D2 in Appendix 5)	The right to assemble is critical for Travelers and Merchants. There is general safety in numbers. The more valuable or bulky that any possessions or goods that are being moved are, the more likely that a greater number of people will be needed to travel in the group.
1st Amendment	Congress shall make no law … abridging … the right of the people to petition their Government for a redress of grievances.	English Bill of Rights (EBR5 in Appendix 4) and Declaration of Independence (D16 in Appendix 5)	The ability to travel to National or State government locations is highly important for any citizen of a free republic.
2nd Amendment	A well regulated Militia, being necessary to the security of a free State, the right of the people to keep and bear Arms, shall not be infringed.	English Bill of Rights (EBR7 in Appendix 4)	The ability to protect yourself and your possessions when traveling is critical. Moving between states, and through unknown regions, can be an extremely vulnerable time for citizens.
3rd Amendment	No Soldier shall, in time of peace be quartered in any house, without the consent of the Owner, nor in time of war, but in a manner to be prescribed by law.	Petition of Right (PR3 in Appendix 2) Declaration of Independence (D10 in Appendix 5)	This has very little affect on Travelers and Merchants.
4th Amendment	The right of the people to be secure in their persons, houses, papers, and effects, against unreasonable searches and seizures, shall not be violated,…		For travelers and merchants, unreasonable searches and seizures are a key means that authoritarians and protectionists could impede and harass them.
4th Amendment	no Warrants shall issue, but upon probable cause, supported by Oath or affirmation, and particularly describing the place to be searched, and the persons or things to be seized.		For travelers and merchants, the risk of being falsely accused and arrested is especially problematic. They are far from home, and in uncertain communities where defending themselves is made all the more difficult.

Source in the Bill of Rights	Constitutional Text	Privilege and Immunity Precedents from the Magna Carta, the Petition of Right, the Habeus Corpus Act, the [English] Bill of Rights and the Declaration of Independence	Explanation and reasoning for importance as a Privilege and Immunity[1] for Travelers
5th Amendment	No person shall be held to answer for a capital, or otherwise infamous crime, unless on a presentment or indictment of a Grand Jury, except in cases arising in the land or naval forces, or in the Militia, when in actual service in time of War or public danger;	Petition of Right (PR2 and PR4 in Appendix 2)	A serious felony charge could bankrupt and destroy a traveler. A Grand Jury indictment means that a corrupt individual can not individually try to destroy a person from another state.
5th Amendment	nor shall any person be subject for the same offence to be twice put in jeopardy of life or limb;		Travelers and merchants who are law abiding, should not normally be exposed to this issue. People who are tried for a serious offense in one state would be best to avoid that state in the future.
5th Amendment	nor shall be compelled in any criminal case to be a witness against himself,		Given that travelers and merchants to other states are expected to be law-abiding, they should not be going to trial where this would be an issue.
5th Amendment	nor be deprived of life, liberty, or property, without due process of law;	Petition of Right (PR2 and PR4 in Appendix 2)	Travelers and Merchants expect to be able to defend themselves and to not be tried in a kangaroo court or using unreasonable processes.
5th Amendment	nor shall private property be taken for public use, without just compensation.	Magna Carta (MC19, MC21 and MC22 in Appendix 1)	This could impact travelers and merchants who possess goods that are valuable to the local authorities.
6th Amendment	In all criminal prosecutions, the accused shall enjoy the right to a speedy and public trial, by an impartial jury of the State and district wherein the crime shall have been committed, which district shall have been previously ascertained by law, …	Magna Carta (MC29 in Appendix 1)	This is very important for travelers and merchants. They are already at a disadvantage being away from their homes, but added delays for a trial are especially problematic. Jury trials are critical to avoid Authoritarians who harass outsiders.

Source in the Bill of Rights	Constitutional Text	Privilege and Immunity Precedents from the Magna Carta, the Petition of Right, the Habeus Corpus Act, the [English] Bill of Rights and the Declaration of Independence	Explanation and reasoning for importance as a Privilege and Immunity[1] for Travelers
6th Amendment	… and to be informed of the nature and cause of the accusation;	Petition of Right (PR2 in Appendix 2)	This is very important for travelers and merchants who are already at a disadvantage by being in unfamiliar territory.
7th Amendment	In Suits at common law, where the value in controversy shall exceed twenty dollars, the right of trial by jury shall be preserved, and no fact tried by a jury, shall be otherwise re-examined in any Court of the United States, than according to the rules of the common law.		This is solely a financial issue, and not a criminal issue that would put a traveler or merchant at risk of life or liberty.
8th Amendment	Excessive bail shall not be required, nor excessive fines imposed …	Magna Carta (MC28 in Appendix 1) English Bill of Rights (EBR11, EBR12 and EBR14 in Appendix 4)	This is extremely critical for travelers and merchants away from home who have limited financial resources at their control.
8th Amendment	… nor cruel and unusual punishments inflicted.	English Bill of Rights (EBR13 in Appendix 4)	This is a qualitative statement. Law-abiding Travelers and Merchants would not normally be exposed to this. They would expect a Nationwide baseline limit on acceptable versus unacceptable punishments.

Appendix 19 - Dueling Provisions in Initial State Constitutions between 1812-1850

State	Date of Constitution	Provision Location	Constitutional Text or {Notes}
Louisiana[1]	April 30, 1812		{Constitutional Provisions added in 1845}
Indiana[2]	December 11, 1816		{Constitutional Provisions added in 1851}
Mississippi [3]	December 10, 1817	Article VI, General Provisions, Section 2.	The General Assembly shall have power to pass such penal laws to suppress the evil practice of dueling, extending to disqualification from office or the tenure thereof, as they may deem expedient.

1 Wikisource.org. (2026, Feb. 24).
https://en.wikisource.org/wiki/Louisiana_State_Constitution_of_1812

In 1845, Louisiana passed a new Constitution that had the following dueling provision. Title VI, Art. 130 "Any citizen of this state who shall, after the adoption of this Constitution, fight a duel with deadly weapons with a citizen of this State, or send or accept a challenge to fight a duel with deadly weapons, either within this state or out of it with a citizen of this State, or who shall act as a second, or knowingly aid and assist in any manner, those thus offending, shall be deprived of holding any office of trust or profit, and of enjoying the right of suffrage under this Constitution."

2 Indiana State Government, Indiana Historical Bureau. (2026, Feb. 24).
https://www.in.gov/history/about-indiana-history-and-trivia/explore-indiana-history-by-topic/indiana-documents-leading-to-statehood/constitution-of-1816/

In 1851, Indiana passed a new Constitution that had the following dueling provision. Article 2, Section 7. "Every person who shall give or accept a challenge to fight a duel, or who shall knowingly carry to another person such challenge, or who shall agree to go out of the State to fight a duel, shall be ineligible to any office of trust or profit."

3 Mississippi Historical Society, Mississippi History Now. (2026, Feb. 24).
https://www.mshistorynow.mdah.ms.gov/issue/mississippi-constitution-of-1817

Appendix 19 - Dueling Provisions in Initial State Constitutions between 1812-1850

State	Date of Constitution	Provision Location	Constitutional Text or {Notes}
Illinois[4]	December 3, 1818	Schedule 11	It shall be the duty of the general assembly to enact such laws as may be necessary and proper to prevent the practice of dueling.
Alabama[5]	December 14, 1819	Article VI, General Provisions, Section 3.	The General Assembly shall have power to pass such penal laws, to suppress the evil practice of Duelling, extending to disqualification from office or the tenure thereof, as they may deem expedient.
Maine[6]	March 15, 1820		{Laws passed against dueling[7]}
Missouri [8]	August 10, 1821		{Laws passed prescribing murder charges.[9]}

4 Wikisource.org. (2026, Feb. 24). https://en.wikisource.org/wiki/Illinois_Constitution_of_1818

5 Yale Law School, Lillian Goldman Law Library, *The Avalon Project.* (2026, Feb. 23). https://avalon.law.yale.edu/19th_century/ala1819.asp

6 Maine State Legislature. (2026, Feb. 24). https://legislature.maine.gov/uploads/originals/const1820.pdf

7 Maine State Legislature. (2026, Feb. 24). https://legislature.maine.gov/statutes/17/title17ch49sec0.html

8 United States Library of Congress. (2026, Feb. 24). https://tile.loc.gov/storage-services/service/ll/llserialset-pdf/00/04/8_/00/_0/0/00048_00_00/00048_00_00-003-0002-0000/SERIAL-SET-00048_00_00-003-0002-0000.pdf

9 Missouri Secretary of State, Missouri State Archives. (2026, Feb. 24 https://www.sos.mo.gov/CMSImages/MDH//1822Anit-DuelingStatute.pdf

State	Date of Constitution	Provision Location	Constitutional Text or {Notes}
Arkansas[10]	June 15, 1836		Constitutional Provisions added in 1874
Michigan[11]	January 26, 1837		Constitutional Provisions added in 1850

10 Wikisource.org. (2026, Feb. 24).
https://en.wikisource.org/wiki/Arkansas_Constitution_of_1836

In 1874, the new Arkansas Constitution added dueling provisions in Article 19, Section 2. Dueling "No person who may hereafter fight a duel, assist in the same as second, or send, accept, or knowingly carry a challenge therefor, shall hold any office in the State, for a period of ten years; and may be otherwise punished as the law may prescribe."

11 Wikisource.org. (2026, Feb. 24).
https://en.wikisource.org/wiki/Michigan_Constitution_of_1835

In 1850, the new Michigan Constitution added a dueling provision in Article 7, Section 8. "Any inhabitant who may hereafter be engaged in a duel, either as principal or accessory before the fact, shall be disqualified from holding any office under the constitution and laws of this state, and shall not be permitted to vote at any election."

Michigan Legislature. (2026, Feb. 24).
https://www.legislature.mi.gov/documents/historical/miconstitution1850.htm

Appendix 19 - Dueling Provisions in Initial State Constitutions between 1812-1850

State	Date of Constitution	Provision Location	Constitutional Text or {Notes}
Florida[12]	March 3, 1845	Article VI, Section 5	No person shall be capable of holding, or of being elected to any post of honor, profit, trust, or emolument, civil or military, legislative, executive, or judicial, under the government of this State, who shall hereafter fight a duel, or send, or accept a challenge to fight a duel, the probable issue of which may be the death of the challenger, or challenged, or who shall be a second to either party, or who shall in any manner aid, or assist in such duel, or shall be knowingly the bearer of such challenge, or acceptance, whether the same occur, or be committed in or out of the State.
Texas[13]	December 29, 1845	Article VII, General Provisions, Section 1	Members of the legislature, and all officers, before they enter upon the duties of their offices, shall take the following oath or affirmation: "I (A. B.) do solemnly swear, (or affirm,) that I will faithfully and partially discharge and perform all the duties incumbent on me as ------, according to the best of my skill and ability, agreeably to the constitution and laws of the United States, and of this State; and I do further solemnly swear, (or affirm,) that since the adoption of this constitution by the Congress of the United States, I, being a citizen of this State, have not fought a duel with deadly weapons within this State, nor out of it; nor have I sent or accepted a challenge to fight a duel with deadly weapons; nor have I acted as second in carrying a challenge, or aided, advised, or assisted any person thus offending--so help me God."

12 Florida Constitution Revision Commission, Florida State University. (2026, Feb. 24) https://library.law.fsu.edu/Digital-Collections/CRC/CRC-1998/conhist/1838con.html

13 University of Texas at Austin, Texas Law, Tarlton Law Library. (2026, Feb. 24). https://tarlton.law.utexas.edu/c.php?g=787754

State	Date of Constitution	Provision Location	Constitutional Text or {Notes}
Texas	December 29, 1845	Article VII, General Provisions, Section 5	Any citizen of this State who shall, after the adoption of this constitution, fight a duel with deadly weapons, either within the State of out of it, or who shall act as second, or knowingly aid and assist in any manner those thus offending, shall be deprived of holding any office of trust or profit under this State.
Iowa[14]	December 28, 1846	Article I, Bill of Rights, Section 5	Any citizen of this State who may hereafter be engaged, either directly, or indirectly, in a duel, either as principal, or accessory before the fact, shall forever be disqualified from holding any office under the Constitution and laws of this State.
Wisconsin[15]	May 29, 1848	(Article XIII) Section 2.	Any inhabitant of this state who may hereafter be engaged, either directly or indirectly, in a duel, either as principal or accessory, shall forever be disqualified as an elector, and from holding any office under the constitution and laws of this state, and may be punished in such a manner as shall be prescribed by law.
California[16]	September 9, 1850	Article XI, Section 2	Any citizen of this state who shall, after the adoption of this constitution fight a duel with deadly weapons, or send or accept a challenge to fight a duel with deadly weapons, either within this state or out of it, or who shall act as a second, or knowingly aid and assist in any manner those thus offending, shall not be allowed to hold any office of profit, or to enjoy the right of suffrage under this constitution.

14 Iowa Legislature. (2026, Feb. 24). https://www.legis.iowa.gov/docs/publications/ICP/1518289.pdf

15 Wisconsin Historical Society. (2026, Feb. 24). https://cdn.wisconsinhistory.org/turning-points/1627.pdf

16 California Secretary of State, California State Archives.(2026, Feb. 24). https://archives.cdn.sos.ca.gov/pdf/1849-california-constitution-for-website-9-16-20.pdf

Appendix 20 - California Constitution of 1849

Declaration of Rights

Section	Text from California Constitution[1]	Notes
1	All men are by nature free and independent, and have certain inalienable rights, among which are those of enjoying and defending life and liberty; acquiring, possessing and protecting property; and pursuing and obtaining safety and happiness.	Strong declaration for "defending life and liberty" and for "protecting property".
2	All political power is inherent in the people. Government is instituted for the protection, security, and benefit of the people; and they have the right to alter or reform the same, whenever the public good may require it.	"protection, security" are the first two listed functions of the Government.
3	The right of trial by jury shall be secured to all, and remain inviolate forever; but a jury trial may be waived by the parties, in all civil cases, in the manner to be prescribed by law.	United States Constitution Amendment VII – "In Suits at common law, where the value in controversy shall exceed twenty dollars, the right of trial by jury shall be preserved, ..."
4	The free exercise and enjoyment of religious profession and worship, without discrimination or preference, shall forever be allowed in this state; and no person shall be rendered incompetent to be a witness on account of his opinions on matters of religious belief; but the liberty of conscience hereby secured, shall not be so construed, as to excuse acts of licentiousness, or justify practices inconsistent with the peace or safety of this state.	United States Constitution Amendment I – "Congress shall make no law respecting an establishment of religion, or prohibiting the free exercise thereof; ..."

1 California Secretary of State, California State Archives. (2026, Feb. 24). https://archives.cdn.sos.ca.gov/pdf/1849-california-constitution-for-website-9-16-20.pdf

Section	Text from California Constitution[1]	Notes
5	The privilege of the writ of habeas corpus shall not be suspended, unless when in cases of rebellion or invasion, the public safety may require its suspension.	United States Constitution Article I, Section 9 – "The Privilege of the Writ of Habeas Corpus shall not be suspended, unless when in Cases of Rebellion or Invasion the public Safety may require it."
6	Excessive bail shall not be required, nor excessive fines imposed, nor shall cruel or unusual punishment be inflicted, nor shall witnesses be unreasonably detained.	United States Constitution Amendment VIII – "Excessive bail shall not be required, nor excessive fines imposed, nor cruel and unusual punishments inflicted."
7	All persons shall be bailable, by sufficient sureties, unless for capital offences, when the proof is evident or the presumption great.	United States Constitution Amendment VIII – "Excessive bail shall not be required, …"
8	No person shall be held to answer for a capital or otherwise infamous crime, (except in cases of impeachment, and in cases of militia when in actual service, and the land and naval forces in time of war, or which this state may keep with the consent of Congress in time of peace, and in cases of petit larceny under the regulation of the Legislature) unless on presentment or indictment of a grand jury: and in any trial in any court whatever, the party accused shall be allowed to appear and defend in person with counsel as in civil actions. No person shall be subject to be twice put in jeopardy for the same offense; nor shall be compelled in any criminal case, to be a witness against himself, nor be deprived of life, liberty, or property, without due process of law; nor shall private property be taken for public use without just compensation.	United States Constitution Amendment V – "No person shall be held to answer for a capital, or otherwise infamous crime, unless on a presentment or indictment of a Grand Jury, except in cases arising in the land or naval forces, or in the Militia, when in actual service in time of War or public danger; nor shall any person be subject for the same offence to be twice put in jeopardy of life or limb; nor shall be compelled in any criminal case to be a witness against himself, nor be deprived of life, liberty, or property, without due process of law; nor shall private property be taken for public use, without just compensation."

Section	Text from California Constitution[1]	Notes
9	Every citizen may freely speak, write, and publish his sentiments on all subjects, being responsible for the abuse of that right; and no law shall be passed to restrain or abridge the liberty of speech or the press. In all criminal prosecutions on indictments fore libels, the truth may be given in evidence to the jury; and if it shall appear to the jury that the matter charged as libelous is true, and was published with good motives and for justifiable ends, the party shall be acquitted; and the jury shall have the right to determine the law and the fact.	United States Constitution Amendment I – "Congress shall make no law … abridging the freedom of speech, or of the press; …"
10	The people shall have the right freely to assemble together to consult for the common good, to instruct their representatives, and to petition the legislature for redress of grievances.	United States Constitution Amendment I – "Congress shall make no law … abridging … the right of the people peaceably to assemble, and to petition the Government for a redress of grievances."
11	All laws of a general nature shall have a uniform operation.	
12	The military shall be subordinate to the civil power. No standing army shall be kept up by this state in time of peace; and in time of war no appropriation for a standing army shall be for a longer time than two years.	
13	No soldier shall in time of peace, be quartered in any house, without the consent of the owner; nor in time of war, except in the manner to be prescribed by law.	United States Constitution Amendment III – "No Soldier shall, in time of peace be quartered in any house, without the consent of the Owner, nor in time of war, but in a manner to be prescribed by law."
14	Representation shall be apportioned according to population.	
15	No person shall be imprisoned for debt, in any civil action on mesne or final process, unless in cases of fraud; and no person shall be imprisoned for a militia fine in time of peace.	*mesne refers to intermediate or intervening.

Section	Text from California Constitution[1]	Notes
16	No bill of attainder, or ex post facto law, or law impairing the obligation of contracts shall ever be passed.	
17	Foreigners who are, or who may hereafter become bona fide residents of the state, shall enjoy the same rights in respect to the possession, enjoyment, and inheritance of property as native born citizens.	This was included to deal with Article VIII of the Treaty of Guadalupe Hidalgo[2] . This pertained to the recognition of the rights of prior citizens of Mexico. It was changed in the Constitution of 1879
18	Neither slavery, nor involuntary servitude, unless for the punishment of crimes, shall ever be tolerated in this state.	The United States Constitution 13th Amendment was ratified 16 years later on December 6, 1865. It said: "Neither slavery nor involuntary servitude, except as a punishment for crime whereof the party shall have been duly convicted, shall exist within the United States, or any place subject to their jurisdiction."
19	The right of the people to be secure in their persons, houses, papers, and effects against unreasonable seizures and searches, shall not be violated, and no warrant shall issue but on probable cause, supported by oath or affirmation particularly describing the place to be searched, and the persons and things to be seized.	United States Constitution Amendment IV – "The right of the people to be secure in their persons, houses, papers, and effects, against unreasonable searches and seizures, shall not be violated, and no Warrants shall issue, but upon probable cause, supported by Oath or affirmation, and particularly describing the place to be searched, and the persons or things to be seized."
20	Treason against the state shall consist only in levying war against it, adhering to its enemies, or giving them aid and comfort. No person shall be convicted of treason, unless on the evidence of two witnesses to the same overt act, or confession in open court.	
21	This enumeration of rights shall not be construed to impair or deny others, retained by the people.	

2 United States National Archives and Records Administration. (2026, Feb. 22). https://www.archives.gov/milestone-documents/treaty-of-guadalupe-hidalgo

Additional California 1849 Constitutional Provisions related to the Militia, the Military, Dueling, Religion, and Ratification

Section	California Constitution of 1849 Text[1]
Article V, Section 5.	The Governor shall be commander-in-chief of the militia, the army, and navy of this state.
Article V, Section 6	He shall transact all executive business with the officers of Government, civil and military, ...
Article V, Section 17	... But when the Governor shall with the consent of the legislature, be out of the state in time of war, at the head of any military force thereof, he shall continue commander-in-chief of all the military force of the State.
Article VII, Section 1	The Legislature shall provide by law for organizing and disciplining the militia in such manner as they shall deem expedient, not incompatible with the Constitution and laws of the United States.
Article VII, Section 2	Officers of the militia shall be elected or appointed in such manner as the legislature shall from time to time direct, and
Article VII, Section 3	The Governor shall have power to call forth the militia to execute the laws of the State, to suppress insurrections, and repel invasions.
Article XI, Section 2	Any citizen of this state who shall, after the adoption of this Constitution, fight a duel with deadly weapons, or send or accept a challenge to fight a duel with deadly weapons, either within this state or out of it, or who shall act as a second, or knowingly aid or assist in any manner those thus offending, shall not be allowed to hold any office of profit, or to enjoy the right of suffrage under this Constitution.
Article XI, Section 12	No contract of marriage if otherwise duly made, shall be invalidated for want of conformity to the requirements of any religious sect.
Schedule, Section 6	This Constitution shall be submitted to the people for their ratification or rejection, at the general election to be held on Tuesday the thirteenth day of November next.

1California Secretary of State, California State Archives. (2026, Feb. 24). https://archives.cdn.sos.ca.gov/pdf/1849-california-constitution-for-website-9-16-20.pdf

Appendix 21 - Slavery in the United States in 1790

State[1]	#Free White Males >=16	#Free White Males <16	#Free White Females	Other Free People	Slaves	Total	% Other	% Slave
Vermont	22,435	22,328	40,505	255	16	85,539	0.3	0.0
New Hampshire	36,086	34,851	70,160	630	158	141,885	0.4	0.1
Maine	24,384	24,748	46,870	538	0	96,540	0.6	0.0
Massachusetts	95,453	87,289	190,582	5,463	0	378,787	1.4	0.0
Rhode Island	16,019	15,799	32,652	3,407	948	68,825	5.0	1.4
Connecticut	60,523	54,403	117,448	2,808	2,764	237,946	1.2	1.2
New York	83,700	78,122	152,320	4,654	21,324	340,120	1.4	6.3
New Jersey	45,251	41,416	83,287	2,762	11,423	184,139	1.5	6.2
Pennsylvania	110,788	106,948	206,363	6,537	3,737	434,373	1.5	0.9
Delaware	11,783	12,143	22,384	3,899	8,887	59,096	6.6	15.0
Maryland	55,915	51,339	101,395	8,043	103,036	319,728	2.5	32.2
Virginia	110,936	116,135	215,046	12,866	292,627	747,610	1.7	39.1
Kentucky	15,154	17,057	28,922	114	12,430	73,677	0.2	16.9
North Carolina	69,988	77,506	140,710	4,975	100,572	393,751	1.3	25.5
South Carolina	35,576	37,722	66,880	1,801	107,094	249,073	0.7	43.0
Georgia	13,103	14,044	25,739	398	29,264	82,548	0.5	35.5
Totals	**807,094**	**791,850**	**1,541,263**	**59,150**	**694,280**	**3,893,637**	**1.5**	**17.8**

1 United States National Archives and Records Administration. (2026, Feb. 24). https://www.archives.gov/research/census/1790

Appendix 22 - Slavery in the United States in 1860

State[1]	White	Free Colored	Slave	Indian	Asian	Total	% Free Colored	% Slave
Alabama	526,271	2,690	435,080	160		964,201	0.3	45.1
Arkansas	324,191	144	111,115			435,450	0.0	25.5
California	323,177	4,086		17,798	34,933	379,994	1.1	0.0
Connecticut	451,504	8,627		16		460,147	1.9	0.0
Delaware	90,589	19,829	1,798			112,216	17.7	1.6
Florida	77,747	932	61,745			140,424	0.7	44.0
Georgia	591,550	3,500	462,198	38		1,057,286	0.3	43.7
Illinois	1,704,291	7,628		32		1,711,951	0.4	0.0
Indiana	1,338,710	11,428		290		1,350,428	0.8	0.0
Iowa	673,779	1,069		65		674,913	0.2	0.0
Kansas	106,390	625	2	189		107,206	0.6	0.0
Kentucky	919,517	10,684	225,483			1,155,684	0.9	19.5
Louisiana	351,556	18,547	326,726	173		697,002	2.7	46.9
Maine	626,947	1,327		5		628,279	0.2	0.0
Maryland	515,918	83,942	87,189			687,049	12.2	12.7
Massachusetts	1,221,432	9,602		32		1,231,066	0.8	0.0
Michigan	736,142	6,799		6,172		749,113	0.9	0.0
Minnesota	169,395	259		2,369		172,023	0.2	0.0
Mississippi	353,899	773	436,631	2		791,305	0.1	55.2
Missouri	1,063,489	3,572	114,931	20		1,182,012	0.3	9.7
New Hampshire	325,570	494				326,064	0.2	0.0
New Jersey	646,699	25,318	18			672,035	3.8	0.0
New York	3,880,735	49,005		140		3,929,880	1.2	0.0

1 United States Department of Commerce, U.S. Census Bureau. (2026, Feb. 24). https://www.census.gov/library/publications/1864/dec/1860a.html

State[1]	White	Free Colored	Slave	Indian	Asian	Total	% Free Colored	% Slave
North Carolina	629,942	30,463	331,059	1,158		992,622	3.1	33.4
Ohio	2,302,808	36,673		30		2,339,511	1.6	0.0
Oregon	52,160	128		177		52,465	0.2	0.0
Pennsylvania	2,849,259	56,949		7		2,906,215	2.0	0.0
Rhode Island	170,649	3,952		19		174,620	2.3	0.0
South Carolina	291,300	9,914	402,406	88		703,708	1.4	57.2
Tennessee	826,722	7,300	275,719	60		1,109,801	0.7	24.8
Texas	420,891	355	182,566	403		604,215	0.1	30.2
Vermont	314,369	709		20		315,098	0.2	0.0
Virginia	1,047,299	58,042	490,865	112		1,596,318	3.6	30.7
Wisconsin	773,093	1,171		1,017		775,281	0.2	0.0
Washington, D.C.	60,764	11,131	3,185			75,080	14.8	4.2
Totals	**26,758,754**	**487,667**	**3,948,716**	**30,592**	**34,933**	**31,260,662**	**1.6**	**12.6**

Appendix 23 - Dred Scott Precedents

Key Privileges and Immunities References

Reference[1]	Dred Scott Privileges and Immunities References (Chief Justice Taney-Opinion of the Court)	Notes[2]
60 U.S. 393, 403	This question is simply this: Can a negro, whose ancestors were imported into this country, and sold as slaves, become a member of the political community formed and brought into existence by the Constitution of the United States, and as such become entitled to all the rights, and privileges and immunities, guarantied by that instrument to the citizen? One of which rights is the privilege of suing in a court of the United States in the cases specified in the Constitution.	Chief Justice Taney's positioning of the case. Question was whether "negros" could be citizens of the United States and receive Privileges and Immunities of citizens.
60 U.S. 393, 404-405	The words "people of the United States" and "citizens" are synonymous terms, and mean the same thing. They both describe the political body who, according to our republican institutions, form the sovereignty, and who hold the power and conduct the Government through their representatives. They are what we familiarly call the "sovereign people," and every citizen is one of this people, and a constituent member of this sovereignty. The question before us is, whether the class of persons described in the plea in abatement compose a portion of this people, and are constituent members of this sovereignty? We think they are not, and that they are not included, and were not intended to be included, under the word "citizens" in the Constitution, and can therefore claim none of the rights and privileges which that instrument provides for and secures to citizens of the United States. On the contrary, they were at that time considered as a subordinate and inferior class of beings, who had been subjugated by the dominant race, and, whether emancipated or not, yet remained subject to their authority, and had no rights or privileges but such as those who held the power and the Government might choose to grant them.	Argument that "negros" cannot be citizens of the United States since they would be entitled to Privileges and Immunities from the Constitution. Fear of Nationwide Privileges and Immunities for "negros" #1

1 Dred Scott v. Sandford, 60 U.S. 393 (1857)
United States Library of Congress. (2026, Feb. 24).
https://www.loc.gov/item/usrep060393a/

2 Generated by the author based upon the text.

Reference[1]	Dred Scott Privileges and Immunities References (Chief Justice Taney-Opinion of the Court)	Notes[2]
60 U.S. 393, 405	In discussing this question, we must not confound the rights of citizenship which a State may confer within its own limits, and the rights of citizenship as a member of the Union. It does not by any means follow, because he has all the rights and privileges of the citizen of a State, that he must be a citizen of the United States. He may have all the rights and privileges of the citizen of a State, and yet not be entitled to the rights and privileges of a citizen in any other State.	Argument that State Citizenship is not equal to National Citizenship. Fear of Nationwide Privileges and Immunities for "negros" #2
60 U.S. 393, 405-406	For, previous to the adoption of the Constitution of the United States, every State had the undoubted right to confer on whomsoever it pleased the character of a citizen, and to endow him with all its rights. But this character of course was confined to the boundaries of the State, and gave him no rights or privileges in other States beyond those secured to him by the laws of nations and the comity of States. Nor have the several States surrendered the power of conferring these rights and privileges by adopting the Constitution of the United States. Each State may still confer them upon an alien, or any one it thinks proper, or upon any class or description of persons; yet he would not be a citizen in the sense in which that word is used in the Constitution of the United States, nor entitled to sue as such in one of its courts, nor to the privileges and immunities of a citizen in the other States. The rights which he would acquire would be restricted to the State which gave them. The Constitution has conferred on Congress the right to establish an uniform rule of naturalization, and this right is evidently exclusive, and has always been held by this court to be so. Consequently, no State, since the adoption of the Constitution, can by naturalizing an alien invest him with the rights and privileges secured to a citizen of a State under the Federal Government, although so far as the State alone was concerned, he would undoubtedly be entitled to the rights of a citizen, and clothed with all the rights and immunities which the Constitution and laws of the State attached to that character.	Argument that prior to the Constitution, States controlled immigration and naturalization. The Constitution made this a Federal issue, so States cannot turn non-citizens into citizens. Fear of Nationwide Privileges and Immunities for "negros" #3
60 U.S. 393, 406	The question then arise, whether the provision of the Constitution, in relation to the personal rights and privileges to which the citizen of a State should be entitled, embraced the negro African race, at that time in this country, or who might afterwards be imported, who had then or should afterwards be made free in any State; and to put it in the power of a single State to make him a citizen of the United States, and endue him with the full rights of citizenship in every other State without their consent? Does the Constitution of the United States act upon him whenever, he shall be made free under the laws of a State, and raised there to the rank of a citizen, and immediately clothe him with all the privileges of a citizen in every other State, and in its own courts?	Argument that States cannot turn members of their State into citizens of the United States. Fear of Nationwide Privileges and Immunities for "negros" #4

Reference[1]	Dred Scott Privileges and Immunities References (Chief Justice Taney-Opinion of the Court)	Notes[2]
60 U.S. 393, 406	It is true, every person, and every class and description of persons, who were at the time of the adoption of the Constitution recognized as citizens in the several States, became also citizens of this new political body; but none other; it was formed by them, and for them and their posterity, but for no one else. And the personal rights and privileges guarantied to citizens of this new sovereignty were intended to embrace those only who were then members of the several State communities, or who should afterwards by birthright or otherwise become members, according to the provisions of the Constitution and the principles on which it was founded. It was the union of those who were at that time members of distinct and separate political communities into one political family, whose power, for certain specified purposes, was to extend over the whole territory of the United States. And it gave to each citizen rights and privileges outside of his State which he did not before possess, and placed him in every other State upon a perfect equality with its own citizens as to rights of person and rights of property; it made him a citizen of the United States.	Nationwide Privileges and Immunities description. Fear of Nationwide Privileges and Immunities for "negros" #5
60 U.S. 393, 411-412	No one of that race had ever migrated to the United States voluntarily; all of them had been brought here as articles of merchandise. The number that had been emancipated at that time were but few in comparison with those held in slavery; and they were identified in the public mind with the race to which they belonged, and regarded as a part of the slave population rather than the free. It is obvious that they were not even in the minds of the framers of the Constitution when they were conferring special rights and privileges upon the citizens of a State in every other part of the Union."	Argument that negros could not be citizens even though some were emancipated at the time of the Constitution. Fear of Nationwide Privileges and Immunities for "negros" #6
60 U.S. 393, 413-414	And certainly nothing which would have led the slaveholding States to suppose, that Connecticut designed to claim for them, under the new Constitution, the equal rights and privileges and rank of citizens in every other State."	Referring to Connecticut law, and claiming they did not intend negros to be United States citizens. Fear of Nationwide Privileges and Immunities for "negros" #7

Reference[1]	Dred Scott Privileges and Immunities References (Chief Justice Taney-Opinion of the Court)	Notes[2]
60 U.S. 393, 416-417	More especially, it cannot be believed that the large slaveholding States regarded them as included in the word citizens, or would have consented to a Constitution which might compel them to receive them in that character from another State. For if they were so received, and entitled to the privileges and immunities of citizens, it would exempt them from the operation of the special laws and from the police regulations which they considered to be necessary for their own safety. It would give to persons of the negro race, who were recognised as citizens in any one State of the Union, the right to enter every other State whenever they pleased, singly or in companies, without pass or passport, and without obstruction, to sojourn there as long as they pleased, to go where they pleased at every hour of the day or night without molestation, unless they committed some violation of law for which a white man would be punished; and it would give them the full liberty of speech in public and private upon all subjects upon which its own citizens might speak; to hold public meetings upon political affairs, and to keep and carry arms wherever they went. And all of this would be done in the face of the subject race of the same color, both free and slaves, and inevitably producing discontent and insubordination among them, and endangering the peace and safety of the State.	Extremely powerful and descriptive block regarding privileges and immunities of United States citizens. Fear of Nationwide Privileges and Immunities for "negros" #8
60 U.S. 393, 417	It is impossible, it would seem, to believe that the great men of the slaveholding States, who took so large a share in framing the Constitution of the United States, and exercised so much influence in procuring its adoption, could have been so forgetful or regardless of their own safety and the safety of those who trusted and confided in them. Besides, this want of foresight and care would have been utterly inconsistent with the caution displayed in providing for the admission of new members into this political family. For, when they gave to the citizens of each State the privileges and immunities of citizens in the several States, they at the same time took from the several States the power of naturalization, and confined that power exclusively to the Federal Government. No State was willing to permit another State to determine who should or should not be admitted as one of its citizens, and entitled to demand equal rights and privileges with their own people, within their own territories."	Fear of Nationwide Privileges and Immunities for "negros" #9

Reference[1]	Dred Scott Privileges and Immunities References (Chief Justice Taney-Opinion of the Court)	Notes[2]
60 U.S. 393, 421-422	But it is said that a person may be a citizen, and entitled to that character, although he does not possess all the rights which may belong to other citizens; as, for example, the right to vote, or to hold particular offices; and that yet, when he goes into another State, he is entitled to be recognized there as a citizen, although the State may measure his rights by the rights which it allows to persons of a like character or class resident in the State, and refuse to him the full rights of citizenship. This argument overlooks the language of the provision in the Constitution of which we are speaking. Undoubtedly, a person may be a citizen, that is, a member of the community who form the sovereignty, although he exercises no share of the political power and is incapacitated from holding particular offices. Women and minors, who form a part of the political family, cannot vote; and when a property qualification is required to vote or hold a particular office, those who have not the necessary qualification cannot vote or hold the office, yet they are citizens. So, too, a person may be entitled to vote by the law of the State, who is not a citizen even of the State itself. And in some of the States of the Union foreigners not naturalized are allowed to vote. And the State may give the right to free negros and mulattos, but that does not make them citizens of the State, and still less of the United States. And the provision in the Constitution giving privileges and immunities in other States, does not apply to them.	Argument that State laws and citizenship do not directly translate to United States Citizenship Fear of Nationwide Privileges and Immunities for "negros" #10

Reference[1]	Dred Scott Privileges and Immunities References (Chief Justice Taney-Opinion of the Court)	Notes[2]
60 U.S. 393, 422-423	Neither does it apply to a person who, being the citizen of a State, migrates to another State. For then he becomes subject to the laws of the State in which he lives, and he is no longer a citizen of the State from which he removed. And the State in which he resides may then, unquestionably, determine his status or condition, and place him among the class of persons who are not recognized as citizens, but belong to an inferior and subject race; and may deny him the privileges and immunities enjoyed by its citizens. But so far as mere rights of person are concerned, the provision in question is confined to the citizens of a State who are temporarily in another State without taking up residence there. It gives them no political rights in the State, as to voting or holding office, or in any other respect. For a citizen of one State has no right to participate in the government of another. But if he ranks as a citizen in the State to which he belongs, within the meaning of the Constitution of the United States, then, whenever he goes into another State, the Constitution clothes him, as to the rights of person, with all the privileges and immunities which belong to citizens of the State. And if persons of the African race are citizens of a State, and of the United States, they would be entitled to all of these privileges and immunities in every State and the State could not restrict them; for they would hold these privileges and immunities under the paramount authority of the Federal Government, and its courts would be bound to maintain and enforce them, the Constitution and laws of the State to the contrary notwithstanding. And if the States could limit or restrict them, or place the party in an inferior grade, this clause of the Constitution would be unmeaning, and could have no operation; and would give no rights to the citizen w hen in another State. He would have none but what the State itself chose to allow him. This is evidently not the construction or meaning of the clause in question. It guaranties rights to the citizen, and the State cannot withhold them. And these rights are of a character and would lead to consequences which make it absolutely certain that the African race were not included under the name of citizens of a State, and were not in the contemplation of the framers of the Constitution when these privileges and immunities were provided for the protection of the citizen in other States	Extremely strong perspective on how Slave States could not restrict "negros" if they were United States citizens. Fear of Nationwide Privileges and Immunities for "negros" #11

Reference[1]	Dred Scott Privileges and Immunities References (Chief Justice Taney-Opinion of the Court)	Notes[2]
60 U.S. 393, 425	This case, however, strikingly illustrates the consequences that would follow the construction of the Constitution which would give the power contended for to a State. It would in effect give it also to an individual. For if the father of young Darnall had manumitted him in his lifetime, and sent him to reside in a State which recognized him as a citizen, he might have visited and sojourned in Maryland when he pleased, and as long as he pleased, as a citizen of the United States; and the State officers and tribunals would be compelled, by the paramount authority of the Constitution, to receive him and treat him as one of its citizens, exempt from the laws and police of the State in relation to a person of that description, and allow him to enjoy all the rights and privileges of citizenship, without respect of the laws of Maryland, although such laws were deemed by it absolutely essential to its own safety.	Referring to the case of Legrand v. Darnall (2 Peters, 664) Fear of Nationwide Privileges and Immunities for "negros" #12

Reference	Dred Scott Privileges and Immunities References (Justice Curtis - Dissent)	Notes
60 U.S. 393, 580	"The citizens of each State shall be entitled to all the privileges and immunities of citizens of the several States." Nowhere else in the Constitution is there anything concerning a general citizenship; but here, privileges and immunities to be enjoyed throughout the United States, under and by force of the national compact, are granted and secured. In selecting those who are to enjoy these national rights of citizenship, how are they described? As citizens of each State. It is to them these national rights are secured. The qualification for them is not to be looked for in any provision of the Constitution or laws of the United States. They are to be citizens of the several States, and, as such, the privileges and immunities of general citizenship, derived from and guarantied by the Constitution, are to be enjoyed by them. It would seem that if it had been intended to constitute a class of native-born persons within the States, who should derive their citizenship of the United States from the action of the Federal Government, this was an occasion for referring to them. It cannot be supposed that it was the purpose of this article to confer the privileges and immunities of citizens in all the States upon persons not citizens of the United States. And if it was intended to secure these rights only to citizens of the United States, how has the Constitution here described such persons? Simply as citizens of each State.	Clear description of Nationwide Privileges and Immunities

Reference	Dred Scott Privileges and Immunities References (Justice Curtis - Dissent)	Notes
60 U.S. 393, 583-584	But whether native-born women, or persons under age, or under guardianship because insane or spendthrifts, be excluded from voting or holding office, or allowed to do so, I apprehend no one will deny that they are citizens of the United States. Besides, this clause of the Constitution does not confer on the citizens of one State, in all other States, specific and enumerated privileges and immunities. They are entitled to such as belong to citizenship, but not to such as belong to particular citizens attended by other qualifications. Privileges and immunities which belong to certain citizens of a State, by reason of the operation of causes other than mere citizenship, are not conferred. Thus, if the laws of a State require, in addition to citizenship of the State, some qualification for office, or the exercise of the elective franchise, citizens of all other States, coming thither to reside, and not possessing those qualifications, cannot enjoy those privileges, not because they are not to be deemed entitled to the privileges of citizens of the State in which they reside, but because they, in common with the native-born citizens of that State, must have the qualifications prescribed by laws for the enjoyment of such privileges, under its Constitution and laws.	Excellent Description of the operation of State Level Privileges and Immunities.
60 U.S. 393, 586	It secured to the citizens of each State the privileges and immunities of citizens in every other State. But it does not allow to the States the power to make aliens citizens or permit one State to take persons born on the soil of another State, and, contrary to the laws and policy of the State where they were born, make them its citizens and so citizens of the United States.	Description that States can not make aliens citizens or take fugitive "negros" from other states and make them citizens against the law of the State where they are from.

Articles of Confederation Discussions

Reference	Dred Scott Articles of Confederation References (Chief Justice Taney-Opinion of the Court)	Notes[1]
60 U.S. 393, 418-419	A clause similar to the one in the Constitution, in relation to the rights and immunities of citizens of one State in the other States, was contained in the Articles of Confederation. But there is a difference of language, which is worthy of note. The provision in the Articles of Confederation was, "that the free inhabitants of each of the States, paupers, vagabonds, and fugitives from justice, excepted, should be entitled to all the privileges and immunities of free citizens in the several States." It will be observed, that under this Confederation, each State had the right to decide for itself, and in its own tribunals, whom it would acknowledge as a free inhabitant of another State. The term free inhabitant, in the generality of its terms, would certainly include one of the African race who had been manumitted. But no example, we think, can be found of his admission to all the privileges of citizenship in any State of the Union after these Articles were formed, and while they continued in force. And notwithstanding the generality of the words "free inhabitants," it is very clear that, according to their accepted meaning in that day, they did not include the African race, whether free or not: for the fifth section of the ninth article provides that Congress should have the power "to agree upon the number of lands forces to be raised, and to make requisitions from each State for its quota in proportion to the number of white inhabitants in such State, which requisition should be binding." Words could hardly have been used which more strongly mark the line of distinction between the citizen and the subject; the free and the subjugated races. The latter were not even counted when the inhabitants of a State were to be embodied in proportion to its numbers for the general defence. And it cannot for a moment be supposed, that a class of persons thus separated and rejected from those who formed the sovereignty of the States, were yet intended to be included under the words "free inhabitants," in the preceding article, to whom privileges and immunities were so carefully secured in every State."	Analyzes the Privileges and Immunities Clause from the Articles of Confederation. Argues that there were no cases under the Articles of Confederation where free members of the African race received the privileges and immunities in other States. Argues that Articles of Confederation only used the number of white citizens to generate military requisitions.

1 Generated by the author based upon the text.

Reference	Dred Scott Articles of Confederation References (Chief Justice Taney-Opinion of the Court)	Notes[1]
60 U.S. 393, 419	But although this clause of the Articles of Confederation is the same in principle with that inserted in the Constitution, yet the comprehensive word inhabitant, which might be construed to include an emancipated slave, is omitted; and the privilege is confined to citizens of the State. And this alteration in words would hardly have been made, unless a different meaning was intended to be conveyed, or a possible doubt removed. The just and fair inference is, that as this privilege was about to be placed under the protection of the General Government, and the words expounded by its tribunals, and all power in relation to it taken from the State and its courts, it was deemed prudent to describe with precision and caution the persons to whom this high privilege was given – and the word citizen was on that account substituted for the words free inhabitant. The word citizen excluded, and no doubt intended to exclude, foreigners who had not become citizens of some one of the States when the Constitution was adopted; and also every description of persons who were not fully recognized as citizens in the several States. This upon any fair construction of the instruments to which we have referred, was evidently the object and purpose of this change of words.	Compares the Privileges and Immunities Clause from the Articles of Confederation with the United States Constitution. Argues that changing "free inhabitants" to "citizens" was to exclude "negros" from these rights.

Reference	Dred Scott Articles of Confederation References (Justice Curtis Dissent)	Notes[2]
60 U.S. 393, 572	At the time of the ratification of the Articles of Confederation, all free native-born inhabitants of the States of New Hampshire, Massachusetts, New York, New Jersey, and North Carolina, thought descended from African slaves, were not only citizens of those States, but such of them as had the other necessary qualifications possessed the franchise of electors, on equal terms with other citizens.	Clear example that "negros" were citizens of five states under the Articles of Confederation.

2 Generated by the author based upon the text.

Reference	Dred Scott Articles of Confederation References (Justice Curtis Dissent)	Notes[2]
60 U.S. 393, 575	The fourth of the fundamental articles of the Confederation was as follows: "The free inhabitants of each of these States, paupers, vagabonds, and fugitives from justice, excepted, shall be entitled to all the privileges and immunities of free citizens in the several States." The fact that free persons of color were citizens of some of the several States, and the consequence, that this fourth article of the Confederation would have the effect to confer on such persons the privileges and immunities of general citizenship, were not only known to those who framed and adopted those articles, but the evidence is decisive, that the fourth article was intended to have that effect, and that more restricted language, which would have excluded such persons, was deliberately and purposely rejected. On the 25th of June, 1778, the Articles of Confederation being under consideration by the Congress, the delegates from South Carolina moved to amend this fourth article by inserting after the word "free," and before the word "inhabitants," the word "white," so that the privileges and immunities of general citizenship would be secured only to white persons. Two states voted for the amendment, eight States against it, and the vote of one State was divided. The language of the article stood unchanged, and both by its terms of inclusion, "free inhabitants," and the strong implication from its terms of exclusion, "paupers, vagabonds, and fugitives from justice," who alone were excepted, it is clear, that under the Confederation, and at the time of the adoption of the Constitution, free colored persons of African descent might be, and, by reason of their citizenship in certain States, were entitled to the privileges and immunities of general citizenship of the United States.	Interesting example that under the Articles of Confederation government, South Carolina requested an amendment that would change "free inhabitants" to "free white inhabitants". They were voted down 2-8 with another state evenly divided.
60 U.S. 393, 584-585	It has been suggested, that in adopting it into the Constitution, the words "free inhabitants" were changed for the word "citizens." An examination of the forms of expression commonly used in the State papers of that day, and an attention to the substance of this article of the Confederation, will show that the words "free inhabitants," as then used, were synonymous with citizens. When the Articles of Confederation were adopted, we were in the midst of the war of the Revolution, and there were very few persons then embraced in the words "free inhabitants," who were not born on our soil. It was not a time when many, save the children of the soil, were willing to embark their fortunes in our cause; and though there might be an inaccuracy in the uses of words to call free inhabitants citizens, it was then a technical rather than a substantial difference.	Response to Justice Taney's claim that the change from "free inhabitants" to "citizens" was to exclude "negros". Shows that this was a technicality.

Appendix 24 - Cruikshank Indictment Count Dispositions

United States v. Cruikshank Commentary on Indictment Counts

Counts	Indictment Count Description	Key parts of the Opinion regarding the Indictment Counts[1]
1, 9	The first and ninth counts state the intent of the defendants to have been to hinder and prevent the citizens named in the free exercise and enjoyment of their "lawful right and privilege to peaceably assemble together with each other and with other citizens of the United States for a peaceful and lawful purpose."	The right of the people peaceably to assemble for lawful purposes existed long before the adoption of the Constitution of the United States. ... It is found wherever civilization exists. It was not, therefore, a right granted to the people by the Constitution.
2, 10	The second and tenth counts are equally defective. The right there specified is that of "bearing arms for a lawful purpose."	This is not a right granted by the Constitution. Neither is it in any manner dependent upon that instrument for its existence. The second amendment declares that it shall not be infringed; but this, as has been seen, means no more than that it shall not be infringed by Congress.
3, 11	The third and eleventh counts are even more objectionable. They charge the intent to have been to deprive the citizens named, they being in Louisiana, "of their respective several lives and liberty of person without due process of law."	This is nothing else than alleging a conspiracy to falsely imprison or murder citizens of the United States, being within the territorial jurisdiction of the State of Louisiana. The rights of life and personal liberty are natural rights of man. "To secure these rights," says the Declaration of Independence, "governments are instituted among men, deriving their just powers from the consent of the governed." The very highest duty of the States, when they entered into the Union under the Constitution, was to protect all persons within their boundaries in the enjoyment of these "unalienable rights with which they were endowed by their Creator." Sovereignty, for this purpose, rests alone with the States.

1 United States v. Cruikshank(1876), 92 U.S. 542, 551-559
United States Library of Congress. (2026, Feb. 24).
https://www.loc.gov/item/usrep092542/

Counts	Indictment Count Description	Key parts of the Opinion regarding the Indictment Counts[1]
4, 12	The fourth and twelfth counts charge the intent to have been to prevent and hinder the citizens named, who were of African descent and persons of color, in "the free exercise and enjoyment of their several right and privilege to the full and equal benefit of all laws and proceedings, then and there, before that time, enacted or ordained by the said State of Louisiana and by the United States; and then and there, at that time, being in force in the said State and District of Louisiana aforesaid, for the security of their respective persons and property, then and there, at that time enjoyed at and within said State and District of Louisiana by white persons, being citizens of said State of Louisiana and the United States, for the protection of the persons and property of said white citizens."	There is no allegation that this was done because of the race or color of the persons conspired against. When stripped of its verbiage, the case as presented amounts to nothing more than that the defendants conspired to prevent certain citizens of the United States, being within the State of Louisiana, from enjoying the equal protection of the laws of the State and of the United States.

Counts	Indictment Count Description	Key parts of the Opinion regarding the Indictment Counts[1]
6, 14	The sixth and fourteenth counts state the intent of the defendants to have been to hinder and prevent the citizens named, being of African descent, and colored, "in the free exercise and enjoyment of their several and respective right and privilege to vote at any election to be thereafter by law had and held by the people in and of the said State of Louisiana, or by the people of and in the parish of Grant aforesaid."	In Minor v. Happersett, 21 Wall. 178, we decided that the Constitution of the United States has not conferred the right of suffrage upon any one, and that the United States have no voters of their own creation in the States. In United States v. Reese et al., supra, p. 214, we hold that the fifteenth amendment has invested the citizens of the United States with a new constitutional right, which is, exemption from discrimination in the exercise of the elective franchise on account of race, color, or previous condition of servitude. ... The right to vote in the States comes from the States; but the right of exemption from the prohibited discrimination comes from the United States. The first has not been granted or secured by the Constitution of the United States; but the last has been. Inasmuch, therefore, as it does not appear in these counts that the intent of the defendants was to prevent these parties from exercising their right to vote on account of their race, &c., it does not appear that it was their intent to interfere with any right granted or secured by the constitution or laws of the United States. We may suspect that race was the cause of the hostility; but it is not so averred. This is material to a description of the substance of the offence, and cannot be supplied by implication. Every thing essential must be charged positively, and not inferentially. The defect here is not in form, but in substance.

Counts	Indictment Count Description	Key parts of the Opinion regarding the Indictment Counts[1]
7, 15	The seventh and fifteenth counts are no better than the sixth and fourteenth. The intent here charged is to put the parties named in great fear of bodily harm, and to injure and oppress them, because, being and having been in all things qualified, they had voted "at an election before that time had and held according to law by the people of the said State of Louisiana, in said State, to wit, on the fourth day of November, A.D. 1872, and at divers other elections by the people of the State, also before that time had and held according to law."	There is nothing to show that the elections voted at were any other than State elections, or that the conspiracy was formed on account of the race of the parties against whom the conspirators were to act. The charge as made is really of nothing more than a conspiracy to commit a breach of the peace within a State. Certainly it will not be claimed that the United States have the power or are required to do mere police duty in the States. If a State cannot protect itself against domestic violence, the United States may, upon the call of the executive, when the legislature cannot be convened, lend their assistance for that purpose. This is a guaranty of the Constitution (art. 4, sect. 4); but it applies to no case like this.
5, 13 8, 16	We come now to consider the fifth and thirteenth and the eighth and sixteenth counts, which may be brought together for that purpose. The intent charged in the fifth and thirteenth is "to hinder and prevent the parties in their respective free exercise and enjoyment of the rights, privileges, immunities, and protection granted and secured to them respectively as citizens of the United States, and as citizens of said State of Louisiana," "for the reason that they, . . . being then and there citizens of said State and of the United States, were persons of African descent and race, and persons of color, and not white citizens thereof;" and in the eighth and sixteenth, to hinder and prevent them "in their several and respective free exercise and enjoyment of every, each, all, and singular the several rights and privileges granted and secured to them by the constitution and laws of the United States." The same general statement of the rights to be interfered with is found in the fifth and thirteenth counts.	So here, the crime is made to consist in the unlawful combination with an intent to prevent the enjoyment of any right granted or secured by the Constitution, &c. All rights are not so granted or secured. Whether one is so or not is a question of law, to be decided by the court, not the prosecutor. Therefore, the indictment should state the particulars, to inform the court as well as the accused. It must be made to appear- that is to say, appear from the indictment, without going further - that the acts charged will, if proved, support a conviction for the offence alleged. But it is needless to pursue the argument further. The conclusion is irresistible, that these counts are too vague and general. They lack the certainty and precision required by the established rules of criminal pleading. It follows that they are not good and sufficient in law. They are so defective that no judgment of conviction should be pronounced upon them.

Appendix 25 - Summary of Privilege and Immunity Related Supreme Court Cases (1873-1899)

Case	State	Year	Proposed Nationwide Privilege and Immunity	Decision Summary	Key Opinion Text
Bradwell v. State	IL	1873	"right for a woman to practice law in any state"	Not a Nationwide Privilege and Immunity.	83 U.S. 130, 139 - We agree with him that there are privileges and immunities belonging to citizens of the United States, in that relation and character, and that it is these and these alone which a State is forbidden to abridge. But the right to admission to practice in the courts of a State is not one of them. This right in no sense depends on citizenship of the United States.
Bartemeyer v. Iowa	IA	1874	"right to sell liquor that was owned before 1860 even though Iowa outlawed sales in 1860"	Not a Nationwide Privilege and Immunity	85 U.S. 129, 132-133 - As regards both branches of this defence, it is to be observed that the statute of Iowa, which is complained of, was in existence long before the amendment of the Federal Constitution, which is thus invoked to render it invalid. Whatever were the privileges and immunities of Mr. Bartemeyer, as they stood before that amendment, under the Iowa statute, they have certainly not been abridged by any action of the State legislature since that amendment became a part of the Constitution. And unless that amendment confers privileges and immunities which he did not previously possess, the argument fails.

Case	State	Year	Proposed Nationwide Privilege and Immunity	Decision Summary	Key Opinion Text
Minor v. Happersett	MO	1874	"right for women citizens to vote"	Not a Nationwide Privilege and Immunity Women received the right to vote by the 19th Amendment in 1920	88 U.S. 162, 165 - It is contended that the provisions of the constitution and laws of the State of Missouri which confine the right of suffrage and registration therefor to men, are in violation of the Constitution of the United States, and therefore void. The argument is, that as a woman, born or naturalized in the United States and subject to the jurisdiction thereof, is a citizen of the United States and of the State in which she resides, she has the right of suffrage as one of the privileges and immunities of her citizenship, which the State cannot by its laws or constitution abridge. 88 U.S. 162, 170 - The fourteenth amendment did not affect the citizenship of women any more than it did of men. In this particular, therefore, the rights of Mrs. Minor do not depend upon the amendment. She has always been a citizen from her birth, and entitled to all the privileges and immunities of citizenship. The amendment prohibited the State, of which she is a citizen, from abridging any of her privileges and immunities as a citizen of the United States; but it did not confer citizenship on her. That she had before its adoption.
Walker v. Sauvinet	LA	1876	"right to a trial by jury for civil suits in state courts"	The 7th Amendment to the United States Constitution does not create a Nationwide Privilege and Immunity	92 U.S. 90, 92 - By art. 7 of the amendments, it is provided, -that "in suits at common law, where the value in controversy shall exceed twenty dollars, the right of trial by jury shall be preserved." This, as has been many times decided, relates only to trials in the courts of the United States.

Case	State	Year	Proposed Nationwide Privilege and Immunity	Decision Summary	Key Opinion Text
United States v. Reese	KY	1876	"the right for an African American to have his vote counted at the voting booth"	Confirmation and further description of a Nationwide Privilege and Immunity to be exempt from discrimination for voting on account of race, color or previous condition of servitude that was initially identified in the Slaughterhouse Cases.	92 U.S. 214, 217-218 - The Fifteenth Amendment does not confer the right of suffrage upon any one. It prevents the States, or the United States, however, from giving preference, in this particular, to one citizen of the United States over another on account of race, color, or previous condition of servitude. Before its adoption, this could be done. It was as much within the power of a State to exclude citizens of the United States from voting on account of race, &c., as it was on account of age, property, or education. Now it is not. If citizens of one race having certain qualifications are permitted by law to vote, those of another having the same qualifications must be. Previous to this amendment, there was no constitutional guaranty against this discrimination: now there is. It follows that the amendment has invested the citizens of the United States with a new constitutional right which is within the protecting power of Congress. That right is exemption from discrimination in the exercise of the elective franchise on account of race, color, or previous condition of servitude. This, under the express provisions of the second section of the amendment, Congress may enforce by "appropriate legislation."

Case	State	Year	Proposed Nationwide Privilege and Immunity	Decision Summary	Key Opinion Text
United States v. Cruikshank	LA	1876	"right for federal protection against heinous criminal acts performed by individuals"	The horrible actions described are those that are left to the State's police powers for prosecution.	92 U.S. 542, 552 - The first amendment to the Constitution prohibits Congress from abridging "the right of the people to assemble and to petition the government for a redress of grievances." This, like the other amendments proposed and adopted at the same time, was not intended to limit the powers of the State governments in respect to their own citizens, but to operate upon the National government alone. 92 U.S. 542, 552-553 - The right of the people peaceably to assemble for the purpose of petitioning Congress for a redress of grievances, or for any thing else connected with the powers or the duties of the national government, is an attribute of national citizenship, and, as such, under the protection of, and guaranteed by, the United States. The very idea of a government, republican in form, implies a right on the part of its citizens to meet peaceably for consultation in respect to public affairs and to petition for a redress of grievances. If it had been alleged in these counts that the object of the defendants was to prevent a meeting for such a purpose, the case would have been within the statute, and within the scope of the sovereignty of the United States. [Continued]

Case	State	Year	Proposed Nationwide Privilege and Immunity	Decision Summary	Key Opinion Text
United States v. Cruikshank [Cont.]					[Continued] 92 U.S. 542, 553 - The second and tenth counts are equally defective. The right there specified is that of "bearing arms for a lawful purpose." This is not a right granted by the Constitution. Neither is it in any manner dependent upon that instrument for its existence. The second amendment declares that it shall not be infringed; but this, as has been seen, means no more than that it shall not be infringed by Congress. This is one of the amendments that has no other effect than to restrict the powers of the national government, leaving the people to look for their protection against any violation by their fellow-citizens of the rights it recognizes, to what is called, in The City of New York v. Miln, 11 Pet. 139, the "powers which relate to merely municipal legislation, or what was, perhaps, more properly called internal police," "not surrendered or restrained" by the Constitution of the United States.

Case	State	Year	Proposed Nationwide Privilege and Immunity	Decision Summary	Key Opinion Text
Hall v. DeCuir	LA	1877	"the right for African Americans to travel in the same ship cabins with whites"	A Louisiana law that gave rights to African American passengers was ruled unconstitutional since it infringed on interstate commerce.	95 U.S. 485, 489 - The river Mississippi passes through or along the borders of ten different States, and its tributaries reach many more. The commerce upon these waters is immense, and its regulation clearly a matter of national concern. If each State was at liberty to regulate the conduct of carriers while within its jurisdiction, the confusion likely to follow could not but be productive of great inconvenience and unnecessary hardship. Each State could provide for its own passengers and regulate the transportation of its own freight, regardless of the interests of others. Nay more, it could prescribe rules by which the carrier must be governed within the State in respect to passengers and property brought from without. On one side of the river or its tributaries he might be required to observe one set of rules, and on the other another. Commerce cannot flourish in the midst of such embarrassments. 95 U.S. 485, 490 - The statute under which this suit is brought, as construed by the State court, seeks to take away from him that power so long as he is within Louisiana; and while recognizing to the fullest extent the principle which sustains a statute, unless its unconstitutionality is clearly established, we think this statute, to the extent that it requires those engaged in the transportation of passengers among the States to carry colored passengers in Louisiana in the same cabin with whites, is unconstitutional and void. If the public good requires such legislation, it must come from Congress and not from the States.

Case	State	Year	Proposed Nationwide Privilege and Immunity	Decision Summary	Key Opinion Text
Strauder v. West Virginia	WV	1880	"the right for African Americans to be on juries"	West Virginia's law was declared unconstitutional based on an Equal Protection Violation of the 14th Amendment.	100 U.S. 303, 307-308 …What is this but declaring that the law in the States shall be the same for the black as for the white; that all persons, whether colored or white, shall stand equal before the laws of the States, and, in regard to the colored race, for whose protection the amendment was primarily designed, that no discrimination shall be made against them by law because of their color? … If in those States where the colored people constitute a majority of the entire population a law should be enacted excluding all white men from jury service, thus denying to them the privilege of participating equally with the blacks in the administration of justice, we apprehend no one would be heard to claim that it would not be a denial to white men of the equal protection of the laws.

Case	State	Year	Proposed Nationwide Privilege and Immunity	Decision Summary	Key Opinion Text
Kirtland v. Hotchkiss	CT	1880	"right for a resident of one State to avoid paying taxes upon a debt upon a resident of another State, and specifically upon real estate located in another state"	Not a Nationwide Privilege and Immunity	100 U.S. 491, 499 - It is consequently for the state to determine, consistently with its own fundamental law, whether such property owned by one of its residents shall contribute, by way of taxation, to maintain its government. Its discretion in that regard cannot be supervised or controlled by any department of the federal government, for the reason, too obvious to require argument in its support, that such taxation violates no provision of the federal Constitution. Manifestly it does not, as is supposed by counsel, interfere in any true sense with the exercise by Congress of the power to regulate commerce among the several states. Nathan v. Louisiana, 8 How. 73; Cooley on Taxation 62. Nor does it, as is further supposed, abridge the privileges or immunities of citizens of the United States, or deprive the citizen of life, liberty, or property without due process of law or violate the constitutional guaranty that the citizens of each state shall be entitled to all privileges of citizens in the several states.

Case	State	Year	Proposed Nationwide Privilege and Immunity	Decision Summary	Key Opinion Text
United States v. Harris	TN	1883	"right to federal protection against criminal acts performed by individuals"	The Supreme Court struck down the KKK Act as an Unconstitutional violation of State power.	106 U.S. 629, 643 - There is only one other clause in the Constitution of the United States which can, in any degree, be supposed to sustain the section under consideration; namely, the second section of article 4, which declares that "the citizens of each State shall be entitled to all the privileges and immunities of citizens of the several States." But this section, like the Fourteenth Amendment, is directed against State action. 106 U.S. 629, 644 It was never supposed that the section under consideration conferred on Congress the power to enact a law which would punish a private citizen for an invasion of the rights of his fellow citizen, conferred by the State of which they were both residents, on all its citizens alike.

Case	State	Year	Proposed Nationwide Privilege and Immunity	Decision Summary	Key Opinion Text
The Civil Rights Cases	KS, CA, MO, NY, TN	1883	"right for African Americans to be customers of all hotels, theatres and railroads on the same terms as white customers"	The Supreme Court held that the 13th and 14th Amendments did not apply to private organizations.	109 U.S. 3, 13 – Opinion of the Court - And so in the present case, until some State law has been passed, or some State action through its officers or agents has been taken, adverse to the rights of citizens sought to be protected by the Fourteenth Amendment, no legislation of the United States under said amendment, nor any proceeding under such legislation, can be called into activity: for the prohibitions of the amendment are against State laws and acts done under State authority. 109 U.S. 3, 41 – Harlan Dissent - These authorities are sufficient to show that a keeper of an inn is in the exercise of a quasi public employment. The law gives him special privileges and he is charged with certain duties and responsibilities to the public. The public nature of his employment forbids him from discriminating against any person asking admission as a guest on account of the race or color of that person. [Continued]

Case	State	Year	Proposed Nationwide Privilege and Immunity	Decision Summary	Key Opinion Text
The Civil Rights Cases [Cont.]					[Continued] 109 U.S. 3, 47-48 – Harlan Dissent - Although this court has wisely forborne any attempt, by a comprehensive definition, to indicate all of the privileges and immunities to which the citizen of a State is entitled, of right, when within the jurisdiction of other States, I hazard nothing, in view of former adjudications, in saying that no State can sustain her denial to colored citizens of other States, while within her limits; of privileges or immunities, fundamental in republican citizenship, upon the ground that she accords such privileges and immunities only to her white citizens and withholds them from her colored citizens. The colored citizens of other States, within the jurisdiction of that State, could claim, in virtue of section 2 of article 4 of the Constitution, every privilege and immunity which that State secures to her white citizens. Otherwise, it would be in the power of any State, by discriminating class legislation against its own citizens of a particular race or color, to withhold from citizens of other States, belonging to that proscribed race, when within her limits, privileges and immunities of the character regarded by all courts as fundamental in citizenship;

Case	State	Year	Proposed Nationwide Privilege and Immunity	Decision Summary	Key Opinion Text
Hurtado v. California	CA	1884	"right to be indicted by a grand jury for state murder charges"	The Supreme Court decided that Grand Jury Indictments for Murder Charges are not covered by "due process of law"	110 U.S. 516, 538 - Tried by these principles, we are unable to say that the substitution for a presentment or indictment by a grand jury of the proceeding by information, after examination and commitment by a magistrate, certifying to the probable guilt of the defendant, with the right on his part to the aid of counsel, and to the cross-examination of the witnesses produced for the prosecution, is not due process of law. It is, as we have seen, an ancient proceeding at common law, which might include every case of an offence of less grade than a felony, except misprision of treason; and in every circumstance of its administration, as authorized by the statute of California, it carefully considers and guards the substantial interest of the prisoner. It is merely a preliminary proceeding, and can result in no final judgment, except as the consequence of a regular judicial trial, conducted precisely as in cases of indictments. 110 U.S. 516, 557-558 - Harlan Dissent - So that the court, in this ease, while conceding that the requirement of due process of law protects the fundamental principles of liberty and justice, adjudges, in effect, that an immunity or right, recognized at the common law to be essential to personal security, jealously guarded by our national Constitution against violation by any tribunal or body exercising authority under the general government, and expressly or impliedly recognized, when the Fourteenth Amendment was adopted, in the Bill of Rights or Constitution of every State in the Union, is, yet, not a fundamental principle in governments established, as those of the States of the Union are, to secure to the citizen liberty and justice,

Case	State	Year	Proposed Nationwide Privilege and Immunity	Decision Summary	Key Opinion Text
Ex Parte Yarbrough	GA	1884	"right for an African American to vote for a member of Congress without being attacked to stop him from doing so"	The Nationwide Privilege and Immunity against discrimination from voting on account of race was confirmed.	110 U.S. 651, 657 - Stripped of its technical verbiage, the offence charged in this indictment is that the defendants conspired .to intimidate Berry Saunders, a citizen of African descent, in the exercise of his right to vote for a member of the Congress of the United States, and in the execution of that conspiracy they beat, bruised, wounded and otherwise maltreated him; and in the second count that they did this on account of his race, color, and previous condition of servitude, by going in disguise and assaulting him on the public highway and on his own premises. 110 U.S. 651, 665 In the case of United States v. Reese, so much relied on by counsel, this court said in regard to the Fifteenth Amendment, that "it has invested the citizens of the United States with a new constitutional right which is within the protecting power of Congress. That right is an exemption from discrimination in the exercise of the elective franchise on account of race, color, or previous condition of servitude." This new constitutional right was mainly designed for citizens of African descent. The principle, however, that the protection of the exercise of this right is within the power of Congress, is as necessary to the right of other citizens to vote as to the colored citizen, and to the right to vote in general as to the right to be protected against discrimination. The exercise of the right in both instances is guaranteed by the Constitution, and should be kept free and pure by congressional enactments whenever that is necessary.

Case	State	Year	Proposed Nationwide Privilege and Immunity	Decision Summary	Key Opinion Text
Presser v. Illinois	IL	1886	"right to parade and drill non state sponsored militia units"	Not a Nationwide Privilege and Immunity to parade and drill non-militia units Implicitly acknowledges a Nationwide Privilege and Immunity for all citizens to bear arms.	116 U.S. 252, 254 - The indictment charged in substance that Presser, on September 24, 1879, in the county of Cook, in the State of Illinois, "did unlawfully belong to, and did parade and drill in the city of Chicago with an unauthorized body of men with arms, who had associated themselves together as a military company and organization, without having a license from the Governor, and not being a part of, or belonging to, 'the regular organized volunteer militia' of the State of Illinois, or the troops of the United States." 116 U.S. 252, 256 - The Second Amendment declares that it shall not be infringed, but this, as has been seen, means no more than that it shall not be infringed by Congress. This is one of the amendments that has no other effect than to restrict the powers of the National government, leaving the people to look for their protection against any violation by their fellow-citizens of the rights it recognizes to what is called in The City of New York v Miln, 11 Pet. [102] 139, the 'powers which relate to merely municipal legislation, or what was perhaps more properly called internal police,' 'not surrendered or restrained' by the Constitution of the United States." 116 U.S. 252, 265-266 - It is undoubtedly true that all citizens capable of bearing arms constitute the reserved military force or reserve militia of the United States as well as of the States, and, in view of this prerogative of the general government, as well as of its general powers, the States cannot, even laying the constitutional provision in question out of view, prohibit the people from keeping and bearing arms, ...

Case	State	Year	Proposed Nationwide Privilege and Immunity	Decision Summary	Key Opinion Text
Mahon v. Justice	KY, WV	1888	"right for a fugitive not to be abducted from one state and removed to another state that has an indictment for them, unless it is done through a writ of habeas corpus."	Not a Nationwide Privilege and Immunity	127 U.S. 700, 715 - But the plain answer to this contention is, that the laws of the United States do not recognize any such right of asylum, as is here claimed, on the part of a fugitive from justice in any State to which he has fled; nor have they, as already stated, made any provision for the return of parties who, by violence and without lawful authority, have been abducted from a State. There is, therefore, no authority in the courts of the United States to act upon any such alleged right.
Cole v. Cunningham	MA, NY	1890	"the right to file suits in other states to assert legal rights for a bankruptcy and have those decisions respected in your state"	The court affirmed that States need to respect the court decisions from other states.	133 U.S. 107, 136 - the courts of Massachusetts must give full credit, by which is meant the same effect to the proceedings in New York which that State gives to them. The constitutional provision which makes this declaration is part of Article IV, and it is in immediate connection with its second section, which declares that "the citizens of each State shall be entitled to all 'the privileges and immunities of citizens in the several States." The meaning of this is to prevent conflicts between courts of the different States, over the same matters, by establishing the rule that whatever is done or decided in one State shall be respected in every other State when properly proved before it. It is one feature of the general idea which is found all through the Constitution.

Case	State	Year	Proposed Nationwide Privilege and Immunity	Decision Summary	Key Opinion Text
In re. Kemmler	NY	1890	"the right not to be executed by the electric chair since it is cruel and unusual punishment"	The electric chair was not considered cruel and unusual.	136 U.S. 436, 449 - The enactment of this statute was in itself within the legitimate sphere of the legislative power of the State, and in the observance of those general rules prescribed by our systems of jurisprudence, and the legislature of the State of New York determined that it did not inflict cruel and unusual punishment, and its courts have sustained that determination. We cannot perceive that the State has thereby abridged the privileges or immunities of the petitioner, or deprived him of due process of law In order to reverse the judgment of the highest court of the State of New York, we should be compelled to hold that it had committed an error so gross as to amount in law to a denial by the State of due process of law to one accused of crime, or of some right secured to him by the Constitution of the United States. We have no hesitation in saying that this we cannot do upon the record before us.
Crowley v. Christensen	CA	1890	"the right to a liquor license to sell alcohol"	Not a Nationwide Privilege and Immunity	137 U.S. 86, 91 - Their sale in that form may be absolutely prohibited. It is a question of public expediency and public morality, and not of federal law. The police power of the State is fully competent to regulate the business to mitigate its evils or to suppress it entirely. There is no inherent right in a citizen to thus sell intoxicating liquors by retail; it is not a privilege of a citizen of the State or of a citizen of the United States.

Case	State	Year	Proposed Nationwide Privilege and Immunity	Decision Summary	Key Opinion Text
McElvaine v. Brush	NY	1891	"right not to be held in solitary confinement when waiting for execution"	Not a Nationwide Privilege and Immunity Uses same reasoning as in re Kemmler, 136 U.S. 436	142 U.S. 155, 160 - The general rule of decision is that this Court will follow the adjudication of the highest court of a state in the construction of its own statutes, and there is nothing in this case to take it out of that rule. We are of opinion that the record does not disclose that the petitioner is restrained of his liberty in violation of the Constitution and laws of the United States,
O'Neil v. Vermont	VT	1892	"right against cruel and unusual punishment"	Only the Dissent of Justice Fields discusses this right.	144 U.S. 323, 338 Justice Field Dissent - The accusation describes only a single offence; yet, by the addition of the words "at divers times," that document is held to justify a trial and uphold a conviction for three hundred and seven distinct offences, only one of which is set forth in the accusation, and that defectively, all the others being brought within it by the use of those words. The punishment imposed was one exceeding in severity, considering the offences of which the defendant was convicted, anything which I have been able to find in the records of our courts for the present century. By the justice of the peace in Vermont, before whom the defendant was accused, he was convicted of four hundred and fifty-seven distinct offences, and sentenced to pay to the treasurer of the State a fine of \$9140 and the costs of prosecution taxed at \$472.96, and be confined at hard labor in the house of correction in the county of Rutland for one month, and, in case the fine and costs should not be paid on or before the expiration of this month's imprisonment, to be confined there at hard labor for the further term of twenty-eight thousand eight hundred and thirty-six days, to be computed from the expiration of the month's imprisonment. This was more than seventy-nine years for selling, furnishing and giving away, as alleged, intoxicating liquor,

Case	State	Year	Proposed Nationwide Privilege and Immunity	Decision Summary	Key Opinion Text
McPherson v. Blacker	MI	1892	"right to choose Presidential electors by popular vote"	Not a Nationwide Privilege and Immunity	146 U.S. 1, 27 - The Constitution does not provide that the appointment of electors shall be by popular vote, nor that the electors shall be voted for upon a general ticket, nor that the majority of those who exercise the elective franchise can alone choose the electors. It recognizes that the people act through their representatives in the legislature, and leaves it to the legislature exclusively to define the method of effecting the object. 146 U.S. 1, 40 If presidential electors are appointed by the legislatures, no discrimination is made ; if they are elected in districts where each citizen has-an equal right to vote the same as any other citizen has, no discrimination is made.
Giozza v. Tiernan	TX	1893	"right to sell intoxicating liquors"	Not a Nationwide Privilege and Immunity Uses the same logic as Bartemeyer v. Iowa, 85 U.S. 129	148 U.S. 657, 661-662 - The privileges and immunities of citizens of the United States are privileges and immunities arising out of the nature and essential character of the national government, and granted or secured by the Constitution of the United States, and the right to sell intoxicating liquors is not one of the rights growing out of such citizenship. Bartemeyer v Iowa, 18 Wall. 129.
Duncan v. Missouri	MO	1894	"right for the United States Supreme Court to rule that a State's Constitutional Amendment changing the structure of the States Supreme Court is an Ex Post Facto violation relative to a convicted murder's proceedings"	Thrown out on procedural grounds.	152 U.S. 377, 383 - To give jurisdiction to this court, the title, right, privilege, or immunity relied on must be specially set up or claimed at the proper time and in the proper way, and the decision must be against it; whereas, in this case, the question was not suggested until after judgment, and after an application for rehearing had been overruled, and only then in the form of a motion to transfer the cause.

Case	State	Year	Proposed Nationwide Privilege and Immunity	Decision Summary	Key Opinion Text
Miller v. Texas	TX	1894	Desperate final appeal after a murder conviction that argued 2nd, 4th, 5th and 14th Amendment violations during the arrest for the first time.	Thrown out on procedural grounds.	153 U.S. 535, 539 - There was no other question under the Fourteenth Amendment to the Constitution. As the proceedings were conducted under the ordinary forms of criminal prosecutions there certainly was no denial of due process of law, nor did the law of the State, to which reference was made, abridge the privileges or immunities of citizens of the United States, as such privileges and immunities are defined in the Slaughter-house Cases, 16 Wall. 36; and in Crandall v. Nevada, 6 Wall. 35; and Ward v. Maryland, 12 Wall. 163.
In re Lockwood	VA	1894	"The right for a woman to be considered a person under Virginia law to permit her to practice law in Virginia"	The Supreme Court upheld Bradwell v. State, 83 U.S. 130. The Supreme Court left it up to Virginia to determine whether "person" was confined to males in their law.	154 U.S. 116, 117 - In Bradwell v. The State, 16 Wall. 130, it was held that the right to practise law in the state courts was not a privilege or immunity of a citizen of the United States ; that the right to control and regulate the granting of license to practice law in the courts of a State is one of those powers that was not transferred for its protection to the Federal government, and its exercise is in no manner governed or controlled by citizenship of the United States in the party seeking such license. 154 U.S. 116, 118 - It was for the Supreme Court of Appeals to construe the statute of Virginia in question, and to determine whether the word "person" as therein used is confined to males, and whether women are admitted to practise law in that Commonwealth.

Case	State	Year	Proposed Nationwide Privilege and Immunity	Decision Summary	Key Opinion Text
Iowa Central Ry. v. Iowa	IA	1896	"the right to specific legal processes in state courts"	As long as there is legal due process, this is not a Nationwide Privilege and Immunity.	160 U.S. 389, 393 - But it is clear that the Fourteenth Amendment in no way undertakes to control the power of a state to determine by what process legal rights may be asserted or legal obligations be enforced, provided the method of procedure adopted for these purposes gives reasonable notice and affords fair opportunity to be heard before the issues are decided. This being the case, it was obviously not a right, privilege, or immunity of a citizen of the United States to have a controversy in the state court prosecuted or determined by one form of action instead of by another.
Plessy v. Ferguson	LA	1896	"right for an African American to travel in any railcar that whites can travel in"	The Supreme Court Created the doctrine of separate but equal	163 U.S. 537, 543 - that its main purpose was to establish the citizenship of the negro; to give definitions of citizenship of the United States and of the States, and to protect from the hostile legislation of the States the privileges and immunities of citizens of the United States, as distinguished from those of citizens of the States. 163 U.S. 537, 545-546 - So, where the laws of a particular locality or the charter of a particular railway corporation has provided that no person shall be excluded from the cars on account of color, we have held that this meant that persons of color should travel in the same car as white ones, and that the enactment was not satisfied by the company's providing cars assigned exclusively to people of color, though they were as good as those which they assigned exclusively to white persons. Railroad Company v. Brown, 17 Wall. 445. [Continued]

Case	State	Year	Proposed Nationwide Privilege and Immunity	Decision Summary	Key Opinion Text
Plessy v. Ferguson [Cont.]					[Continued] 163 U.S. 537, 551 - We consider the underlying fallacy of the plaintiff's argument to consist in the assumption that the enforced separation of the two races stamps the colored race with a badge of inferiority. If this be so, it is not by reason of anything found in the act, but solely because the colored race chooses to put that construction upon it. 163 U.S. 537, 560 – Harlan Dissent The present decision, it may well be apprehended, will not only stimulate aggressions, more or less brutal and irritating, upon the admitted rights of colored citizens, but will encourage the belief that it is possible, by means of state enactments, to defeat the beneficent purposes which the people of the United States had in view when they adopted the recent amendments of the Constitution, by one of which the blacks of this country were made citizens of the United States and of the States in which they respectively reside, and whose privileges and immunities, as citizens, the States are forbidden to abridge.
Holden v. Hardy	UT	1898	"the right to work longer hours in an underground mine than state law allows"	Not a Nationwide Privilege and Immunity	169 U.S. 366, 395 - Upon the principles above stated, we think the act in question may be sustained as a valid exercise of the police power of the State. The enactment does not profess to limit the hours of all workmen, but merely those who are employed in underground mines, or in the smelting, reduction or refining of ores or metals. These employments, when too long pursued, the legislature has judged to be detrimental to the health of the employes, and, so long as there are reasonable grounds for believing that this is so, its decision upon this subject cannot be reviewed by the Federal courts.

Appendix 25 - Summary of Privilege and Immunity Related Supreme Court Cases (1873-1899)

Case	State	Year	Proposed Nationwide Privilege and Immunity	Decision Summary	Key Opinion Text
Blake v. McClung	TN, OH	1899	"right for out of state creditors of a bankrupt company to be treated equally with in state creditors"	Nationwide Privilege and Immunity was recognized for individual citizens of other states to be treated equally to in-state citizens with respect to bankruptcy proceedings. Corporations were excluded from this right based upon Paul v. Virginia, 75 U.S. 168	172 U.S. 239, 254-255 - We hold such discrimination against citizens of other States to be repugnant to the second section of the Fourth Article of the Constitution of the United States, although, generally speaking, the State has the power to prescribe the conditions upon which foreign corporations may enter its territory for purposes of business. Such a power cannot be exerted with the effect of defeating or impairing rights secured to citizens of the several States by the supreme law of the land. Indeed, all the powers possessed by a State must be exercised consistently with the privileges and immunities granted or protected by the Constitution of the United States. 172 U.S. 239, 256 - There are privileges that may be accorded by a State to its own people in which citizens of other States may not participate except in conformity to such reasonable regulations as may be established by the State. For instance, a State cannot forbid citizens of other States from suing in its courts, that right being enjoyed by its own people; but it may require a non-resident, although a citizen of another State, to give bond for costs, although such bond be not required of a resident. Such a regulation of the internal affairs of a State cannot reasonably be characterized as hostile to the fundamental rights of citizens of other States. So, a State may, by rule uniform in its operation as to citizens of the several States, require residence within its limits for a given time before a citizen of another State who becomes a resident thereof shall exercise the right of suffrage or become eligible to office.

Case	State	Year	Proposed Nationwide Privilege and Immunity	Decision Summary	Key Opinion Text
Orient Insurance Co. v. Daggs	CT, MO	1899	"right for an insurance company to limit its liability to actual damages caused by a fire"	Corporations are not citizens as decided in Paul v. Virginia, 75 U.S. 168	172 U.S. 557, 561 - A corporation is not a citizen within the meaning of the provision, and hence has not "privileges and immunities" secured to "citizens" against state legislation. This was decided in Paul v. Virginia, 8 Wall. 168 …
Cumming v. Board of Education	GA	1899	"right to have equal education spending for African American kids as for white kids"	Not a Nationwide Privilege and Immunity	175 U.S. 528, 545 Under the circumstances disclosed, we cannot say that this action of the state court was, within the meaning of the Fourteenth Amendment, a denial by the State to the plaintiffs and to those associated with them of the equal protection of the laws or of any privileges belonging to them as citizens of the United States. We may add that while all admit that the benefits and burdens of public taxation must be shared by citizens without discrimination against any class on account of their race, the education of the people in schools maintained by state taxation is a matter belonging to the respective States, and any interference on the part of Federal authority with the management of such schools cannot be justified except in the case of a clear and unmistakable disregard of rights secured by the supreme law of the land.

Appendix 26 - Summary of Privilege and Immunity Related Supreme Court Cases (1900-2025)

Case	State	Year	Proposed Nationwide Privilege and Immunity	Decision Summary	Key Opinion Text
Maxwell v. Dow	UT	1900	"right to be tried by a jury of 12 people in state trials"	Not a Nationwide Privilege and Immunity based on the view that the Bill of Rights did not extend to the States from Barron v. Baltimore.	175 U.S. 581, 594 - There is no intimation here that among the privileges or immunities of a citizen of the United States are the right of trial by jury in a state court for a state offence and the right to be exempt from any trial for an infamous crime, unless upon presentment by a grand jury. And yet if these were such privileges and immunities, they would be among the first that would occur to any one when enumerating or defining them. Nor would these rights come under the description, given by the Chief Justice in the Kemmler case, supra. Such privileges or immunities do not arise out of the nature or essential character of the National Government. 175 U.S. 581, 612 – Harlan Dissent - For if prior to the adoption of the Fourteenth Amendment it was one of the privileges or immunities of citizens of the United States that they should not be tried for crime in any court organized or existing under National authority except by a jury composed of twelve persons, how can it be that a citizen of the United States may be now tried in a state court for crime, particularly for an infamous crime, by eight jurors, when that amendment expressly declares that "no State shall make or enforce any law which shall abridge the privileges or immunities of citizens of the United States"? It does not meet the case to say that a trial by eight jurors is as much a trial by jury as if there were twelve jurors; for if a citizen charged with crime can be subjected to trial by a less number of jurors than that prescribed by the Constitution, the number may be reduced to three.

Case	State	Year	Proposed Nationwide Privilege and Immunity	Decision Summary	Key Opinion Text
Williams v. Fears	GA	1900	"right not to have a tax on labor that could be used interstate".	Not a Nationwide Privi-lege and Immunity since it only incidentally affects egress from the State.	179 U.S. 270, 274 - On behalf of plaintiff in error it is insisted that paragraph ten is in conflict with the Fourteenth Amendment because it restricts the right of the citizen to move from one State to another, and so abridges his privileges and immunities; impairs the natural right to labor; and is class legislation, discriminating arbitrarily and without reasonable basis. 179 U.S. 270, 278 - These labor contracts were not in themselves subjects of traffic between the States, nor was the business of hiring laborers so immediately connected with interstate transportation or interstate traffic that it could be correctly said that those who followed it were engaged in interstate commerce, or that the tax on that occupation constituted a burden on such commerce. Nor was the imposition in violation of section 2 of Article.IV, as there was no discrimination between the citizens of other States and the citizens of Georgia.

Case	State	Year	Proposed Nationwide Privilege and Immunity	Decision Summary	Key Opinion Text
Orr v. Gilman	NY	1902	"the right not to have a state estate tax charged"	Not a Nationwide Privilege and Immunity	183 U.S. 278, 282-283 - Whatever be the technical source of title of a grantee under a power of appointment, it cannot be denied that, in reality and substance, it is the execution of the power that gives to the grantee the property passing under it. The will of Dows, Senior, gave his son a power of appointment to be exercised only in a particular manner, to-wit, by last will and testament. If, as said by the Supreme Court of the United States, the right to take property by devise is not an inherent or natural right, but a privilege accorded by the state, which it may tax or charge for, it follows that the rights of a testator to make a will or testamentary instrument is equally a privilege, and equally subject to the taxing power of the state. When David Dows, Senior, devised this property to the appointees under the will of his son, he necessarily subjected it to the charge that the state might impose on the privilege accorded to the son of making a will. That charge is the same in character as if it had been laid on the inheritance of the estate of the son himself -- that is, for the privilege of succeeding to property under a will.

Case	State	Year	Proposed Nationwide Privilege and Immunity	Decision Summary	Key Opinion Text
Board of Education v. Illinois	IL	1906	"right not to pay inheritance tax on charitable donations made to out of state charities."	Not a Nationwide Privilege and Immunity	203 U.S. 553, 562 - It must be kept in mind that the controversies in this case depend upon the power of the state over inheritances, and the conditions she may put upon them in the exercise of that power. 203 U.S. 553, 563 - A federal court would hesitate indeed to put impediments on this power or declare invalid any classification of persons or corporations that had reasonable regard to the purposes of the state and its legislation. And it cannot be said that, if a state exempt property bequeathed for charitable or educational purposes from taxation, it is unreasonable or arbitrary to require the charity to be exercised or the education to be bestowed within her borders and for her people, whether exercised through persons or corporations.

Case	State	Year	Proposed Nationwide Privilege and Immunity	Decision Summary	Key Opinion Text
Ballard v. Hunter	AR	1907	"right to have equal tax summons service times for in state and out-of-state residents"	Not a Nationwide Privilege and Immunity	204 U.S. 241, 254 - The assignments of error present the contention that plaintiff in error have been deprived of their property without due process of law. One of them urges, in addition, the clauses of the Fourteenth Amendment, which prohibit a State from making or enforcing any law which shall abridge the privileges or immunities of citizens of the United States, and from depriving any person within her jurisdiction of the equal protection of the laws. Plaintiffs in error invoke those provisions against the statutes of Arkansas, because of the different manner and time of service of summons of the suit authorized by said statutes to enforce the payment of the levee taxes. It is contended that, by requiring personal service of summons upon resident owners or occupants of lands for at least twenty days before the rendition of the decree of sale, and providing for- constructive service by publication, upon non-resident owners of only four weeks, a discrimination is made between owners of lands, and that non-resident owners are thereby denied the rights secured to them by the Constitution of the United States. We have no doubt of the power of the State to so discriminate, nor do we think extended discussion is necessary.
Western Turf Assn. v. Greenberg	CA	1907	"the right to publish a horse racing chart at an establishment where the association had sold this right to another company."	Corporations are not citizens as decided in Paul v. Virginia, 75 U.S. 168	204 U.S. 359, 363 - Of still less merit is the suggestion that the statute abridges the rights and privileges of citizens, for a corporation cannot be deemed a citizen within the meaning of the clause of the Constitution of the United States which protects the privileges and immunities of citizens of the United States against being abridged or impaired by the law of a State.

Case	State	Year	Proposed Nationwide Privilege and Immunity	Decision Summary	Key Opinion Text
Halter v. Nebraska	NE	1907	"right to use the United States flag in advertising"	Not a Nationwide Privilege and Immunity	205 U.S. 34, 42- By the statute in question the State has in substance declared that no one subject to its jurisdiction shall use the flag for purposes of trade and traffic, a purpose wholly foreign to that for which it was provided by the Nation. Such an use tends to degrade and cheapen, the flag in the estimation of the people, as well as to defeat the object of maintaining it as an emblem of National power and National honor. And we cannot hold that any privilege of American citizenship or that any right of personal liberty is violated by a state enactment forbidding the flag to be used as an advertisement on a bottle of beer.
Wilmington Star Mining Co. v. Fulton	IL	1907	"right to operate mining property without employing licensed managers and following other requirements"	Not a Nationwide Privilege and Immunity	205 U.S. 60, 73 - In legal effect, duties are imposed upon the mine owner, customarily performed for him by certain employees -- duties which substantially relate to the furnishing of a reasonably safe place for the workmen. The subject was one peculiarly within the police power of the state, and the enactment of the regulations counted upon we think was an appropriate exercise of such power. The use and enjoyment of mining property being subject to the reasonable exercise of the police power of the state, certainly the rights, privileges, and immunities of a mine owner as a citizen of the United States were not invaded by the regulations in question,

Case	State	Year	Proposed Nationwide Privilege and Immunity	Decision Summary	Key Opinion Text
Twining v. New Jersey	NJ	1908	"right against self-incrimination"	Not a Nationwide Privilege and Immunity Exhaustive historical analysis including English law and State Constitutions.	211 U.S. 78, 99 - We conclude, therefore, that the exemption from compulsory self-incrimination is not a privilege or immunity of National citizenship guaranteed by this clause of the Fourteenth Amendment against abridgment by the States. 211 U.S. 78, 211 - Thus it appears that four only of the thirteen original States insisted upon incorporating the privilege in the Constitution, and they separately and simultaneously with the requirement of due process of law, and that three States proposing amendments were silent upon this subject. 211 U.S. 78, 119 - Harlan Dissent - Can there be any doubt that at the opening of the War of Independence the people of the colonies claimed as one of their birthrights the privilege of immunity from self-incrimination? This question can be answered in but one way. If at the beginning of the Revolutionary War any lawyer had claimed that one accused of crime, could lawfully be compelled to testify against himself, he would have been laughed at by his brethren of the bar, both in England and America. 211 U.S. 78, 126-127 Harlan Dissent - I cannot support any judgment declaring that immunity from self-incrimination is not one of the privileges or immunities of National citizenship, nor a part of the liberty guaranteed by the Fourteenth Amendment against hostile state action. The declaration of the court, in the opinion just delivered, that immunity from self-incrimination is of great value, a protection to the innocent and a safeguard against unfounded and tyrannical prosecutions, meets my cordial approval.

Case	State	Year	Proposed Nationwide Privilege and Immunity	Decision Summary	Key Opinion Text
Graham v. West Virginia	WV	1912	"right not to have increased penalties for repeat offenders"	Not a Nationwide Privilege and Immunity	224 U.S. 616, 631 - What has been said, and the authorities which have been cited, sufficiently show that there is no basis for the contention that the plaintiff in error has been put in double jeopardy or that any of his privileges or immunities as a citizen of the United States have been abridged.
Selover, Bates & Co. v. Walsh	MN	1912	Interstate Land Contract Dispute.	Corporations are not citizens as decided in Paul v. Virginia, 75 U.S. 168	226 U.S. 112, 126 - And we may say further, it is well settled that a corporation cannot claim the protection of the clause of the Fourteenth Amendment which secures the privileges and immunities of citizens of the United States against abridgment or impairment by the law of a state. Western Turf Asso. v. Greenberg, 204 U. S. 359.
Rosenthal v. New York	NY	1912	"the right to accept junk metal that might be stolen property without checking on the source"	Not a Nationwide Privilege and Immunity	226 U.S. 260, 266 - No serious argument was made to support the contention that the act in any way abridged the privileges or immunities of the plaintiff in error as a citizen of the United States. This part of the prohibition of the Fourteenth Amendment refers only to such privileges and immunities as pertain to citizenship of the United States, as distinguished from state citizenship.
Waugh v. Board of Trustees of the University of Mississippi	MS	1915	"the right to be in a fraternity when a student at the University of Mississippi"	Not a Nationwide Privilege and Immunity	237 U.S. 589, 597 - It is very trite to say that the right to pursue happiness and exercise rights and liberty are subject in some degree to the limitations of the law, and the condition upon which the State of Mississippi offers the complainant free instruction in its University, that while a student there he renounce affiliation with a society Which the State considers inimical to discipline, finds no prohibition in the Fourteenth Amendment.
Crane v. Campbell	ID	1917	"the right to carry a bottle of whiskey on your person in a prohibition district"	Not a Nationwide Privilege and Immunity	245 U.S. 304, 308 We further think it clearly follows from our numerous decisions upholding prohibition legislation that the right to hold intoxicating liquors for personal use is not one of those fundamental privileges of a citizen of the United States which no State may abridge.

Case	State	Year	Proposed Nationwide Privilege and Immunity	Decision Summary	Key Opinion Text
Armour & Co. v. Virginia	VA	1918	"the right for there not to be tax breaks for manufacturers who offer for sale at the place of manufacture."	Not a Nationwide Privilege and Immunity	246 U.S. 1, 6-7 - In the third place, we also conclude that, as the subject matter of the statute was plainly within the legislative authority of the State and as the previous conclusions exclude the conception of the repugnancy of the statute to the provisions of the Constitution just considered, it necessarily follows that there is no ground for the assertion that the 'statute conflicted with the privileges and immunities clause of Article IV of the Constitution or of the clause in the Fourteenth Amendment providing that, "No State shall make or enforce any law which shall abridge the privileges or immunities of citizens of the United States."
Omaechevarria v. Idaho	ID	1918	"right for sheep owners to use the public lands equally with cattle ranchers."	Not a Nationwide Privilege and Immunity	246 U.S. 343, 346-348 - First: It is urged that the statute denies rights guaranteed by the Fourteenth Amendment, namely: Privileges of citizens of the United States, in so far as it prohibits the use of the public lands by sheep owners; and equal protection of the laws, in that it gives to cattle owners a preference over sheep owners. These contentions are, in substance, the same as those made in respect to the "Two Mile Limit Law," in Bacon v. Walker, supra; and the answer made there is applicable here. The police power of the State extends over the federal public domain, at least when there is no legislation by Congress on the subject.' We cannot say that the measure adopted by the State is unreasonable or arbitrary. It was found that conflicts between cattle rangers and sheep herders on the public domain could be reconciled only by segregation

Case	State	Year	Proposed Nationwide Privilege and Immunity	Decision Summary	Key Opinion Text
Maxwell v. Bugbee	NJ	1919	"the right not to pay an inheritance tax since you are not a resident of the state where the person dies"	Not a Nationwide Privilege and Immunity	250 U.S. 525, 538-539 - We are unable to discover in the statute before us, which regulates and taxes the right to succeed to property in New Jersey upon the death of a non-resident owner, any infringement of the rights of citizenship either of the States or of the United States, secured by either of the constitutional provisions referred to. We have held that the protection that they afford to rights inherent in citizenship are not infringed by the taxation of the transfer of property within the jurisdiction of a State passing by will or intestacy where the decedent was a non-resident of the taxing State, although the entire succession was taxed in the State where he resided. Blackstone v. Miller, 188 U. S. 189, 207. Upon this point it is unnecessary to decide whether the case might not be rested on a much narrower ground. The alleged discrimination, here complained of, so far as privileges and immunities of citizenship are concerned, is not strictly applicable to this statute because the difference in the method of taxation rests upon residence and not upon citizenship. La Tourette v. McMaster, 248 U. S. 465.
United States v. Wheeler	AZ	1920	"the right to reside and remain in a state and to be immune from unlawful deportation from that State by a conspiracy of individuals"	Not a Nationwide Privilege and Immunity Similar to United States v. Harris (1883), 106 U. S. 629, since the violation is by individuals and not the State.	254 U.S. 281, 297-298 - Undoubtedly the right of citizens of the States to reside peacefully in, and to have free ingress into and egress from, the several States had, prior to the Confederation, a twofold aspect: (1) as possessed in their own States and (2) as enjoyed in virtue of the comity of other States. But although the Constitution fused these distinct rights into one by providing that one State should not deny to the citizens of other States rights given to its own citizens, no basis is afforded for contending that a wrongful prevention by an individual of the enjoyment by a citizen of one State in another of rights possessed in that State by its own citizens was a violation of a right afforded by the Constitution.

Case	State	Year	Proposed Nationwide Privilege and Immunity	Decision Summary	Key Opinion Text
Ferry v. Spokane, P. & S. R. Co.	OR	1921	"the right to dowry rights for a widow who is living in another state to inherit property in a different state"	Not a Nationwide Privilege and Immunity	258 U.S. 314, 318 Dower is not a privilege or immunity of citizenship, either state or federal, within the meaning of the provisions relied on. At most it is a right which, while it exists, is attached to the marital contract or relation; and it always has been deemed subject to regulation by each State as respects property within its limits.
Prudential Ins. Co. v. Cheek	MO	1922	"the right to refuse to provide a letter describing a former employee's service with a company"	Not a Nationwide Privilege and Immunity	259 U.S. 530, 539 - It appears rather that the right to discharge a servant for any reason or for no reason was thought to be one of the "privileges or immunities of citizens of the United States." But, as this court more than once has pointed out, the privileges or immunities of citizens protected by the Fourteenth Amendment against abridgment by state laws are not those fundamental privileges and immunities inherent in state citizenship, but only those which owe their existence to the Federal Government, its national character, its constitution, or its laws.
New York ex rel. Bryant v. Zimmerman	NY	1928	"the right not to file an organization's Constitution, By-laws and membership lists for secret organizations such as the Ku Klux Klan"	Not a Nationwide Privilege and Immunity	278 U.S. 63, 71-72 - There are various privileges and immunities which under our dual system of government belong to citizens of the United States solely by reason of such citizenship. It is against their abridgement by state laws that the privilege and immunity clause in the Fourteenth Amendment is directed. But no such privilege or immunity is in question here. If to be and remain a member of a secret, oath-bound association within a State be a privilege arising out of citizenship at all, it is an incident of state rather than United States citizenship; and such protection as is thrown about it by the Constitution is in no wise affected by its possessor being a citizen of the United States. Thus there is no basis here for invoking the privilege and immunity clause.

Case	State	Year	Proposed Nationwide Privilege and Immunity	Decision Summary	Key Opinion Text
Helson and Randolph v. Kentucky	KY	1929	"the right to import gasoline into a state without being taxed by the state on the importation"	Switched Taxation of movement of people between states to Interstate Commerce Clause Regulation	279 U.S. 245, 251 - To impose a tax upon the transit of passengers from foreign countries or between states is to regulate commerce and is beyond state power. The doctrine of Crandall v. Nevada, 6 Wall. 35, so far as it is to the contrary, has not been followed.
Hamilton v. Regents	CA	1934	"the right to refuse to take a required military science class at the University of California which is a land-grant University."	Not a Nationwide Privilege and Immunity	293 U.S. 245, 261-262 - Appellants assert-unquestionably in good faith-that all war, preparation for war, and the training required by the university, are repugnant to the tenets and discipline of their church, to their religion and to their consciences. The " privilege " of attending the university as a student comes not from federal sources but is given by the State. It is not within the asserted protection. The only " immunity" claimed by these students is freedom from obligation to comply with the rule prescribing military training. But that 'immunity ' cannot be regarded as not within, or as distinguishable from the "liberty" of which they claim to have been deprived by the enforcement of the regents' order. If the regents' order is not repugnant to the due process clause, then it does not violate the privileges and immunities clause. Therefore we need only decide whether by state action the "liberty" of these students has been infringed.

Case	State	Year	Proposed Nationwide Privilege and Immunity	Decision Summary	Key Opinion Text
Colgate v. Harvey	VT	1935	"the right not to be taxed at a higher rate on out-of-state dividends or interest for state tax purposes"	Identified a new Privilege and Immunity that was overruled 5 years later.	296 U.S. 404, 433 - The statute, as here applied, says that if a citizen resident in Vermont loan his money at 5% or less in another state, he must pay a tax upon the income; but if he loan money in Vermont at the same rate, no tax whatever shall be imposed. The power to tax income here asserted by Vermont is, in the final analysis, the power to tax so heavily as to preclude loans outside the state altogether. It reasonably is not open to doubt that the discriminatory tax here imposed abridges the privilege of a citizen of the United States to loan his money and make contracts with respect thereto in any part of the United States. Stone Dissent 296 U.S. 404, 443 - Feeble indeed is an attack on a statute as denying equal protection which can gain any support from the almost forgotten privileges and immunities clause of the Fourteenth Amendment. The notion that that clause could have application to any but the privileges and immunities peculiar to citizenship of the United States, as distinguished from those of citizens of states, has long since been rejected. [Continued]

Case	State	Year	Proposed Nationwide Privilege and Immunity	Decision Summary	Key Opinion Text
Colgate v. Harvey {Cont.}					[Continued] Stone Dissent 296 U.S. 404, 445 The reason for this reluctance to enlarge the scope of the clause has been well understood since the decision of the Slaughter-House Cases, supra. If its restraint upon state action were extended more than is needful to protect relationships between the citizen and the national government, and it did more than duplicate the protection of liberty and property secured to persons and citizens by the other provisions of the Constitution, it would enlarge judicial control of state action and multiply restrictions upon it to an extent difficult to define, but sufficient to cause serious apprehension for the rightful independence of local government. Stone Dissent 296 U.S. 404, 448 - The contention that a state tax indirectly affecting transactions carried on across state lines, not forbidden by the commerce clause or by Art. IV, § 2, can be condemned under the privileges and immunities clause, was definitely rejected by this Court in Williams v. Fears, supra. There a state occupation tax upon those engaged in hiring laborers for employment outside the state was held not to infringe "the privileges and immunities clause or the equal protection clause. Stone Dissent 296 U.S. 404, 450 - We are thus returned to the point of beginning, to a discussion of the question whether the exemption in them present tax is so unreasonable, so without support of a permissible state policy, as to infringe constitutional limitations. If the exemption does not merit condemnation as a denial of the equal protection which the Fourteenth Amendment extends to every person, nothing can be added to the vehemence or effectiveness of the denunciation by invoking the command of the privileges and immunities clause.

Case	State	Year	Proposed Nationwide Privilege and Immunity	Decision Summary	Key Opinion Text
Whitfield v. Ohio	OH, AL	1936	"the right to sell prison made goods from one state in another state"	As long as a state restricts its own people the same as those from other states, there is not a Constitutional conflict.	297 U.S. 431, 437 The effect of the privileges and immunities clause of the Fourteenth Amendment, as applied to the facts of the present case, is to deny the power of Ohio to impose restraints upon citizens of the United States resident in Alabama in respect of the disposition of goods within Ohio, if like restraints are not imposed upon citizens resident in Ohio.
Breedlove v. Suttles	GA	1937	"the right not to pay a poll tax to vote"	Not a Nationwide Privilege and Immunity. The poll tax was invalidated by the 24th Amendment which was ratified in 1964.	302 U.S. 277, 283 To make payment of poll taxes a prerequisite of voting is not to deny any privilege or immunity protected by the Fourteenth Amendment. Privilege of voting is not derived from the United States, but is conferred by the State and, save as restrained by the Fifteenth and Nineteenth Amendments and other provisions of the Federal Constitution, the State may condition suffrage as it deems appropriate.
Palko v. Connecticut	CT	1937	"right not to be retried by a State as a result of a State Appeal to correct an error, and then to receive a greater sentence: in this case death versus life imprisonment."	Not a Nationwide Privilege and Immunity	302 U.S. 319, 328 - The conviction of appellant is not in derogation of any privileges or immunities that belong to him as a citizen of the United States.

Case	State	Year	Proposed Nationwide Privilege and Immunity	Decision Summary	Key Opinion Text
United States v. Miller	AR	1939	"right to carry an unregistered sawed-off shotgun"	The Supreme Court ruled that the National Firearms Act of 1934 was not unconstitutional	307 U.S. 175 – Statement of the Indictment – "did unlawfully, knowingly, wilfully, and feloniously transport in interstate commerce from the town of Claremore in the State of Oklahoma to the town of Siloam Springs in the State of Arkansas a certain firearm, to-wit, a double barrel 12-gauge Stevens shotgun having a barrel less than 18 inches in length, bearing identification number 76230, said defendants, at the time of so transporting said firearm in interstate commerce as aforesaid, not having registered said firearm as required by Section 1132d of Title 26, United States Code (Act of June 26, 1934, c. 737, Sec. 4 [§ 5], 48 Stat. 1237), and not having in their possession a stamp-affixed written order for said firearm as provided by Section 1132c, Title 26, United States Code (June 26, 1934, c. 737, Sec. 4, 48 Stat. 1237) and the regulations issued under authority of the said Act of Congress known as the 'National Firearms Act' approved June 26, 1934, contrary to the form of the statute in such case made and provided, and against the peace and dignity of the United States." 307 U.S. 178 - In the absence of any evidence tending to show that possession or use of a "shotgun having a barrel of less than eighteen inches in length" at this time has some reasonable relationship to the preservation or efficiency of a well regulated militia, we cannot say that the Second Amendment guarantees the right to keep and bear such an instrument. 307 U.S. 182 - Most if not all of the States have adopted provisions touching the right to keep and bear arms. Differences in the language employed in these have naturally led to somewhat variant conclusions concerning the scope of the right guaranteed.

Case	State	Year	Proposed Nationwide Privilege and Immunity	Decision Summary	Key Opinion Text
Hague v. Committee for Industrial Organization	NJ	1939	"right to assemble in public parks and streets to discuss the National Labor Relations Act"	Rights were protected by the Due Process Clause of the 14th Amendment.	307 U.S. 496, 515-516 Roberts Opinion - Wherever the title of streets and parks may rest, they have immemorially been held in trust for the use of the public and, time out of mind, have been used for purposes of assembly, communicating thoughts between citizens, and discussing public questions. Such use of the streets and public places has, from ancient times, been a part of the privileges, immunities, rights, and liberties of citizens. The privilege of a citizen of the United States to use the streets and parks for communication of views on national questions may be regulated in the interest of all; it is not absolute, but relative, and must be exercised in subordination to the general comfort and convenience, and in consonance with peace and good order; but it must not, in the guise of regulation, be abridged or denied. 307 U.S. 496, 519-520 Stone Opinion - Hence there is no occasion, for jurisdictional purposes or any other, to consider whether freedom of speech and of assembly are immunities secured by the privileges and immunities clause of the Fourteenth Amendment to citizens of the United States, or to revive the contention, rejected by this Court in the Slaughter-House Cases, supra, that the privileges and immunities of United States citizenship, protected by that clause, extend beyond those which arise or grow out of the relationship of United States citizens to the national government [Continued]

Case	State	Year	Proposed Nationwide Privilege and Immunity	Decision Summary	Key Opinion Text
[Cont.] Hague v. Committee for Industrial Organization					[Continued 307 U.S. 496, 522 Stone Opinion - It has been said that the right of citizens to assemble for the purpose of petitioning Congress for the redress of grievances is a privilege of United States citizenship protected by the privileges and immunities clause. United States v. Cruikshank, 92 U. S. 542, 552-553. We may assume for present purposes, although the step is a long and by no means certain one, see Maxwell v. Dow, 176 U. S. 581; Twining v. New Jersey, supra, that the right to assemble to discuss the advantages of the National Labor Relations Act is likewise a privilege secured by the privileges and immunities clause to citizens of the United States, but not to others, while freedom to assemble for the purpose of discussing a similar state statute would not be within the privileges and immunities clause. But the difficulty with this assumption is, as the record and briefs show, that it is an afterthought first emerging in this case after it was submitted to us for decision, and like most afterthoughts in litigated matters it is without adequate support in the record.
Madden v. Kentucky	KY	1940	"the right not to pay higher state taxes on interest from out-of-state banks"	Not a Nationwide Privilege and Immunity Overruled Colgate v. Harvey 296 U.S. 404 (1935)	309 U.S. 83, 92-93 - We think it quite clear that the right to carry out an incident to a trade, business or calling such as the deposit of money in banks is not a privilege of national citizenship. In the states, there reposes the sovereignty to manage their own affairs except only as the requirements of the Constitution otherwise provide. Within these constitutional limits the power of the state over taxation is plenary. An interpretation of the privileges and immunities clause which restricts the power of the states to manage their own fiscal affairs is a matter of gravest concern to them." It is only the emphatic requirements of the Constitution which properly may lead the federal courts to such a conclusion.

Case	State	Year	Proposed Nationwide Privilege and Immunity	Decision Summary	Key Opinion Text
Edwards v. California	CA	1941	"the right to transport indigent people across state lines"	The Supreme Court distances itself from the "paupers" classification in the Articles of Confederation and declares that there is a right for able-bodied but unemployed people to be transported across state lines.	314 U.S. 160, 176-177 - There remains to be noticed only the contention that the limitation upon State power to interfere with the interstate transportation of persons is subject to an exception in the case of "paupers." It is true that support for this contention may be found in early decisions of this Court. In City of New York v. Miln, 11 Pet. 102, at 143, it was said that it is "as competent and as necessary for a State to provide precautionary measures against the moral pestilence of paupers, vagabonds, and possibly convicts, as it is to guard against the physical pestilence, which may arise from unsound and infectious articles imported,." This language has been casually repeated in numerous later cases up to the turn of the century. See, e. g., Passenger Cases, 7 How. 283, 426 and 46-467; Railway Company V. Husen, 95 U. S. 465, 471; Plumley v. Massachusetts, 155 U.S. 461, 478; Missouri, K. & T. Ry. Co. v. Haber, 169 U. S. 613, 629. In none of these cases, however, was the power of a State to exclude "paupers" actually involved. Whether an able-bodied but unemployed person like Duncan is a "pauper" within the historical meaning of the term is open to considerable doubt. See 53 Harvard L. Rev. 1031, 1032. But assuming that the term is applicable to him and to persons similarly situated, we do not consider ourselves bound by the language referred to. City of New York v. Miln was decided in 1837. Whatever may have been the notion then prevailing, we do not think that it will now be seriously contended that because a person is without employment and without funds he constitutes a "moral pestilence." Poverty and immorality are not synonymous. [Continued]

Case	State	Year	Proposed Nationwide Privilege and Immunity	Decision Summary	Key Opinion Text
[Cont.] Edwards v. California					[Continued] 314 U.S. 160, 181 - The conclusion that the right of free movement is a right of national citizenship stands on firm historical ground. If a state tax on that movement, as in the Crandall case, is invalid, a fortiori a state statute which obstructs or in substance prevents that movement must fall. That result necessarily follows unless perchance a State can curtail the right of free movement of those who are poor or destitute. But to allow such an exception to be engrafted on the rights of national citizenship would be to contravene every conception of national unity. It would also introduce a caste system utterly incompatible with the spirit of our system of government. It would permit those who were stigmatized by a State as indigents, paupers, or vagabonds to be relegated to an inferior class of citizenship. It would prevent a citizen because he was poor from seeking new horizons in other States. It might thus withhold from large segments of our people that mobility which is basic to any guarantee of freedom of opportunity. The result would be a substantial dilution of the rights of national citizenship, a serious impairment of the principles of equality. Since the state statute here challenged involves such consequences, it runs afoul of the privileges and immunities clause of the Fourteenth Amendment.
Henderson v. United States	MD	1950	"the right for an African American to dine at a table with white passengers on a train"	Discriminatory law was invalidated using the Interstate Commerce Clause	339 U.S. 816, 825 - Discriminations that operate to the disadvantage of two groups are not the less to be condemned because their impact is broader than if only one were affected. Cf. Shelley v. Kraemer, 334 U. S. 1, 22. Since § 3 (1) of the Interstate Commerce Act invalidates the rules and practices before us, we do not reach the constitutional or other issues suggested.

Appendix 26 - Summary of Privilege and Immunity Related Supreme Court Cases (1900-2025)

Case	State	Year	Proposed Nationwide Privilege and Immunity	Decision Summary	Key Opinion Text
Brown v. Board of Education	KS, SC, VA, DE	1954	"the right for African American children to attend schools with white children"	Segregated Schools were found to be unconstitutional based upon the Equal Protection Clause of the 14th Amendment	347 U.S. 483, 495 - We conclude that in the field of public education the doctrine of "separate but equal" has no place. Separate educational facilities are inherently unequal. Therefore, we hold that the plaintiffs and others similarly situated for whom the actions have been brought are, by reason of the segregation complained of, deprived of the equal protection of the laws guaranteed by the Fourteenth Amendment. This disposition makes unnecessary any discussion whether such segregation also violates the Due Process Clause of the Fourteenth Amendment.

Case	State	Year	Proposed Nationwide Privilege and Immunity	Decision Summary	Key Opinion Text
Kent v. Dulles	DC	1958	"the right for a Communist to obtain a passport"	Decided on Due Process grounds.	357 U.S. 116, 125 - The right to travel is a part of the "liberty" of which the citizen cannot be deprived without due process of law under the Fifth Amendment. So much is conceded by the Solicitor General. In Anglo-Saxon law that right was emerging at least & early as the Magna Carta. 357 U.S. 116, 129 - …the issuance of the passport carries some implication of intention to extend the bearer diplomatic protection, though it does no more than "request all whom it may concern to permit safely and freely to pass, and in case of need to give all lawful aid and protection" to this citizen of the United States. But that function of the passport is subordinate. Its crucial function today is control over exit. And, as we have seen, the right of exit is a personal right included within the word "liberty" as used in the Fifth Amendment. If that "liberty" is to be regulated, it must be pursuant to the law-making functions of the Congress. 357 U.S. 116, 130 - To-repeat, we deal here with a constitutional right of the citizen, a right which we must assume Congress will be faithful to respect. We would be faced with important constitutional questions were we to hold that Congress by § 1185 and § 211a had given the Secretary authority to withhold passports to citizens because of their beliefs or associations. Congress has made no such provision in explicit terms; and absent one, the Secretary may not employ that standard to restrict the citizens' right of free movement.

Case	State	Year	Proposed Nationwide Privilege and Immunity	Decision Summary	Key Opinion Text
Boynton v. Virginia	VA	1960	"the right for an African American bus passenger to eat in a restaurant at a route stop that serves interstate customers"	Decided based on the Interstate Commerce Act	364 U.S. 454, 463-464 - Because of some of the arguments made here it is necessary to say a word about what we are not deciding. We are not holding that every time a bus stops at a wholly independent roadside restaurant the Interstate Commerce Act requires that restaurant service be supplied in harmony with the provisions of that Act. We decide only this case, on its facts, where circumstances show that the terminal and restaurant operate as an integral part of the bus carrier's transportation service for interstate passengers. Under such circumstances, an interstate passenger need not inquire into documents of title or contractual arrangements in order to determine whether he has a right to be served without discrimination.
Aptheker v. Secretary of State	DC	1964	"the right for a member of the Communist Party to receive a passport"	The passport could not be withheld, and the law was found Unconstitutional on Due Process Grounds	378 U.S. 500, 514 - In our view the foregoing considerations compel the conclusion that § 6 of the Control Act is unconstitutional on its face. The section, judged by its plain import and by the substantive evil which Congress sought to control, sweeps too widely and too indiscriminately across the liberty guaranteed in the Fifth Amendment. The prohibition against travel is supported only by a tenuous relationship between the bare fact of organizational membership and the activity Congress sought to proscribe. The broad and enveloping prohibition indiscriminately excludes plainly relevant considerations such as the individual's knowledge, activity, commitment, and purposes in and places for travel.

Case	State	Year	Proposed Nationwide Privilege and Immunity	Decision Summary	Key Opinion Text
Hearts of Atlanta Motel v. United States	GA	1964	"the right for African Americans to use a hotel that advertises along interstate highways used for interstate commerce."	The Civil Rights Act of 1964 was found Constitutional under Congress' power under the Commerce Clause.	379 U.S. 241, 250-251 - In light of our ground for decision, it might be well at the outset to discuss the Civil Rights Cases, supra, which declared provisions of the Civil Rights Act of 1875 unconstitutional. 18 Stat. 335, 336.- We think that decision inapposite, and without precedential value in determining the constitutionality of the present Act. Unlike Title II of the present legislation, the 1875 Act broadly proscribed discrimination in "inns, public conveyances on land or water, theaters, and other places of public amusement," without limiting the categories of affected businesses to those impinging upon interstate commerce. In contrast, the applicability of Title II is carefully limited to enterprises having a direct and substantial relation to the interstate flow of goods and people, except where state action is involved. Further, the fact that certain kinds of businesses may not in 1875 have been sufficiently involved in interstate commerce to warrant bringing them within the ambit of the commerce power is not necessarily dispositive of the same question today. Our populace had not reached its present mobility, nor were facilities, goods and services circulating as readily in interstate commerce as they are today. 379 U.S. 241, 261 - We, therefore, conclude that the action of the Congress in the adoption of the Act as applied here to a motel which concededly serves interstate travelers is within the power granted it by the Commerce Clause of the Constitution, as interpreted by this Court for 140 years. It may be argued that Congress could have pursued other methods to eliminate the obstructions it found in interstate commerce caused by racial discrimination. But this is a matter of policy that rests entirely with the Congress not with the courts.

Case	State	Year	Proposed Nationwide Privilege and Immunity	Decision Summary	Key Opinion Text
Katzenbach v. McClung	AL	1964	"the right for African Americans to eat in a restaurant that serves interstate travelers and gets significant food from outside of the state"	The Civil Rights Act of 1964 was found Constitutional under Congress' power under the Commerce Clause.	379 U.S. 294, 304 - Confronted as we are with the facts laid before Congress, we must conclude that it had a rational basis for finding that racial discrimination in restaurants had a direct and adverse effect on the free flow of interstate commerce.
Zemel v. Rusk	CT	1965	"the right to travel to Cuba when the State Department has banned it"	Not a Nationwide Privilege and Immunity	381 U.S. 1, 15-16 - The right to travel within the United States is of course also constitutionally protected, cf. Edwards v. California, 314 U. S. 160. But that freedom does not mean that areas ravaged by flood, fire or pestilence cannot be quarantined when it can be demonstrated that unlimited travel to the area would directly and materially interfere with the safety and welfare of the area or the Nation as a whole. So it is with international travel. That the restriction which is challenged in this case is supported by the weightiest considerations of national security is perhaps best pointed up by recalling that the Cuban missile crisis of October 1962 preceded the filing of appellant's complaint by less than two months.

Case	State	Year	Proposed Nationwide Privilege and Immunity	Decision Summary	Key Opinion Text
United States v. Guest	GA	1966	"the right for African Americans to equally use public facilities without being falsely arrested."	Case was allowed to proceed based on Equal Protection Clause violations.	383 U.S. 745, 756 - This case, however, requires no determination of the threshold level that state action must attain in order to create rights under the Equal Protection Clause. This is so because, contrary to the argument of the litigants, the indictment in fact contains an express allegation of state involvement sufficient at least to require the denial of a motion to dismiss. One of the means of accomplishing the object of the conspiracy, according to the indictment, was "By causing the arrest of Negroes by means of false reports that such Negroes had committed criminal acts." 383 U.S. 745, 758 - Although the Articles of Confederation provided that "the people of each State shall have free ingress and regress to and from any other State," " that right finds no explicit mention in the Constitution. The reason, it has been suggested, is that a right so elementary was conceived from the beginning to be a necessary concomitant of the stronger Union the Constitution created." In any event, freedom to travel throughout the United States has long been recognized as a basic right under the Constitution.
United States v. Price	MS	1966	"the right to protection against a conspiracy between local law enforcement and private individuals"	Known as the Mississippi Burning Case. The Supreme Court ruled that the action was clearly a violation of the 14th Amendment Due Process Clause	383 U.S. 787, 799 - This is an allegation of state action which, beyond dispute, brings the conspiracy within the ambit of the Fourteenth Amendment. It is an allegation of official, state participation in murder, accomplished by and through its officers with the participation of others. It is an allegation that the State, without the semblance of due process of law as required of it by the Fourteenth Amendment, used its sovereign power and office to release the victims from jail so that they were not charged and tried as required by law, but instead could be intercepted and killed. If the Fourteenth Amendment forbids denial of counsel, it clearly denounces denial of any trial at all.

Case	State	Year	Proposed Nationwide Privilege and Immunity	Decision Summary	Key Opinion Text
Shapiro v. Thompson	CT, PA, DC	1969	"the right to collect welfare benefits without needing to meet a residency requirement"	The Supreme Court declared that residency requirements violated the Equal Protection Clause of the 14th Amendment.	383 U. S. 618, 629 - We do not doubt that the one-year waiting-period device is well suited to discourage the influx of poor families in need of assistance. An indigent who desires to migrate, resettle, find a new job, and start a new life will doubtless hesitate if he knows that he must risk making the move without the possibility of falling back on state welfare assistance during his first year of residence, when his need may be most acute. But the purpose of inhibiting migration by needy persons into the State is constitutionally impermissible.
Saenz v. Roe	CA	1999	"the right to collect higher welfare benefits than you would have been entitled to in your previous state for the first year of residence in a new state"	The Supreme Court used a combination of the Privileges and Immunities Clause and the Equal Protection Clause of the 14th Amendment to create a right to collect full welfare benefits without a residency requirement	526 U.S. 489, 502 - What is at issue in this case, then, is this third aspect of the right to travel-the right of the newly arrived citizen to the same privileges and immunities enjoyed by other citizens of the same State. That right is protected not only by the new arrival's status as a state citizen, but also by her status as a citizen of the United States. 526 U.S. 489, 504 - That newly arrived citizens "have two political capacities, one state and one federal," adds special force to their claim that they have the same rights as others who share their citizenship. Neither mere rationality nor some intermediate standard of review should be used to judge the constitutionality of a state rule that discriminates against some of its citizens because they have been domiciled in the State for less than a year. The appropriate standard may be more categorical than that articulated in Shapiro, see supra, at 499, but it is surely no less strict. [Continued]

Case	State	Year	Proposed Nationwide Privilege and Immunity	Decision Summary	Key Opinion Text
[Cont.] Saenz v. Roe					[Continued] 526 U.S. 489, 527-528 – Thomas Dissent – Because I believe that the demise of the Privileges or Immunities Clause has contributed in no small part to the current disarray of our Fourteenth Amendment jurisprudence, I would be open to reevaluating its meaning in an appropriate case. Before invoking the Clause, however, we should endeavor to understand what the Framers of the Fourteenth Amendment thought that it meant. We should also consider whether the Clause should displace, rather than augment, portions of our equal protection and substantive due process jurisprudence. The majority's failure to consider these important questions raises the specter that the Privileges or Immunities Clause will become yet another convenient tool for inventing new rights, limited solely by the "predilections of those who happen at the time to be Members of this Court." Moore v. East Cleveland, 431 U. S. 494, 502 (1977).

Case	State	Year	Proposed Nationwide Privilege and Immunity	Decision Summary	Key Opinion Text
District of Columbia v. Heller	DC	2008	"the right to bear arms for self-defense within the home"	Supreme Court ruled that this right existed as defined by the 2nd Amendment for individuals as opposed to just members of militias.	554 U.S. 570, 592 - Putting all of these textual elements together, we find that they guarantee the individual right to possess and carry weapons in case of confrontation. This meaning is strongly confirmed by the historical background of the Second Amendment. We look to this because it has always been widely understood that the Second Amendment, like the First and Fourth Amendments, codified a pre-existing right. The very text of the Second Amendment implicitly recognizes the pre-existence of the right and declares only that it "shall not be infringed." 554 U.S. 570, 620 - The limited discussion of the Second Amendment in Cruikshank supports, if anything, the individual-rights interpretation. There was no claim in Cruikshank that the victims had been deprived of their right to carry arms in a militia; indeed, the Governor had disbanded the local militia unit the year before the mob's attack, see C. Lane, The Day Freedom Died 62 (2008). We described the right protected by the Second Amendment as " 'bearing arms for a lawful purpose' " 22 and said that "the people [must] look for their protection against any violation by their fellow-citizens of the rights it recognizes" to the States' police power. 92 U. S., at 553. That discussion makes little sense if it is only a right to bear arms in a state militia.

Case	State	Year	Proposed Nationwide Privilege and Immunity	Decision Summary	Key Opinion Text
McDonald v. Chicago	IL	2010	"the right to bear arms in the states"	The Supreme Court found that the 2nd Amendment applies to the States	561 U.S. 742, 822-823 – Thomas Concurrence – I start with the nature of the rights that § 1's Privileges or Immunities Clause protects. Section 1 overruled Dred Scott's holding that blacks were not citizens of either the United States or their own State and, thus, did not enjoy "the privileges and immunities of citizens" embodied in the Constitution. 19 How., at 417. The Court in Dred Scott did not distinguish between privileges and immunities of citizens of the United States and citizens in the several States, instead referring to the rights of citizens generally. It did, however, give examples of what the rights of citizens were -- the constitutionally enumerated rights of "the full liberty of speech" and the right "to keep and carry arms." Ibid. Section 1 protects the rights of citizens "of the United States" specifically. The evidence overwhelmingly demonstrates that the privileges and immunities of such citizens included individual rights enumerated in the Constitution, including the right to keep and bear arms.

Appendix 27 - Wong Kim Ark Opinion Quotes, Sections 1-7

Sec#	Reference[1]	Quote	Notes
1	169 U.S. 649, 653-654	I. In construing any act of legislation, whether a statute enacted by the legislature, or a constitution established by the people as the supreme law of the land, regard is to be had, not only to all parts of the act itself, and of any former act of the same law-making power, of which the act in question is an amendment; but also to the condition, and to the history, of the law as previously existing, and in the light of which the new act must be read and interpreted.	Section 1 analyzes the usage of "citizenship" in the Constitution
	169 U.S. 649, 654	The Constitution nowhere defines the meaning of these words, either by way of inclusion or of exclusion, except in so far as this is done by the affirmative declaration that "all persons born or naturalized in the United States, and subject to the jurisdiction thereof, are citizens of the United States." In this, as in other respects, it must be interpreted in the light of the common law, the principles and history of which were familiarly known to the framers of the Constitution.	

1 United States v. Wong Kim Ark, 169 U.S. 649
United States Library of Congress. (2026, Feb. 24).
https://www.loc.gov/item/usrep169649/

Sec#	Reference[1]	Quote	Notes
2	169 U.S. 649, 655	II. The fundamental principle of the common law with regard to English nationality was birth within the allegiance, also called "ligealty," "obedience," " faith" or "power," of the King. The principle embraced all persons born within the King's allegiance and subject to his protection. Such allegiance and protection were mutual-as expressed in the maxim, protectio trahit subjectionem, et subjectio protectionem - and were not restricted to natural-born subjects and naturalized subjects, or to those who had taken an oath of allegiance; but were predicable of aliens in amity, so long as they were within the kingdom. Children, born in England, of such aliens, were therefore natural-born subjects. But the children, born within the realm, of foreign ambassadors, or the children of alien enemies, born during and within their hostile occupation of part of the King's dominions, were not natural-born subjects, because not born within the allegiance, the obedience, or the power, or, as would be said at this day, within the jurisdiction of the King.	Section 2 analyzes English Common Law prior to the founding of the United States. It identifies "allegiance" as being within the "ligealty", "obedience", "faith" or "power" of the King.
	169 U.S. 649, 658	And he adds: "The exceptional and unimportant instances in which birth within the British dominions does not of itself confer British nationality are due to the fact that, though at common law nationality or allegiance in substance depended on the place of a person's birth, it in theory at least depended, not upon the locality of a man's birth, but upon his being born within the jurisdiction and allegiance of the King of England; and it might occasionally happen that a person was born within the dominions without being born within the allegiance, or, in other words, under the protection and control of the Crown." Dicey Conflict of Laws, pp. 173-177, 741. It thus clearly appears that by the law of England for the last three centuries, beginning before the settlement of this country, and continuing to the present day, aliens, while residing in the dominions possessed by the Crown of England, were within the allegiance, the obedience, the faith or loyalty, the protection, the power, the jurisdiction, of the English Sovereign;	This Quotation from Mr. Dicey regarding English Law was published in 1896 which was 110 years after the signing of the United States Constitution. Dicey recognizes Common Law birth as being within the jurisdiction and allegiance of the King

Sec#	Reference[1]	Quote	Notes
3	169 U.S. 649, 658	III. The same rule was in force in all the English Colonies upon this continent down to the time of the Declaration of Independence, and in the United States afterwards, and continued to prevail under the Constitution as originally established.	Section 3 analyzes how English Common Law applied to the early United States
	169 U.S. 649, 660	"Nothing is better settled at the common law than the doctrine that the children, even of aliens, born in a country, while the parents are resident there under the protection of the government, and owing a temporary allegiance thereto, are subjects by birth." 3 Pet. 164.	Quotation is from Inglis vs. the Trustees of the Sailor's Snug Harbour, 28 U.S. 99, 164 (1830)

Sec#	Reference[1]	Quote	Notes
4	169 U.S. 649, 666	IV. It was contended by one of the learned counsel for the United States that the rule of the Roman law, by which the citizenship of the child followed that of the parent, was the true rule of international law, as now recognized in most civilized countries, and had superseded the rule of the common law, depending on birth within the realm, originally founded on feudal considerations.	Section 4 analyzes International Law regarding citizenship and the citizenship of children of Americans born abroad.
	169 U.S. 649, 668	Nor can it be doubted that it is the inherent right of every independent nation to determine for itself, and according to its own constitution and laws, what classes of persons shall be entitled to its citizenship. Both in England and in the United States, indeed, statutes have been passed, at various times, enacting that certain issue born abroad of English subjects, or of American citizens, respectively, should inherit, to some extent at least, the rights of their parents. But those statutes applied only to cases coming within their purport; and they have never been considered, in either country, as affecting the citizenship of persons born within its dominion.	
	169 U.S. 649, 674	It thus clearly appears that, during the half century intervening between 1802 and 1855, there was no legislation whatever for the citizenship of children born abroad, during that period, of American parents who had not become citizens of the United States before the act of 1802; and that the act of 1855, like every other act of Congress upon the subject, has, by express proviso, restricted the right of citizenship, thereby conferred upon foreign-born children of American citizens, to those children themselves, unless they became residents of the United States. Here is nothing to countenance the theory that a general rule of citizenship by blood or descent has displaced in this country the fundamental rule of citizenship by birth within its sovereignty.	

Sec#	Reference[1]	Quote	Notes
5	169 U.S. 649, 675	V. In the fore front, both of the Fourteenth Amendment of the Constitution, and of the Civil Rights Act of 1866, the fundamental principle of citizenship by birth within the dominion was reaffirmed in the most explicit and comprehensive terms.	Section 5 analyzes the Civil Rights Act of 1866 and the 14th Amendment
	169 U.S. 649, 679-680	"At common law, with the nomenclature of which the framers of the Constitution were familiar, it was never doubted that all children, born in a country, of parents who were its citizens, became themselves, upon their birth, citizens also. These were natives, or natural-born citizens, as distinguished from aliens or foreigners. Some authorities go further and include as citizens children born within the jurisdiction, without reference to the citizenship of their parents. As to this class there have been doubts, but never as to the first. For the purposes of this case it is not necessary to solve these doubts. It is sufficient, for everything we have now to consider, that all children, born of citizen parents within the jurisdiction, are themselves citizens." Minor v.Happersett, (1874) 21 Wall. 162, 166-168.	

Sec#	Reference[1]	Quote	Notes
5	169 U.S. 649, 680	The only adjudication that has been made by this court upon the meaning of the clause, "and subject to the jurisdiction thereof," in the leading provision of the Fourteenth Amendment, is Elk v. Wilkins, 112 U. S. 91, in which it was decided that an Indian born a member of one of the Indian tribes within the United States, which still existed and was recognized as an Indian tribe by the United States, who had voluntarily separated himself from his tribe, and taken up his residence among the white citizens of a State, but who did not appear to have been naturalized, or taxed, or in any way recognized or treated as a citizen, either by the United States or by the State, was not a citizen of the United States, as a person born in the United States, "and subject to the jurisdiction thereof," within the meaning of the clause in question.	Analysis of Elk v. Wilkins, 112 U.S. 91 (1884)
	169 U.S. 649, 681	… that the Indian tribes, being within the territorial limits of the United States, were not, strictly speaking, foreign States, but were alien nations, distinct political communities, the members of which owed immediate allegiance to their several tribes, and were not part of the people of the United States; that the alien and dependent condition of the members of one of those tribes could not be put off at their own will, without the action or assent of the United States; and that they were never deemed citizens, except when naturalized, collectively or individually, under explicit provisions of a treaty, or of an act of Congress;	

Sec#	Reference[1]	Quote	Notes
5	169 U.S. 649, 684-685	He then stated, and supported by argument and illustration, the propositions, that "this full and absolute territorial jurisdiction, being alike the attribute of every sovereign, and being incapable of conferring extra-territorial power," has "given rise to a class of cases in which every sovereign is understood to waive the exercise of a part of that complete exclusive territorial jurisdiction, which has been stated to be the attribute of every nation " - the first of which is the exemption from arrest or detention of the person of a foreign sovereign entering its territory with its license, because "a foreign sovereign is not understood as intending to subject himself to a jurisdiction incompatible with his dignity and the dignity of his nation;" "a second case, standing on the same principles with the first, is the immunity which all civilized nations allow to foreign ministers;" "a third case, in which a sovereign is understood to cede a portion of his territorial jurisdiction, is where he allows the troops of a foreign prince to pass through his dominions;" and, in conclusion, that "a public armed ship, in the service of a foreign sovereign, with whom the Government of the United States is at peace, and having entered an American port open for her reception, on the terms on which ships of war are generally permitted to enter the ports of a friendly power, must be considered as having come into the American territory, under an implied promise, that while necessarily within it, and demeaning herself in a friendly manner, she should be exempt from the jurisdiction of the country." 7 Cranch, 137-139, 147.	Chief Justice Marshall quotations from the Schooner Exchange v. McFaddon 11 U.S. 116 (1812)

Sec#	Reference[1]	Quote	Notes
5	169 U.S. 649, 686	In short, the judgment in the case of The Exchange declared, as incontrovertible principles, that the jurisdiction of every nation within its own territory is exclusive and absolute, and is susceptible of no limitation not imposed by the nation itself; that all exceptions to its full and absolute territorial jurisdiction must be traced up to its own consent, express or implied; that upon its consent to cede, or to waive the exercise of, a part of its territorial jurisdiction, rest the exemptions from that jurisdiction of foreign sovereigns or their armies entering its territory with its permission, and of their foreign ministers and public ships of war; and that the implied license, under which private individuals of another nation enter the territory and mingle indiscriminately with its inhabitants, for purposes of business or pleasure, can never be construed to grant to them an exemption from the jurisdiction of the country in which they are found.	The implied license for private individuals entering a country does not grant them an exemption from jurisdiction.
	169 U.S. 649, 693	The foregoing considerations and authorities irresistibly lead us to these conclusions: The Fourteenth Amendment affirms the ancient and fundamental rule of citizenship by birth within the territory, in the allegiance and under the protection of the country, including all children here born of resident aliens, with the exceptions or qualifications (as old as the rule itself) of children of foreign sovereigns or their ministers, or born on foreign public ships, or of enemies within and during a hostile occupation of part of our territory, and with the single additional exception of children of members of the Indian tribes owing direct allegiance to their several tribes.	

Sec#	Reference[1]	Quote	Notes
6	169 U.S. 649, 694	VI. Whatever considerations, in the absence of a controlling provision of the Constitution, might influence the legislative or the executive branch of the Government to decline to admit persons of the Chinese race to the status of citizens of the United States, there are none that can constrain or permit the judiciary to refuse to give full effect to the peremptory and explicit language of the Fourteenth Amendment, which declares and ordains that "All persons born or naturalized in the United States, and subject to the jurisdiction thereof, are citizens of the United States."	Section 6 reviews how laws and executive decisions cannot remove the Constitutional requirement.
	169 U.S. 649, 694	Chinese persons, born out of the United States, remaining subjects of the Emperor of China, and not having become citizens of the United States, are entitled to the protection of and owe allegiance to the United States, so long as they are permitted by the United States to reside here; and are "subject to the jurisdiction thereof," in the same sense as all other aliens residing in the United States.	
	169 U.S. 649, 699	The acts of Congress, known as the Chinese Exclusion Acts, the earliest of which was passed some fourteen years after the adoption of the Constitutional Amendment, cannot control its meaning, or impair its effect, but must be construed and executed in subordination to its provisions. And the right of the United States, as exercised by and under those acts, to exclude or to expel from the country persons of the Chinese race, born in China, and continuing to be subjects of the Emperor of China, though having acquired a commercial domicil in the United States, has been upheld by this court, for reasons applicable to all aliens alike, and inapplicable to citizens, of whatever race or color.	

Sec#	Reference[1]	Quote	Notes
6	169 U.S. 649, 704	The fact, therefore, that acts of Congress or treaties have not permitted Chinese persons born out of this country to become citizens by naturalization, cannot exclude Chinese persons born in this country from the operation of the broad and clear words of the Constitution, "All persons born in the United States, and subject to the jurisdiction thereof, are citizens of the United States."	

Sec#	Reference[1]	Quote	Notes
7	169 U.S. 649, 704	VII. Upon the facts agreed in this case, the American citizenship which Wong Kim Ark acquired by birth within the United States has not been lost or taken away by anything happening since his birth. No doubt he might himself, after coming of age, renounce this citizenship, and become a citizen of the country of his parents, or of any other country; for by our law, as solemnly declared by Congress, "the right of expatriation is a natural and inherent right of all people," and "any declaration, instruction, opinion, order or direction of any officer of the United States, which denies, restricts, impairs or questions the right of expatriation, is declared inconsistent with the fundamental principles of the Republic."	Section 7 shows that nothing could have taken away Wong Kim Ark's citizenship from birth unless he renounces it as an adult.
	169 U.S. 649, 705	The evident intention, and the necessary effect, of the submission of this case to the decision of the court upon the facts agreed by the parties, were to present for determination the single question, stated at the beginning of this opinion, namely, whether a child born in the United States, of parents of Chinese descent, who, at the time of his birth, are subjects of the Emperor of China, but have a permanent domicil and residence in the United States, and are there carrying on business, and are not employed in any diplomatic or official capacity under the Emperor of China, becomes at the time of his birth a citizen of the United States. For the reasons above stated, this court is of opinion that the question must be answered in the affirmative.	

Bibliography

Balcerski, Thomas. *The 175-Year History of Speculating About President James Buchanan's Bachelorhood.* Smithsonian Magazine, August 27, 2019, Washington, DC.

Blackstone, William. *Commentaries on the Laws of England Book 1: The Rights of Persons.* Wallachia Publishers, 2015, New York, New York (First published 1769)

Canellos, Peter. *The Great Dissenter: The Story of John Marshall Harlan, America's Judicial Hero.* Simon and Schuster, 2021, New York, New York

Carey, Henry Charles. *The Harmony of Interests, Agricultural, Manufacturing and Commercial.* Myron Finch, 122 Nassau Street, 1852, New York, New York

Coke, Sir Edward. *The Second Part of the Institutes of the Laws of England: The Exposition of many ancient, and other Statutes.* 6th Edition, Printed by Miles Flesher and Robert Young, 1642, Fleetstreet, London

Finkelman, Paul. *Scott v. Sandford: The Court's Most Dreadful Case and How It Changed History.* Chicago-Kent Law Review, 2007, https://scholarship.kentlaw.iit.edu/cklawreview/vol82/iss1/2/

Goodwin, Doris Kearns. *Team of Rivals: The Political Genius of Abraham Lincoln.* Simon & Schuster, 2005, New York, New York

Gordon, Thomas. (see Trenchard, John for *Cato's Letters*)

Hamilton, Alexander with Madison, James and Jay, John. *The Federalist Papers: A Collection of Essays Written in Favour of the New Constitution, As Agreed Upon by the Federal Convention, September 17, 1787.* Dover Publications, 2014, Garden City, New York

Ketcham, Ralph. *The Anti-Federalist Papers and the Constitutional Convention Debates.* Signet Classics, 1986

Lane, Charles. *The Day Freedom Died: The Colfax Massacre, The Supreme Court, and the Betrayal of Reconstruction.* Henry Holt and Company, LLC, 2008, New York, New York

Locke, John. *The Second Treatise of Government & A Letter Concerning Toleration.* Dover Publications, 2002, Garden City, New York

Lucas, Samuel. *Charters of the Old English Colonies in America*, John W. Parker, West Strand, 1850, London

Madison, James [see Hamilton, Alexander for *The Federalist Papers*]

Mchangama, Jacob. *Free Speech: A History from Socrates to Social Media.* Basic Books, 2022, New York, New York

Meacham, Jon. *American Lion: Andrew Jackson in the White House.* Random House, 2008, New York, New York

Millard, Candice. *Destiny of the Republic: A Tale of Madness, Medicine and the Murder of a President.* Doubleday, 2011, New York, New York

O'Donnell, Patrick K. *The Indispensables: The Diverse Soldier-Mariners Who Shaped the Country, Formed the Navy, and Rowed Washington Across the Delaware.* Atlantic Monthly Press, 2021, New York, New York

Paine, Thomas. *Common Sense.* Dover Publications, 1997, Garden City, NY (Originally published by William and Thomas Bradford, Philadelphia, 14 February 1776)

Reynolds, David. *John Brown Abolitionist: The Man Who Killed Slavery, Sparked the Civil War, and Seeded Civil Rights.* Vintage Books, 2005, New York, New York

Story, Joseph. *Commentaries on the Constitution of the United States Volume I, Volume II and Volume III.* Cosmo Classics, 2020, New York, New York (Originally published in 1833 by Hilliard, Gray and Company, Boston)

Trenchard, John and Gordon, Thomas (Edited by Ronald Mamowy). *Cato's Letters: Or, Essays on Liberty, Civil and Religious, and other Important Subjects.* Liberty Fund Inc., 1995, Carmel, Indiana (Originally appeared from Nov. 1720 to Dec. 1723 in the London journal)

Vincent, Professor Nicholas. *Magna Carta Translation.* Sotheby's Inc., New York, New York, https://www.archives.gov/files/press/press-kits/magna-carta/magna-carta-translation.pdf

Online Reference Website Sources

American Battlefield Trust. Washington, DC.
https://www.battlefields.org/

California Office of Attorney General. Sacramento, CA
https://oag.ca.gov/

California Secretary of State, California State Archives. Sacramento, CA
https://www.sos.ca.gov/archives

Florida Constitution Revision Commission, Florida State University. Tallahassee, FL.
https://library.law.fsu.edu/Digital-Collections/CRC/CRC-1998/conhist/1838con.html

Illinois Institute of Technology, Chicago-Kent Law Review. Chicago, IL
https://scholarship.kentlaw.iit.edu/cklawreview/

Indiana State Government, Indianapolis, IN
https://www.in.gov/core/index.html

Iowa Legislature, Des Moines, IA
https://www.legis.iowa.gov/

Maine State Legislature, Augusta, ME
https://legislature.maine.gov/

Maryland State Archives. Annapolis, MD
https://msa.maryland.gov/

Massachusetts, The 194th General Court of the Commonwealth of Massachusetts. Boston, MA
https://malegislature.gov/

Mississippi Historical Society, Mississippi History Now. 2026, Jackson, MS
https://www.mshistorynow.mdah.ms.gov/

Missouri Secretary of State, Missouri State Archives. Jefferson City, MO
https://www.sos.mo.gov/

National Constitution Center. Philadelphia, PA
https://constitutioncenter.org/

National Right to Life. Alexandria, VA
https://nrlc.org/

New Jersey, Department of State, New Jersey State Archives. Trenton, NJ
https://www.nj.gov/state/archives/

New York, Historical Society of the New York Courts. White Plains, NY.
https://history.nycourts.gov/

North Carolina History Project, John Locke Foundation. Raleigh, NC.
https://northcarolinahistory.org/

Rhode Island Secretary of State. Providence, RI.
https://docs.sos.ri.gov/documents/civicsandeducation/teacherresources/DeclarationOfRights.pdf

Supreme Court of the United States. Washington, DC.
https://www.supremecourt.gov/

Teaching American History, 2026, Ashland, OH
https://teachingamericanhistory.org/

United Kingdom National Archives.
https://www.legislation.gov.uk/

United States Department of Agriculture, National Agricultural Statistics Service. Washington, DC.
https://www.nass.usda.gov/

United States Department of Commerce, United States Census Bureau. Suitland, MD
https://www.census.gov/

United States Department of Homeland Security, U.S. Citizenship and Immigration Services. Camp Springs, MD
https://www.uscis.gov/

United States Department of the Interior, National Park Service. Washington, DC.
https://www.nps.gov/index.htm

United States Library of Congress. Washington, DC.
https://www.loc.gov/

United States National Archives. College Park, MD
https://www.archives.gov/

United States Senate, Washington, DC.
https://www.senate.gov/

United States Supreme Court. Washington, DC.
https://www.supremecourt.gov/

University of Texas at Austin, Department of History, Immigration History. 2019, Austin, TX
https://immigrationhistory.org/

University of Texas at Austin, Texas Law, Tarlton Law Library. 2024, Austin, TX
https://tarlton.law.utexas.edu/home

University of Wisconsin-Madison, Department of History, Center for the Study of the American Constitution. 2026, Madison, WI
https://csac.history.wisc.edu/

Virginia Humanities, Encyclopedia Virginia. 2026, Charlottesville,VA,
https://encyclopediavirginia.org/

Wikisource.org
https://en.wikisource.org/wiki/Main_Page

Wisconsin Historical Society, Madison, WI
https://www.wisconsinhistory.org/

Yale Law School, Lillian Goldman Law Library. *The Avalon Project: Documents in Law, History and Diplomacy.* 2008, New Haven, Connecticut
https://avalon.law.yale.edu/

Index

www.ingramcontent.com/pod-product-compliance
Lightning Source LLC
LaVergne TN
LVHW101118240926
848814LV00016B/58/J
9798218938499